HOME OFFICE

YOUNG ADULT OFFENDERS

Report of the Advisory Council on the Penal System

LONDON
HER MAJESTY'S STATIONERY OFFICE
1974

ISBN 0 11 340559 6

ADVISORY COUNCIL ON THE PENAL SYSTEM

Members who took part in the review:

The Right Honourable Sir Kenneth Younger, KBE (Chairman)
The Right Reverend Dr. R. C. Mortimer, lately Bishop of Exeter
    (Vice-Chairman)
Mr. Leo Abse, MP
Mr. Louis Blom-Cooper, QC
Mr. D. A. Fiske
The Honourable Mr. Justice Griffiths, MC[1]
His Honour Judge Hines, QC
The Lady James of Rusholme
Mr. Richard Lowry, QC
Mr. R. E. Millard, CBE
Professor Sir Leon Radzinowicz
Mr. Timothy Raison, MP
The Lady Rothschild, MBE
The Reverend the Right Honourable Lord Sandford, DSC[2]
Dr. Peter Scott
Mr. W. R. Stirling
Professor G. B. Trasler
Mr. George Twist, CBE, QPM
Professor Nigel Walker
The Honourable Mr. Justice Waller, OBE
The Baroness Wootton of Abinger

Secretaries:

Mr. S. G. Norris (until April 1973)
Mr. N. R. Varney (from April 1973)

---

[1] Mr. Justice Griffiths resigned from the Council in August 1971 following his appointment as a Judge of the Queen's Bench.
[2] Lord Sandford resigned from the Council in June 1970 following his appointment as Parliamentary Under Secretary of State.

Home Office
Whitehall
London SW1A 2AP

8 November 1973

Sir,

In April 1970 your predecessor, Mr. Callaghan, asked the Advisory Council on the Penal System to carry out a review of the treatment of young offenders aged 17 and over. I now have the honour, on behalf of the Council, to submit for your consideration our report of that review.

The proposal that a comprehensive review of this kind should be undertaken arose out of the earlier reference to the Council to examine detention centres, on which a report was submitted in January 1970. The Council made a number of recommendations for improving, within the framework of the existing law, the operation of detention centres. We found it impossible, however, to consider that system fully without wider enquiry into the custodial system for young adult offenders as a whole, and accordingly recommended that a wider review should be carried out.

The principal theme of the report is that a shift is needed in emphasis, and therefore in deployment of resources, from custodial treatment to treatment in the community. The Council's main recommendations for bringing about this change are:

(*a*) A new sentence of custody and control with an emphasis on early release to supervision in the community, linked with the development of a network of custodial establishments serving localised areas.

(*b*) A new non-custodial sentence of supervision and control designed to give the supervising probation service stronger and more flexible measures of control over individual offenders.

Every member of the Council has signed the report. A number of members have also signed notes which set out dissenting views on various points. Only one requires comment here: that is the note by Mr. Abse, who proposes special sentencing provisions for young women offenders, aimed at eliminating the use of custody altogether for certain offences. This possibility is not canvassed in the body of the report. The Council considered various sentencing proposals which would have differentiated young women from young men. Its conclusion was that, given in particular the great flexibility which the proposed custody and control order would possess, there was no need or justification for differentiating between young men and young women in respect of the sentencing powers of the courts. For this reason the particular proposals put forward by Mr. Abse are not discussed in the report.

I am, Sir,

Your obedient Servant,

KENNETH YOUNGER.

The Rt. Hon. ROBERT CARR, M.P.
Her Majesty's Principal Secretary of State
for the Home Department

CONTENTS

CHAPTER 1

PREFACE

1. We were given in April 1970 the following terms of reference:

> "to review the arrangements for the treatment of young offenders aged 17 and over, with particular reference to custodial methods of treatment (including after-care arrangements), and the powers of the courts; and to make recommendations."

2. The singling out of this age group, which we have called in this report "young adults", for special treatment within the penal system had its origin in the Gladstone Committee's Report of 1895 and was given practical effect through the inauguration of the borstal system in the Prevention of Crime Act 1908. For the ensuing 40 years custodial sentences for offenders between 17 and 21 years of age comprised prison and borstal training. The Criminal Justice Act 1948 introduced a third custodial sentence for this age group to be served in a new type of establishment, the detention centre. There are thus today three types of establishment for the custody of young adults—prison (young prisoners' centres), borstal and detention centre. (For young women offenders, however, only one detention centre was ever established and it was discontinued in 1969, following the recommendation made in the Council's interim report on detention centres for girls.)[1] Over the same period the treatment of offenders in the community has been greatly developed through the probation system, which has been widely used for the young adult age group.

3. During this period of some 60 years the only wide-ranging review made of arrangements for dealing with young adult offenders was that of the Departmental Committee on Young Offenders which reported in 1927 (Cmd 2831). A later enquiry by the Home Secretary's Advisory Council on the Treatment of Offenders (ACTO) in 1959 was much more limited in scope.

4. In the report which follows we have reviewed the evolution of the system since its inception and have offered our conclusions on the lessons to be learned from this experience, from the results of research and from changes in penal thinking about the effectiveness of various ways of dealing with young adult offenders, whether custodial or in the community; and about the sentencing structure best suited to protect the public and reduce future offences. We have sought to place our recommendations for changes in existing law and practice in the wider social context within which a modern penal system has to operate, including the increase in recorded crime during the last quarter of a century, the increasing cost of the penal system, and the transformation of social life and social values which has taken place, especially in the great urban centres from which most young adult offenders come and to which they must return after a period in custody.

---

[1] *Detention of Girls in a Detention Centre* (HMSO, 1968).

1

5. Chapter 2 contains a review of the report as a whole and Chapter 3 a summary of our principal recommendations. Part I of the report, which follows, contains an account of the evolution of the young adult offender system and an analysis of the problems which now have to be faced. Part II contains our proposals. A description of our proceedings and methods of work is to be found in Appendix A: we are grateful to all those listed and referred to in it who in various ways have assisted us in carrying out this review.

6. We were particularly fortunate in the appointment as secretary of the Council, at the outset of the review, of Mr. S. G. Norris, who brought with him exceptional knowledge of criminological and penal matters, in the United States as well as in this country, and guided our deliberations, discussions with witnesses and overseas visits with great skill. It was therefore a severe loss to us when early last year, at an early stage in the drafting of our report, he was withdrawn from the service of the Council in order to become Principal Private Secretary to the Home Secretary; glad though we were at the distinction that this appointment conferred on him, we could have wished that he could have been spared for the final stages of the review. In his place we were happy to welcome Mr. N. R. Varney, who successfully picked up the threads of the review, and of the compilation of the report, at a difficult time.

7. We also wish to record that we could scarcely have completed the drafting process within our allotted time without the invaluable assistance given to us after Mr. Norris's departure by Mr. M. J. Moriarty, who had been associated with the Council's inquiry from the outset. In addition we express our gratitude to other members of the secretariat, and to other staff in the Home Office who have supplied the various supporting services—such as typing, copying and distribution of documents—on which an enterprise of this kind so much depends. Space does not permit a mention of all those whose assistance we acknowledge, and the singling out of individuals can be invidious: nevertheless we allow ourselves a particular word of thanks to Mr. A. D. Burgess, who joined the secretariat in 1969 and has put a great deal of careful and conscientious work into the review, and Miss M. M. White, who ever since the Council was set up in 1966 has been tireless in assuring the smooth running of its business.

CHAPTER 2

REVIEW

Young adult offenders as a separate legal category

8. Every developed penal system makes provision for treating child offenders separately from adults, the dividing line usually being drawn at the age of about 17 or 18, but the recognition of a distinct category of young adult offender is less common. As explained in the Preface above, such a category, comprising (in recent years) offenders aged 17 and under 21, has been recognised in the United Kingdom since the beginning of the century and special establishments have been maintained for over 60 years. We have considered whether there is still a valid case for maintaining this separate category and have concluded that there is.

9. We have been impressed by the purely practical consideration that for more than half a century both the courts and those responsible for dealing with offenders have been accustomed to regard this group as requiring special handling and have therefore accumulated useful experience on which to build. But there are also arguments of a more general nature. This is a highly delinquent group making a major demand on the penal system. While offenders in the group often have records of serious delinquency behind them, many are not yet set in their ways. They may be failures of the school system or immature in other respects and the few years after leaving school may offer a last chance of helping them to make good the ground they have lost. A special concentration of public effort upon this group of young adults, who are in danger of going on to long and costly criminal careers, is a sensible investment by society at a time when resources, both human and material, are too scarce to allow a similar degree of attention to be paid to all age groups. While there may be little evidence that this age group is, as the Gladstone Committee believed, especially malleable, there is evidence that these are particularly vulnerable years and that delinquent tendencies are apt to diminish thereafter. To give special support and assistance during this period is therefore still a rational policy.

10. The most appropriate limits of the young adult offender age group are a matter for practical judgment rather than scientific calculation. Since our terms of reference refer to young offenders aged 17 and over, and since comprehensive new legislation dealing with young people below that age, the Children and Young Persons Act 1969, has not been long enacted, we have accepted 17 as the obvious lower limit. Like the Latey Committee on the Age of Majority, we see no special reason for adopting 18, the new age of majority, as a dividing line for penal purposes.

11. As regards the upper age limit, at present 21, there is no one age which marks a uniquely appropriate point at which to make the dividing line. We have had suggestions to substitute 23 or even 25 for the present limit. To raise

the limit even to 23, let alone 25, would bring in so high a proportion of all offenders as to frustrate our purpose of securing a special concentration of effort and resources upon the young adult age group. We therefore conclude that the limit should remain at 21, but that provision should be made for this to be raised by statutory instrument as experience suggests and available resources permit. We have made detailed recommendations designed to achieve some flexibility at both the upper and lower age limits.

12. The special arrangements which at present exist for this age group extend to the sentences available to the courts and to special establishments provided for it within the custodial system. They do not include the provision of special courts for young adults. Although suggestions have been made to us that this should be done, there is no strong weight of opinion in support of it and we ourselves do not favour it.

The evolution of the young adult offender system

13. The essential element in the reform introduced following the Gladstone Committee's Report was the establishment, alongside the traditional method of imprisonment, of the borstal system, a new type of custodial treatment for carefully selected types of young adult offender. The purpose of this was to be primarily reform and rehabilitation, and this involved a change both in the length of sentences, which were to be determined within fairly wide discretionary limits by the time thought to be needed for effective training rather than by the gravity of the offence; and also in the attitudes to be adopted by staff towards the offenders. In accordance with the accepted standards of the time, stress was placed upon a brisk and disciplined regime, hard work of a more constructive kind than was available in prisons and as much trade training and education as could be provided. The moral quality and personal example of the staff, whose relationship was to be more like that of a boarding-school master to his pupils than of prison staff to prisoners, was considered to be of prime importance. To allow time for these influences to take effect, a substantial period of training was thought necessary, one year being originally seen as a practical minimum, irrespective of the offence committed.

14. For a long period both before and after the First World War borstal training, which was applied only to those offenders whom the court considered reasonably likely to respond to rehabilitative treatment, produced results (in terms of relatively low reconviction rates) which were found encouraging. Techniques of training were developed and borstal staff acquired a distinct morale and tradition of their own. This has proved to be of great value in the face of mounting difficulties and has enabled them to maintain a high standard right up to the present time. But since 1945 the problems with which the borstal system has had to deal have radically changed, with the result that its success has become less marked in terms of reconviction rates and its philosophy more open to question. If the quality and enthusiasm of the service is to be maintained, the purposes of the system now need to be reformulated and clearer guidance needs to be given about what society expects of it in the radically changed conditions of today. The principal changes which have occurred may be summarised as follows.

15. The borstal system is now required to deal with more difficult types of

4

offender than those for whom the system was developed. There are several reasons for this. Firstly, with the development of the probation system many relatively promising offenders, who might previously have been sent to borstal, are now supervised in the community. Secondly, there has since the 1950s been available the sentence of three to six months detention in a detention centre, and some relatively "low risk" offenders may have received this sentence rather than borstal training. Thirdly, the Criminal Justice Act 1961, by placing restrictions on the passing of prison sentences on young adults, has made borstal the standard medium-term custodial sentence within this age range, thus largely superseding the original idea that borstal training should be given only to those specially selected as being likely to respond to it.

16. The increase in delinquency in this age group and in the numbers sentenced to borstal training has caused strains due to overcrowding which have led to a shortening, for purely practical reasons, of the average time spent in borstal. While there are differences of opinion about the extent to which the effectiveness of training has been impaired by the shortening of the time spent in custody, it has called in question the basic principle of the borstal sentence that, within a fixed maximum period of custody laid down by statute, the borstal authorities should decide the date of release on the basis of the training needs of the individual offender and of the progress made by him.

17. The experience of the last half century and the results of a growing volume of research into penal questions have increasingly emphasised the intrinsic difficulty of providing training or treatment which will fit an offender, in the artificially segregated and disciplined conditions of custody, to face the problems of managing his own life on release. Borstal administrators have always been aware of this difficulty and have attempted to meet it by the development of open borstals and by maximising contacts with the world out-side the establishment. Nevertheless the constant emphasis in modern thinking and writing upon the potentially damaging effects of custody, even under an enlightened regime, has tended to undermine confidence in what can be achieved within a custodial system. Moreover research and experiment, both in the United Kingdom and elsewhere, appear to indicate that for offenders of comparable background, time spent in custody cannot be shown to produce any better results than supervision in the community.

18. These doubts have been accentuated by the rapid changes in social values which have been taking place in modern society. A form of institutional training, originally based upon confidence in military training methods and the boarding-school ethos, now increasingly seems, despite many adjustments which have been made in its application, to be of doubtful relevance to the conditions in which most young adult offenders will find themselves on release.

19. Finally, in view especially of the growing doubts about the efficacy of custodial forms of treatment, the question is increasingly being asked whether it is justifiable for society to deprive an offender of his liberty for a longer period than might be thought appropriate to the seriousness of his offence or the nature of his record, simply in order to subject him to prolonged treatment whose reformative effect is so open to question.

5

20. None of this, in our view, alters the unhappy fact that there are considerable numbers of young adult offenders whose persistently anti-social behaviour requires that they should be held in custody, or our conviction that something can be done to help them while they are there, despite the intrinsic difficulties referred to above. On the question of how to help them, the experience of borstal training as it has evolved over the years provides a sound basis for future experiment and progress. The general concept of constructive training pioneered by the borstal system has indeed won such wide acceptance that it is largely applied not only in borstals but throughout young prisoners' centres and detention centres as well. The result is that the supposed distinctions, which were once real and significant, between prisons, borstals and detention centres, as establishments offering alternative ways of dealing with young adult offenders in custody, have now become blurred and indeed misleading.

21. The corollary to the growing awareness of the difficulties inherent in preparing young adults in custody to deal with the problems which will face them on release is that new ways must be found of controlling as many young adult offenders as possible without committing them to custody and of bringing constructive influences to bear upon them while they continue to live and work in the community. Probation was, of course, the first major step in this direction. Further steps now need to be taken. This will involve leaving in the community offenders who are more likely to offend again than those who would today be considered suitable for probation. To make this acceptable to the courts and the public, there must be assurance that the control exercised is real and that it is supported by adequate sanctions. This can be achieved only by a deliberate switch of resources into a new system of control in the community.

Changes in penal philosophy

22. The Gladstone Committee Report of 1895 opened a new chapter in British thinking about the purposes of the penal system. For a selected category of young adult offender it established the primacy of reform among the objectives of the new borstal system. Since then, as already stated, the borstal concept has become more and more widely accepted in all types of establishment for young adult offenders. Nevertheless, even in the years when borstal sentences were passed on a highly selective basis, motives other than reformation, in particular individual and general deterrence, also played their part in the sentencing decisions of the courts. Now that, as explained above (paragraph 15), borstal has become the standard custodial sentence for a very wide range of young adult offender, considerations connected directly with the protection of the public may often become more important in the mind of the court when passing a borstal sentence, while the offender's probable response to reformative training may become secondary in determining the decision.

23. The difficulty experienced by borstal staff when faced with the sort of offender who seems very unlikely to respond to attempts at reformation, and was not sentenced by the court with that primarily in mind, is obvious. There is a need for a clearer formulation of the respective functions of the courts and of the treatment authorities in this matter. Over the years there has been a continuing debate on the respective roles within the penal system of deterrence

6

and reformation. As regards deterrence, the doctrine, formulated at an early stage, that offenders should be sent to custody "as a punishment and not for punishment" has steadily gained acceptance: the logic of this is that the deterrent element should be expressed by the court's choice of length of sentence and not by any especially deterrent nature of the regime, which should rather be concerned with helping the offender to avoid reverting to crime on his return to the community. On reformation, the doctrine has been gaining ground that, while this should indeed be the main objective of a custodial regime, it is wrong to send an offender to custody, or to decide how long he should be kept in custody, purely on reformative grounds, since it is only in a relatively small proportion of cases that custody is a condition of constructive treatment, and indeed it may often be an obstacle to it.

24. The borstal sentence, with its relatively long statutory maximum period in custody (formerly three years and now two), unrelated as it is to the gravity of the particular offence in respect of which the sentence was passed, and with its emphasis on treatment needs as the criterion for deciding the length of time to be actually served in custody, is now in conflict with both the doctrines mentioned above. Added to this is the relatively recent anomaly that, because of overcrowding, the timing of releases from borstal has frequently to be determined on administrative grounds, with neither deterrence nor reformation playing any significant part in the decision.

25. Informed opinion now increasingly sees the period in custody as only one part of a continuous process which should include supervision and control in the community. It is thought unsound to consider a propensity to commit offences as a kind of sickness which, on the medical analogy, can be rectified by relatively brief treatment in an institution from which the offender will emerge cured. While there are of course cases in which ascertainable and treatable defects may be at least partially the cause of delinquency, the medical model ignores the social pressures which may well have been more important in determining criminal conduct and will re-assert themselves when the offender is released from custody into his former surroundings.

26. If then the need is, on the one hand, to enable the court to express its judgment upon the offence on behalf of the community, and on the other, to meet the individual's need of reformative treatment, provided where possible in the community rather than in custody, then it seems to follow that the sentence of the court should be one of determinate length and should represent a maximum period to be spent under some form of control. Within this maximum those who are in continuing contact with the offender, and are thus in a position to assess changes in his disposition and behaviour, should have a wide discretion to decide what proportion of the total term is to be spent in custody and what under supervision and control in the community. A system based on this principle would enable the court both to relate the length of sentence to its assessment of the seriousness of the offence and also to ensure that an offender's liberty was not interfered with, purely for the purposes of treatment or training, for a period disproportionate to the offences committed. At the same time it would enable the treatment authorities to determine the degree of control to be exercised over the offender at each stage of his sentence, primarily with a view to his re-integration into the community.

Sentencing proposals

27. On the basis of the arguments outlined in the preceding paragraphs we propose that the three separate custodial sentences which courts can now pass on young adult offenders—imprisonment, borstal training and detention in a detention centre—should be discontinued and replaced by two new sentences. The first of these would be a *custody and control order* which would be available when a court decided that a custodial sentence was unavoidable. The second would be a *supervision and control order,* a non-custodial order which would enable supervision in the community to be conducted with a greater measure of control over the offender's life and behaviour than would be customary or appropriate under a probation order. The remaining non-custodial orders available now to the courts, including the power to make a probation order or to order community service, would remain unchanged, except that we now recommend that the two experimental senior attendance centres should be discontinued.

The Custody and Control Order

28. Where a court has power to pass a sentence of imprisonment on an adult, we recommend that it should have power to make a custody and control order on a young adult offender for any period not exceeding the maximum period of imprisonment which it could pass upon an adult for the same offence (for a magistrates' court this would normally be six months).

29. The effect of the custody and control order would be that the offender would be committed to a Prison Department establishment designated for the purpose by the Secretary of State. This might be either a closed or open establishment, and the full range of facilities linked with custody, such as satellite hostels and outside working, would be available. The present distinction between young prisoners' centres, borstals and detention centres would disappear. The custody and control order would thus become the only custodial order available to courts for young adult offenders, apart from those convicted of murder, who would be detained during Her Majesty's Pleasure.

30. The length of the custody and control order would be fixed by the court in each case in the light of the seriousness of the offence, the offender's record and circumstances and the public interest generally. The order would provide for a period spent in custody followed by supervision in the community by a probation officer: these periods would be regarded as a single continuum, the timing of the offender's transfer from custody to supervision being a matter of executive decision reached by the process described in paragraphs 33 and 34 below.

31. We also recommend that the courts when making a young adult subject to a custody and control order for the first time should be required, as they are at present in passing a first sentence of imprisonment (though not borstal training or detention), to satisfy themselves after considering a social enquiry report that no other method of dealing with him is appropriate.

32. We have concluded after careful consideration that custody and control orders of less than three months should not be made. The deterrent value of very

8

short sentences is at best dubious. They offer little possibility of devising planned or constructive treatment during the period of custody, while absorbing a considerable amount of staff time in the routine processes of reception, custody and discharge.

Release to supervision in the community under a Custody and Control Order

33. The constitutional responsibility for the decision when to transfer an offender from custody to supervision would rest with the Secretary of State who we envisage would delegate this function to a considerable extent. It is fundamental to our concept of the custody and control order that an important part in deciding the right time for transfer from custody to supervision in the community should be played by those who have the responsibility for the offender's treatment and are in a position to make a continuing assessment of his needs and prospects. Where the duration of the custody and control order is of less than three years—that is in the great majority of cases—we recommend that the Secretary of State should be advised by a new local advisory body, which we have called the licence advisory committee and which we envisage being similar in many respects to the local review committee which at present makes recommendations to the Parole Board. This new body would include the governor of the establishment, a representative of the local probation service, a member of the Board of Visitors of the establishment and another member of the local community. In the case of a custody and control order of three years or more we recommend that release to supervision should be ordered only with the approval of the Parole Board.

Restricted release orders

34. Cases involving those offences which cause the greatest public concern will thus, like serious offences at the present time, come under the scrutiny of the Parole Board. There are, however, among young adult offenders who may be the subject of custody and control orders for periods of less than three years, some whose offences are of considerable gravity. It is unlikely that the Secretary of State would in any event be advised to release such offenders to supervision without the most careful consideration of every aspect of the public interest. Nevertheless, we consider that it would be of advantage in a new system of this kind if the Crown Court were enabled, when making a custody and control order of at least 12 months but less than three years, to add to it in exceptional cases a *restricted release order*, the effect of which would be to ensure that the offender would not, without reference to the court, be released to supervision before one third of the custody and control order had been served. (This one third period would be common to all restricted release orders: the proportion could, we envisage, be changed by statutory instrument.) We do not consider it necessary to apply this provision to custody control orders of less than 12 months since it is our intention that restricted release orders should be regarded as exceptional and only to be used in particularly serious cases.

Criteria for release to supervision

35. It is not possible to lay down precise criteria which the staff of an establishment, the licence advisory committee and the Parole Board could apply generally in deciding upon the timing of release from custody to

9

supervision. It is of the essence of the problem that considerations will vary widely from one case to another and it is the intention that the fullest account should be taken of the circumstances of individual offences and offenders. Release to supervision does not mean the end of control. On the contrary, as stated in paragraph 36 below, our recommendations would strengthen the control in the community, thus encouraging, it is hoped, a transfer of substantial numbers of young adult offenders from control in an establishment to control in the community. It must be emphasised that, under our proposals, the sentence of the court would not be a sentence of custody for a fixed period, but a sentence laying down the maximum period during which the offender would be subject either to custody or to control in the community. For the authorities to transfer an offender from custody to control in the community at some time within that period would be an implementation of and not a departure from the court's decision. The licence advisory committee should ask itself whether there are compelling reasons why the sentence must continue to be served in custody rather than under supervision. The decision will be related to the individual, but that does not mean that those advising the Secretary of State should ignore all other considerations, nor is it at all likely that they would be tempted to do so. The court's view of the seriousness of the offence—as expressed by the length of the order—would clearly be one consideration, which would be relevant though not decisive. Public confidence in the operation of the system is, after all, an obvious condition of its success, as it has been in the operation of the parole system in recent years, and neither the Secretaty of State nor his advisers would be likely to forget this.

Supervision and licence requirements

36. Under our proposals, no less than at present, young adult offenders released from serving the custodial part of their sentence will face daunting problems—accommodation, work and coming to terms generally with the community—and if they are to surmount them will need all the help and support that they can be given. In this process of resettlement the probation and after-care service will play the key role, within the framework of the custody and control order licence. We recommend that on release an offender should be under supervision for the balance of the term of the order or for six months, whichever is the longer. At the time of sentence the court should make it clear that supervision is an integral part of the sentence. While this minimum period of six months is short compared with the periods which now follow a short prison sentence or a sentence of detention on a young adult offender, and more particularly the liability to two years' supervision on release from borstal, we envisage that the supervision given will often be more intensive than is at present usual either as after-care or under a probation order. We propose that, for the period of supervision, the Secretary of State should be able to prescribe a wide range of requirements including some which could be applied within the discretion of the supervisor. These would relate to such matters as place of residence, nature of employment, the undertaking of courses of education or training, avoidance of certain places of resort and participation in prescribed activities. Since some offenders, who are released from custody at a fairly early stage of their sentence, may be liable to a lengthy period of supervision, the supervising officer should consider at regular intervals whether the order is still serving a useful purpose and in appropriate cases should recommend its termination.

Recall to custody from supervision

37. A young adult offender released to supervision would be liable to be recalled to custody at any time during the period of supervision. On recall his liability to detention would be the balance of the term of the custody and control order or 30 days, whichever is the longer. Recall during the term of the order should be seen as part of the implementation of the sentence, whether it occurred as a result of a deterioration in the offender's behaviour and prospects or as a sanction for a breach of licence requirements. If, as we hope, release under supervision at an early stage is to be recommended with a measure of boldness, the possibility of fairly ready recall if things are going wrong may be thought to be essential. We should therefore like to see more flexible recall than is at present practised under the borstal system, as well as the provision of effective but less severe sanctions for breach of licence by an offender.

38. We are aware that the recall to custody of an offender who has been living in the community for a substantial time without committing further offences, or being in serious breach of his licence, is a drastic measure which could cause great resentment if used in circumstances which the offender himself might not fully understand. While recall in order to forestall a foreseeable breach of licence or a fresh offence may be used for constructive purposes, it may also make the offender feel that he is being subjected to a "cat and mouse" type of interference, especially if release followed by recall is repeated. Under the present borstal recall system, concern for the liberty of the offender is one of the reasons for infrequent resort to recall. We have therefore considered carefully what restrictions should be placed upon this power.

39. We recommend that when a young adult is first released, he should for a period of two months be regarded as being on extended leave from the establishment. During this period he should remain subject to the authority of the governor and liable to recall by him, after consultation with the probation service, on any reasonable grounds. On completing the two month period satisfactorily he should be regarded as being on licence, and liable to recall only on clear breach of a requirement. The procedure for recall would be carefully regulated and the offender would be able to make representations against a decision to recall him. These representations would be made to the advisory body which had recommended his release.

40. In the event of a young adult offender under supervision committing further offences, the court could make a new custody and control order of any length appropriate to the circumstances of the case.

41. A number of detailed problems result from the proposal to introduce a novel sentence such as the custody and control order, to be applied only to a limited age-group of offenders. We have made recommendations regarding the status and liabilities of offenders who attain 21 years of age during the currency of a custody and control order. We have also considered the possibility of suspending for a short time the implementation of a custody and control order. None of these recommendations raises matters of major principle and they are accordingly omitted from this review. Argument on them will be found in Part II of the report.

A non-custodial Supervision and Control Order

42. Our second main sentencing proposal is designed to develop and expand non-custodial treatment, building upon the existing probation system but with important new elements. The purpose of the proposed supervision and control order is to make available to the courts an order which would impose a new form of control in the community. While not involving committal to custody, it would be markedly stricter in its requirements than a probation order, which would however remain as an option available to the courts in dealing with young adult offenders. It would be appropriate for a fairly wide range of young adult offenders some of whom the courts at present feel obliged to sentence to custody—for instance some whom the courts send to detention centres, rather than place on probation, because a number of offences is involved or because they have already committed further offences while subject to an earlier probation order.

43. A court making a supervision and control order would lay down the range of requirements which, as in the case of supervision under a custody and control order, could be applied at the discretion of the supervisor. The supervision would be carried out by a probation officer who, because of the strict control envisaged and because the offender would often be of a more difficult type than the offenders at present handled on probation, might have to accept more of a controlling function than has been customary under the probation system. The probation service has already moved some way along this road in its administration of both after-care and parole, so that the change, though real, would not involve a new departure of principle. Since the purpose of the new order is to keep in the community offenders who would otherwise go into custody, its operation would in our view be entirely consistent with the basic traditions of the probation and after-care service.

44. The most important change which will be required in order to make supervision effective under a supervision and control order (and also of course on release under licence under a custody and control order) will be a major increase in the resources available. First and foremost this means human resources—more probation officers, with work loads such that they can give young adults the close attention which we envisage, with a greater readiness to intervene in their lives; and more varied—and often more intensive—supervision. Secondly, there will need to be an increase in the facilities which back up supervision—hostels and other accommodation, day training and so on. We appreciate that the service is already expanding at the present time and that some improvement in facilities is provided for in the 1972 Criminal Justice Act. Our proposals would require that both processes be intensified.

45. It follows from the character of the proposed supervision and control order that there should be no requirement that the offender should consent to it. It should however be a normal procedure that before making a supervision and control order the court should consider a social enquiry report, one purpose of which would be to ensure that the probation and after-care service saw a reasonable prospect of securing compliance by the offender with the requirements of the order.

46. On breach of a requirement of the order the supervisor could bring the

12

offender back to court, where he would be liable to a fine or other non-custodial measure. Alternatively, if the court considered that the order had wholly failed, he could be sentenced for the original offence.

47. We propose the introduction of a further sanction to support the supervision and control order, namely that power be given to the supervising officer to obtain a warrant from a magistrate for the temporary detention of the offender at short notice for a period of up to 72 hours. This could be used when either a serious breach had occurred, or the officer could show that temporary detention was required in order to forestall a breach or the commission of an offence. This proposal borrows from what we have learned of a practice developed in California where a supervising officer sometimes has an offender removed to temporary detention in order to make it possible for supervision in the community to be resumed, when otherwise custody would have become inevitable. This would be the primary object of its introduction here.

48. The proposal for temporary detention set out in the preceding paragraph, because it would be an innovation in the British system, would require particularly full discussion with the probation and after-care service, as indeed would other aspects of the operation of the supervision and control order. The purpose of the supervision and control order being to provide the means for exercising close control of offenders without committing them to custody, it is the view of the majority of us that the addition of the power of detention which we propose would enhance the order's effectiveness, thus making it more acceptable as an alternative to more severe action. Although the power may seem a drastic one by comparison with those which probation has already made familiar, this need not, in our view, prevent it from gaining acceptance if it can contribute to the important objective of achieving a major switch from custody to supervision in the community.

The organisation of the custodial system

49. It would be easier to translate into practice the concept of custody forming a continuous process with control in the community if offenders were normally held in custody near to where they are later to be released to supervision in the community. The evolution of the borstal system and the location of young prisoners' centres have precluded this in the past. Although great efforts have been made to ensure good liaison between the staff of establishments and probation officers in the offenders' home areas, distance usually restricts the opportunities for a probation officer to get to know an offender in advance of his release. For the same reason some families find frequent visiting difficult. We think that it should be an object of policy so to reorganise the pattern of location of establishments and the allocation of young adult offenders to them that periods in custody will normally be spent in establishments situated nearer to their home areas. This is already the case with offenders who are sent to detention centres and we would wish to see the system extended to all young adult offender establishments.

50. At present the choice among young prisoners' centres is small and they are not divided on a regional basis. There are now 23 training borstals for young men, widely scattered throughout the country (with one or two areas poorly

13

served) and divided, for purposes of the allocation of offenders, into two regions only, covering respectively the northern and southern halves of the country. Offenders sentenced to borstal training are sent first to an allocation centre, either at Manchester or at Wormwood Scrubs in London, before going on to their training establishment. Many of them, therefore, find themselves in custody a long way from home.

51. The process of assessment and allocation has become fairly elaborate and makes a substantial demand upon skilled staff. Recent research and the experience of those who operate the process suggest that the time and effort involved may have become disproportionate to the practical benefits derived from the attempt to classify offenders with a view to assigning them to specialised regimes precisely appropriate to their particular needs. While a simple form of classification is obviously required before a decision is made, for instance between open and closed conditions, the choice of different kinds of custodial regimes is not so varied as to justify prolonged assessment of the personal characteristics of most offenders. Any custodial establishment with an adequate induction system and reasonable flexibility in its facilities should be capable of receiving satisfactorily all offenders sent to it and of picking out for transfer the small minority who require specialist attention which cannot be provided within it. Some psychiatric cases, and possibly some with unusual educational requirements, might come within this category.

52. We therefore believe that it should be an aim of policy to regroup establishments for young adult offenders (which will in any case cease to be divided into young prisoners' centres, borstals and detention centres) in such a way that each area has one or more establishments covering a reasonable variety of regimes—including open and closed conditions and hostels—and developing links with the community which they serve. A young adult offender should then normally be sent for custody to an establishment serving his own area. This is what we have called the "neighbourhood" concept in Part II of the report. We have not attempted to decide how large these areas should be, but clearly they would have to be smaller than those at present recognised by the Prison Department for administrative purposes.

53. For such a system it would no longer be necessary to maintain allocation centres to which offenders would be sent after sentence. We are satisfied that a much simpler and more rapid system of allocation could be devised which would be entirely adequate and would release skilled personnel for more productive work.

54. We recognise that it would not be practicable to apply these proposals to young women offenders sentenced to custody, whose numbers are too small to justify the setting up of separate establishments in each area. Our recommendations contemplate some reorganisation of custodial establishments for young women, based upon a north-south division of the country and a flexible relationship between this and other age groups.

The nature and objectives of custodial regimes
55. If our sentencing proposals are accepted those who spend substantial periods in custody will in future be more strictly limited than at present to

14

those from whom the courts find it necessary to protect society. There will be no implication that the court thought them likely to respond to treatment. Moreover, under the proposal for neighbourhood establishments offenders with widely differing requirements will be found in the same establishment. No one type of approach can be laid down for such a heterogeneous collection of people, and variety of regime within each establishment and flexibility in application will be essential. In any event every custodial establishment must provide safe custody (though not always at the same level of security) and an adequate standard of physical care in terms of food, accommodation and health. Beyond that it must exert whatever influences may seem most likely to prepare offenders to return to life in the community with an improved prospect of keeping out of crime.

56. While this formulation of the problem may seem to present custodial staffs with a stern challenge, the experience already gained of the handling of difficult offenders with complex problems, both in borstal and in prison, shows that they can be effectively helped. Following the period in custody some are not reconvicted at all, while others after further minor convictions settle down and avoid the career of crime to which they had previously seemed committed. To achieve this is immensely worthwhile, and we believe that the prospects of success can be further improved if custody is seen increasingly as a preparation for return to and supervision in the community and if the co-operation between the custodial and supervising staff can be made even closer than at present.

57. Since the first condition of living a satisfactory life in the community is an ability to take one's own decisions and since this is precisely the area in which most offenders have proved inadequate, the custodial regime must have as its aim to motivate the offender to change his attitudes and to give him opportunities for exercising choice. This is intrinsically difficult to achieve within the framework of an institution whose inmates are being detained against their will and where some degree of discipline is imposed by the necessities of communal life. The borstal system, however, has long experience in this field and has had no small measure of success. Rule 1 of the Borstal Rules[1] is still a good general statement of what has to be attempted, though the wording has an old-fashioned ring. The problem is to translate such generalisations into specific programmes which meet individual needs and to make correct use of modern ideas and techniques in education, psychology and the social sciences. We have confined our main observations in this varied field to one or two main areas, where we believe that we have something to add to the thought already being given within the service to methods of improving custodial regimes.

Education, training and work
58. Education in custodial establishments, which was once seen as being limited to class-room schooling, an activity pursued largely in the evening after the serious day's work was done, is now increasingly recognised as an integral part of a wider learning process, which includes vocational and trade training and work as much as academic teaching. We welcome this change and wish to see it taken further. Education should have a status equal with other forms of training and work, both as regards trainees' earnings and as an activity to be

[1] See paragraph 329 below.

15

pursued in appropriate cases on a full-time basis during the day and not only in the evenings. In particular we should like to see increasing emphasis on social education relating to the behaviour which has brought the individual young adult offender into custody and the problems that he will have to face in the community.

59. The education officer should be a full member of the management team in every establishment. Since it is important that he should bring with him the most up-to-date expertise available in the education system, we prefer that he should, as at present, be employed by the local education authority rather than by the Prison Department. In a system of neighbourhood establishments this should have the additional advantage of facilitating the continuation in the community of courses begun in custody.

60. Further progress needs to be made in securing recognition that the education of offenders in custody is an integral though specialised part of the national education system and that a period of teaching in custodial establishments is an accepted part of a teacher's career. For this and other reasons set out in our report we recommend that a formal investigation should be made of the numerous administrative problems involved in the provision of education in establishments, including the level of resources required for their solution.

61. For many offenders vocational or trade training and work will be a more important part of the educational pattern than academic classes. Much useful development has taken place in these fields in recent years, but there is a constant need to keep forms of training and work in tune with outside conditions and to relate them more closely to probable employment opportunities. Although better success rates occur among those who receive vocational training and later obtain jobs where they can use their acquired skills, this applies only to a small minority, and indeed some offenders find that their criminal records virtually debar them from obtaining the work for which they have been trained while in custody. There is, too, a tendency to assume that most offenders will be seeking work in factories, whereas for many there may be at least equally good opportunities in catering, in the retail trades and even in office work. In this aspect of custodial regimes, good and continuous liaison between establishments and outside bodies concerned with employment, including the trade unions, is particularly important.

Punishments and rewards

62. The system of punishments and rewards, inherited from the past though greatly modified, still lies heavy upon attempts to make custodial regimes primarily therapeutic. In certain special establishments, of which the psychiatric prison at Grendon is the outstanding example, formal "tariff" punishments, including loss of remission, have to a large extent been superseded by more sophisticated means of control designed to fit the needs of the individual. This is a goal for all to aim at, but we recognise that it may not be attainable in establishments containing more widely varying types of offender and enjoying a less favourable ratio of staff, especially of skilled staff, to inmates. In the system as a whole some use of "tariff" penalties may be essential in order to maintain a smooth-running and reasonably civilised social unit, without which constructive policies could not be carried out.

63. Subject to that qualification, efforts should be made in all establishments to use penalties and methods of control for constructive purposes related to the individual's needs. Where, for instance, segregation is necessary, it should not be seen as a purely penal form of solitary confinement but also as an opportunity to persuade the offender to understand his situation better and so facilitate his return to normal conditions. We welcome the Home Secretary's decision to complete the abolition of dietary punishments.

64. The nature of the system of rewards and punishments and the spirit in which it is operated go to the heart of the all-important relationship between offenders and custodial staff. We are anxious to see custodial staff increasingly involved in the therapeutic and constructive aspects of their work and we believe that this is the predominant wish of the service. A constructive attitude is more likely to be engendered and staff will more easily see the positive side of their work if there is an increase in emphasis on rewards rather than punishments. Traditionally the authority of custodial staff has depended very largely upon the disciplinary sanctions at their disposal. In asking them to exert the authority which is necessary by more sophisticated means and on a more individual basis, we are making new demands upon their patience and skill and are assuming that they can be given the support and training to enable them to take on these responsibilities without loss of control or damage to their status. We believe that this can be done and that the end result will be as beneficial to staff as to offenders and to society as a whole.

Administration and staffing of establishments

65. Our recommendations, involving as they do the retention of separate establishments for young adult offenders, raise the question whether these ought not to be administered by a separate youth authority. We do not recommend this. One consideration that has weighed with us is that, if a separate youth authority were to be created, it would be natural to entrust it not only with control of custodial establishments but also with the control of young adult offenders in the community. The implications of this for the probation system would be drastic and we have not seen any sufficient advantages to be gained from the change to justify such dislocation of existing arrangements. The establishment of a youth authority running only custodial establishments would likewise involve a major disruption of the Prison Department, and could hardly be done without duplication of many common services. The organisation of the Prison Department has in the past enabled a sufficient share of the available resources and expertise to be channelled to the young adult system, and with some changes which we later recommend we consider that it can continue to maintain a distinct approach towards young adults. Moreover we have concluded after full discussion that both sets of establishments are most appropriately served by a single service with full inter-changeability of staffs throughout the whole system. This is clearly the wish of the prison service itself.

66. The Prison Department has the inherently difficult task of providing a unified national service offering satisfactory career prospects to its staff and meeting the reasonable requirements of staff associations for fair and uniform practices, while at the same time making the best use of individual skills and talents in a widely diversified range of establishments. We have not thought it

17

our task to investigate in detail the Department's management problems, but our enquiries have convinced us that there are some shortcomings in the present system and that their effect upon the treatment of young adult offenders deserves attention.

67. In recent years there has in our view been excessive mobility of senior staff between establishments. If particular methods of approach are to be developed and operated for long enough to show results or to provide a basis for research, continuity of direction by the same governor is important and may sometimes be indispensable. Changes have taken place more frequently than is desirable in many establishments with an adverse effect upon the morale of the establishment. The unsettling effect has been all the greater because it is rarely possible to promote to a vacant governorship the deputy governor already serving in the same establishment and able to ensure continuity of methods. There have been cases where the deputy governor has been transferred almost at the same time as the governor. Rigidity of the rules of the service governing the grading of posts and promotion are we believe at least partly responsible for this, and we consider that more flexibility is required.

68. We have also been struck by the limited extent to which governors are consulted, even in highly specialised establishments, about the suitability of staff who are allocated to them. Other public services, we believe, find it possible to allow such consultations to play a bigger part. The same comment applies to consultation with staff about their own career development. We appreciate, of course, that appointments made in one establishment have repercussions in others and that neither the needs of one particular establishment nor the wishes of an individual can always be decisive. Nevertheless, we believe that in the past excessive weight has been given, in filling vacant posts throughout the system, to considerations of grading and promotion, and that morale has suffered because staff feel that they are moved about in too impersonal and mechanical a manner. We are aware that the maintenance of personal relations with staff on the ground is one of the functions of the relatively recently established Regional Offices of the Prison Department, but these offices do not appear to the staffs of establishments to have much effect upon postings and promotions, which are nationally determined. Nor are they able to provide for the staff of young adult offender establishments the kind of moral support which, we were frequently told, used to be offered by the Director of Borstal Administration.

69. Complaints on these scores have been widely voiced to us in the course of our enquiry, and we hope that early attention will be given to them. We feel it is for the Department rather than for us to devise specific remedies. However, two particular recommendations that we make are, first, the appointment at a high level in the Prison Department of someone with sole responsibility for the young adult custodial system, and, secondly, the setting up of a standing advisory body with terms of reference extending over the young adult offender system as a whole.

Hostels
70. We have laid great emphasis throughout our report on our wish to see a substantial switch from custody to supervision in the community. The key to

effective supervision in the community is the relationship between the supervising officer and the offender; but a substantial number of the offenders whom we should like to see treated in the community will require residential support, and there is a clear need for an expansion of hostel and other accommodation. Hostels are neither cheap nor easy to operate effectively, but there can be no doubt of their value for particular categories of offenders, some at least of which can be fairly readily identified. These include the completely homeless and those in conflict with their homes; those who need to be insulated from destructive influence of either a home or a peer group; and those who, by reason of personality disorder or other cause, cannot order their own lives satisfactorily unless given continuing residential support. It is our belief that if the right kind of accommodation could be more widely available for such people, courts and supervisors alike would gladly make use of it in many cases where now custody seems unavoidable.

71. Hostels need to be varied in character. Some would need well-qualified staff, capable of providing skilled support; in others the relationship of a benevolent landlady to a young lodger might provide the necessary sense of security. We believe that the system of administration of hostels by a variety of agencies—both voluntary bodies, supported by public funds, and the probation committees under their new statutory powers—should continue. Material conditions and staff training in voluntary hostels should be improved so that common national standards may be established. Additional public money will be necessary for this purpose.

72. Hostels attached to Prison Department establishments such as Hollesley Bay should remain under Prison Department administration and more should be created. We do not, however, believe that the prison service should become generally involved in the running of hostels in the community.

73. We think that hostels should, as a general rule, serve a nearby area. Our proposal for reorganising custodial establishments on a "neighbourhood" basis reinforces the argument for this. We would wish to see the question of the number and range of hostels required investigated in each region in relation to local circumstances. These investigations should be set in motion by the Home Office, the purpose being to ensure that programmes for extension of the hostel system would be so adapted to the services available in each region as to facilitate to the maximum extent the treatment of offenders in the community.

Remand

74. In our view there is scope for the increased use of bail for young adult offenders, both before conviction and before sentence. Remand in custody should be used only where there are exceptionally strong reasons for it, and never as a simply punitive measure.

Information requirements

75. We have made a number of detailed recommendations about the collection and provision of information for the courts and for those who deal with the offender after sentence. In particular we have sought to improve and systematise further the present provision of social enquiry reports and have proposed a limited trial of a system of correctional assessment of offenders,

to be carried out at an early stage in an offender's career for future use by both courts and those responsible for carrying out the courts' orders.

76. While our sentencing recommendations may simplify the task of the court in reaching its decision at the time of conviction, nevertheless it will still be important for it to have all available information about an offender, for instance to enable it to decide whether to make a custody and control order or a supervision and control order. We recommend strongly that, where the court feels the need to remand for further information, it should whenever possible remand on bail. There is reason to believe that, at least in some areas, many offenders are now remanded in custody for psychiatric reports which could equally well be made in the community. An additional reason for requiring efficient reporting is that an adequate social enquiry report will, under our proposals, be expected to provide the basis for a simplified form of allocation to a particular establishment.

77. Finally, both the systematising of social enquiry reports and the proposal for the experimental introduction of correctional assessments should be seen as additional tools for improved analysis of the effects of particular sentences and forms of treatment. Adequate research into these problems should, in our view, be regarded not only as an academic matter but as an essential pre-condition of the rational development of methods of dealing with young adult offenders.

CHAPTER 3

SUMMARY OF PRINCIPAL RECOMMENDATIONS

78. In this chapter we summarise our principal and specific recommendations. For detailed reference, recommendations are printed in italics where they occur in the body of the report and in some of the appendices.

The young adult offender

79. (1) There should continue to be special sentencing and treatment arrangements for an intermediate category of young adult offenders, starting at the age of 17. The upper age limit should remain at 21, but the Secretary of State should have power to raise it by statutory instrument (paragraphs 86 and 91). Some special arrangements for flexibility around the age limits are proposed in Appendix E.

(2) Whatever arrangements are made for offenders under 17, young adults who receive custodial sentences should be dealt with separately from them (paragraph 89).

Custodial sentences

(3) The existing custodial sentences of imprisonment of young adults, borstal training and detention in a detention centre should be combined into a single "generic" sentence to be called a custody and control order; and the separate systems of establishments catering for the three sentences should be merged into a single system. The sentence should be available in respect of any offence punishable in the case of an adult by imprisonment, except murder. The court would determine the length of the order in each case without restriction other than the statutory maximum for the offence, which would be the same as the statutory maximum prison sentence. A court should not, in pursuit of a "treatment" objective, make a longer order than the sentence of imprisonment it would pass on an adult who had committed the same offence and had similar antecedents (paragraphs 182 and 186).

(4) The penalty for murder by a person aged 18 and under 21 should be the same as is provided for murder committed by a person under the age of 18, namely detention during Her Majesty's Pleasure, or such sentence as the Criminal Law Revision Committee recommends to replace that sentence (paragraph 184).

(5) The maximum length of custody and control order that a magistrates' court should be able to impose should in general be six months. Magistrates' courts should have power to commit to the Crown Court for sentence after summary trial if they consider their powers insufficient. The minimum length for all courts should be three months. Unless the offence is sufficiently serious to warrant a sentence of that length the court should employ a non-custodial measure (paragraphs 176, 187 and 188).

(6) There should be a statutory requirement that a court should not make

21

a custody and control order in respect of a young adult who has not previously been subject to such an order unless it is of opinion that no other method of dealing with him is appropriate; and it should state the reasons for that opinion (paragraph 190).

(7) Subject to the arrangements and restrictions in recommendations 8 to 13 following, it should be possible at any time during the period of a custody and control order to release an offender from custody to control under licence in the community (paragraph 181).

(8) Constitutional responsibility for decisions to release to control in the community should continue to rest with the Secretary of State, decisions being taken, as far as practicable, on his behalf at a local or regional level (paragraph 192).

(9) For the purpose of making recommendations for the release of offenders on licence there should be set up in respect of each establishment (or group of establishments) a licence advisory committee (paragraph 193).

(10) In respect of custody and control orders of less than three years, recommendations regarding release should be made to the Secretary of State by the licence advisory committee direct. Cases involving orders of three years or more would be referred by the committee to the Parole Board, who would make the recommendation to the Secretary of State (paragraphs 193 and 196).

(11) Irrespective of the opportunities for early release referred to above, a young adult subject to a custody and control order should in any event have a statutory entitlement, subject to good behaviour, to release on licence after not more than two thirds of the term of the order has elapsed (paragraphs 198 to 205).

(12) Where it is necessary for the protection of the public, the Crown Court when making a custody and control order of at least 12 months and less than three years should be empowered exceptionally to make a restricted release order, the effect of which would be that release should not take place without reference to the Court until a specified proportion of the sentence had been served. That proportion should be common to all cases in which a restricted release order is made, and should be fixed by statutory instrument. Initially it should be set at one third (paragraphs 206 to 208).

(13) Time spent on remand in custody before conviction or sentence should count towards sentence for the purposes of calculating the length of the custody and control order, the entitlement to release, and the expiration of any restricted release order (paragraph 211).

(14) In general the decision to release on licence should be based on an assessment of the individual's needs, but regard should also be had to the likelihood of further offences, the damage they would cause, and the potential effect on public confidence in the sentencing and release arrangements (paragraphs 212 to 217).

(15) On release from custody an offender subject to a custody and control order should normally be under supervision for the balance of the term of the order, or for six months, whichever is longer. Licence requirements on release should be stronger and more specific than those at present and should give greater flexibility to the supervisor (paragraphs 220 and 223).

(16) A person released on licence under a custody and control order should be liable to recall during the period of supervision (paragraph 224). The first two months after release should be regarded as a period of "long leave" during which the offender could be recalled by the governor on any reasonable grounds without right of appeal (paragraph 229). Thereafter an offender should be liable to recall only where there has been a clear breach of the licence requirements, and he should then have a right of appeal (paragraphs 230 to 233). An offender's maximum liability to detention on recall should be the balance of the term of the custody and control order or 30 days, whichever is longer. The supervising officer should alternatively be able to take the offender before a magistrates' court for breach of the licence requirements. The court should be able to impose any of the available non-custodial penalties or, exceptionally, order return to custody (paragraph 226).

(17) A court should have power in exceptional circumstances to postpone the commencement of the custodial element of the sentence for a short specified period on the application of the defence, or for not more than seven days on the application of the Prison Department (paragraphs 235 to 238).

(18) Arrangements should be developed to facilitate early consideration of appeals by young adult offenders against short custodial sentences; and the courts should be encouraged to adopt a more liberal policy than hitherto in the granting of bail pending appeal (Appendix F).

(19) Discharge grants for young adults should be at least as generous as for older prisoners; they should be regularly reviewed, and in particular should keep pace with the cost of living (paragraphs 255 to 259).

Non-custodial sentences
(20) As a means of promoting the use, and the acceptance by the public, of non-custodial measures for many offenders who are not at present dealt with in the community, there should be a new and stronger non-custodial sentence for young adults, the supervision and control order, to be available (in addition to the existing probation order) in respect of any offence punishable in the case of an adult by imprisonment (paragraph 260). This should be operated by the probation service; the supervisor should have available a wide range of potential requirements to be invoked as and when he considers their use desirable. The making of an order should not require the offender's consent (paragraphs 269 to 278).

(21) In the event of breach of requirements of a supervision and control order, the supervisor should be empowered to take the offender before a magistrates' court. The court should then be able to impose any non-custodial measure available to it, in which case the supervision and control order would remain in force, or revoke the order and sentence the offender afresh for the original offence (paragraphs 281 and 282).

(22) The supervisor should also be able, where a breach of the order has been committed or he has grounds for believing that the offender is contemplating a breach or the commission of an offence, to apply to a magistrate for the offender's detention for up to 72 hours. The offender would normally be detained in the nearest young adult establishment (paragraphs 283 to 288).

(23) The two existing senior attendance centres should be discontinued.

23

There should however be an experimental attendance centre, properly equipped for the purpose, specially for the training of traffic offenders (paragraph 298).

The organisation of custodial establishments

(24) As indicated earlier, the existing young prisoners' centres, borstals and detention centres should be combined in a single system of establishments; and the present borstal allocation system should be abandoned. As a means of maintaining and developing ties with offenders' home areas and with the supervising service, young adult offender establishments should be developed in the form of "neighbourhood" establishments, serving limited committal areas and situated in or near to the areas from which their trainees come. They should provide for a wide range of trainees (although one or two specialist establishments may need to be retained) under the control of a single governor; their facilities should include a range of security conditions, and a hostel in which offenders would still be regarded as legally in custody (paragraphs 317 to 321).

(25) Because of the much smaller number in custody similar arrangements are not feasible for young women, and allocation should be on the basis of suitability for open and closed conditions and whether the offender lives in the north or south of the country. Young women need not be separated from older women (paragraphs 322 to 324).

Custodial regimes

(26) The objectives of custodial establishments for young adult offenders, which should be formulated in a statutory rule, should be educational in the broadest sense, and such as to motivate the offender towards change and maturation. Classroom education, vocational and trade training, industrial work and ordinary institutional maintenance work should all be regarded as ways of meeting the overall educational objective (paragraphs 338 and 339).

(27) The content of educational activities in this wide sense should be related to the needs of the individual and his future educational needs and employment prospects. Education courses should not be planned in isolation, but should be designed to prepare the offender for further education or training in the community after release to supervision. Greater use should be made during the custodial element of the sentence of day release courses in the community. The present statutory rules which provide for a minimum number of hours per week of formal classroom education should be revoked. Individual trainees should have a greater choice of activities, and pay should not differ according to whether they are engaged in study, vocational training or work (paragraphs 339 to 347 and 350).

(28) The Prison Department should continue to look to local education authorities for the provision of staff for education arrangements. A period of service in a custodial establishment should be seen as an integral part of a teacher's career, and should not be a handicap to subsequent promotion (paragraph 348). Education staff should be more fully integrated into the life of the establishment as a whole, and the education officer should always be a full member of the management team (paragraph 349). Each local education authority should be invited to designate an adviser or inspector responsible for education of delinquents, both in custody and in the community. There should be a formal examination by the Home Office, the Department of Education and Science and other interested bodies of the objectives and content of

education in custody and ways of integrating education in custodial establishments more fully into the national education system (paragraph 351).

(29) All work undertaken in a custodial establishment should have a practical and intelligible purpose, using up-to-date methods and no unnecessary manual labour: with this in mind, the Department should review the value of certain kinds of work, specifically metal recovery and domestic work (paragraph 356).

(30) Officers in young adult establishments should wear civilian clothes (paragraphs 369 and 370).

Management and resources

(31) A senior official should be designated within the Prison Department to co-ordinate policy on young adult matters, with no other responsibilities (paragraph 385).

(32) There should be a standing advisory body, whose terms of reference would extend over the young adult offender system as a whole, consisting of officials of the Prison Department and persons from outside including judges, magistrates and representatives of voluntary bodies. Its purpose would be to provide a forum for an informal exchange of views and review of policy (paragraphs 386 and 387).

(33) The Prison Department, in consultation with the staff associations, should draw up procedures to avoid frequent movement of senior staff where this would cause instability in establishments. This may necessitate more flexible grading structures (paragraphs 388 to 395).

(34) Staff should be brought more fully into the planning of their own careers; and governors should be more closely consulted about the appointment of senior staff to their establishments. A person with a particular aptitude for work with young adults should be able to make a satisfactory career in that work (paragraphs 396 and 397).

(35) The Prison Department should continue to seek sites in or near urban areas for establishments for young adult offenders; and planning authorities should recognise, and give proper priority to, the obligation of the community to make provision for the treatment of young adult offenders in the places where it is most likely to be effective (paragraph 403).

(36) In framing future forecasts of probation service manpower, the Department should consider, and where necessary allow for a reduction in, workloads in the context of the supervision and control order. Additional physical resources should also be made available in connection with this order (paragraphs 404 to 407).

Hostels and other accommodation

(37) Priority should be given to the provision of a range of accommodation in the community for young adult offenders. The main need for expansion is in hostels of the existing approved probation hostel type; but the role of hostels should be expanded, so as to include some young adults who on existing criteria might not be regarded as suitable for a non-custodial sentence. There is a particular need for hostels for homeless young recidivists (paragraphs 415 to 424).

(38) The rules about admission to hostels should be amended to allow the admission of young women who are pregnant. Where residents have the ability and motivation to engage in full-time education this should be encouraged, and the rules should be amended to relieve them of the obligation to seek work and contribute to maintenance (paragraphs 425 to 427).

(39) There should be provision, including financial support from public funds, for voluntary residence in a hostel where a supervisor thinks this appropriate (paragraph 433).

(40) Further hostels outside the custodial system should in the main be provided and managed by probation and after-care committees. Public funds should bear a greater share of the cost of after-care hostels run by voluntary bodies. To determine how great an expansion is needed the Home Office should survey the existing supply of, and demand for, hostel places. The survey should include other forms of accommodation available for offenders. Planning authorities should consider sympathetically whether hostels can be provided for in plans for urban development and renewal, and there may be value in planning hostels as part of wider treatment complexes (paragraphs 434, 435 and 439).

(41) Changes are needed in staffing arrangements to deal with the problems of low pay, the lack of a unified career structure, and the isolation of hostel staff from the main-stream of social work. Greater co-operation and co-ordination of the various agencies involved, a system of comprehensive regional planning, and the provision of new hostels by public authorities should all help in this respect (paragraph 441).

(42) Lodgings may be especially useful for young people who are un-acceptable as residents in a hostel of the traditional type, or as a transition from such a hostel to complete independence. The probation service should continue to develop ways of supporting landladies who run lodging schemes so that they are assured of help in times of crisis (paragraphs 442 to 446).

Remand and assessment

(43) Bail should be granted to a young adult before conviction or sentence unless there are particularly strong reasons for refusing it (paragraph 449). The likelihood of a custodial sentence should not in itself be regarded as a conclusive argument in favour of remanding in custody. The law should be amended to prohibit remand in custody where the offence of which the person is accused or convicted is not punishable by a custodial sentence (paragraph 450). Remand in custody should never be used for punitive purposes (paragraphs 452 to 455).

(44) Courts should be encouraged to make fuller use of arrangements recently introduced with a view to reducing the remand population, in particular the facilities for psychiatric assessment on bail. In a number of ways there is scope for improving the machinery for obtaining psychiatric reports on bail. There should be further provision of hostel places for persons on remand who are required to reside in a hostel as a condition of bail (paragraphs 456 and 457).

(45) Where it is necessary to remand a young adult in custody he should be remanded to the nearest available remand centre, provided this is within a reasonable distance, or, if it is not, to a local prison (paragraph 462).

(46) Present arrangements for the preparation by the Prison Department of reports on response to previous custodial sentences should be discontinued. Instead a more thorough discharge report should be prepared than at present, which would be forwarded to the court in the event of a further court appearance, as well as constituting the discharge report to the supervisor and "feedback" to those preparing correctional assessments (paragraphs 483 to 485).

(47) A field trial should be undertaken of a new system of correctional assessments, embracing information about an offender's history, social background and educational achievements, personal characteristics and intellectual status, aptitudes and interests. Its purpose should be to provide staff with a more carefully formulated starting point in dealing with the offender; it would also provide a basis for research into the characteristics of offenders and the suitability of different treatment approaches (paragraphs 489 to 497).

CHAPTER 4

YOUNG ADULT OFFENDERS AS A SEPARATE LEGAL CATEGORY

80. The recognition of a separate legal category of young adult offender within the English penal system dates from the recommendations of the Gladstone Committee of 1895 and the Prevention of Crime Act 1908, which established a separate borstal sentence[1] for this age group and began the development of borstal institutions. The new arrangement was applied only to carefully selected offenders within the age group. Nevertheless it was a major breakthrough in penal thinking, and over the years the influence of the borstal system has spread outwards to more varied types of young adult offender and to numerous other countries, and its principles have also influenced thinking about the treatment of older offenders.

81. A natural question to ask at the outset of any examination of the system of treatment of young offenders aged 17 and under 21 is whether, in the light of the many social changes which have occurred, offenders in this particular age group should still be treated as a distinct legal category, separate from children and young persons (ie persons under 17)[2] on the one hand and persons aged over 21 on the other; if so, whether this distinction should apply, as at present, both to the sentencing and to the subsequent handling of offenders; and whether the concept should be extended to include separate youth courts.

82. The most obvious reason for considering this question afresh is the recent lowering of the age of majority from 21 to 18. It has been argued from this that it would be logical to treat those over 18 years of age as fully adult for all purposes. Some have suggested that, if this were done, a new category of young offender might be created to bridge the gap between the present compulsory school-leaving age of 16 and the attainment of majority at 18. We consider that such proposals are misconceived; and in this we are supported by most of the evidence submitted to us, which favours the continuance of separate sentencing and treatment arrangements for young adults. The Latey Committee, while recommending 18 as the age of majority, argued that the general capacity of young people to order their personal affairs should not affect the criminal or penal field.[3] We agree with them that the age selected for the general exercise of civic rights and responsibilities need not dictate the age limits for special treatment under the criminal law.

83. Nor does it seem to us that the new age of compulsory school-leaving

---

[1] In the words of the Act, "a sentence of detention under penal discipline in a Borstal Institution".

[2] Offences by persons aged under 17 are dealt with under the provisions of the Children and Young Persons Acts 1933 to 1969. In general for the purposes of those Acts a child is a person aged under 14 and a young person is one aged 14 and under 17. We refer to the position regarding implementation of the Children and Young Persons Act 1969 in paragraphs 87 to 89 below.

[3] Report of the Committee on the Age of Majority (Cmnd 3342), paragraph 27.

should necessarily, or even logically, form the dividing line between different types of penal provision. Since in this review we have been invited to consider only offenders aged 17 and over, we have not given detailed attention to those who are below that age. But it seems a reasonable view that in the year after leaving school, when young people are meeting new social and commercial pressures without the control and support which school formerly provided, they may well have a special need for the type of educational and welfare approach to their problems which is implicit in the Children and Young Persons Acts. We therefore see no reason to suggest that they should, instead, be put into a new group together with those aged between 17 and 18.

84. Accepting, then, that there are no convincing arguments for replacing 17 as the lower age limit for the group which we are considering, we have also concluded that there is still a sound case for maintaining and developing separate provisions for young adult offenders in the years after they have attained that age. From this age until the early or middle twenties, young people are going through a process of trying to find a role and identity as adults. They are not yet set in their ways and their images of themselves and of society at large are subject to rapid changes. Of those who are convicted of criminal offences, many will have been failures at school and a good proportion will already have been in conflict with the law and subject to various forms of social intervention. A period under some special form of control may offer the last chance of helping some of them to avoid becoming recidivists; we hope in this report to outline some of the ways in which we think this can be done. But many of these offenders appear to become less prone to commit offences as they enter their middle twenties and at the least the treatment of young adult offenders can be viewed as a process of helping them through this difficult period. It was the Gladstone Committee, reporting in 1895, who first expressed the view that there should be a concentration of reformative effort in dealing with offenders during this particular period of their development. We consider that there remains a strong case, in terms of the protection of the public as well as in the interests of offenders themselves, for making the concentrated effort to which the Gladstone Committee referred.

85. To make this a reality the necessary administrative resources have to be made available and the courts must have appropriate sentencing powers. Enough staff must be provided, both in custodial establishments and in the community, to make possible continuous assessment of the offender's attitudes and prospects and to enable staff members to take continuous responsibility for small manageable groups and to pay particular attention to the most deprived, disturbed and institutionalised offenders. The courts, for their part, must have available a form of sentence which gives to those responsible for handling offenders after sentence the necessary discretion to alter the form and content of treatment in response to changing requirements.

86. While, ideally, one might wish to apply these principles to offenders of all ages, material resources and skilled manpower are limited, and it is necessary to make choices in the priorities to be accorded to the competing claims of different groups, as well as among the competing claims of the different social services. We believe that, for the reasons given above, a special effort should be made with this particularly vulnerable age group; and that the necessary

29

effort is possible. The existence of a separate legally recognised age group for both sentencing and treatment purposes is, we believe, already acceptable to the courts, to those who deal with offenders, and to the public through familiarity with borstal and, to a lesser extent, with detention centres. There is therefore much useful experience upon which to build. Indeed, for some of us the mere fact that special sentences and treatment facilities already exist for this age group is the decisive factor. Many features of borstal have permeated the prison system. In the same way we are sure that experiments started in the young adult system will be capable of extension when they have proved their value and become accepted by the public. *We accordingly recommend that a separate category of young adult offenders starting at the age of 17 should continue to be recognised* and all our recommendations are, unless otherwise stated, related to this group.

87. Under present arrangements, and pending full implementation of the Children and Young Persons Act 1969, there is not a clean dividing line at age 17. The present position is that the Crown Court may sentence a young person of 15 or 16 years of age to borstal training if it is of opinion that no other method of dealing with him is appropriate.[4] With the consent of the Secretary of State for Social Services[5] it is also possible—although cases are very few—for a juvenile court to transfer a person aged 15 or over who is subject to a care order from a community home to borstal "if his behaviour is such that it will be detrimental to the persons accommodated in any community home for him to be accommodated there".[6] It is not necessary that such a person should have been convicted of any offence. The Prison Department is also responsible for providing detention centre facilities for boys under 17: the minimum age for a sentence of detention in a detention centre is 14.[7] Separate senior and junior centres are provided for the 17–20 and 14–16 age groups respectively.

88. The Children and Young Persons Act 1969 permits the minimum age for sentences of detention in a detention centre to be raised to 17,[8] and the minimum age for a sentence of borstal training to be raised from 15 to 17[9]. The Act also allows the minimum age for removal from a community home to a borstal to be adjusted correspondingly.[10] These provisions have not been brought into force. The present Government indicated in 1970 that they did not intend to do so until they had received our report, and that in any case they will not withdraw the power to commit persons under 17 to borstal until the system of community homes has developed sufficiently to deal with them.

89. Young people under 17 are outside our terms of reference for the present review, and it is not for us to say what their treatment should be save to the extent that it impinges on the young adult system. From this angle we are bound to observe that our recommendations for the reorganisation of the

---

[4] Criminal Justice Act 1961, s. 1: 15 and 16 year olds make up about 10% of the present borstal population, and are not kept separate from all older offenders.
[5] In Wales, the Secretary of State for Wales.
[6] Children and Young Persons Act 1969, s. 31.
[7] Criminal Justice Act 1961, s. 4.
[8] Section 7(3).
[9] Section 7(1): section 34(1)(d) permits the minimum age to be raised to 16 as a transitional measure.
[10] Section 34(1)(f).

custodial system, which are designed to meet the needs of offenders between the ages of 17 and 21, will be more difficult to implement if the system continues to have to cope with large numbers of younger people. Our proposals involve the abolition of borstals and senior detention centres as such. There will instead be a single system of custodial establishments for young adults, organised as far as possible on a "neighbourhood" basis, and each taking, with a few exceptions, the whole range of young adults from the area who receive custodial sentences. The regime should include scope for full-time education for those who are educationally backward or unusually gifted, but it should recognise that the population will see themselves as adults with their school days behind them and that they should be treated as such. A different orientation is needed for those who are still schoolboys and schoolgirls, perhaps with the prospect of returning to ordinary full-time education still before them. We do not consider that both groups can be accommodated successfully in the same establishment and we understand that difficulties arise where this has to be done in the system as it is at present. The new system we propose could hardly include separate establishments in each area for those who are below the minimum school-leaving age and the task of providing full-time school-type education for those under 16 would therefore be much more difficult than at present, unless separate establishments covering much wider areas were provided for them, and this would depart from the "neighbourhood" principle in which we see so many advantages. It is therefore our view that the arrangements for the treatment of young offenders aged 17 and over should not be complicated in this way, and *we recommend that juvenile offenders under 17 should be dealt with entirely separately.*

90. Our recommendations generally are not intended to affect the existing powers in section 53 of the Children and Young Persons Act 1933 to deal with the very small number of persons under 18 convicted of murder, or persons under 17 convicted of grave crimes, who may be detained "in such place and under such conditions as the Secretary of State may direct", nor to conflict with whatever the Criminal Law Revision Committee may eventually[11] recommend regarding the penalty for murder by a person under 18. We recognise that the Secretary of State may decide, as now, that such people should spend part of their sentences in establishments for young adults.

The upper age limit

91. Young people become fully mature at widely differing ages. Suggestions have been made to us that the upper age limit for young adults, at present 21, should be extended to 23 or even to 25. A case can be made for either of these but clearly no one age can be uniquely appropriate for all offenders; yet courts and administrative authorities alike require an overall limit to which they can work. Examination of current statistics shows that, if the limit were to be raised immediately to 25, more than half of the present daily average population of Prison Department establishments would come within the young adult category. This would be bound to defeat the objective of achieving a significant concentration of all kinds of resources upon this age group. Even a decision to raise the limit immediately to 23 would involve a similar though

---

[11] In paragraph 184 we refer to an interim report of the Committee, in which they have made a provisional recommendation on this subject.

reduced risk. *We therefore recommend that the upper limit should remain at 21, but that new legislation should include a power to raise the age by statutory instrument to such higher age as the Secretary of State may determine.* We see no need to place a limit on the age which the Secretary of State may specify, since this will inevitably be governed by the future availability of resources capable of handling a larger number and wider range of offenders within the system.

Exceptions to age limits

92. Since the choice of age limits cannot take account of the many divergencies in the rate of development and the treatment needs of different offenders, we think it right to provide for exceptions to be made in special cases. In Appendix E we add to our new sentencing proposals in Chapter 8 detailed provisions to enable courts exceptionally to sentence an offender over 21 as though he were under 21. In addition where a young adult offender is still in custody when he reaches the age of 21 there will often be advantage in his remaining in the young adult establishment. On the other hand we shall also propose that it should be possible to transfer to an adult establishment a person who was sentenced as a young adult and is still under 21 years of age. We do not envisage that cases of the latter type should be numerous or that they should make any significant inroad upon the general proposition that the young adult offender system is designed for the treatment of those who are between 17 and 21 years of age.

93. At the other end of the scale, we do not propose a general power to sentence young adults over 17 as if they were juveniles. It is obvious that if an offender has recently been in local authority care the court before which he is brought should take full account of his response to earlier treatment, and we shall recommend that in this situation the court should be required to consult the local authority concerned. But we do not consider that any special powers of sentence are needed: where the right course is to secure a continuation of local authority care, this can be arranged informally.

Youth courts

94. From time to time in the past it has been suggested that there should be separate courts for young offenders in this age group[12] or that they should be subject to the jurisdiction of juvenile courts, or that after conviction the court's functions should cease, leaving sentence to be determined by a sentencing panel composed of people with academic knowledge or practical experience of the treatment of young adult offenders. Such possibilities have been raised by a small number of witnesses who submitted written evidence to us, but the majority made no recommendation for changes in court procedures and it is clear that the idea of introducing special court arrangements for dealing with this age group attracts only limited support. We have considered each of the

---

[12] Some members of the Committee on Children and Young Persons (the Ingleby Committee), which reported in 1960, favoured a "youth court" to deal with offenders aged 17 up to 20 or 21, mainly it would appear as a means of reducing delays in dealing with young offenders committed to a higher court for trial or sentence. The Committee refrained from making a recommendation, since the matter was not within its terms of reference, but suggested that it called for further examination. More detailed proposals appeared in the White Paper *The Child, the Family and the Young Offender,* published in 1965, but have not since been pursued.

proposals put to us, but *we recommend that offenders aged 17 and under 21 should continue to be dealt with by the same courts and court procedures as those over 21.*

95. In part the reasoning behind proposals for youth courts has been that they would reduce delays in dealing with young adults charged with the more serious offences and committed for trial or sentence. We believe that this argument has been weakened by the experience of the operation of the new Crown Court which over the country as a whole has already markedly reduced the delays in bringing people to trial. It is further argued that special expertise is needed to deal with this age group. If the sentence selected by the court had the effect of defining in detail and once for all the form of treatment which an offender was to receive, a case could be made out for a separate court composed of people with special knowledge of the problems of dealing with young adults. But our sentencing proposals do not take this form, and do not call for a separate court system. It would of course be desirable for court clerks to arrange wherever practicable that a court trying and sentencing young adults should include one or more persons with experience of dealing with late adolescents and young adults in their ordinary lives, but we do not think it necessary to lay down separate legal requirements for the composition of such courts.

CHAPTER 5

THE SOCIAL CONTEXT OF THE YOUNG ADULT OFFENDER SYSTEM

96. One of the most fundamental changes brought about by the borstal sentence has been the notion that borstal training, unlike the essentially punitive prison sentence which preceded its introduction, should be seen in the context of the offender's previous life and, above all, of the social conditions and pressures to which he would return after completing his sentence. This has influenced both the nature of the training provided and the timing of the offender's release to a period of supervision on licence. It has stood the test of time and is still valid, but the great changes which have taken place in society during this century have profoundly altered the outlook and status of young people in the community and the nature of the problems which bring them into conflict with the law. This is too obvious to require lengthy general comment from us, but one or two factors which are particularly relevant to the handling of this age group of offenders should be mentioned.

97. Opinions will no doubt differ on the question of what is relevant in this connection, for the causes of crime seem as complex to us as they have done to our predecessors. Criminological research has not established indubitable causal connections between particular social factors or personal characteristics and the commission of offences. Even if a disproportionate number of delinquents come from certain social groups and certain kinds of family situation, a larger number of those who have the same background do not become involved with the penal system. Nevertheless it is highly probable that in individual cases delinquency is partly an adaptation to such factors as instability in family life, blocked aspirations at school or at work and poor material conditions generally. For this reason, in considering the treatment of young adult offenders we have been conscious that social intervention of one kind or another at an earlier age might often have had a better prospect of affecting delinquent habits than any training that can be given in the course of a relatively short penal sentence at a later stage.

98. To discuss this problem in detail would be outside our terms of reference. But it would be unrealistic, in describing the background against which our review has been conducted, to ignore the adverse influence of the social environment from which many young adult offenders come and to which they will almost inevitably return after a custodial sentence. In some neighbourhoods many young adults repeatedly commit crime as part of their normal pattern of life. Young men to whom we have spoken in borstals have attributed their offences simply to "boredom". What they need are legitimate outlets for their energies.

99. A young man serving a custodial sentence is insulated from many of the social pressures of ordinary life. Some, especially those with long institutional

34

experience, aim to get by simply by superficial conformity with the requirements of staff and the regime. But others, under the positive influence of staff, mature and undergo a real change of attitude, leaving the establishment with every intention of trying to lead a good, useful and law-abiding life on release. But returning as they often must to adverse home surroundings, to old associates, possibly to a period of unemployment, and generally to the problems which beset them before their offence, their task in keeping clear of further trouble is a daunting one, however close the support and control of those responsible for post-release supervision. Although there is evidence that in the longer term most offenders will settle down to a law-abiding life as they become older and take on the responsibilities of marriage and parenthood, it is hardly surprising that in the short term so many quickly return to crime. This is the sombre background against which staff, both in Prison Department establishments and in the probation service, have to work, and the so-called failure rates must be viewed against this perspective: the agencies which deal with young adult offenders cannot be blamed if they do not succeed in overcoming deep-rooted social influences of the kind that we have described.

100. We therefore wish to stress the importance that we attach to any action, public or private, that can be taken to improve the quality of home life and the stability of families, and to provide children and young people with schooling, leisure activities and work that will give them satisfaction and a sense of personal value. The prevention of crime is a broad social problem requiring measures which cannot be taken exclusively—or even mainly—within the field of the criminal law and the penal system.

101. The growing awareness of the complex origins of criminal behaviour has been accompanied by widespread questioning of many conventional standards which, half a century ago, seemed to have a sufficient weight of religious authority and social consensus behind them to justify society, and especially its penal institutions, in attempting to impose them firmly upon those young people who did not willingly accept them. Thus in the early years of borstal it was reasonable to assume that most young adults would be released into an essentially hierarchical society in which their status would be a fairly humble one; and that regular habits of work, a reasonably conformist attitude to the group in which they worked and respect for authority were among the main qualities which would help offenders to take their expected place in society. Even if a fair number of offenders reacted against this stereotyped picture of what their life should be, it was nevertheless a sufficiently accurate description of what they knew they would encounter on release to persuade most of them that it was inevitable. In any case this picture of society gave to borstal staff a reasonably clear idea of what the task of training these young people involved.

102. Since the end of the Second World War the scene has been transformed. Long periods of relatively full employment in most areas have given to most young people, soon after they leave school, a measure of economic independence which has reduced parental control. It has also made them a target for commercial advertising, which was previously concentrated upon more mature groups, and this in turn has stimulated their material ambitions. Many influences including those of the mass media have made them conscious of

themselves as members of a distinct group in society, with its own tastes and aspirations. The influence of peer groups among young people has consequently greatly increased at the expense of deference to the older generation and to authority generally. In terms of employment, the problem of finding work for the kind of unskilled school-leaver who is apt to drift into delinquency remains very real in some areas. Nevertheless the availability of some kind of work for most school-leavers and the rapidity of technological changes in the pattern of industry have between them greatly reduced the incentive to undergo prolonged trade training in the expectation of relying on the skills thus acquired to provide a livelihood throughout a whole career.[1]

103. Borstal staff since the earliest days have recognised the inherent difficulty of ensuring that the training offered in an organised and disciplined establishment is relevant to the problems which will face offenders who are released into the much less stable conditions of urban life. As society has changed they have sought to adjust their methods, and can claim some success. But it is undeniable that the social changes noted above have widened the gap which separates even the most imaginative institutional regime from the mode of life of a young person in a modern industrial city. Accordingly, whereas in earlier days borstal represented an attempt to transfer young adults from a largely punitive prison regime to a form of institutional training which was to be closely related to the demands of a largely hierarchical and deferential society, the very different social conditions of today now dictate a determined effort to provide the necessary training so far as possible in the community itself.

The incidence of crime among young adults

104. The number of indictable offences known to the police has risen during most of this century. There was a decrease in the early 1930s and another in the early 1950s, and provisional figures for the first quarter of 1973, published right at the end of our review, showed what might prove to be the beginning of a new downward trend. The rate per 100,000 of the population tripled between 1901 and the early 1940s and has increased $4\frac{1}{2}$ times since then. Whatever the effects of changes in reporting and recording practice, it is widely accepted that there has been a considerable increase in crime, which inevitably affects the demands made of the penal system.

105. It is an obvious point—though one that is often overlooked—that the proportion of all recorded crime that is attributable to a particular age group cannot be stated, since the offender's age is not known unless he is detected and rather more than half the indictable offences recorded as known to the police are not "cleared up". It cannot simply be assumed that the proportion of total crime for which young adults are responsible is the same as the proportion that convicted young adults bear to the total of convicted persons.

106. However, figures of the number of persons in the young adult age group

---

[1] For an interesting comparison of problems facing young delinquents in Liverpool in 1934–36 and 1965–66 see David Murray Lowson: *City Lads in Borstal* (Liverpool University Press, 1970).

36

who are found guilty of, or cautioned for,[2] an indictable offence are the best available statistical guide to the extent of criminal activity among young adults. In Appendix C there is a series of tables which show, over a period of time, the number of young people dealt with for indictable crime, their proportion of the total, and the way in which they are dealt with by the courts. Probably the most meaningful comparison of the relative criminality of people in different age groups is that provided by the number of persons found guilty of, or cautioned for, an indictable offence as a proportion of the population of that age "at risk" (that is in the population of that age as a whole at the time), since absolute numbers may be misleading depending on the extent of the age ranges being compared and hence the numbers within them "at risk". The age group with which we are concerned in this review contains for young men the age—17[3]—at which the "peak" of offending appears to be reached: the number of young men aged 17 found guilty of, or cautioned for, an indictable offence in 1971 per 100,000 of the population of that age was 6,449. The proportion fell to 4,345 per 100,000 at the age of 20 and, as table 3 of Appendix C shows, young men in the age group 17 and under 21 as a whole appear to be less prone to commit offences than those aged 14 and under 17. In 1971 5,502 were found guilty or cautioned per 100,000 of the population, compared with 6,155 per 100,000 in the 14 and under 17 age group. However, since 1960 the rate of increase has been higher among young men aged 17 and under 21: an estimated increase of 106.8% between 1960 and 1971.[4] In 1971 about one young man in 20 in the age group 17 and under 21 was convicted of an indictable offence. Over the period covered by Appendix C there has been a very much smaller increase in the number of men aged 17 and under 21 found guilty of non-indictable offences other than traffic offences (see table 8 of the Appendix).

107. There are far fewer female offenders of all ages. For girls the "peak" in terms of the number found guilty or cautioned per 100,000 of the population occurs at the age of 14,[5] after which there is a progressive decline. The 14 and under 17 and 17 and under 21 age groups may be compared in table 4 of Appendix C. In the 17 and under 21 age group the proportion of young women to young men convicted of, or cautioned for, indictable offences is about 1 to 9; over the last decade the rate of increase related to the population at risk has been approximately the same for both sexes. In the 14 and under 17 age group the rate of increase has been higher among females than males.

108. As regards road traffic offences, for which the opportunities have been increasing rapidly as the number of motor vehicles on the road grows, in terms of absolute numbers (and without allowance for the population "at risk") the number of young adult men found guilty increased between 1960 and 1971 by just over 60% and the number of young adult women found guilty trebled.

The implications for the penal system

109. It is plain from these figures that this age group poses a major problem

---

[2] An explanation of the statistics of persons cautioned, and of the reason for aggregating these figures with those of persons found guilty of indictable offences, is given in paragraph 2 of Appendix C.
[3] See Appendix C, table 3; 17 also appears as the "peak age" if cautions are disregarded.
[4] See Appendix C, paragraph 5 and table 3.
[5] See Appendix C, table 4; if findings of guilt alone are considered the peak occurs at the age of 17.

for the whole penal system and that the burden which it imposes upon resources threatens to increase rapidly if the trends of recent years in crime and methods of dealing with young adult offenders remain unchanged.

110. The daily average population of young men aged 17 and under 21 under sentence in Prison Department establishments in 1972 was about 7,500[6] out of a total daily average sentenced population of 32,372 males. The number of young men aged 17 and under 21 received into prison, borstal or senior detention centres under sentence without the option of a fine more than doubled from 6,548 in 1960 to 15,337 in 1971. This means that about one young man in 89 in this age group is now received into custody each year. In the same period the number of young women aged 17 and under 21 received into borstal or prison under sentence without the option of a fine has also increased, though the numbers are far less dramatic, from 238 to 357. If society through the criminal justice system continues to use custody on this scale, the cost of providing the necessary increase in resources will be substantial. The Home Office estimated in 1972 that there would be over 17,000 young offenders in custody by the early 1980s if the prevailing trends in the number of young men in this age group convicted of criminal offences were to persist, and there were no major change in the sentencing practice of the courts in dealing with them. This estimate expressly made no allowance for any changes following our report. The projections may vary from year to year, but there seems little reason to doubt that, without changes of policy on the part of the courts, the number of young adults committed to custody will in the long term continue to rise. It is noteworthy that, while in recent years the courts in dealing with adult offenders have shown an increasing tendency to use non-custodial measures, so that there has been a steady decline in the proportion of adult offenders sent to custody, there has been no corresponding shift in the sentencing practice of the courts in dealing with young adults so that the proportion sent to custody among those convicted of indictable offences has remained more or less constant. For example, in 1958 there were 218 young men aged 17 and under 21 received into custody per 1,000 convicted of indictable offences and 396 men aged 21 and over per 1,000 convicted of indictable offences. By 1972 the adult figure had fallen to 197 (a drop of about 50%) while the young adult figure had fallen only to 211.

111. These figures present the penal system and the public with important questions about the resources to be made available for dealing with offenders and the way in which they should be used. Detaining people in custody is expensive. If the Prison Department were to have to look after an average of more than 17,000 young adults in the early 1980s the cost of maintaining these offenders in custody would be more than £30m a year at 1972 prices. Substantial capital expenditure would also be required if offenders were to be housed in modern buildings giving even the minimum facilities for decent living. Young adults consume per head a higher proportion of the Prison Department's resources than prisoners aged over 21. For example, young men detained in borstals, detention centres and young prisoners' centres constitute less than 20% of the population of adult male custodial establishments

---

[6] A more precise figure cannot be given since the average number of trainees aged under 17 is not known.

(excluding the remand centres), but the young adult establishments contain over 30% of governor grade staff, and nearly 30% of instructor staff.[7] These differences, together with the provision for formal education, no doubt substantially account for the differences in unit running costs: the average weekly cost per head was reckoned in 1971–72 to be about £30 in prison and over £35 in borstals and detention centres[8]. The average cost of residence in probation hostels for young men is about £25 per week; this figure takes into account minor capital expenditure. Supervision on probation was reckoned in 1971 to cost a maximum of £2 per head per week,[9] though more intensive supervision with smaller caseloads would clearly cost more. In addition to these costs there are frequently social security costs arising, in the case of an offender in custody, from his separation from his family; in the case of supervision in the community costs of this kind may also be incurred in respect of the offender himself.

112. In our view the time has come to contemplate changes in the methods of dealing with this difficult age group which will both help to reduce recidivism, or at least prevent its increase, and keep within tolerable limits the social and financial costs which, if present trends are allowed to continue, could reach alarming proportions.

---

[7] The young adult establishments do not have a more than proportionate share of discipline officer staff: security and escort duties demand high levels of staffing in these grades in prisons.

[8] Report of the work of the Prison Department 1972 (Cmnd 5375) Appendix 4. These figures exclude capital expenditure on buildings, vehicles and "plant maintenance" (which includes building repair costs, rates and rents).

[9] First Report from the Expenditure Committee Session 1971–72 Probation and After-Care, p XXII and p 249, Q. 1185–6.

CHAPTER 6

THE EVOLUTION OF THE YOUNG ADULT OFFENDER SYSTEM

113. The present system for dealing with young adult offenders includes both special forms of sentence and special establishments for their treatment and training. These are the product of more than 60 years of evolution and adaptation. A detailed factual statement provided by the Home Office, describing the system as it exists today, is contained in Appendix B. The most recent statistics available to us give the following picture of the manner of disposal by the courts of young adults at the present time.

The disposal of young adult offenders

114. The majority of young adults are dealt with by the simple punishment of a fine—in 1971 just over 50% (41,071) of those who were convicted of indictable offences or committed by magistrates' courts to a higher court for sentence, and 80% of those convicted of all types of offence, were fined. Positive measures of "treatment" are applied to a minority, though a large minority, in the young adult age group. In the same year 14,867 (12,136 young men and 2,731 young women) were placed on probation, while 14,700 received the distinctive custodial sentences applicable to this age group of detention centre or borstal training (borstal, 6,068 young men and 228 young women aged 17 and under 21; detention centre, 8,404 young men). Immediate sentences of imprisonment were passed on 2,942 young men and 94 young women, and a further 3,443 young men and 284 young women received suspended prison sentences.

115. There is a great deal of ambiguity about the purposes for which sentences of detention in a detention centre and borstal training are passed. Statutory provisions can be read to imply that a supposed need for reformative treatment can be sufficient justification for passing a sentence of borstal training or detention centre training on an offender. Section 1 of the Criminal Justice Act 1961 states that the power to pass a sentence of borstal training

"shall be exercisable in any case where the court is of opinion, having regard to the circumstances of the offence and after taking into account the offender's character and previous conduct, that it is expedient that he should be detained for training for not less than six months".

Neither the Criminal Justice Act 1948 nor the Criminal Justice Act 1961 specifies the purpose of a detention centre sentence. The Home Office publication *The Sentence of the Court*[1] states, under the heading "What detention is designed to achieve":—

"Detention centres provide a means of treating young offenders for whom a long period of residential training away from home is not yet necessary or justified by their offence, but who cannot be taught respect for the law by such non-custodial measures as fines or probation."

---

[1] *The Sentence of the Court—A Handbook for Courts on the Treatment of Offenders*, (HMSO, 1969) paragraph 99; *Supplement on Detention Centres*, 1971, paragraph 10.

116. On the whole however it is not a belief in the peculiar effectiveness of custodial regimes to change the offender's behaviour which leads the court to pass a detention centre or borstal sentence in preference to a non-custodial sentence, but rather a wish to ensure that the offender has no immediate prospect of repeating the offence, to discourage others from following his example, or to assure the public that the offence is one which the courts treat seriously and for which they will impose restrictions on liberty in keeping with its gravity. All too often the reason is simply that everything else has been tried and failed. In these cases the court may hope that something will be done to assist the offender or to alter his behaviour while he is detained, but such considerations will usually be secondary. In other cases, however, the court may favour a custodial sentence not because it discerns any special need to keep the offender out of circulation, or to deter others, but because it believes that a period of full-time exposure to the influence of institutional staff or of subjection to a disciplined routine may produce desirable changes that would not take place if the offender were left in the community. These are the two extremes. In practice most custodial sentences probably fall between them, and it is not clear which consideration is uppermost in the court's mind: a custodial sentence of some kind may seem justified by the offence alone, but its length may be influenced by hopes—which, as we shall show, we would regard as sanguine—of what custodial "treatment" will do for the offender.

117. These uncertainties about the intentions of the court in passing sentence can cause corresponding uncertainties about the goals which custodial staff should be pursuing. The wording of the Criminal Justice Act 1961 is a particularly potent source of confusion. The Act retains borstal as a sentence "for training" but under its provisions a court wishing to pass a custodial sentence of between six months and three years, for whatever reason, can only pass a borstal sentence,[2] with the implication that the provision of training is the justification for the sentence, when in fact this is not the reason for the offender's detention.

118. These problems do not arise to the same degree in relation to imprisonment, which is generally recognised as a form of deprivation of liberty, imposed to show that the law cannot be broken with impunity, to ensure a respite for society from offences, to deter the offender from committing further offences or to deter others from emulating him. One or more of these considerations should apply in every case where an offender is sentenced to imprisonment—even in those cases where the court reluctantly sends the offender to prison because it sees no alternative means of disposal.

119. The Prison Department clearly distinguishes the reasons for which sentences of imprisonment are passed from the aims and principles that should guide staff in dealing with prisoners and deciding how the time in custody should be spent. Among the latter is the encouragement of a good and useful life, and the regime in young prisoners' centres has accordingly developed on borstal lines. In local prisons, however, where most young adults subject to sentences

---

[2] This general rule is subject to the exception that, if an offender has already served a sentence of imprisonment of six months or more or a sentence of borstal training, a sentence of imprisonment of 18 months or more may be passed, and the restrictions do not apply where the offender is already serving a sentence of imprisonment.

of imprisonment of less than three months serve the whole of their sentence, little more can be done than an attempt to segregate them from older prisoners and provide some work and recreation.

120. The regime in detention centres, where the sentence was originally thought to last too short a time to allow for constructive treatment, has evolved even further in the direction of borstal training. However, until fairly recently those running the centres were given little guidance regarding the development of their regimes: there were at one time marked differences between establishments, and some misunderstanding on the part of the courts as to the nature of the establishments to which they were sending offenders when they passed a detention centre sentence. We hope that our earlier report on detention centres[3] has been of help here.

121. These doubts and ambiguities are partly the product of the way in which the system for young adult offenders has evolved since its inception, through the interaction of changes in penal philosophy with the lessons of practical experience. The central feature of this system has been borstal, one of the great constructive experiments of the century. A brief analysis of the evolution of the borstal system may accordingly provide the best explanation of the present situation and point to the changes which now need to be made.

The origins and early decades of the system

122. When in 1895 the Gladstone Committee recommended the development of special institutions for young offenders it reported Sir Godfrey Lushington's views on imprisonment:

> "I regard as unfavourable to reformation the status of a prisoner throughout his whole career; the crushing of self-respect; the starving of all moral instinct he may possess; the absence of all opportunity to do or receive a kindness; the continual association with none but criminals, and that only as a separate item amongst other items also separate; the forced labour, and the denial of all liberty. I believe the true mode of reforming a man or restoring him to society is exactly in the opposite direction of all these. But, of course, this is a mere idea. It is quite impracticable in a prison. In fact, the unfavourable features I have mentioned are inseparable from a prison life."[4]

The Committee accepted this as an accurate description of prison life at the time, but concluded that the unfavourable features were not irremovable. They noted that in many respects and in individual cases these features had already been modified, and expressed the view that this modification could be carried further in the direction of the treatment adopted and practised by the best of the reformatories which existed for juvenile offenders.[5] The development of custodial regimes during this century has been an attempt to give effect to the Gladstone Committee's view.

123. In the years between the Gladstone Committee report in 1895 and the introduction of a separate borstal sentence by the Prevention of Crime Act 1908

---

[3] *Detention Centres.* Report of the Advisory Council on the Penal System, HMSO 1970.
[4] Report of the Departmental Committee on Prisons, 1895 (C. 7702) Minutes of Evidence Q 11482.
[5] ibid, paragraph 25 of the Report.

the Prison Commissioners experimented with reformative treatment of young prisoners and established to their satisfaction that a minimum of one year was required for such treatment to have an effect. This was consistent with the recommendations of the Gladstone Committee. Section 1 of the Prevention of Crime Act accordingly enabled the higher courts when sentencing an offender aged over 16 and under 21 to pass a sentence of "detention under penal discipline in a Borstal Institution" for a term of not less than one year or more than three years instead of a sentence of imprisonment or penal servitude. Before passing a borstal sentence the court was required to be satisfied that "by reason of his criminal habits or tendencies or association with persons of bad character, it is expedient that [the offender] should be subject to detention for such term and under such supervision and discipline as appears most conducive to his reformation and the repression of crime." Section 5 of the Act empowered the Prison Commissioners to release an offender on licence at any time after he had served six months (three months for girls), and there was provision for compulsory supervision after the expiry of the sentence. The new sentence was brought into use in 1910 and within four years the minimum sentence the court could pass was raised to two years by section 11 of the Criminal Justice Administration Act 1914. This does not appear to have been a matter of bringing the law into line with judicial practice, but rather of giving notice to the courts that the objectives of reform required a longer period of detention than they might be prepared to order in accordance with the normal tariff for imprisonment.[6]

The period of custody and selection of offenders for borstal training

124. By the 1920s the normal programme of borstal training took two years, and releases after less than two years were rare. The sentence was more like a determinate sentence of three years with one year's remission than a genuinely indeterminate sentence between a statutory minimum and a maximum fixed by the court. Proponents of borstal training argued against sentences of less than three years on the grounds that less than two years detention for training was likely to be ineffective, and therefore a two-year sentence left no scope for the offender to earn an earlier release. An advocate of borstal, writing with undoubted official blessing, said "It is kinder, and far better for his morale, that he should be sentenced to three years and feel that it is largely in his own hands to reduce it to two, than to give him two only and remove a powerful stimulus".[7]

125. Another argument was that a two-year sentence left insufficient time for supervision. Section 11 of the Criminal Justice Administration Act 1914 had extended from six months to one year the period after the end of the sentence during which the offender would remain under the supervision of the Borstal Association and liable to recall by the Prison Commissioners. It had also extended from three months to one year the period for which a person could be detained on recall. A person receiving a sentence of two years borstal training was therefore subject to compulsory supervision and liable to recall for 12 months after release, even if he had been detained for the full period selected by the court. Nevertheless the Departmental Committee on the Treatment of Young Offenders in 1927 was persuaded that this was inadequate and recommended that, in order to ensure two years' supervision (a year of remission

---

[6] *Borstal Reassessed* by Roger Hood (Heinemann, 1965), page 25.
[7] *Boys in Trouble* by L. Le Mesurier (John Murray, 1931), page 215.

43

and the compulsory year after the end of sentence), the borstal sentence should be a standard one of three years.[8]

126. Borstal training was then a special form of detention available at three establishments for a minority of selected offenders aged 16 and under 21.[9] The Departmental Committee agreed with the view expounded by the Prison Commissioners and others that young offenders should be dealt with either by probation or by long terms of "training" in custody which would influence and equip them to become law-abiding members of the community. Accordingly over the ensuing years borstal training became a major method of dealing with young offenders, and by the Second World War there were nine establishments receiving over half the young adult offenders sent to custody. The Prison Commissioners claimed that 60% of young men released from borstal were not reconvicted within three years of release, and borstal training inspired developments of treatment for young people in their late teens and early twenties in the United States and many other parts of the world. Borstal showed, perhaps most significantly through the development of open establishments, that it was practicable to detain offenders in more relaxed and humane conditions than had been contemplated in the past and exerted considerable influence on penological thinking about adult imprisonment.

127. The Departmental Committee on the Treatment of Young Offenders also advocated a change in the criteria for selection for borstal training. Initially the sentence had been intended for those who already seemed to have advanced some way along a criminal career but might still be diverted away from crime. The wording of the Prevention of Crime Act 1908 had been designed to achieve that effect and various circulars sent by the Home Office to courts and to prison governors were intended to help them in identifying those who were criminal enough, but not too criminal, for borstal training. The Departmental Committee proposed that these provisions should be rephrased to give greater prominence to the need for training than to the existence of formed criminal habits in the criteria for a borstal sentence. They observed that it was rare for those committed to borstal to have many previous findings of guilt and sentences of imprisonment; this they thought was due to the growing use of probation and of the practice of allowing time for payment of fines. Those received were "usually not so hardened" but "none the less in need of training".[10]

128. These changes, which accorded with the view of Sir Alexander Paterson[11] and others associated with borstal, were included in the Criminal Justice Bill 1938 and eventually enacted in the Criminal Justice Act 1948. Section 20 of the Act provided that a higher court sentencing a person aged 16 and under 21 on the date of his conviction for an offence punishable with imprisonment, "may, in lieu of any other sentence, pass a sentence of Borstal training" provided that the court was "satisfied having regard to his character and

---

[8] Report of the Departmental Committee on Young Offenders, 1927, Cmd 2831, pp 102–103.

[9] The history of the borstal system is the subject of a number of published works, notably *Borstal Reassessed* by Roger Hood (Heinemann, 1965) and *The English Prison and Borstal System*, by Sir Lionel Fox (Routledge and Kegan Paul, 1952; now out of print). A description of existing sentencing powers and treatment arrangements is in Appendix B. In this Chapter references to young offenders and young offender institutions apply solely to males and in general to males over 16 and under 21.

[10] ibid, P. 99 of their Report.

[11] A Commissioner of Prisons (1922–46) with special responsibility for borstals.

44

previous conduct, and to the circumstances of the offence, that it is expedient for his reformation and the prevention of crime that he should undergo a period of training in a Borstal institution". The Act provided that the period of detention should be not less than nine months and not more than three years at the discretion of the Prison Commissioners and that supervision and liability to recall should continue for four years from the date of sentence.[12]

129. The changes over the years in sentencing philosophy did not go unopposed. Particularly in the early years of borstal, some judges at least were reluctant to pass sentences which were as long as the Prison Commissioners thought necessary for reformative training. Judicial opposition seems to have been overcome first by the belief (not wholly justified) that those receiving borstal training were commonly given an opportunity to acquire a trade,[13] and in subsequent years by the belief that they gained some of the benefits offered by a boarding school education. An important factor in removing opposition was no doubt the high proportion of former borstal inmates whom the Borstal Association records showed throughout the inter-war period to have settled down on release without committing further offences. It was not possible to compare the success rates with those for other methods of dealing with offenders because comparable statistics did not exist.

130. The idea that borstal training should continue for longer than the period of deprivation of liberty which the courts might otherwise have imposed became so well entrenched as to be rarely questioned. Commenting in 1959 on the Prison Commissioners' proposal to make borstal training a sentence with a liability to custody in every case of between six months and two years, the Advisory Council on the Treatment of Offenders said: "the minimum period of detention should be sufficient to afford a penalty which will be regarded by the courts as appropriate to the offence" and "the maximum period of detention should be determined by the requirements of training".[14] Admittedly the Prison Commissioners' selection of two years as the maximum period indicated a certain change of view compared with their predecessors. They told the Council that there were "very few youths whose training can usefully be extended beyond a period of two years"[15] and offenders "would be encouraged to co-operate more fully in their training by the knowledge that such co-operation would earn them release on licence after a period of detention substantially shorter than two years".[16] However, the intention was still to keep offenders in custody for longer, in the interests of training, than the courts might otherwise have thought fit. Both the ACTO report[17] and the White Paper *Penal Practice in a Changing Society* in presenting these proposals[18] said that the continuance of medium-term imprisonment for young adults was not justified by deterrent effect: most young people preferred a prison sentence because it was likely to be much shorter than a borstal sentence, as well as carrying a more certain date of release.

131. The borstal philosophy has almost certainly increased the lengths of

[12] Criminal Justice Act 1948, Second Schedule.
[13] *Borstal Reassessed* pp 25–28 and 34–38.
[14] *The Treatment of Young Offenders,* a report by the Advisory Council on the Treatment of Offenders (HMSO, 1959), paragraph 52.
[15] ibid, paragraph 53.
[16] ibid, paragraph 54.
[17] ibid, paragraph 14.
[18] *Penal Practice in a Changing Society: Aspects of Future Development (England and Wales)* (Cmnd 645) February 1959, paragraph 42.

sentence that are publicly acceptable for young adults. In the period before the Second World War the Prison Commissioners and other advocates of borstal training were so confident of the effectiveness of this training, and so persuaded that it was more akin to education in a school than to incarceration in a prison, that they consistently encouraged the courts to use borstal training, which in effect meant two years' detention, instead of terms of imprisonment of less than six months. The power to pass a borstal sentence has always been confined to the higher courts,[19] but section 10 of the Criminal Justice Administration Act 1914 gave magistrates power to commit an offender aged 16 and under 21 to quarter sessions for sentence of borstal training provided that the offence was one for which a maximum sentence of at least one month was available and that the offender had been convicted before (or had been discharged on probation and had failed to observe the conditions of the recognizance).[20] From time to time the Prison Commissioners expressed regret at the evident reluctance of magistrates to make use of this power and their apparent preference for short sentences of imprisonment.[21] In line with the Commissioners' views the Departmental Committee of 1927 dismissed the idea of short-term training establishments for young offenders as a "fatally easy solution", and recommended that short sentences of imprisonment should be eliminated and supervision on probation or borstal training used instead. However, short-term detention in detention centres, for periods of from three to six months, were introduced by the Criminal Justice Act 1948, though the Act went some way in the direction of the Departmental Committee's views by broadening the criteria for committal to a higher court for a borstal sentence, so that magistrates' courts were given power to commit for a sentence of borstal training in any case where they were satisfied that the new criteria for borstal training in section 20(1) of the new Act applied (see paragraph 128 above).

132. In Appendix D (paragraphs 8 to 10) we refer to two studies carried out at our own request which are relevant to the question whether the provision of special sentences offering training leads to a greater use of custody by the courts. The conclusions from these studies are negative or at best neutral on the question whether the courts make extensive use of custodial sentences in the hope of effecting reformation in cases where they would not do so on more traditional sentencing principles. However the effect of the 1961 Act, described in paragraph 117 above, is that some offenders may spend longer in custody under a borstal sentence than they would do if the courts were free to impose a prison sentence of any determinate length related to the gravity of the offence. It seems likely that the rhetoric of borstal training has influenced the general climate of public opinion in the direction of regarding a lengthy period in custody as the natural alternative if ordinary supervision on probation does not keep the offender out of trouble, and has encouraged the view that if one custodial sentence has not stopped a person committing offences this indicates a need for "further treatment and training" and consequently for a longer sentence next time.

---

[19] Attempts by back-bench Members of Parliament to amend the 1914 and 1938 legislation so as to confer on magistrates' courts a direct power to pass a borstal sentence were unsuccessful.

[20] A magistrates' court was also required to be satisfied that the criteria relating to "criminal habits or tendencies, or association with persons of bad character" and the need for "such instruction and discipline as appears most conducive to his reformation and the repression of crime" (see paragraph 123 above) were met.

[21] *Borstal Reassessed*, page 38. Cf Criminal Statistics 1937 Introductory Note Page XV and *Boys in Trouble*, page 173.

133. We now briefly look back again in time in order to examine the influences which seem to have led to reliance on long periods of "reformative treatment" in custody on young adult offenders. The Gladstone Committee and the Prison Commissioners were greatly influenced by the fact that short sentences in the deterrent regime of prison at the turn of the century appeared to have no impact on young adults. If familiarity did not breed contempt it bred a cynical indifference. The Prison Commissioners were as impressed as their critics with the fact that what was intended as a deterrent did not seem to deter those who experienced it. When the records were studied of adult habitual prisoners who appeared to be professional criminals they were often found to have begun in youth and to have served many previous sentences.[22]

134. At the same time the Gladstone Committee had before it statistics which suggested (as statistics in this and other countries have continued to do) that while the age group 16 to 21 contributed more than its fair share of crime, offenders seemed to commit fewer offences the older they got. The rate of convictions for indictable offences per 100,000 of the population at risk was the highest for those aged 16 and under 21 and declined steadily for older age groups. Statistics of the ages of offenders in prison for certain offences showed that young people of 17, 18 and 19 were the most numerous and the number in each age group declined considerably after the early twenties. The Committee decided that this tendency for people to cease committing offences in their twenties and thirties could be reinforced and speeded up by introducing new treatment methods, aimed at reform, for people in their late teens and early twenties. Its members were undoubtedly impressed by the claim of a 91% success rate for Redhill Reformatory made by its Head Mr. Trevarthen, and by the 80% success rate attributed to the penal reformatory at Elmira in New York State. The Committee was convinced that the period 16 to 21 was crucial in the development of the majority of habitual criminals and that the years 17, 18 and 19 were "most fatal in the formation of lasting criminal habits". It concluded that "the most determined effort should be made to lay hold of these incipient criminals and to prevent them by strong restraint and rational treatment from recruiting the habitual class".[23]

135. It was natural for the Gladstone Committee to see the solution in terms of prolonged institutional treatment. At the time probation was not as widely recognised as a distinct way of dealing with offenders as it became following the Probation of Offenders Act 1907 and subsequent legislation.[24] The fine was relatively little used. Neither the Gladstone Committee Report, nor the reports of the Prison Commissioners, betrayed any suspicion that long separation from ordinary life could itself make it harder for a person to resume the responsibilities of living and working outside after release. They clearly did not doubt that the

---

[22] Cf the Prison Commissioners' statement announcing the intention to set up a reformatory regime at Borstal, "It may be said to be established by experience that the professional criminal of later years . . ., who reverts again and again, with a cynical indifference, to the prison from which he has only just been discharged, is only a later development of the juvenile offender whom a succession of short sentences in his youth have made familiar with prison life, of which the mystery and the fear must always constitute the principal deterrent" (Report of the Commissioners of Prisons and the Directors of Convict Prisons, 1900–01, p 13).

[23] Report of the Departmental Committee on Prisons 1895 (C. 7702) paragraphs 29 and 84.

[24] The Probation of First Offenders Act 1887 had made probation available for certain first offenders; it did not specify a supervising authority, although some courts had the services of "missionaries" of the Church of England Temperance Society.

highly disciplined life and "healthful influences" which could be provided in a penal institution would be better for the offender than the slum conditions under which he would live outside.[25] In the penological climate of the early 20th century, penal reformers could be confident of the superiority of their own values. Incarceration was the natural way to deal with repeated offenders and there had been no research to cast doubt on the success of treatment or to point to damaging effects that institutional life could have.

136. More recent experience has produced greater scepticism about the wisdom of relying upon long terms of "reformative treatment" in custody to prevent recidivism. Sentences of the kind recommended by the Gladstone Committee have now been in general use over a long period, yet it is still common to find among adult offenders many who have received a succession of custodial sentences of what were intended to be a reformative character during their youth.[26] Where those receiving such sentences do not offend again, it is impossible to be sure whether this result is due to the training they received or to the tendency, which remains unchanged, for people to commit fewer offences as they get older. In short, experience gained over the years since the Gladstone Committee reported produces no firm presumption about the peculiar effectiveness of custodial training of the kind which it advocated.

137. Nor does such research as there has been on the effects of different lengths of custodial treatment on people who have similar likelihood of offending again support the view that longer treatment produces greater success, though it does not conclusively prove the reverse. Complex and interesting studies have been made of the relationship of the length of time spent in borstal to reconviction after release. We refer to some of these in Appendix D. The results are open to a variety of interpretations. They do not prove that longer detention for treatment produces worse results, though some of them suggest that there is some association between longer periods of detention and a *higher* rate of conviction, and that reducing periods of detention improves some offenders' chances of avoiding reconviction rather than the reverse. At least it can be said that it would be a rash assumption to assert that long-term custodial treatment is more likely than short-term to reduce recidivism either generally or for identifiable individuals.

---

[25] Cf the chaplain of Brecon Prison speaking of juveniles under 16 committed to prison for less than a month in default of fines for trivial offences:
  "A longer term of imprisonment, say 3 months, is better for a boy than a month. The sentence should be such as to allow the boy sufficient time to reap the full advantages of the moral and intellectual training which the prison affords".
(Quoted with approval in the report of the Prison Commissioners for 1902–03, page 19.)

[26] 25% of adult men received into prison under sentence without the option of a fine in 1971 had previously been sentenced to borstal training, and 14% to detention centre training. 15% had been to approved schools. 37% of young adults received into borstal had previously been to approved school and 42% had previously been sentenced to detention centre training, 11% to borstal training and 1% to imprisonment. 46% had not previously received a custodial sentence. Of men under 21 received under sentence of imprisonment without the option of a fine during 1971, 49% had previously been to approved school, 36.8% were known to have previously been sentenced to detention centre training and 61% to borstal training. 18.6% were known to have had no previous custodial sentence. The position is different in relation to women. 7% of adult women prisoners received under sentence without the option of a fine in 1971 and 7% of young women received into borstal had previously served sentences of borstal training. 84% of borstal trainees were known to have had no previous custodial sentence. 19% of young prisoners received under sentence were known to have previously been sentenced to borstal training and 16% to imprisonment. 48% had not previously had a custodial sentence.

138. It is not possible to say what proportion of young adults coming before the courts continue to commit offences and could be said to "recruit the habitual class", or to make a judgment about the chances of influencing them away from crime. The standard statistics merely show reconvictions over a period of three years from release. It is clear that only a proportion, even of those reconvicted within this period, go on to become persistent serious offenders.[27]

The system since 1945

139. The confident inter-war period of expansion of the borstal system, during which judicial and public opinion was progressively convinced that long terms in custody were desirable in the interests of reformation, has been followed by a phase of doubt and questioning about the success and relevance of treatment in custody. During the Second World War pressures on resources required the release of all those in borstal who had served the minimum statutory period of six months and the closure of five borstals. Naturally many experienced staff were lost to the borstal system. Over 1,000 young adult offenders continued to be received each year under sentence of borstal training, but many served their sentences in prison. Following the war the borstal tradition was revived, and new establishments were developed in a variety of Prison Department and ex-service accommodation. But the pre-war "success rates" were never again achieved and repeatedly in the post-war years the Prison Commissioners noted that borstal was receiving more difficult and less responsive young people than in the past.

140. During the years immediately after the Second World War the annual number of young men received under sentence of borstal training was about 2,000 and the average training period was 18 months. Between 1956 and 1958 the annual number of receptions rose to over 3,000. In the ensuing seven years it increased nearly 1,000 to just under 4,000 in 1965; in 1966 alone it rose by a further 900. In the four years 1966 to 1970 the annual number of receptions went up from nearly 5,000 to over 7,000, and the average period in custody under a borstal sentence dropped from 13 months to $10\frac{1}{2}$ months; by the end of 1971 it was down to $9\frac{1}{2}$ months, and was 10 months in September 1973. Borstal was being asked to perform a new kind of role, for which it was not designed, as the standard sentence for all young adult offenders for whom a medium-term custodial sentence was thought necessary, and no longer as a selective sentence for those expected to benefit from it. As its pre-war advocates wished, borstal training was increasingly replacing imprisonment. The Criminal Justice Act 1948 allowed courts to pass sentences of imprisonment on persons under 21 only if no other course of action was appropriate, and prevented magistrates' courts from passing sentences of imprisonment on those under 17. Some of those who would previously have gone to prison were therefore presumably sentenced to borstal training.

141. From 1955 onwards senior detention centres gave the courts an alternative custodial sentence, which was probably used for many who might otherwise have gone to borstal and been among the more amenable of the inmates. The

[27] See for example T. C. N. Gibbens and J. Prince, "The results of borstal training", in *Sociological Studies within the British Penal Services,* edited by P. Halmos. (Monographs of the Sociological Review, No. 9, 1965). The authors estimated that, in the case of two samples of young men sent to borstal in 1951 and 1953 for offences committed in the Metropolitan police area, the proportion of persistent serious offenders after 10–12 years was 20%.

49

courts were discouraged from using detention centre sentences for those who had experienced institutional treatment in the past, and so while borstal lost some of those with a good chance of success it continued to receive many who were highly likely to fail. It is not surprising that these changes increased the proportion of people sentenced to borstal whose probability of reconviction was high and whose likelihood of being influenced was low—people with established criminal ways of life; people who had repeatedly committed offences despite efforts to alter their behaviour; and people ill-equipped, unwilling or unable to make personal relationships and adjust to the demands of others and of the law.

142. The provision of the Criminal Justice Act 1961 quoted in paragraph 115 above was intended to eliminate as far as practicable the imposition of sentences of imprisonment of less than three years upon young adult offenders. The scheme of the Act was that if the court considered detention for a short period appropriate, it should make a detention centre order; if for an intermediate period short of three years, it should order borstal training. However, the restriction on short-term prison sentences has not been implemented: in earlier years the supply of detention centre places was insufficient to make it practicable, and in our report on detention centres we recommended against implementation pending the outcome of the present review. The implication of the Act was that all sentences of under three years were to be "training" sentences with a predominantly reformative purpose. At the same time the Act deprived the courts of the power to pick out those offenders whom they considered to be most likely to respond to training.

143. When, as a consequence of the 1961 Act, borstal training thus became the standard medium-term custodial sentence for young adults, it was envisaged that a variety of approaches and methods of treatment would be employed to deal with the greater range of offenders that would come into borstals. This has to some extent been achieved. The borstal system has retained the basic principles of influencing young men through the establishment of personal relationships, trying to preserve personal responsibility and a degree of choice, and attempting to equip young men by education and work training to live a good and useful life on release. There are now 23 borstals for young men, excluding the two allocation centres and the special psychiatric centre at Grendon. Personal characteristics, previous criminal record and past institutional experience are among the factors which influence the choice of the borstal to which a young man should go. Clearly they also affect the degree to which staff can afford to trust inmates and to give them the opportunity to exercise choice and responsibility. Establishments differ in the scope for amicable personal relationships between staff and trainees and in the degree of optimism with which staff can approach the task of encouraging and assisting young people to lead a good and useful life. Borstal training in some establishments must seem to the staff to be very different from the impressions of pre-war borstal given by oral tradition and the writings of Alexander Paterson.[28] It is natural that some staff should see the changes following the 1961 Act as the destruction of borstal training. While we sympathise with this reaction we believe that these changes should more usefully be regarded as an extension of its scope to wider categories of offender and therefore an application of its principles to meet a greater challenge.

---

[28] However, the difference between borstal training in closed establishments now and in the thirties may be exaggerated; cf *Borstal Reassessed*, pp 119 and 120.

144. The Criminal Justice Act 1961 has also led to difficulties for the courts, who find that its restrictions from time to time prevent them from passing the sentences they would think fit, either because they cannot influence the length of sentence between the statutory limits (six months and two years), or because for one of a variety of reasons[29] they consider imprisonment more suitable than borstal training but are not allowed to order it. Shortly after the 1961 Act came into operation the Court of Criminal Appeal[30] pointed out in a judgment[31] that borstal training now consisted of a variety of establishments and regimes, some not differing markedly from prison while others had a strong educational emphasis. However the retention of the name "borstal training", which before 1939 acquired connotations first of trade training and then of boarding school education, has tended to perpetuate in the mind of the public, and possibly even of some courts, an unrealistic image of what borstal training now means.

145. It also seems to us highly likely that the restrictions on medium-term imprisonment imposed by the 1961 Act have resulted in a number of young adults spending longer periods in custody than would be the case if the courts had complete discretion to pass a sentence of a length related to the offence and the offender's past record. We have already observed how, in a general sense, the borstal philosophy may have led to longer terms of custody for young adults because of the belief that it will assist their rehabilitation. But we also believe that the present statutory restrictions may have had the effect of increasing the periods which young adults spend in custody above what the court would normally have ordered, in two quite specific ways. First, there seems to us little reason to doubt that many, if not a majority, of young adults receiving borstal sentences (with a minimum period of detention of six months and in practice an average of 10 months), would, if the courts had complete discretion in the length of sentence, receive sentences of nine months (effectively six months with full remission) or one year (effectively eight months with full remission). Table D1 of the Statistical Tables to the report on the Work of the Prison Department for 1971[32] shows the distribution of lengths of sentences of adult prisoners received into custody in that year without the option of a fine. Of a total of 29,641 received, 14.2% had sentences of up to three months; 21.6% had sentences of over three and up to six months; 27.4% had sentences of over six and up to 12 months; 14.0% sentences of over a year and up to 18 months; 8.5% over 18 months and up to two years; and 14.3% sentences of over two years. Above the six months level (the maximum detention centre sentence and the minimum period of detention on a borstal sentence), sentences of up to 12 months—in practice probably nine month and 12 month sentences—were the most numerous. We have no reason to think that if the courts had complete discretion in the length of sentence, the pattern of the sentences they would impose on young adults would be significantly different from that for adults.

146. Secondly, there is reason to believe, although in the nature of things it cannot be proved conclusively, that courts occasionally impose sentences of

[29] For example because they believe that the case is one which requires "punishment" rather than "training" or because they judge the particular offender to be "untrainable" or not in need of "training".

[30] The Court that until 1966 heard criminal appeals from the higher courts. The Criminal Appeal Act 1966 set up in its place the Criminal Division of the Court of Appeal and conferred on it the jurisdiction of the former Court.

[31] *R v Angell* [1964] 4.5.64, 484/64 Crim. L R 553.

[32] *Report on the Work of the Prison Department 1971, Statistical Tables* (Cmnd 5156).

three years' imprisonment in cases where, but for the restrictions, they would have given prison sentences of, say, two years or 30 months. There have been a number of cases where a trial judge has in fact indicated that he was passing a sentence as long as three years only because he considered borstal unsuitable. (In such cases if there has been an appeal a sentence of borstal training has generally been substituted.)[33] These are clear examples, quickly remedied: but there may well also be cases where a court has made a similar calculation without announcing that fact and the sentence of three years falls within the normal range for the offence and cannot therefore be held on appeal to be excessive.

147. The present position can be summed up by saying that the borstal system, which is at the heart of custodial provision for young adults, has for some years been suffering as a result of the imposition of a load for which it was never designed. It is ironic that this has come about at a time when many of the principles underlying borstal training have been adopted generally in penal treatment. The influence of the borstal philosophy has extended to imprisonment many of the features which made borstal training a distinct form of treatment, thus making the regimes of young prisoners' centres and some closed borstals indistinguishable in many ways. Many of the features of borstal between the wars are now also recognised as desirable features of humane imprisonment. There is widespread acceptance of Sir Alexander Paterson's dictum that people are sent to prison as a punishment, not for punishment, with the implication that any deterrent or retributive element should be in the deprivation of liberty rather than in conditions and activities deliberately intended to be punitive. The belief that the objective of reformation requires offenders to be treated as far as possible in conditions of freedom, which found expression in the 1930s in open borstals and home leave, has led to similar developments in adult prisons. What is needed now is a sustained effort to adapt what is best and most relevant in the borstal system to the changed conditions of the present day.

---

[33] *R v Angell* is one example. The leading case is *R v Lowe* [1964]2 All E R 116, 48 Cr App R 165. The trial judge originally imposed a sentence of two years for the principal offence but, when reminded of the restrictions, brought the offender back and raised the sentence to three years. The Court of Criminal Appeal in substituting a borstal sentence observed that "Where the Court feels that the judge erred was in putting up that sentence of two years' imprisonment to three years' imprisonment because he felt that training was not called for. It seems to this Court that at that stage . . . he should have said that since the appropriate prison sentence, which otherwise he would have given, was two years, he must give the indeterminate sentence of borstal training."

CHAPTER 7

CONCLUSIONS TO BE DRAWN FROM EXPERIENCE AND RESEARCH

148. We now draw some general conclusions from the experience gained in the course of the evolution of the system described in the last chapter, noting both the substantial successes achieved and the recent ambiguities and frustrations which have resulted from piecemeal attempts to adjust old methods to suit changed conditions. In doing this we have had the benefit of studying the results of a growing body of research, undertaken both in the United Kingdom and elsewhere, which has sought to test accepted assumptions about the effectiveness of different ways of handling young adult offenders.

149. In general, experience and research have tended to support one another, but the difficulties of research in this field are such that it is rarely possible as yet to derive from it alone clear guidance on which to base major changes in methods of treatment of offenders. Research has so far been more successful in shaking some old conventional assumptions, in itself a valuable contribution to penal thinking, than it has in providing judges and administrators with new certainties. We set out in Appendix D particulars of some of the research projects which we have found most helpful.

The courts and the executive

150. One need which we have identified is to redefine the respective roles of the courts and those responsible for executing their sentences in such a way as to give to each a more effective discretion in the exercise of their particular functions and to make sure that these functions are seen to be complementary. rather than conflicting.

151. We accept for instance that, while reformative treatment is a natural and proper objective of staff in the custodial and probation services, it cannot always be the overriding factor in sentencing decisions. In passing sentence a court may have one or more of a number of objectives in mind: to make it clear to the offender and to the public that offences cannot be committed with impunity; to impose some penalty or obligation which may discourage others from committing offences; to make clear the seriousness with which the courts, on behalf of the community, view the offending behaviour; and to prevent the individual concerned from committing offences in the short term, whether or not he can be induced to stop in the long term. Essentially the court's requirement in passing a "treatment" sentence, whether custodial or supervisory, is that some person in authority should accept responsibility for supervising or controlling the offender's behaviour. Sometimes this can be achieved by placing the offender under supervision in the community. A custodial sentence is an extreme measure of control but obviously there will always be some circumstances in which courts find it necessary to use it. This may be because it seems to be the minimum likely to deter potential offenders, or in order to

53

remove from the community for a time someone whose frequent offences can no longer be tolerated or whose offence is so serious that any risk of a repetition must be avoided for some time to come. There may also be cases causing public disquiet in which some period of withdrawal from the community is essential in order to avoid retaliation.

152. It follows from this that a number of offenders will continue to be received into custody, as they are now, who were sentenced by the courts not with reformation primarily in view or with any expectation of their responding readily to attempts to achieve that end, but on some different ground of public policy. It does not, however, follow that those responsible for deciding how to treat the offender should have the same objective as the court had in sentencing him. We see their task as, first, to support the system of law by carrying out the sentence of the court; and, secondly, to return the offender to the community in as healthy a state as possible, as soon as possible, and in a frame of mind such that he is less likely to offend again and is willing and able to take his part in society and to co-operate with his supervising officer in seeking to achieve those ends. In order to do this they must have not only wide discretion in devising custodial regimes, but also the discretion to decide to release an offender under control within the community at a time judged most likely to secure those objectives.

153. The Secretary of State at present has discretion, within fairly wide statutory limits, to release a young adult from borstal but not from prison (save for the availability of parole in certain cases) or a detention centre. We think that there is a strong case for generalising a power of this kind throughout the whole young adult offender system.

154. On the sentencing side, as we have seen in the previous chapter, the power of the courts to suit the length of their custodial sentence to their assessment of the gravity of the offence and of other aspects of the public interest has been greatly limited by the restrictions on medium-term prison sentences and the obligation to pass a borstal sentence where they consider a sentence in this range appropriate. This loss of flexibility has been found irksome by the courts and does not seem to have had corresponding advantages. The statutory maximum laid down for borstal has raised a presumption that long periods of training in custody have peculiarly reformative merits, which experience suggests may be illusory. At the same time the 1961 Act has resulted in courts being obliged to sentence to borstal training, with its maximum liability of two years in custody, a number of offenders for whom they believe neither that two years' custody is required nor that borstal training is appropriate.

155. We propose that these anomalies should be remedied by restoring to the courts the right to pass sentences of determinate length, during which young adult offenders will be liable to custody or other forms of control; by ensuring the maximum flexibility in the type of establishment and the type of regime which can be chosen for the offender while he is in custody; and by affording to the authorities during the period of the sentence a wider discretion than they now have to choose when to substitute control in the community for custody in an establishment.

The choice between custodial and non-custodial treatment

156. It is in our view a source of surprise and regret that, whereas in recent years there has been a proportionate reduction in the use of custodial sentences on adults found guilty of offences, this has not occurred in respect of young adults. As we have recognised above, the courts will continue to find it necessary to pass custodial sentences upon young adults for reasons unconnected with the expected effect upon the offender himself of any treatment or training which he may receive while in custody. It can be claimed for such sentences that at least they prevent the commission of further offences during the actual period of detention and also, though with less certainty, that they have a deterrent effect both on the offender and on others. But we have seen in the last chapter that custody has been and still is ordered a good deal more widely than these considerations of public protection and deterrence would imply. Traditionally imprisonment was society's normal response to any substantial crime. The development of the borstal system encouraged a belief in the efficacy of training given in custody, first to carefully selected categories of young adults and then more generally, so that the desire to reduce and finally eliminate imprisonment for young adults has been matched by a belief that what should replace it is some more constructive kind of custodial regime. Training given in the community under the probation system, though ordered for widening categories of offender, still remains a form of disposal which the courts are reluctant to use where the offence is relatively serious or the offender has a substantial previous record; and the resources devoted to developing probation have not been comparable with what society spends on custody.

157. To some extent this reflects a feeling that custody is a measure ordered to protect the public, while probation is a solution devised for the benefit of the offender. We believe this distinction to be misleading. Sooner or later almost every offender sent to custody must rejoin society; and a way should be found of dealing with young adult offenders which does not defeat the object of protecting the public by eventually releasing from custody a more determined offender. Neither practical experience nor the results of research in recent years have established the superiority of custodial over non-custodial methods in their effect upon renewed offending: this is still an open question. Some aspects of custodial treatment may even contribute to recidivism. Moreover, comparisons of different types of custodial regime have so far shown little or no difference in effects upon offending again. This suggests that the treatment effort, whatever its nature, has very little impact compared with the general social experiences and pressures of living in a custodial establishment, and with the environmental influences and opportunities which the offender meets on release.

158. These considerations point in the direction of trying to achieve change not by withdrawing a person from the community but by supervising and influencing him while he remains within it. A number of studies[1] show past institutional experience in penal establishments or other residential institutions to be correlated with reconviction after release. While the research results do not indicate that the general effect of detention in a custodial establishment must be deleterious, they do show that there is a significant number of young adult offenders whose behaviour seems to be little improved as a result of

---

[1] See, for example, paragraph 17 of Appendix D.

serving custodial sentences. Research and experimentation on this question in California have pointed in the same direction and have taken the argument a stage further by suggesting that many types of offender who have in the past been sentenced to custody might well be supervised in the community without any increase in the rates of reoffending at the conclusion of the sentence. There is no reason to assume that the broad conclusions reached in California would be invalid in the United Kingdom.

159. Research in this field is not conclusive by itself but, on the basis of the research results which are available, evidence submitted to us, and what we saw abroad, we believe that the goal of helping, assisting and influencing the offender to live his life and manage his affairs without committing offences has a better chance of being achieved by supervision in the community than by committing him to custody. In an assessment of the validity of this proposition, much no doubt depends on the degree to which supervision in the community can be made more effective than it is at present. The only way to put this to the test is to make greater resources available for the purpose, both in men and money, and to provide the supervisory services with improved facilities, such as hostels, and with the necessary authority to enable them to deal adequately with more difficult types of offender than are customarily put on probation. We make proposals for this purpose in Part II because we are impressed by the considerable impediments to producing a lasting change in a person's behaviour and way of life if he is dealt with in an artificial situation separate from the social situations to which he will return. The social changes which we have noted in Chapter 5 have weakened the former external constraints on behaviour, and make it now more than ever necessary to attempt to motivate offenders in terms of self-reliance rather than of obedience and conformity, so that they can make their own judgments on matters of conduct soundly. They will learn new responses to the situations with which they will be faced in the future only if they continue to be faced with them. This condition can be fully met only in the community and it is worth a major effort to make this possible.

160. These needs have of course been recognised in the philosophy of borstal training, from which comes the concept of the open institution. Paterson stated the importance of the exercise of free choice in the much quoted sentence, "It is impossible to train men for freedom in a condition of captivity", when explaining and justifying the opportunities then afforded to borstal trainees to go out by themselves for walks or to attend church, educational classes or concerts.[2] Borstal training still retains, and in some ways has further developed, the idea of providing young people with opportunities to exercise responsibility and freedom of choice both in the establishment and in the community in which it is based, and of attempting to offer situations similar to those which they will meet in the community to which they will return. But the logic of Paterson's proposition takes us further, to the recognition that there must be difficulties in effecting lasting changes in a young person's behaviour, or indeed knowing whether the method of approach being adopted is likely to succeed, unless the attempt is made while he is subject to the pressures and temptations of life in his own community. Our recommendations therefore have as one of their aims the encouragement of treatment of an increasing proportion of young adults in

---

[2] A. Paterson: *The Principles of the Borstal System*, Prison Commission, Home Office, 1932, p 12.

the community, and the necessary switch of resources within the penal system in order to implement this change of policy to the benefit of public and offenders alike. We believe that in the long term this will be both the most economical and the most effective way of preventing further crime. An important lesson that we have learned on our visits to the United States and to parts of Europe, notably perhaps Holland, is that the public can sustain a considerable degree of tolerance of minor offences by young people, provided that they are satisfied that someone is taking real responsibility for their treatment and future behaviour. Similarly we believe that, while the public in this country are naturally worried by the increase in violent crime among young people, equally there is increasing interest, sympathy and concern for the problems of those inadequate offenders, often from underprivileged social environments, who present no serious physical threat but rather are a nuisance. The trend in this country has been towards an increasing use of non-custodial measures in respect of adult offenders. We believe that under appropriate conditions the public would be ready to accept a similar change of sentencing policy in respect of young adults.

161. It is important not to jump from these propositions to the conclusion that custodial treatment must necessarily be damaging or at least that it cannot do anything worthwhile. Even the present borstal "success rates", so often unfavourably compared with the corresponding rates before 1939, show that 30 out of every 100 young men released from borstal are not reconvicted within three years of release. When the previous record of many of these offenders is taken into account, this figure is not unimpressive, and reflects credit on the efforts of borstal staff.

162. Moreover custodial treatment, for all its inherent disadvantages, does offer some possibilities at the beginning of a sentence which do not occur outside. It can, for instance, provide the opportunity for closer acquaintance with the offender, during which needs may become apparent which would be less likely to be observed during supervision in the community. It can also provide a period of removal from outside criminal contacts, during which the offender can be given time to consider with some measure of objectivity the course upon which he has embarked. Time in custody can be seen therefore as one stage on the way to rehabilitation, which will in any case have to be completed in the community.

163. Before passing from this topic we should refer to one suggestion for dealing with the present dilemmas of borstal staff, which we have considered but felt bound to reject. This is a return to the earlier system of rigorous selection of young adults for this particular type of training. This, it has been put to us, would again show the substantial benefits which can result from custodial training, provided that the system is asked to deal only with offenders who have been carefully assessed and pronounced likely to respond satis-factorily. The borstal system, of course, still handles a substantial number of young adult offenders of the kind who would have been accepted for borstal training in earlier days, but it is now expected to handle many others as well. The report of the Advisory Council on the Treatment of Offenders in 1959[3] specifically endorsed the view that borstal training should in future embrace

---

[3] *The Treatment of Young Offenders.*

diverse treatment approaches suitable for a wide range of types of offender. The implications of this have created some confusion among borstal staff as to their proper role, and they may have found it difficult and often unrewarding to apply traditional borstal principles to offenders who cannot readily be persuaded to co-operate, either because of their hostility to authority or because of the degree to which they have become inured to institutional life.

164. In our view it is unrealistic to think in terms of a return to the situation which existed before the 1961 Act, when courts could either select offenders for borstal training or pass a medium-term prison sentence, as a solution to the problems facing establishments and staff today. It would leave the worst risks and most difficult young adult offenders as likely to fail as now, and as difficult to deal with. It would involve maintaining special prisons for young adults, operating essentially on borstal principles. If this method of dealing with people were adopted many of the present borstal staff who wish to see a return to a selective approach would have to serve in the new establishments to look after the same type of offender as prompts their misgivings at present. Clearly there is some dissatisfaction among borstal staff with the problems of trying to apply borstal principles to many of those who are sent to borstal, but like the Advisory Council on the Treatment of Offenders we consider that the need is not to separate out the more difficult for a different form of sentence, but to try to develop new, more suitable approaches. Where segregation of some offenders from others is required it should be possible to achieve this, normally in separate wings of establishments or occasionally in separate establishments within the young adult system.

Amalgamation of the separate custodial sentences

165. We have already described in Chapter 6 how the existence of separate sentences of borstal training and longer-term imprisonment for young prisoners has become misleading to the courts and the public and how it perpetuates certain ideas about both prison and borstal which, though once accurate enough, are now largely divorced from reality. This has led us to the conclusion that the separate sentences ought now to be replaced by a single sentence, with a consequential amalgamation of the separate systems of establishments. These changes would eliminate the rigidity of the system as it has developed and provide greater flexibility both to the courts and to those running the custodial system.

166. It has been put to us, however, that it might be desirable to retain a separate sentence of longer-term imprisonment as a deterrent for some types of young adult offender. We believe that this proposition derives from precisely the supposed distinction between prison on the one hand and borstal training on the other which, as we have shown in Chapter 6, has for many years past ceased to be significant. We see no reason to suppose that imprisonment, as opposed to other forms of detention, has the special deterrent effect which this solution would imply. What counts with the offender is the length of time during which he suffers loss of liberty, not the type of establishment in which the sentence is served. There are indications from the period when sentences of borstal training mostly involved custody for 12 months or more that offenders feared this more than they feared a shorter sentence of imprisonment.[4] The

---

[4] See footnotes 17 and 18 to Chapter 6.

argument for retaining a separate prison sentence is based largely on the belief that it has peculiarly deterrent qualities: prison is seen primarily as a place of punishment, in contrast to borstal where "training" is provided. This is a misunderstanding of the actual position, and any attempt to make it a reality would involve a reversal of the long process by which the principles of borstal training have come to be adopted throughout the whole young adult system. This we would deplore.

167. The existence of the three separate sentences for young adults also limits the capacity of the executive to use the available custodial facilities in the most flexible and effective way. There are 23 training borstals[5] for young men with some 5,300 places, 13 senior detention centres with 1,500 places and five young prisoners' centres able to house about 800 people. (The total number of young prisoners at the end of 1972, however, was 1,455 and many were in local prisons.)[6] Those receiving one kind of sentence have to be kept separate from those receiving another, and this has particularly undesirable effects for young prisoners: the total number of young men serving substantial prison sentences is too small to enable the Prison Department to provide the range of security conditions and training facilities that might be desirable.

168. There is no open prison for young men sent to prison, although some may well be suitable for open conditions; and while one solution suggested to us was to develop special young prisoners' centres that would offer a variety of security conditions, we think that the better solution would be to merge the sentences. Again, the relatively small number of young prisoners means that young prisoners' centres have to serve a large geographical area. It is therefore necessary to place many young adults sentenced to imprisonment further from their homes than would be necessary if the two sentences were amalgamated and borstals and young prisoners' centres formed part of one system of young adult establishments.

169. We also see considerable advantages in combining the existing standard short-term and medium-term sentences of detention in a detention centre and borstal training. Although they were once intended to provide quite distinctive forms of sentence, the influence of the borstal philosophy on the original "short, sharp shock" approach of detention centres—both before, and subsequently with encouragement from, our own detention centre report—has been such that it is doubtful whether sufficient difference remains between the regimes of borstals and detention centres for there to be any value in maintaining the distinction. The point made earlier, that the existence of separate sentences prevents the best use being made of the available facilities, applies in this context also. For example, some detention centre trainees might be able to derive benefit from facilities for work training, education or medical treatment that it would be uneconomic to provide in a short-stay establishment.

170. These conclusions make it unnecessary for us to consider in detail whether the power in section 3(5) of the Criminal Justice Act 1961[7] to abolish by Order in Council sentences of imprisonment of six months or less on young adults

---

[5] ie excluding the two allocation centres and the psychiatric centre at Grendon.
[6] Prison Department Annual Report for 1972.
[7] See paragraph 19 of Appendix B.

should now be exercised. Our own report on detention centres[8] recommended that, pending the outcome of the wider review on which we are now reporting, short-term imprisonment of young offenders aged 17 and under 21 should continue to be available. Our recommendation for the amalgamation of the different custodial sentences which can be passed upon young adults into a single generic sentence providing for custody and control (see Chapter 8 below) will have the effect of abolishing imprisonment for young adults, so that the considerations which were present in 1961 and at the time of our previous report will no longer have any relevance.

171. We have emphasised in Chapter 5 the problems that many young adult offenders have to face in their home environment. It is essential that if they are committed to custody the time should be used to help them to come to terms with these problems. Offenders and staff should look forward to the future and outward to the community, concentrating throughout the period of detention on how the offender can be re-established in society. The nature of the new custodial order which we propose is designed to facilitate this: it will permit flexibility in the timing of the transition from detention to further support in the community, so that support in custody and support in the community may be regarded as parts of the same process. But, for this to be fully possible, arrangements are also needed to keep offenders in custody closer to their home area. Our proposal to combine the existing custodial sentences applicable to young adult offenders, and consequently the establishments in which the sentences are served, offers one step towards being able to keep young men near to their home areas. But we would wish to go further than this, and later in this report (in Chapter 12) we make proposals for the development of a system of establishments for young adults which will serve particular geographical areas: the result will be to strengthen links with the home area.

Length of sentences

172. Our account in the last chapter of the evolution of the custodial system for young adults shows clearly how the early belief in the need for sentences long enough to provide for adequate training in custody resulted in young people spending longer in custody than would otherwise have seemed justified on the basis of the offences committed. More recently this belief has to a large extent given way to the view that offenders should not be sent to custody, nor should their periods in custody be prolonged, simply in order to meet needs which can be provided for in the community; and we are sympathetic to this change of outlook. In our view considerations of the offender's individual needs can and should be given their proper weight within the limits of a sentence of custody or control. The maximum length of such a sentence would be fixed by the court and would not involve any judgment of what period in custody might achieve reformation.

173. There remains the question of the value of very short custodial sentences. The abolition of sentences of imprisonment of less than six months on young offenders would under present sentencing arrangements leave three months in a detention centre as the minimum length of custody that a court could order; and we consider that three months should become the minimum sentence that a

[8] See *Detention Centres*, paragraph 59.

court could impose if our proposal to combine the existing sentences is accepted. Some organisations which submitted evidence to us in the course of our present study suggested that it should be possible for courts to pass shorter custodial sentences than this.[9] Sentences shorter than three months would not be entirely compatible with our view that the time provided by the court's sentence should be used to influence the offender. A short period of detention, if followed by compulsory supervision, could no doubt be regarded as the first stage of a continuum of treatment in custody and in the community. It could provide an opportunity to assess a person's needs and attitudes and to decide what kind of care or supervision in the community on release might contribute to his avoiding offences in the future. But for this to be accomplished and the necessary administrative arrangements made preparatory to release, a certain minimum period of detention would need to be available.

174. Those who have advocated very short custodial sentences have therefore done so not so much on these grounds as because they believe that custody would have a specially deterrent effect. We do not believe this to be the case. When short terms of imprisonment were more freely available for young adults it was generally agreed that they did not deter but rather the reverse. The Prison Commissioners regularly made this point at the beginning of the century, when prison conditions were harsher than would be acceptable today. It was still the experience in 1938 when the Home Secretary said in the Second Reading of the Criminal Justice Bill 1938: "A short sentence cannot give a boy or girl any kind of useful training. It often destroys any deterrent effect that imprisonment may have . . ."[10] There is no reason to think that detention for a matter of days for deterrent purposes would be any more successful now than it was then or that it would make any difference if the detention took place not in a prison but in a special establishment for young adults.

175. Short detention of the kind envisaged by these witnesses exists in the Federal Republic of Germany and was the subject of comment in our report on Non-Custodial and Semi-Custodial Penalties.[11] Officials of the Federal Ministry of Justice expressed some doubts to us about its value and considered that there was no virtue in a sentence so short as to preclude any attempt to influence the offender by constructive and positive action. It might be said that such short-term detention would have an effect on some offenders though not on others. But even if this were accepted as possibly valid, the courts could not hope to distinguish in advance those who would be influenced by a short period of custody from those who would not. It would certainly seem pointless to pass such a sentence on a person who had already been remanded in custody, since any special effect of detention would presumably have already resulted from the remand itself.

176. We regard as useful simple penalties of a deterrent nature such as fines, which as we have noted are the most common penalty passed on young adults. We think it likely that those who would be influenced by very short periods of custody would also be influenced by fines, or by other forms of penalty

---

[9] In 1971 some 200 young offenders received immediate prison sentences of two months or less, and about as many again received a suspended prison sentence of two months or less.
[10] House of Commons, Official Report, Volume 342, col. 272.
[11] *Non-Custodial and Semi-Custodial Penalties*. (Chapter 7 and Appendix D of that Report).

such as community service or by an order for compensation. The great majority of young adults receiving custodial sentences at present have had offences proved against them on one or more previous occasions and have already been subject to non-custodial penalties or supervision in the community. Very short periods of detention have not in the past appeared to be more successful in changing the behaviour of young adults than other penalties. We therefore consider that it is better to avoid sentencing powers that might lead courts to pass short custodial sentences more readily than they do at present, and that unless the court concludes that in all the circumstances it has no alternative but to pass a custodial sentence of three months or more, it is in general better that it should employ a non-custodial measure.

177. We do see attractions, however, in the prospect of introducing weekend detention on the lines of the periodic detention work centres operating in New Zealand. These were described in our report on Non-Custodial and Semi-Custodial Penalties.[12] We have received further information about them and are convinced that they have many advantages over other forms of short custodial sentence. Residential centres similar to the periodic detention work centres could provide a form of punishment by deprivation of liberty that did not involve imprisonment or serious risk of contamination and required effort and active co-operation by the offender in purposeful work for the benefit of individuals in need, charitable institutions or publicly owned establishments in the community. Under the Criminal Justice Act 1972 community service is now available as a penalty which can be imposed by the courts and it has been introduced experimentally in a number of probation areas. We do not wish to distract effort and resources from the development of community service by recommending that periodic detention work centres should be established at this stage. *But as community service develops consideration should be given to the possible value of residential centres from which community service projects could be operated and at which offenders could be ordered by the courts to spend their weekends.*

---

[12] See paragraphs 161, 162 and Appendix E of that Report.

CHAPTER 8

THE CUSTODY AND CONTROL ORDER

178. In this chapter and in Chapter 10 we set out in detail our proposals for two new sentences which we intend to replace the existing custodial sentences for young adults. The custody and control order, which is the subject of the present chapter, would be the only custodial sentence which the courts could pass on a young adult.[1] The supervision and control order which we propose in Chapter 10 would be a non-custodial sentence, providing strong and effective controls in the community over offenders on whom the courts would at present feel it necessary to pass a custodial sentence.

THE GENERAL NATURE OF THE CUSTODY AND CONTROL ORDER

179. The term "custody and control order" emphasises our view that detention in a custodial establishment is to be seen not as an isolated experience at the end of which the offender is abruptly released to freedom (if possible "cured" of his criminality) but as the beginning of a period of control and supervision, partly in custody and partly in the community. The problems which have led a person into crime cannot easily be dealt with in a custodial establishment, isolated from the offender's normal social circumstances; nor as we have noted in the previous chapter is there any evidence from research studies that committal to custody necessarily improves an offender's chances of avoiding further offences. It is therefore one of the primary aims of the custody and control order that—so far as may be consistent with the aim of protecting the public from further offences of a dangerous or persistent nature—an offender's transfer from custody to control in the community should be arranged at as early a stage as possible.

180. In each case the court would fix the length of the custody and control order, ie the maximum period during which the offender should be liable to detention and subsequently to restrictions on his freedom when at liberty.[2] Our proposal thus restores to courts the means of marking the gravity of a particular offence and distinguishing degrees of culpability, the loss of which (under section 3 of the Criminal Justice Act 1961) has been a cause of complaint.

181. The sentence pronounced by the court would be for a determinate period during which the offender would be liable to either custody or control. The conditions in which the sentence is served, the actual period spent in custody, and the timing and conditions of release to control in the community, would be decided by or on behalf of the Home Secretary in accordance with the restrictions, machinery and criteria set out in this chapter. Release of the offender to supervision and control in the community, at as early a stage as is practicable, should be seen as being consistent with, and indeed in furtherance of, the sentence of the court, and in no sense as a reversal of it. When a

[1] Except for the crime of murder: see paragraph 184.
[2] Subject to what is said in paragraph 221 below about a minimum period of control after release.

person is released under control in the community the court's sentence will continue to operate, though in a different form, and there will be a sanction of recall to custody to ensure that offenders comply with the reasonable requirements which are made of them during the control element of the sentence.

182. The custody and control order would be a "generic" sentence for young adult offenders, that is to say it would be the only custodial sentence available for offenders aged 17 and under 21 except for the crime of murder. We have explained in Chapter 7 why we conclude that the existing distinctions between sentences of imprisonment, borstal training and detention serve no purpose which cannot be achieved at least as well as by other means. *Accordingly we recommend that the existing sentences of imprisonment of young adults, borstal training, and detention in a detention centre should be abolished and that, except in the case of murder, the only custodial sentence available to the courts in respect of young adult offenders should be the custody and control order.* We believe that this solution will command wide acceptance among those responsible for dealing with young adult offenders.

183. It would follow that the three separate systems of custodial establishments for young adults should be amalgamated into a single system. Our proposals for the future organisation of these establishments, and the regimes to be offered in them, are worked out in Chapters 11 and 12.

184. At present a person convicted of murder committed while under the age of 18 is sentenced to detention "during Her Majesty's Pleasure";[3] over that age the sentence is life imprisonment. It would be anomalous to retain the sentence of imprisonment for persons under the age of 21 for murder alone and *we accordingly recommend that the sentence applying to those aged under 18 should be extended to offenders up to 21*. The Criminal Law Revision Committee in their interim report on the penalty for murder[4] provisionally recommended that the mandatory sentence for murder for persons under the age of 18 should be changed to detention "in such place and for such period and subject to such conditions as to release as the Secretary of State may direct". If that provisional recommendation were to be confirmed by the Committee and accepted by the Government, we would wish to see it similarly extended to murderers up to the age of 21. This would not involve any substantive change in the sentence. Custodial establishments for young adult offenders would, as now, be among the places in which a young offender subject to this sentence might be detained.[5]

185. The effect of a custody and control order would be that the offender would be immediately[6] committed to a Prison Department establishment. With the amalgamation of detention centres, borstals and young prisoners centres into one system, the Department would have a much wider range of establishments: open and closed conditions, and residence in hostels administered by the Department, would all be available. On release from custody the offender would be placed under the control of a probation and after-care officer either for the remainder of the period covered by the order or for six months, whichever was

---

[3] Children and Young Persons Act 1933, s.53(1).
[4] Cmnd 5184.
[5] See also paragraph 90 above.
[6] Subject to the exceptional arrangements proposed in paragraphs 235 to 238 below.

the longer.[7] We prefer not to call the period of control "after-care" so as to avoid the implication that the probation officer's role is simply one of resettlement. On the contrary, control in the community is an integral part of the implementation of the order of the court and lasts as long as the order is in force.

Length of the Custody and Control Order

186. *Where a court has power to pass a sentence of imprisonment on an adult we recommend that on a young adult it should have power to make a custody and control order.* Save possibly in the circumstances referred to in paragraph 188 below, a young adult should not receive a longer custody and control order than the prison sentence that an adult would receive for the same offence; and we believe we can rely on the usual checks of appeal procedures to ensure this. The length of a custody and control order would be subject to no statutory maximum other than the statutory maximum prison sentence for the particular offence. It would thus be possible, though in practice extremely rare, for a young adult to be the subject of a custody and control order for life for a grave crime other than murder.

187. *We recommend that the maximum length of custody and control order that a magistrates' court should have power to impose should be the same as the maximum sentence of imprisonment that it is able to pass, that is (save in certain exceptional cases) six months.*[8] Where a young adult is found guilty of an indictable offence following summary trial, and the magistrates' court considers that its powers of punishment are insufficient, there should be power to commit to the Crown Court for sentence, on the lines of the power at present available in section 29 of the Magistrates' Courts Act 1952.

188. For the reasons set out in paragraphs 173 to 176 above, *we recommend that the minimum length of custody and control order available to the courts should be three months.* Unless the offence is sufficiently serious to justify a sentence of that length, the court should instead employ a non-custodial measure. If the circumstances require a high degree of social control, the supervision and control order which we propose in Chapter 10 will be available. There are some offences for which the maximum sentence of imprisonment is less than three months[9] and we have considered carefully whether, in such cases, it should be

---

[7] Subject to the possibility of earlier termination of supervision in appropriate cases (see paragraph 222 below).

[8] Magistrates' courts have power in relation to certain offences under the Customs and Excise Act 1952 and the Misuse of Drugs Act 1971 to impose sentences of imprisonment of up to 12 months; and on summary conviction for a second or subsequent offence of an assault on a constable they may impose a sentence of imprisonment of up to nine months. We consider that they should have similar powers in respect of custody and control orders.

[9] For example, certain offences involving drunkenness carry a liability to a maximum prison sentence of one month; but a small number of young adults are quite legally given a three month detention centre sentence and even on occasion a borstal sentence for offences involving drunkenness. Section 4(2) of the Criminal Justice Act 1961 provides that for any case in which the court may pass a sentence of imprisonment of up to three months it may pass a three month detention centre sentence; and the courts have held in relation to borstal training that it is permissible to pass such a sentence for an offence for which the maximum prison sentence is such that the offender might be kept in custody longer under the borstal sentence than under the maximum available term of imprisonment (*R v Amos* [1961] 1 All E.R. 191, 45 Cr App R. 42).

open to the court in dealing with a young adult to make a custody and control order despite the fact that the minimum duration of such an order is three months. We have concluded that this should not be legally ruled out, but it should be regarded as wholly exceptional and the court should be required to state its reasons for the view that no other sentence would be appropriate. We prefer this solution to either accepting very short custodial sentences for this small group of offences, or depriving the courts of the power to pass a custodial sentence which they would have if the offender were 21 or over.

Appeals against short Custody and Control Orders

189. In Appendix F we set out proposals for expediting the consideration of appeals against short custody and control orders and for a more liberal policy with regard to the granting of bail pending appeal. During our visits to detention centres we have been told of a number of cases in which, because of delays in considering appeals, offenders do not bother to proceed with them because by the time the appeal has been determined the offender has largely or completely served the custodial sentence. This is an obvious source of potential injustice and one which we are most concerned to overcome. Our proposals on this point are independent of our recommendation for a custody and control order and could in our view be brought quickly into operation even while the present sentences for young adults continue in existence.

Limitations on the use of custodial sentences and consideration of information about offenders

190. Section 14 of the Criminal Justice Act 1972 provides that a court shall not pass a prison sentence on a person over 21 who has not previously served a sentence of imprisonment unless it is of opinion that no other method of dealing with him is appropriate; and a magistrates' court must record its reasons in the court register and in the warrant of commitment. There is no corresponding provision discouraging the passing of a custodial sentence on a young adult who has not previously served one. Section 17 of the Criminal Justice Act 1948, together with section 107 of the Magistrates' Courts Act 1952, discourages the courts (in language on which the 1972 provision is based) from passing a *prison* sentence on a young adult unless satisfied that no other method of dealing with him is appropriate; but this is a restriction only on imprisonment, not on custodial sentences as such, and presumably was intended to steer the courts towards borstal and the (then) new detention centre sentence and away from imprisonment,[10] as a part of the strategy of successive statutes of keeping young offenders under 21 out of prison and hence away from the influence of adult offenders. We think that there is every reason to apply restrictions to the use of custody and control orders similar to those which apply to prison sentences. *We therefore recommend that it should be a statutory requirement that a court should not make a custody and control order in respect of a young adult who has not previously been subject to such an order,[11] unless it is of*

---

[10] Section 18 of the Criminal Justice Act 1948 prevented a court from passing a detention centre, sentence unless it had considered every other method of dealing with the offender that was open to it (except imprisonment) and was of the opinion that none of them was appropriate. This restriction on the use of detention centre sentences was removed by the Criminal Justice Act 1961, under which they became the standard short-term custodial sentence, intended to replace imprisonment.

[11] Transitionally a sentence of detention or borstal training since the age of 17 or a sentence of imprisonment.

opinion that no other method of dealing with him is appropriate, and that it should state the reasons for that opinion. For the purpose of deciding whether any other method of dealing with the offender is appropriate the court should be required, before passing a custody and control order on an offender who has not previously received one, to obtain and consider a social enquiry report.[12] If a court, however, should accidentally overlook this requirement this should not automatically invalidate the sentence, although such failure might occasionally provide good ground for an appeal[13].

191. As well as making it mandatory to consider a social enquiry report, this recommendation goes somewhat beyond the requirements of section 14 of the 1972 Act in that it requires a statement of reasons not only by magistrates' courts but also by the Crown Court. We see no good reason for making a distinction between magistrates' courts and the Crown Court in this respect.

ARRANGEMENTS FOR DECIDING DATES OF RELEASE FROM CUSTODY

192. *We recommend that constitutional responsibility for decisions to release offenders from custody to serve the remainder of their sentence under control in the community should rest with the Home Secretary* (as is now the case with young adults released from borstal). He would act on the advice of an advisory body, which for the shorter sentences would be the new local body proposed in paragraph 193 below and for sentences of three years or more would be the Parole Board. This, of course, could not mean that each decision to release an individual offender should be personally approved by the Home Secretary. The more serious cases, which have attracted long sentences, would no doubt require consideration at a high official level, or in some cases by Ministers. But in the case of shorter sentences, broadly equivalent to the present sentences of detention centre and borstal training, the actual decision to release should be taken at local or regional level without undue delay or formality. Even so it would require the formal approval of an official acting in the Home Secretary's name and thus maintaining his constitutional control over and responsibility for the release of each individual offender.

Release advisory bodies

193. *For the purposes of making recommendations for the release of offenders subject to custody and control orders we propose the establishment of a new local advisory body, to be named the licence advisory committee.*[14] This body would consist of the governor of the establishment or his deputy; a

---

[12] It should be noted that the requirement we are recommending is more specific and goes beyond the terms of section 14 of the 1972 Act which require only in general terms that "the court shall obtain and consider information about the circumstances" as well as considering any other information available about his character and his physical and mental condition. In Chapter 15 we make a number of other recommendations regarding the provision of social enquiry reports to courts as an aid to sentencing. These include a general recommendation, though not a universal requirement, that a social enquiry report should be considered by the court before passing a custody and control order on a young adult, whether or not it is his first.

[13] The courts have held in a similar context that failure to state reasons for passing a sentence of imprisonment on a young adult does not automatically invalidate the sentence. (*R v Chesterfield Justices ex parte Hewitt* [1973] Crim. L.R. 181; *R v Jackson* [1966] 1.W.L.R. 528).

[14] We have thought in terms of a separate body of this nature for each establishment, but conceivably one body could serve several establishments. This is a matter which could be settled as turns out to be most convenient in the course of implementing our proposals, as could the consequential arrangements for representation of the prison service and Boards of Visitors.

representative of the local probation service; a member of the Board of Visitors; and one other member of the local community drawn from a panel appointed for the purpose by the Home Secretary.

194. Such a body would provide a fair balance between professionals responsible for dealing with the offender and representatives of the public interest and local opinion. It is important that the governor and the probation officer should both be full members and not merely advisers, in order that proper weight may be given both to the offender's progress in the establishment and to the likely problems of resettlement.

195. We think it right that Boards of Visitors should be represented in the release procedure, but we do not think that Boards should themselves constitute the advisory bodies. The primary function of Boards of Visitors is to act as independent observers and advisers to the governor and the Home Secretary, to hear complaints and to deal with certain questions of discipline. We believe that this function is not easily combined with that of advising on release, and that the latter could with more advantage be discharged by a separate body. Furthermore, governors are not members of Boards of Visitors, nor is the probation and after-care service represented on them. As we have indicated above, we think that the release body should not only have the advice of the governor and of a probation officer, but should include them in its membership.

196. *We propose that young adults subject to custody and control orders of three years or more should be released from custody and transferred to control in the community only with the approval of the Parole Board.*[15] Cases would be referred to the Board through the licence advisory committee described above.[16] The Board has a broadly-based membership,[17] and is accustomed to taking account of the public interest in balancing the probability of the offender's remaining free of trouble against the risk of his committing further offences and the danger of a loss of public confidence in the sentencing system. Offenders with custody and control orders of three years and above would therefore be dealt with in much the same way as young prisoners with sufficiently long sentences are now, and as adults will continue to be. The arrangements would however differ from consideration of prison sentences on adults in two ways—one statutory, the other largely practical.

197. Firstly it should be open to the licence advisory committee to recommend release of a young adult at any stage. We see no need for the restriction which applies to adults that a case may not be referred to the Parole Board until a minimum time or a minimum proportion of the sentence has been served.[18]

---

[15] Subject to any Rules made under section 35 of the Criminal Justice Act 1972—which should be amended to apply to custody and control orders as to prison sentences—enabling the Secretary of State to release certain offenders on the recommendation of the local review committee (or in the young adult context the local advisory body we propose) without reference to the Parole Board.

[16] Or by the appropriate parole local review committee where the offender has been transferred to an adult prison under the arrangement proposed in paragraph 3 of Appendix E.

[17] Schedule 2 of the Criminal Justice Act 1967 provides that the membership of the Board shall include representation from the judiciary, psychiatric medicine, criminology, and persons with experience of the supervision of offenders discharged from custody. A full list of members of the Board, with their occupations, is included in the Board's Annual Report.

[18] A prisoner may not be released on parole until he has served one third of his sentence (including any time spent in custody on remand), or 12 months from the date of sentence, whichever occurs the later.

While we recognise that very early release of a young adult who has attracted a custody and control order of three years or more is likely to be recommended only with especial caution, we think that the Parole Board should have the opportunity in suitable cases of responding flexibly to the changes in attitude and behaviour which characterise many people in this age group. Secondly, where a recommendation for release is rejected by the Parole Board it should be open to the staff and the local advisory body to refer the case to the Board again at any time.[19] It should be a duty of the staff of establishments to maintain a continuing review of the circumstances of each trainee, whatever the length of the order he is serving, and to refer his case back to the Parole Board whenever they think reconsideration of it is justified.

Entitlement to release

198. *We recommend that a young adult subject to a custody and control order should have a statutory entitlement, subject to good behaviour, to be released when not more than two thirds of the order has elapsed.* In reaching this conclusion we have been substantially influenced by existing practice, especially in relation to adult prisoners. Any adult sentenced to imprisonment for more than one month is granted remission of the final one third of his sentence, unless all or part of it is forfeited as a punishment for misconduct. In origin, remission was something which a prisoner positively earned by his conduct and industry. Since the enactment of the Criminal Justice Act 1948 one third remission of sentence has, as it were, been credited in advance to a prisoner, though he can lose that credit through misconduct. Remission of sentence is judged to be a powerful disincentive to bad behaviour, and forfeiture of quite small amounts of remission is regarded by prisoners as a severe penalty.

199. The remission system as such does not apply to young prisoners serving sentence of 18 months or more;[20] they are released on licence, subject to supervision and recall. In practice, however, the two thirds point in the sentence is taken as the latest date for release unless there has been misconduct. Young men in detention centres earn remission, although they too are released on licence to supervision. Borstal training is thus the only sentence in which the concept of guaranteed release after two thirds of the sentence plays no part.

200. Remission is a long established feature of the prison system. It is widely held to have advantages and its abolition seems unlikely. That being so, we have had to consider what would be the consequences of juxtaposing prison sentences for adults with remission after two thirds of the sentence (and parole for some after one third) and custodial sentences for young adults where the courts would fix the maximum using criteria essentially the same as they follow in passing prison sentences but there was no assurance of release after two thirds of the period has expired. We believe that the consequences would be adverse, making the courts' task more difficult and creating a sense of grievance among young adults. Young adult offenders attach great importance to being treated

---

[19] An adult whose parole recommendation is refused normally has his case reviewed again by the local review committee after one year (if his sentence is long enough to permit this); the Board may however recommend that an early review be directed by the Secretary of State, usually after another six months.

[20] Remission does apply to shorter prison sentences—most of which, because of the restrictions on imprisonment, are of six months or less; and the licence and recall arrangements are as for detention centre trainees. (See paragraph 21 of Appendix B.)

no less favourably than if they were adults. If an adult offender receives a 12 months' sentence he is assured of release, unless he misbehaves to an extent that loses him remission, after eight months. It seems to us to be reasonable that a young adult offender should have a similar entitlement in addition to the prospect of even earlier release under the terms of the custody and control order.

201. This argument has special force when the courts have to deal with cases involving young adults and older offenders jointly. They may be equally culpable and the difference in their ages may be no more than a few weeks. Where both offenders are given a three-year sentence the young adult will feel unfairly treated if he has no guarantee of release after two years, while if the young adult is given a shorter sentence to reflect the lack of guaranteed remission the adult might feel a similar grievance and the court's judgment of relative culpability would be obscured.

202. While our proposal in respect of young adult offenders provides a parallel to the adult remission system, it also provides a contrast which we want to stress. For an adult prisoner the remission date is the date on which, if not granted parole, he is actually released, free from all restrictions. (If he is paroled, it is the date on which supervision ceases.) Under the custody and control order the guaranteed release date must not be regarded in any sense as a guide to the normal period of detention. We would expect the great majority of young adults to have been released well before this date, which is no more than a kind of back stop, assuring an offender from the outset of his period in custody that if he does not misbehave he will be out by then at the latest.

203. We do not base the case for remission for young adults solely on the need to keep in step with the adult remission system. Guaranteed release at the two thirds point also helps in ensuring that a young adult, even if his release has had to be delayed until close to, or even at, the two thirds point, will still be under supervision in the community, with a liability to recall if necessary, for a reasonable period before the custody and control period expires. It is true that, later in this chapter, we recommend a minimum period of supervision, which may if necessary extend beyond the terminal date of the custody and control order, but it is desirable to limit such cases as narrowly as possible.

204. The ability to postpone an offender's release beyond the date on which he would normally be entitled to expect it can also be an effective disciplinary sanction. We do not believe that this proposition is invalidated by the fact that, whenever possible, a young adult will be released well before two thirds of his sentence has elapsed. At the time of a disciplinary award postponing a guaranteed release date the offender will have no assurance of release at any time before that date, and the addition of a determinate period of time to the effective maximum period of his detention will be likely to have a clear and immediate effect upon him. We understand that the Parole Board, in deciding the release date of adult prisoners, consider themselves free either to take into account or to ignore any loss of remission through misconduct. The assimilation in this respect of the disciplinary systems applicable to young adults and adults respectively would be particularly useful in the case of young adults who finish the custodial part of their sentences in adult prisons (see paragraph 5 of Appendix E).

70

205. We therefore do not see any incompatibility between a system of remission, with the possibility of postponement for misconduct, and a system of flexible release of the kind envisaged under a custody and control order, while we see substantial advantages to be gained from combining them. The absence of a power to order brief postponements of release as a disciplinary sanction seems to us to be one of the disadvantages of the present borstal sentence. Certain institutional offences may be punished by delaying a trainee's promotion to the discharge grade or by demoting him from it. The effect of this may be a delay in release not of a few days (such as might be effected by loss of remission in prison or detention centre) but of one or two months in the trainee's progress through the establishment. Although the borstal trainee can make good this loss of time by extra effort, he may not be able to see practical steps that he can take to influence his release date. The disciplinary action thus has no precise and evident impact on the offender's expectation regarding release. In this respect our proposed adaptation of the remission system appears to us likely to be more effective.

Restricted release orders

206. We see no need to specify a general statutory minimum period (by analogy with the six months' normal minimum under the borstal sentence) which all offenders must spend in custody under a custody and control order. Cases in which a court has judged committal to custody to be unavoidable and staff then take the view that release is justifiable almost immediately will be rare[21]— indeed, a system in which they were common would quickly lose public confidence. But where they do occur, the staff and the advisory bodies should be able to deal with them on their merits without being fettered by a statutory limitation, and we believe that they can be relied upon to act responsibly in this matter. In any event staff will need a certain minimum period of assessment of the offender's needs and prospects before they could contemplate making a recommendation for early release.

207. There may however be some exceptional cases where because of the nature of the offence or the conduct of the offender the court should have power to ensure that a particular offender is not released without further reference to that court, until a certain minimum proportion of the term of the order has been spent in custody. *We therefore recommend that the Crown Court should, where it is necessary for the protection of the public, be empowered to make a restricted release order.* The effect of the order would be to prevent the offender's release until the expiry of a specified proportion of the period of the custody and control order. This proportion would not be fixed by the court in the individual case, but would be common to all cases in respect of which a restricted release order is made, and should be specified by statutory instrument. We suggest that initially the proportion should be set at one third, but this might be varied in the light of experience.

---

[21] We were told in the course of our enquiries, particularly by detention centre staff, that there are some offenders, recognisable by their behaviour and reactions after arrival in an establishment, who would stand a better chance of avoiding further offences if they were released within a few days, while they were still shocked by the sentence. If they were released then, we were told, the prospect of another sentence of the same kind would be a much more potent deterrent than it would be once they had had time to adjust to the demands of the regime and begun to be influenced by the inmate culture. We see no reason to doubt that there are such cases.

208. We do not attempt a comprehensive definition of the cases in which it would be appropriate to make such an order. We believe that the courts will have no difficulty in identifying those exceptional cases where the offence and the previous behaviour of the offender suggest that he presents a special danger to the public, requiring particular circumspection regarding early transfer to non-custodial treatment. These considerations can hardly arise in cases in which a custody and control order of less than 12 months is the sentence which the court deems appropriate to the offence and the offender. *We accordingly propose that the power to make a restricted release order, if it is necessary for the protection of the public, should be available only when the Crown Court makes a custody and control order of at least 12 months and less than three years.* Orders of three years and above are adequately covered by our proposal that release should be considered by the Parole Board. Restricting the power to cases involving a custody and control order of 12 months or more will in effect confine it to the Crown Court; and in any case this seems to us the kind of power appropriate to a court of superior jurisdiction.

209. Where there is a special reason for considering the early release of an offender, even though he is subject to a restricted release order, *the executive should have power to refer the case to the Crown Court with a view to the order being rescinded.* Where possible, arrangements should be made for the judge who passed a sentence to consider the application for removal of the restriction.

210. An incidental advantage of the power to impose a restricted release order would be that it would assist the executive in identifying certain cases where the court had judged the protection of the public to be the predominant factor in sentencing, and so in developing a liberal release policy in cases in which no such order is made. It would also emphasise to staff that they were not expected to set conventional minimum periods of detention related to the offence rather than the offender.

211. *Any time spent in custody on remand before conviction or sentence should count towards the sentence* for purposes of calculating the length of the custody and control order, the guaranteed date of release, and the expiration of any restricted release order. For example, if a young adult has spent two months in custody before sentence and receives a two-year custody and control order, his guaranteed date of release, subject to any disciplinary awards affecting that date, should be 14 months after sentence, not 16; and if a restricted release order has been made his earliest date of release should be after six months rather than eight. Similar arrangements already apply to prison sentences, but not to sentences of detention centre and borstal training; this is a source of grievance among young adult offenders, who expect equal treatment with adults in terms of calculation of liability to custody.

Criteria and procedures for release to supervision
212. It is of the essence of the proposal for a custody and control order that the decision about the timing of the transfer of an offender from custody to control in the community should be taken in the light of the characteristics of each offender, of his prospects in the event of release from custody and of the danger which he might represent to the public. It follows that no detailed criteria can be laid down for general application to all offenders, but certain principles may be stated.

213. The decision which has to be made is not one which will bring the operation of the court's sentence to an end, but rather one designed to change the method of implementing its sentence, in which custody and control were envisaged as equally valid methods. From the beginning of the sentence staff should concentrate their attention on the best strategy to improve the offender's capacity to live satisfactorily in the community after release without breaking the law. Having established what needs to be done, they should decide whether it must be done in custody or could not equally be done in the community. To this extent the decision will be primarily one based on the offender's needs and circumstances and will take into account both the offender's progress while in custody and his probable circumstances on release, including his relations with his family, or the availability of a job and suitable accommodation.

214. It may be said that there is some unfairness in a system which takes account of social circumstances such as these, and that offenders from poor social circumstances may fear that they will be doubly punished, once for the offence and again because of their background. This is a real dilemma: but it is also a challenge to Government and to the staff both of establishments and of the probation and after-care services. Clearly the release of offenders who can safely be allowed back into the community cannot be delayed simply because there are others of whom, for whatever reasons, this unfortunately cannot be said. Fairness therefore demands that, where these reasons lie in circumstances beyond the offender's control, positive efforts should be made to give him an equal chance. We believe that the development of hostels and other sheltered accommodation, together with more effective help in securing employment and other forms of assistance—perhaps through more intensive work by the supervising officer—can help to make possible the early release of offenders whose prospects in the community would otherwise be poor. Indeed, where an offender's delinquency appears to be largely a reaction to or consequence of poor social circumstances, this may provide an especially strong case for the gradual removal of restrictions and hence for early release, initially, in his case, into relatively sheltered conditions. This will provide the longest possible period of support during which he may be brought face to face again with the problems which led him into trouble.

215. The staff, and subsequently the advisory body to which the staff submits its recommendation, should ask themselves whether there is any compelling reason why the offender should not be released to control in the community and whether anything can be achieved in custody which cannot be achieved as well or better in the community. Only if the answers to these questions are on balance affirmative should custody continue. It has been said that, because courses of education and work training in young adult establishments require certain minimum periods, their provision would impose constraints on the flexible use of the discretion to release. Some young adults, it is argued, might be reluctant to take part in courses if they thought that this might prejudice their chance of early release. We believe that this difficulty can be overcome if courses form part of an individual training programme, which is related as far as possible to a target date for release. Industrial training courses in establishments for young adult offenders are in any case being increasingly organised on a basis compatible with courses outside, so that an offender can finish his course after release. If, unpredictably, release appears advisable on other grounds, it should not be delayed only in order that a course may be completed.

73

216. An important ingredient in the release decision, in addition to the considerations referred to in the previous paragraph, will be the advisory body's assessment of the likelihood of the offender committing further offences, the degree of damage which such offences would cause and, in some cases, the effect of the offender's release upon public confidence in the release system as a whole. In making this judgment, the court's opinion of the seriousness of the offence, as indicated by the length of the sentence, will clearly be relevant, though not necessarily decisive.

217. Forecasting the chances that an offender will commit further offences is notoriously difficult. Some of those released on licence will undoubtedly offend again, but the great majority of them would in any case be released within a comparatively short time, and there is little advantage from any point of view in keeping them in custody for a few weeks or months longer if their chance of avoiding crime in future is judged likely to be improved by releasing them a little earlier under appropriate control. If the policy of the authorities in this matter is clearly explained, we do not believe that public opinion will jump to the conclusion that there has been an error of judgment every time an offender commits a further offence soon after his release. For many young adults who have previous convictions it is more realistic to hope that the frequency and severity of future offences may be reduced than that they will never again commit an offence.

218. In order to make our approach to release decisions a reality, suitable arrangements will be needed for the review of cases by staff and by the licence advisory committee. Obviously every case should be kept under review by the staff of the establishment, as is the case at present with young adults in custody; and there should be a formal review of the case by a board of staff members about once a month. In addition there should be some provision for formal review by the advisory body, as a check on staff decisions and so that trainees may know that their cases are being considered by an independent body and that their fate does not lie entirely in the hands of the staff. It would impose an undue burden on the review committee if they had to consider the case of every trainee at monthly intervals, but they should carry out an early initial review of each case, say within a month of an offender's reception at his training establishment. In the meantime the staff would assess his needs and prospects, with a view to the recommending of a "target release date"[22], which would then be referred to the advisory committee for approval. Shortly before the "target date" the offender's case should again be referred to the committee with a view to consideration being given to release on that date or, in the case of longer sentences, with a view to a recommendation for release being forwarded to the Parole Board. A maximum period between reviews of an offender's case by the advisory committee—perhaps six months—should be laid down where the date is beyond that period. Meanwhile the staff should consider at monthly intervals whether there should be any change in each offender's target date for release.

---

[22] Staff of some establishments, notably those based on therapeutic regimes with emphasis on psychiatric treatment, are opposed to target dates, on the basis that offenders are more likely to co-operate in a programme of treatment if they are in uncertainty as to their date of release. We do not deny that in some exceptional establishments this technique if properly used has merit and we do not wish to rule it out. What we describe in the text however should be the normal procedure for most establishments.

219. In the exceptional case in which the court has made a restricted release order, the staff will of course take the length of the order into account when they put a "target date" proposal to the review committee for endorsement. Such cases should however be reviewed monthly by the staff in just the same way as any other; in this way cases might exceptionally be brought to light in which it would be justifiable to refer the case back to the Crown Court with a view to the restricted release order being rescinded.

Period of supervision

220. *We recommend that on release from an establishment an offender subject to a custody and control order should be under the supervision of a probation officer for the balance of the term of the order or for six months, whichever is longer.* It should be made clear to him by the court at the time of sentence that this supervision represents an integral part of the sentence.

221. The minimum period of 6 months under supervision would apply to short custody and control orders, where the balance of the sentence on release must in any case be extremely short, as well as to longer sentences where the trainee has been detained beyond two thirds of the sentence as a result of disciplinary awards. The minimum period of six months may seem short compared to the maximum of two years' supervision that follows release from borstal and the one year that follows release of a young adult after a sentence of less than 18 months' imprisonment or a detention centre sentence. But we think that concentrated supervision and assistance in the six months following release is likely to be more effective and a better use of resources than a one year or two year commitment, which stimulates no sense of urgency.

222. Anyone released with more than six months of the custody and control order to serve will be under supervision for a longer period. Every young adult will be under control in one form or another for at least the term set by the court, except that *we recommend that the Secretary of State should have power, on the recommendation of the probation service and on the advice of the licence advisory committee or the Parole Board (depending on the length of the order), to terminate supervision before the order expires.* If supervision is terminated liability to recall should also cease. We do not think it necessary to impose any overall limit to the period of supervision. There might for example be a case of an offender released after one year of a three-year custody and control order whose circumstances were such that he needed support and control for the whole of the remaining two years. There may on the other hand be cases where the supervisor considers that the offender has settled down well, is unlikely to offend again, and has no continuing need of supervision. In order to ensure that supervision does not continue unnecessarily, *we recommend that supervising officers should be required to consider at intervals—perhaps every six months—the need for its continuation.*

Requirements on release to supervision

223. At present the standard requirements imposed on a young adult released on licence are to keep in touch with his supervisor, to be of good behaviour and to lead an industrious life. This last requirement in particular, needs to

be made more precise: we think that the supervisor should have power to approve or disapprove a specific job. But, more generally, we do not consider that these requirements are sufficient to supply the degree of control, direction and support that many young adults leaving establishments will need if they are to be helped to establish themselves adequately in society and keep out of trouble, and if the public are to be satisfied that the degree of control provided is sufficient to warrant the early release of offenders for whom the courts have seen no alternative to a custodial sentence. We consider therefore that the requirements need to be strengthened and made more specific. *Accordingly we recommend that the Secretary of State, when releasing an offender, should have power to impose in the notice of supervision handed to the offender any or all of the following requirements:*

(*a*) to keep in touch with the supervisor as required by him;

(*b*) to be of good behaviour;

(*c*) to work in employment approved by the supervisor;

(*d*) to reside in a place approved by the supervisor (including an approved probation hostel);

(*e*) if required by the supervisor, to undertake a specified course of education or work training, whether residential or non-residential; and

(*f*) to avoid any places of resort specified in the notice or by the supervisor.

To these requirements might be added any other requirement which, in the special circumstances of a particular case, the Secretary of State might authorise.

Recall and other sanctions

224. *We recommend that a person released from an establishment should be liable to be recalled to custody at any time during the period of supervision. On recall his liability to detention should be the balance of the term of the custody and control order or 30 days, whichever is the longer,* but the period actually served should be based on an assessment of the offender's deficiencies, the events leading to his recall, and the prospects of avoiding a repetition. Within the period of the custody and control order recall may be seen as a normal part of the implementation of the court's sentence, as would be a transfer from open to closed conditions or return after a period of home leave. But liability to recall will also serve as a sanction to enforce compliance with the requirements of supervision, and where supervision continues beyond the end of the custody and control order this will inevitably be seen as its predominant purpose.[23] It would be consistent with our earlier recommendation about an offender's maximum liability to custody (paragraphs 198 to 205 above) that, subject to any disciplinary awards having the effect of increasing the liability to custody, *the offender should be released again under supervision after not more than two thirds of the maximum liability to detention on recall, and we so recommend.* On being again released the offender would be subject to such requirements as the Secretary of State considered appropriate (paragraph 223 above), and to further recall (for the balance of the term of the custody and control order or for 30 days, whichever is longer). The period during which he should be liable to supervision and recall should again be the balance of the term of the custody and control order or six months, whichever is longer, except that, *we recommend there should*

---

[23] At present a similar liability to recall continues throughout the period of supervision which follows a young adult's release from borstal, detention centre or prison.

*be an automatic termination of all such liabilities six months after the termination
of the custody and control order made by the court.*

225. At present detention on recall is usually quite lengthy—frequently three or
four months in the case of borstal. Recall to borstal tends to be seen as the
commencement of a further period of training, rather than as a simple penalty
or as a temporary withdrawal to prepare for another attempt to settle down in
ordinary life. This is because it is normally ordered only in comparatively serious
cases, where the offender has persistently evaded the attempts of his supervisor
to keep in touch with him. Recall is thus regarded as a somewhat extreme
reaction to a failure to comply with licence requirements: supervisors are
reluctant to recommend it and the Home Office to order it. Shorter periods of
recall are occasionally used where the need is to forestall a breakdown or to
help the offender to overcome some temporary set-back; but we should like to
see a greater readiness to use short periods of recall in this way.

226. It should not, however, be necessary to fall back upon the power to recall
merely for want of other suitable means of dealing with a breach of the licence
requirements; and we consider that there is a need for a wider range of sanctions
of a less extreme kind. Where a probationer is in breach of a probation order
the court has a choice between the extreme sanction of sentencing him for the
original offence (which can mean a custodial sentence), or imposing a non-
custodial penalty (such as a fine or—when section 49 of the Criminal Justice
Act 1972 is brought into effect[24]—a community service order). There would be
advantages in having sanctions less drastic than recall available for breach of
the conditions of supervision, and accordingly *we recommend that the supervising
officer should have power to bring the offender before a magistrates' court for
breach of the licence, and the court should be empowered to impose any of the
available non-custodial penalties.* The supervising officer, in consultation with his
superiors and if necessary with the Home Office, should first rule out the need,
in his own judgment, for recall before initiating breach proceedings. Nevertheless
there might be room for the court to take a different view, or further facts
might come to light in the course of the court proceedings. *We therefore
think it right to provide the court with a power to return an offender to custody
if he is in breach of the licence requirements,* provided the court has first
considered a report from the Secretary of State and from the probation service
on the offender and his prospects. Where however the original custody and
control order was made by the Crown Court and the magistrates' court dealing
with a breach considers return to an establishment to be the right course, we
recommend that the magistrates' court should commit the offender to the
Crown Court to be dealt with. Otherwise a situation could arise in which a
magistrates' court could render an offender on licence liable to a longer period
of detention than if they were dealing with him for an offence (ie normally
6 months—see paragraph 187).

227. In putting into practice the concept of a more flexible use of recall powers
a careful balance has to be struck between conflicting requirements. On the one
hand, if the aim of the release policy is to ensure that offenders are not kept
in custody without good cause, and if the authorities are to be encouraged to
exercise control in the community over offenders about whose response they

---

[24] See paragraph 31 of Appendix B.

77

cannot feel fully confident, then there must be a fairly ready way in which offenders can be recalled to custody if the control is breaking down. On the other hand, the authorities should not lightly take a decision to recall to custody an offender who has already begun to find a place again in the community and expects to be considered as a free man who has already paid his penalty. Whatever explanations may be given to him at the time of his release, he is likely to misunderstand and resent the suggestion that he may be recalled, not because he has broken a requirement of his licence, but because his supervisor fears that he is about to do so and wishes to forestall a breakdown in the order.

228. Under present arrangements recall is employed only in limited circumstances where there has been a clear breach of the licence requirements[25] and we believe that some strengthening of the power of recall is required. The proposals which follow aim to do this, while maintaining the essential rights of the offender.

229. *We recommend that when a young adult is first released he should for a period of 2 months be regarded as being on extended leave from the establishment.* During this period of "long leave" the offender would continue to be subject to the authority of the governor of the establishment from which he had been released, although he would already be under the supervision of a probation officer. The governor, in consultation with the probation service, could recall him on any reasonable grounds. Recall in this period would not need to be limited to circumstances in which there had been a clear breach of the licence requirements but could be employed if the offender's general mode of life and failure to settle down showed that there was a serious risk of his getting into trouble again and that the release decision had been premature. There would be no appeal against recall during this period, but the governor would inform the licence advisory committee of the decision, and it would be open to them to review it if they wished.

230. *At the end of two months of satisfactory compliance with the conditions of supervision the offender should be regarded as released on licence.* The circumstances in which recall could thereafter be initiated should accord with the more limited criteria at present obtaining for administrative recall, namely that there has been a clear breach of the licence requirements. The recall order would be issued on behalf of the Secretary of State and the procedure would be as it is now. That is to say, a recommendation for recall is initiated by the supervising probation officer, and if supported by the principal probation officer is passed on to the Prison Department. If the conclusion is that the person on licence needs to be recalled, the proposal for recall is referred to a senior official in the Prison Department of at least Assistant Secretary rank. Recall takes place only if the person concerned is in breach of one or more of the requirements of his supervision order (normally failure to keep in touch with his supervisor or to try to keep in work).

231. The offender should have a right to make representations against a decision to recall him at this stage. We do not regard the present arrangement for appeal by way of a petition to the Secretary of State as wholly satisfactory,

---

[25] See paragraphs 119 to 121 of Appendix B.

even though the appeal is dealt with at a higher level than the original order of recall. The decisions are more likely to be recognised as reasonable and fair by the offender if the appeal is made to a body which is not part of the Executive and has no responsibility for the decision to recall.

232. *Accordingly we recommend that where an offender is recalled to custody during the licence period and after the expiry of the period of long leave, he should have a right of appeal to the licence advisory committee* which is responsible for recommending releases from the establishment to which the offender is returned. So far as possible this should be the same establishment from which he was released, and there should not be a separate "recall" establishment. The appeal body would then be that which authorised the offender's release.[26] The members would be able to consider all the circumstances of the case, not only the behaviour which had led to recall but also the impact of recall, the offender's present behaviour, and the possibility of further release. They could resume their ongoing review of the case, with a view to releasing the offender again as soon as possible without necessarily concluding that the decision to recall him had been wrong. The licence advisory committee should automatically be informed of recall decisions whether or not the offender wished to appeal. This practice would provide it with information about the effects of its decisions and so help to improve decision-making in the future.

233. *For those serving sentences of three years and above, we recommend that the same procedures should apply except that the licence advisory committee would make its recommendations in the first instance to the Parole Board* rather than to the Secretary of State. We are confident that suitable procedures can be worked out for "long leave" in the case of those within the Parole Board's jurisdiction.

Further offences during a Custody and Control Order

234. At present, if someone who is under supervision on borstal licence or unlawfully at large from a sentence of borstal training is convicted of an offence punishable with imprisonment, the courts have power, under section 12 of the Criminal Justice Act 1961, to order his return to borstal instead of dealing with him in any other way. This is a far more common means of being returned to borstal than recall by administrative action; in 1972 1,182 young men and 18 young women were returned by a court under section 12 for a further offence, while recall orders were issued in respect of 56 young men and seven young women. *Under the arrangements we propose we see no need for a similar provision,* since the courts would have power to make a new custody and control order of whatever length they considered appropriate (subject to the minimum of three months).

POSTPONED EXECUTION OF CUSTODY AND CONTROL ORDERS

235. The arrangements outlined in this chapter presuppose that in all cases the first part of a custody and control order will be spent in custody. We can however envisage circumstances where a court would consider a custodial

---

[26] Strictly speaking the outcome of a successful appeal would be a recommendation to the Secretary of State to revoke the recall order.

sentence unavoidable but in view of some imminent event in the life of the offender, or some aspect of personal or family circumstances, would think it inappropriate or unduly oppressive for him to be committed to custody immediately. He might for example be about to undergo a surgical operation for which he had waited a long time or be about to take examinations. There would be no virtue in disrupting these arrangements in cases where there was little probability of the offender absconding if left at large for a week or two more. A remand on bail with a view to sentencing later, or a formal deferment of sentence under section 22 of the Criminal Justice Act 1972, might have the drawback of encouraging the offender to expect a non-custodial sentence. Recognition of these expectations might inhibit the court from making a custody and control order when he came up for sentence. To meet circumstances such as these *we recommend that when making a custody and control order the court should have power in exceptional circumstances to postpone execution of the custodial element for a short, specified period* in order to enable an offender to put his affairs in order or fulfil immediate obligations.

236. A proposal for a "suspended execution order" with similar intent, which would have enabled courts to suspend the execution of a sentence of imprisonment for up to three months, was considered by the House of Lords during the Committee and Report stages of the Criminal Justice Act 1972.[27] The proposal was withdrawn on the Government's commitment to give the matter further consideration. We see merit in giving the courts this power in dealing with young adults, whether or not it is extended to other age groups (a question which lies outside our terms of reference). There would be no anomaly in differentiating young adults from adults in this respect, since there is no adult sentence that closely resembles our proposed custody and control order, embracing both custody and supervision in the community. It would be only the custodial element which the court would defer; in the meantime the offender would be subject to control in the community. It should be open to the police to make representations to the court where it is considering use of this power, in the same way as they can when bail is considered.

237. The main purpose of postponed execution of the custodial part of the sentence is to avoid unnecessary disruption of an offender's personal arrangements, but where postponement has been ordered there are other uses that can be made of the time thus gained. The Prison Department should be informed and a supervisor appointed from the local probation service. In appropriate cases the offender might be required to present himself for any interviews, examinations and tests which would enable the Prison Department to decide on his allocation. He could then be instructed to report to the establishment at which he would serve the custodial element of the order.

238. Normally the application for postponement of execution would be made by the defence. We are divided on the question whether it should also be open to the Prison Department to apply for postponement to enable them to decide on allocation or because there was no immediate vacancy in the appropriate establishment. We would not wish to see suspended execution used as a means of solving accommodation problems which require more long-term solutions,

---

[27] House of Lords Official Report, Vol 333, No. 109, cols 982–1,000, and Vol 335, No. 133, cols 1,320–1,335.

but we recognise that this measure might sometimes be useful for meeting purely temporary administrative difficulties. A majority of us have concluded that there is no reason to rule out the possibility of the Prison Department applying for a short postponement. *We therefore recommend that, provided that no objection is raised by the defence, the court may order postponement of the custodial part of a custody and control order at the request of the Prison Department for a period of not more than seven days.*

239. Under the Criminal Justice Act 1967 (as amended by the Criminal Justice Act 1972) a court which passes a sentence of imprisonment of two years or less has power to order that the sentence shall not take effect for a period of between one year and two years specified by the court, unless the offender commits a further offence punishable by imprisonment. This power to suspend sentence is not available in relation to borstal training and detention centre training and we see no need for it in relation to custody and control orders. The reasons for not providing for the suspension of borstal and detention centre sentences have been, first, that these have been seen as training sentences reflecting individual needs more than general considerations of deterrence, and second, that young offenders change and mature rapidly and, by the time a suspended sentence fell to be implemented, an offender's needs and characteristics might have changed substantially. Our general view is that a court should not make a custody and control order unless it is of the opinion that no method of dealing with the offender other than his immediate—or almost immediate—committal to custody is appropriate. If the nature of the offence and offender is not such that the court considers an immediate custodial sentence necessary, but at the same time a considerable degree of social intervention and control over the offender's leisure time is warranted, the court should seriously consider whether it could not use a non-custodial measure such as community service or, more particularly, the supervision and control order which we propose in Chapter 10.

TRANSFER AND RECLASSIFICATION ARRANGEMENTS, AND EXCEPTIONS TO AGE LIMITS

240. We have assumed throughout this chapter that the offenders being dealt with are aged 17 and under 21 at the time of sentence (subject to a power to raise the upper age limit by statutory instrument—see paragraph 91). It remains to consider, first, the position of young adults who receive custody and control orders which extend beyond their 21st birthday: we have proposals designed to ensure that they are not treated less favourably in terms of restrictions on their liberty and leisure than their contemporaries who may be released at the same age from shorter sentences of adult imprisonment. Secondly, a frequent theme in the evidence we have received regarding appropriate age limits for the young adult category has been the need for flexibility—the recognition that young people develop to physical, mental and emotional maturity at different rates, and that chronological age alone may be a poor guide to an individual's needs. The age limits which are necessary for delineating a distinct category of offenders may occasionally fail to meet in the best way the needs of certain individuals and should not therefore be immutable in every case. We have therefore considered whether courts should have discretion to deal exceptionally with certain offenders over the age of 21 as though they were young adults, and also whether there should be provision to deal with particularly immature young adults as though

they were under 17 and thus bring them within the scope of the provisions of the Children and Young Persons Acts.

241. We have not thought it necessary to deal with these questions in the main body of our report: the arrangements which we propose are set out in some detail in Appendix E.

CHAPTER 9

RESETTLEMENT OF OFFENDERS IN THE COMMUNITY AFTER CUSTODY

242. In Chapter 8 we described our proposed custody and control order as a measure that would provide a continuum of treatment in custody and in the community, supervision in the community being as much a part of the sentence as time spent in custody. Thus what is usually referred to as "after-care supervision" is to be seen not as an appendage to custodial treatment but as an essential element of the process of custody and control, the supervisor using the powers available to him to meet the offender's needs as identified both during custody and after he has returned to the community. It should be seen as a particular sort of community treatment, for while it exhibits many of the characteristics of community treatment generally, often there are, in addition, particularly acute problems associated with resettling offenders in society after a period of isolation in custody. This is not a novel doctrine: in particular for young adults sentenced to borstal training, the aim has always been to regard the period of supervision after release as an integral part of the sentence.

243. Probation officers have for many years been concerned with the after-care of young adults released from borstal. During the 1960s the service took on the statutory after-care of detention centre trainees, and became involved in the supervision of adult offenders in large numbers, on a voluntary basis and subsequently through the parole scheme. These developments in the last ten years have meant that the probation and after-care service has now become the general agency for the supervision of offenders released from Prison Department establishments; and this in turn has helped it to build up an understanding of the special problems of the discharged offender, and to improve its techniques. A welcome development, which we wish to encourage, is the increasing tendency of probation officers to advocate and practise "through care"—the probation officer being in contact with an individual offender from the beginning of the custodial order through to the end of supervision in the community. Over the last two to three years probation officers have been encouraged to strengthen their working relationships with penal establishments and it is common practice for officers to visit offenders for whom they will have responsibility on discharge in order to build up a relationship with them and to discuss with staff in the establishments any problems which might affect resettlement prospects. The involvement of probation officers with borstal trainees in these ways is however often hindered by the distance between the establishment and the offender's home area. This problem would be greatly eased by our proposals in Chapter 11 under which establishments would serve particular areas so that offenders will so far as possible serve the custodial part of their sentence in the area where they will be supervised.

244. We have received evidence from both the probation and prison services describing new developments in giving support to young adults in the period following release from establishments. Progress has been made in this direction particularly in inner urban areas where attention has been given to the creation of special community support through, for example, the establishment of clubs, support groups and lodging schemes in which borstal staff, probation officers and volunteers have joined in providing continuing support. The successful promotion of such schemes as exist has depended on close collaboration between establishments and probation staff and we believe that much more could be achieved in developing such an approach.

245. In the largest cities the establishment by probation and after-care committees of specialised after-care units has helped to stimulate co-operation with both public institutions and voluntary effort. We are content to leave it to local committees to decide whether the volume of work with discharged offenders justifies this degree of specialisation. We should, however, deprecate specialisation being carried to the point where it might become impossible to release an offender to the care of a probation officer who had supervised him in the past and already had a good understanding of his needs.

246. It has been put to us that the role of staff of young adult establishments should be broadened so that they could be involved with trainees after discharge. There have been experiments in which custodial staff have spent some time in this way. We would not wish to discourage limited experiments of this kind, but we do not think that they should become the general practice. Dealing with offenders in the community—and perhaps most of all offenders discharged from custody—is work that requires its own training and skills, and is the particular province of the probation and after-care service. At the same time the prison service needs to concentrate on and develop its own equally important skills in dealing with offenders in custody. We do not think it practicable for either service to accept major responsibility in the field of the other.

247. It is, however, important that Prison Department staff should be able to relate their work to that of the probation service in carrying out supervision after discharge, and vice versa, and we believe that our proposal that young adult establishments should serve particular areas would, by bringing custodial and community treatment closer together geographically, facilitate closer co-operation between the two services.

Problems of resettlement

248. Young adults, on leaving penal establishments, face all the problems common to their age-group, but in a much more acute form; and they compete on disadvantageous terms with others on low income in obtaining both accommodation and work. As regards accommodation, many will be able to return to their families but for some this may not be a practicable solution. Others may be rejected by their families or be homeless. Particularly for those who do not return home, financial and accommodation problems loom large. The scarcity of public housing provision for single people of any age except the elderly means that the homeless ex-offender is likely to be entirely

dependent on the private landlord or landlady. The wages currently paid to people of this age are barely sufficient to enable a discharged offender to pay the rent normally required for furnished accommodation in big cities and at the same time to lead a reasonably independent existence. A person in full-time employment is not eligible for supplementary benefit, although he may be entitled to a rent rebate or allowance from a local authority and, if he has a family, family income supplement may be payable.

249. It may be said that these difficulties do not differ radically from those which have to be faced by non-offenders in large cities and must therefore be dealt with in the context of services provided for the community in general. Consideration of these falls, of course, outside our terms of reference. Nevertheless it is relevant to our enquiry to note that offenders recently released from custody are a group whose social problems, as they try to reintegrate themselves into the community, require the special attention not only of the probation and after-care service but of other social services and voluntary bodies as well. One way of meeting their needs is through an expansion of hostel facilities, and related types of accommodation for offenders: we discuss this at more length in Chapter 14.

Employment

250. The problems of offenders leaving penal establishments in finding and keeping suitable work can be severe: the adverse effect on the prospects for rehabilitation if they are not surmounted is obvious. It is therefore an important part of the efforts of the staff both of penal establishments and of the probation and after-care service, not to mention the offender himself (eg during home leave), to attend to this aspect of resettlement. This is familiar ground—though there are no easy solutions—and we have no specific recommendations to make.

"New careers"

251. This is, however, a suitable point in our report in which to note the growing significance, in particular in the United States, of what has become known as the *new careers movement*.[1] This term covers a number of schemes in which people from deprived or disadvantaged social groups have been selected, trained and employed in various kinds of social work, the main fields being education and social welfare. It is claimed for these developments that they tap a new and hitherto disregarded source of social work manpower which not only helps to ease the growing problem of manning the social services but has a particular contribution to make, since helpers and helped will be likely to share more of a common background. The work done by "new careerists" has included work with offenders, and some of those selected for "new careers" are themselves former offenders. Those of us who visited the United States learned something of these experiments as they involve former offenders, though we did not examine them in detail.

252. We have also received information about some rather similar experiments which are being carried out on a small scale in this country. Perhaps the most

---

[1] A brief account of the movement is given in *New Careers for the Disadvantaged* published by the National Association for the Care and Resettlement of Offenders in June 1973.

notable of these is an experiment in which the Bristol Association for the Care and Resettlement of Offenders has set up a hostel which is used as a base for a social work training programme. Young adult offenders who might otherwise have been likely to receive a borstal sentence have been identified as suitable for the programme, and have been placed on probation with a condition of residence at the hostel. The object is to equip these young men for employment in various social work openings.

253. These approaches represent a challenge to traditional thinking which for obvious reasons has in general seen a previous criminal history as a disqualification for occupying positions of responsibility, and in particular positions of influence over offenders. Probably in the light of the United States experience this is too rigid a view. We are sceptical about the argument that former offenders, having been "through the mill" and being close in background and outlook to those whom they are helping, are specially suitable to work with offenders; but we do not consider that they should be ruled out for such work if on other grounds they are judged to have the right qualities. It is certainly our experience, in talking to offenders about their hopes for the future, that many of them say they would like to do "work with people". *We welcome the experiments now going on for training offenders in social work, and recommend that the possibility of involving suitable individuals with offenders should be kept in view.*

Clothing

254. Clothes have an important bearing on self-confidence, particularly where young people are concerned, and self-confidence is precisely what many newly released offenders lack. Until recently the choice of discharge clothing, which was usually made by the establishment, was often not to their liking, and differed embarrassingly from what was being worn by their contemporaries. We therefore welcome the recent changes in the system which allow trainees a degree of choice in the kind of clothes available to them on release. Governors may now arrange for trainees to choose clothing, within a fixed price limit, in the following ways:
  (i) from a range of mail order firms;
 (ii) from an outfitter who is invited to visit the borstal to take orders; and
(iii) by trainees being allowed out unsupervised, to select and purchase items from a nearby outfitter nominated by the governor.

Financial assistance on release

255. While in general we believe that those released from establishments should look to the community services for assistance on the same terms and in the same way as other people, there is a need for special arrangements for financial assistance for young adults on release from custody to cover immediate needs. The arrangements that obtained during much of our review were in our view anomalous and unsatisfactory, and we were glad to learn, towards the end of it, that the Prison Department had secured agreement to new arrangements which would bring those for young adults and adults more closely into line. The new arrangements, and those that they have replaced, are summarised below.

256. Since 1964 discharge grants of up to £4 have been available for adult offenders who have served a prison sentence of over three months. Provision was recently made for up to an extra £4 to be available for homeless adult prisoners. Young prisoners (ie those sentenced under the age of 21) are included in the scheme if they have been reclassified as "adult" prisoners during their period of detention. There have until recently been no similar arrangements for young men or young women released from borstals or detention centres, or from prisons if they complete their sentences as young prisoners. Young prisoners and borstal trainees were originally excluded from the discharge grant scheme because they had access to financial aid given by the Borstal Division of the Central After-Care Association. When the Borstal Division was wound up in 1967 authority was given for the average per capita sum which the Division had previously spent on young adults to be available to an offender's supervising officer from public funds through local probation and after-care committees. The amount was £3.50 for young men and £3.75 for young women (whether released from prison or borstal) and these figures have never been increased. The position regarding young men released from detention centres has been that up to £2.50 (or more if he is homeless) may be spent on any one individual. There have also been subsistence payments at various rates for the journey home.

257. We regarded these arrangements for financing young adults on release as unsatisfactory. The amounts were inadequate (they have not been increased to keep pace with living costs) and compared unfavourably with the amounts paid to adult offenders (whose needs are not necessarily greater), and payments through probation committees often cannot be made promptly enough to meet immediate needs at the time of discharge.

258. Under the revised arrangements which have now been adopted, an offender who is released on licence from a sentence of borstal training, or a young prisoner released from a sentence of over three months, is eligible for a discharge grant of up to £4 on the same basis, and subject to the same conditions, as adult prisoners. The grants are paid from Prison Department funds in the same way as grants for adults. Not every young adult eligible for a discharge grant will necessarily receive one, since grants are paid only to those who are homeless or whose circumstances are such that their return without financial help would place a difficult burden on a family; the extent of need is established in the course of the usual discussions between the establishment and the probation officer before the offender is released. Where grant is not paid the offender receives merely a subsistence payment. After release young adults, like adults, will continue to look to the probation and after-care service for financial assistance to meet exceptional needs which are not provided for by other statutory sources.

259. Young adults will not at this stage be eligible for the additional payment which is available to homeless adults as an advance payment of rent. We understand that the arrangements for this payment are now being examined as part of a more general review which will in due course embrace the arrangements for financial help for all offenders on release from custody and this review will include the needs of young adults. We welcome this review and hope it will quickly lead to a system

which ensures that payments automatically keep pace with changes in the cost of living and avoids the serious time lags which have occurred in the past before adjustments are made.

CHAPTER 10

TREATMENT IN THE COMMUNITY

260. In this chapter we set out our proposals for developing and expanding the arrangements for the non-custodial treatment of young adult offenders, building upon the existing probation system. *In particular, we propose the introduction of a new non-custodial order which we have called a supervision and control order*. The purpose of this order is to give to the courts a means of imposing on a young adult offender to whom they might at present feel obliged to give a custodial sentence a degree of supervision and control which would enable him to be dealt with in the community. The new order would be administered by the probation and after-care service but would be distinct from a probation order—which would remain available to the courts—and is intended to deal with a class of offender who would not normally be considered suitable for probation. The order would include a wide range of standard requirements—discussed in greater detail later on—which could be invoked at the supervisor's discretion. *The making of the order, unlike a probation order, would not require the consent of the offender,* and the order would not be "instead of sentencing him".[1]

261. In putting this proposal forward we recognise that new sentencing measures, be they custodial or non-custodial, cannot in themselves have more than a limited effect upon the penal system. Ultimately what is crucial is the manner in which sentencing measures are used, and the resources that are made available for their implementation. Nevertheless, the introduction of a new measure can in itself be important if it stimulates the growth in resources, enables them to be deployed in the most effective way, and brings about beneficial changes in the sentencing practice of the courts. It is in these ways that we hope the proposals described in this chapter will have an impact.

262. Earlier chapters have not discussed the existing arrangements for non-custodial treatment—in particular the probation system—in the same detail as they have discussed custodial treatment.[2] It is therefore necessary, before we proceed to a general description of our proposed new order, to place it in the context of the continuing scope for a greater use of probation. The terms of a probation order are broadly designed to ensure personal contact between the probation officer and the offender by imposing requirements that he reports regularly to the probation officer and receives visits at his home. The development of a personal relationship between the probation officer and the offender remains at the core of social work. However the probation and after-care service, in common with developments in social casework generally, has placed increasing emphasis on community influences in the treatment of offenders. This is illustrated by the use of groups, by the involvement of volunteers, and by the employment of ancillary workers in the work of the service, all of which

---

[1] Criminal Justice Act 1948, section 3(1).
[2] Probation is briefly dealt with in paragraphs 163 to 166 of Appendix B.

indicate that a broader base is being continually established for probation treatment. It has long been the practice of probation officers to encourage persons under their supervision to take part in camps, adventure courses and similar activities, and since 1971 probation and after-care committees have been empowered to incur expenditure for this and similar purposes. Many local probation services now organise camps, and there are examples of probation groups involved in a variety of activities including office-based activity groups and other out-of-door pursuits. A few probation services have permanent camp sites and outdoor pursuit centres.

263. Two current experiments should, if successful, give added impetus to these developments in probation practice. The first is the experimental establishment (under the Criminal Justice Act 1972) of day training centres; the second is a study of "intensive supervision" being undertaken in five areas which is the subject of research by the Home Office Research Unit.

264. It is too soon to say how the day training centres, which were being established in four probation and after-care areas during the course of our review, will develop. These centres, we understand, are aimed at providing community support for the inadequate adult probationer with a chronic unemployment record and a history of repeated offences. Early reports of the first centres indicate that they can be developed so that in addition to using the probation and other staff specifically assigned to the centres they provide a focus for community involvement drawing upon and stimulating the interest of local educational, industrial and voluntary organisations. We were particularly interested to hear of the development of one of the experimental centres on these lines in conjunction with a bail hostel and an approved probation hostel in Sheffield.

265. The second experiment, known as IMPACT (Intensive Matched Probation and After-Care Treatment) consists of a series of co-ordinated controlled experiments in five probation and after-care areas covering serious and high-risk offenders supervised by probation officers. In the ordinary course probation officers provide treatment both in their own offices and in the offenders' environment, the main emphasis generally being on office interviews. The IMPACT experiments seek ways to diversify and extend the range of treatment in particular by attempts to give relatively greater emphasis to meetings outside the office—for example, in the home, at the place of work and in places where the offender spends his leisure time. The final results of this research are expected in 1976.

266. We recognise that there has been a considerable expansion of community facilities which form the basis for the supervision and control of offenders within the context of the statutory provisions for probation orders, and we wish to see these developments gather increasing momentum. We expect this will naturally follow as experience gained from the experimental schemes is applied nationally. We have also considered the general effect on the skills and experience of probation officers that will follow as community service schemes, established under provisions of the 1972 Criminal Justice Act, are extended, and believe that the closer links which result between community organisations and the probation and after-care service will lead to a

strengthening of the community basis for probation treatment. Our recommendations concerning the supervision and control order are therefore not to be interpreted as in any sense an adverse judgment on the existing probation system or the methods and facilities for the administration of probation orders. In our earlier report on non-custodial and semi-custodial penalties we commented (paragraph 193) on the widening scope of the probation and after-care service, and we reiterate the acknowledgment made there of the important part which probation by itself plays in the non-custodial treatment of offenders.

267. Our proposal for a new type of non-custodial sentence is based on two important considerations. First, the supervision and control order gives the supervising probation officer a greater measure of control and freedom of action in exercising supervision. Because the order would be made without the consent of the offender, the probation officer would have a different kind of responsibility for intervening in the conduct of the case by bringing into effect any requirements contained in the order without having to rely on the agreement of the offender. Though the techniques used in the treatment involved in implementing a particular condition would be comparable to techniques used in probation, the authority given to the probation officer implies powers of enforcement in bringing the condition into operation. The sanctions available to the supervising authority in case of the offender's failure to co-operate or in the event of breach of conditions of the order are discussed below. In particular, an entirely new proposal is made that, in certain circumstances, the supervising officer should have power to detain the offender temporarily on application to a magistrate.

268. Our second important consideration in proposing the new power is that it should encourage the courts to use, and the public to accept the use of, non-custodial measures on relatively serious offenders for whom an order of the court which depended on their consent does not seem appropriate. This wider judicial and public acceptance would, we hope, in turn stimulate further provision of resources and facilities in the community which would be available for use both in support of the new measure and for supervision of those released to the community under a custody and control order.

269. Underlying both the considerations outlined above is the contrast between the probation order and the supervision and control order in regard to the need for the offender's consent. We recognise that there are some who will not easily accept a new form of supervision by probation officers which does not require consent. But supervision imposed without the offender's consent and administered by the probation service is not a novelty. It is a feature of statutory after-care supervision and of the new suspended sentence supervision order. A statutory requirement of consent to a supervision and control order would not be appropriate, since it is intended that the order should permit the imposition of types of control to which it would be unrealistic to expect the offender to give genuine consent at the outset of the order. It is of course true that, if the order is to be effective, there must be a measure of acquiescence on the offender's part, but the relationship between supervisor and offender will, at least initially, be based more on obligation than on consent. *Before imposing the order, the court should consider a social enquiry report and*

91

satisfy itself that there is at least a reasonable probability of the obligations being accepted by the offender. If, in the event, they were not, the order would no doubt break down and the offender would have to be brought back to court. But to pretend that the order was based on freely given consent would be unreal.

The order and its requirements

270. Thus, the supervision and control order would supply a means of placing a young adult offender under a quite strict form of control by a probation officer. *The order would be available in respect of any offence punishable by imprisonment in the case of an adult* (ie in a narrower class of case than a probation order). *We recommend that the maximum duration of a supervision and control order should be two years* rather than the three year maximum for probation, in recognition of the greater element of control and intensity of contact: *provision should be made for early termination on the application of the supervising officer, given a good response on the part of the offender.*

271. It would be an important feature of the order that it would make available to the individual supervisor a standard range of requirements which could be invoked at his discretion unless the court in making the order had specifically excluded any of them. *The requirements of the order would be substantially the same as those which we recommend that the Secretary of State should be enabled to apply at the time of releasing an offender from custody under a custody and control order* (see paragraph 223 above). *Thus the requirements would be*
- (a) to keep in touch with the supervisor as required by him;
- (b) to be of good behaviour;
- (c) to work in employment approved by the supervisor;
- (d) to reside in a place approved by the supervisor (including an approved probation hostel);
- (e) to avoid any places of resort specified by the supervisor; and
- (f) if required by the supervisor, to undertake a specified course of education or work training, whether residential or non-residential.

We envisage that *the Secretary of State would have power to add to or modify the available requirements by statutory instrument.*

272. *It is essential that the court, when making a supervision and control order, should explain to the offender what the potential liabilities under the order are,* including his liability to temporary detention (see paragraphs 283 to 288 below) *and that the offender should be given a notice in writing setting them out.* The court should ensure that he clearly understands that any requirements imposed upon him during the course of the order are authorised by the court at the time of sentence and are not to be regarded as being arbitrarily imposed by the supervisor. The latitude allowed to the supervisor in deciding the timing or precise incidence of the conditions allowed by the court order has as its object to permit treatment to be varied flexibly in accordance with the offender's changing needs, without the necessity for reference back on each occasion to the court.

273. We shall not attempt to spell out in detail how the supervising officer would use his discretion, within the terms of the supervision and control order,

to carry out his obligation to supervise and control. This would be determined by the needs of the individual offender. We limit our comments to a few points which seem to us to involve new administrative provisions or a novel approach.

274. Clearly a requirement with regard to residence will be important. Under our proposals hostel residence will continue to be available both as a requirement of a probation order and also as an option available to the supervisor under a supervision and control order. There is a particular need for an increase in non-custodial residential provision for offenders in the form of hostels, lodgings and flatlets which will enable young adult offenders to be kept in the community while at the same time giving them a stable background which may have been lacking in their normal environment. This will be the more important if a greater proportion of offenders in this age-group is to be treated non-custodially. We give a more detailed account of the needs which hostels must satisfy, and the way in which we believe they should be administered, in Chapter 14.

275. As regards education, work training and similar activities, we see scope for a range of different approaches. One approach which may well prove valuable and relevant to the needs of young adults is the day training centre, particularly if (as the initial experience of the experimental centres set up under the 1972 Act seems to suggest) the centres can develop not as premises where educational and training activities take place exclusively but as somewhere for people to meet and develop a common identity and purpose and from which they could go out to make use of existing community facilities. The impression of those members of the Council who visited the United States and saw day centres for young adult offenders, particularly in California, was that this kind of facility should be developed for young adult offenders here also. *Consideration should be given, in the light of further experience of the experimental centres, to adding attendance at a day training centre to the list of standard requirements available in a supervision and control order,* just as it is a requirement that can be inserted in a probation order.

276. But non-residential training of the kind we envisage does not necessarily require the formality of a centre from which it is organised. As indicated above probation officers are accustomed to encouraging those under their supervision to make use of many kinds of community facility which bring them into contact with non-delinquents—for example specifically educational activities, social and recreational clubs, and adventurous outdoor activities of the Outward Bound type. There is every reason to suppose that this process would extend to young offenders made subject to a supervision and control order. Indeed, the greater emphasis on control which the order will impart into the supervisor/offender relationship, and the greater concentration of supervising effort which will be necessary under the order, should mean that more can be done under a supervision and control order than under a probation order to influence an offender in these ways. Whether it is done under the aegis of a formal requirement (paragraph 271 (*f*)), or informally, will vary with the circumstances and indeed, once a proper relationship has been established under the supervision and control order, will probably not greatly matter. These are after all activities towards which the offender can be led but not driven.

277. Some of these considerations apply to *community service*. As introduced in the 1972 Act this is a separate court order and not a condition in a probation order.[3] It will be apparent from what has been said about our concept of the supervision and control order that community service is the kind of activity which it would be useful to be able to require an offender to carry out under a supervision and control order as well as under the existing community service order under the 1972 Act. The Home Office Guide to the Act, prepared for the use of magistrates and others, describes the community service provisions as aimed at providing "a power which the courts and the public will see as a viable alternative to the shorter custodial sentence", and "envisaged as a means of imposing the sanction of deprivation of leisure for a constructive and outward-looking purpose, which will enable the offender to give something back to the community against which he has offended and will in some cases bring him into direct contact with members of the community who most need help and support". These features of community service would make it particularly valuable as an instrument of control available to the supervising officer under a supervision and control order.

278. There is a complication in adding the performance of community service to the list of standard requirements available in a supervision and control order. It arises from the question of consent. Section 15(2) of the 1972 Act provides that a court shall not make a community service order unless the offender consents. We understand that a condition requiring an offender to perform community service would, if imposed without the offender's consent, be held to contravene Article 4(2) of the European Convention for the Protection of Human Rights and Fundamental Freedoms, and the International Labour Office Convention of 1930 for the Suppression of Forced or Compulsory Labour. Therefore, if the performance of community service were made a standard supervision and control order requirement, it would have to be subject to the qualification that the formal consent of the offender had first been obtained. We do not regard this as a serious obstacle, particularly since the performance of community service, like participation in the educational and other activities discussed above, must involve the *de facto* consent of the offender whether or not there is a formal requirement; we should therefore like to see community service made, with the qualification about consent, one of the possible requirements under a supervision and control order. If, however, it were decided to leave the performance of community service outside the formal scope of a supervision and control order, it could still be treated as an example of the involvement in community activity towards which a supervising officer should guide an offender under his charge. This would then be no more than has been the position under the probation system. But in any event, what matters is that young adult offenders subject to a supervision

---

[3] In our report on non-custodial penalties, in which we recommended the introduction of community service, we took the view that either a separate order, or a condition in a probation order, would be a suitable vehicle for ordering community service. The Government, accepting the advice of an official working party with substantial probation service representation, came down in favour of the former approach alone, on the ground that "to incorporate community service in a probation order would be likely to blur the traditional concept of a probation order; it would emphasise the probation officer's controlling function rather than his role of advising and assisting" (House of Commons Official Report, Standing Committee G on Criminal Justice Bill, 8th February 1972, column 480).

Community service is briefly described in paragraphs 168 and 169 of Appendix B.

and control order should where appropriate take part in this sort of activity; the precise means by which it is arranged is of secondary importance.

Provisions for dealing with breach of requirements of a Supervision and Control Order

279. Since it is the intention that the supervision and control order should be used to deal with offenders of a more difficult kind than those who are at present put on probation, and since the order is to be imposed without the offender's consent, the demands made upon supervisors will be heavy and it is important to consider carefully what powers they may need to secure compliance and deal with breaches of requirements.

280. A main purpose of the order being to avoid committing the offender to custody, the supervising officer must in the first instance attempt to deal by persuasion, rather than sanctions, with a failure on the part of an offender to co-operate. He will have considerable latitude in the application of requirements, for instance with regard to residence or avoidance of certain places of resort, but such variations are to be seen as treatment measures rather than as sanctions for failure to carry out other aspects of the order.

281. *We propose that, if the offender shows whether by failing to keep in touch with the supervising officer or by committing specific breaches, that he does not intend to carry out the requirements of the order, the supervisor should have power to take him before a magistrates' court. The court should then have power to deal with the breach by fine or any other non-custodial disposal available to it.* This would include the power to make a community service order; if an order was to be used in this way, we recommend that the minimum of 40 hours to be worked, as laid down in the present Act, should not apply.

282. The imposition of a non-custodial penalty by the court would not terminate the supervision and control order. *There should however be the power in extreme cases,* such as blatant refusal by the offender to comply with the requirements of the order, *to revoke the order and substitute an alternative sentence, which should take account of the extent to which the offender had complied with the original order.*

Temporary detention

283. In the discussions which we have had both in this country and abroad about the difficulties of handling young adult offenders in the community, our attention has been called to the view of experienced supervising officers that a breakdown of a supervision order might sometimes be prevented if they were able to take quick and decisive but essentially short-term action to detain an offender, either on the commission of a breach or in anticipation of some behaviour on the part of the offender which would threaten the continuance of the order. We have therefore given careful thought to the possibility of providing supervising officers with a power which might meet this requirement and so permit the treatment of offenders in the community to continue despite some temporary crisis in the supervisory relationship.

284. In our investigation of methods employed in California we found that a

practice has developed whereby a supervising officer occasionally has an offender removed to temporary detention. The detention of a probationer has to be followed within 48 hours by a court appearance unless, as is frequently the case, he is released by that time. The practice is used in order to provide a short-term penalty for misbehaviour under supervision or a cooling-off period when a breakdown is feared. The most significant feature of this arrangement is that detention is essentially an interlude in the course of supervision in the community and is used with the specific purpose of making it possible for the supervision to continue and of avoiding resort to a custodial sentence. Those who have experience of this practice emphasise the importance of being able to take immediate action, so that the offender sees his detention as a direct consequence of what he has done.

285. Adapting this system to conditions in this country, *we recommend that a supervisor administering a supervision and control order should be empowered to apply to a magistrate for a warrant authorising the arrest of the offender giving reasons why he thinks such action is justified. The magistrate would then have power to issue a warrant, which would be executed by the police, permitting the offender's detention for a maximum period of 72 hours.*

286. We propose that the ground on which a magistrate might make an order of this kind would be that he was satisfied either that a breach of the requirements of the order had been committed, or that the supervising officer had reasonable ground for believing that the commission of an offence or other breach of the order was in contemplation; and that in either case the temporary detention of the offender might avoid the necessity of taking the offender before the court for revocation of the order.

287. It follows from what has been said that the period of temporary detention should be used by the supervising officer to bring home to the offender the likely consequences of his behaviour, so that supervision in the community could be resumed. It would therefore be necessary to hold the offender in detention reasonably near to where he lived and for the supervisor to have easy access to him. We do not think that police cells would be an appropriate place of detention. In cases where the offender offered some measure of co-operation, it might be sufficient to order him to reside in a hostel, but *in most cases he would have to be detained in the nearest establishment designated for the reception of young adults.*

288. We appreciate that this proposal for the temporary detention of a young adult offender, to whom the court has given a non-custodial sentence, would be an innovation in the present British system and raises questions both of principle and of practical administration, which will require full discussion among the various authorities involved in its implementation. We feel sure that the practical problems can be solved if the principle is accepted. The principle which has underlain our thinking on this issue has been that, if difficult and unstable offenders are to be effectively supervised in the community instead of being placed in custody, the supervising officer must be given adequate means of dealing with temporary periods of crisis, which are bound to arise. These means must provide a way of surmounting a passing crisis in such a way that supervision can be resumed when it is over.

Breaches of the requirements of a supervision and control order are to be expected, and the purpose of this new provision will be frustrated if a breach is normally followed by return to the court and termination of the supervision. Arrangements are however needed to ensure that the offender's rights are protected and that the courts retain ultimate control over the decision whether a person should be deprived of his liberty. We consider that the arrangements we have proposed provide sufficient protection.

Implications of these proposals for the probation service

289. Our proposals for making wider use of supervision and control of young offenders in the community, both in this chapter and in Chapter 8, have important implications for the probation service. This is particularly true of the proposal for a supervision and control order, which will call for the exercise of more extensive and intensive supervision and control of categories of offender who are likely to prove more difficult than those who are customarily put on probation. We have had some discussion of our proposals with representatives of the probation service, but we have thought it best that formal consultations with the service should take place at a later stage, when these proposals can be considered in the wider context of our published report.

290. We see the role of the probation and after-care service in regard to the new supervision and control order as consistent with recent developments in the functions of the service. We have stressed the differences between the new order and a probation order, and these will inevitably be reflected in the daily duties of probation officers. But the functions of the service have long since been extended beyond the administration of probation orders into after-care and more recently parole. Under the Criminal Justice Act 1972 they are being further extended into responsibilities for community service, day training and suspended sentence supervision. In all these the traditional duty of the probation officer to "advise, assist and befriend" has been preserved, but the concept of the consent of the person supervised has been eroded and the element of control has been increasingly emphasised. Similarly, while the final decision on the disposal of a probationer following a breach of a probation order remains with the judicial authority, in parole and after-care the decision to recall or to revoke a licence is taken by the executive authority, after receiving a report from the officer in charge of the case, whose opinion on the need for recall or revocation of licence plays an important part. It is true that in these cases the responsibility of the individual probation officer is modified to the extent that the final recommendation rests with his superiors. Similar protection could be provided under our proposals to probation officers administering a supervision and control order, subject only to the need to avoid administrative delay in the operation of temporary detention.

291. For these reasons we do not think that our proposals involve any violation of the basic principles of the probation and after-care service. On the contrary, since their fundamental purpose is to keep as many young offenders as possible out of custody, we believe rather that they represent a realistic modification of traditional practice, which is essential if the underlying objectives of the service are to be attained in the conditions which exist today.

292. In the course of our report we have frequently referred to the imperative need to provide whatever new resources in money, manpower and facilities may be needed for the implementation of new policies. The application of this principle to the probation and after-care service is discussed in Chapter 13 (paragraphs 404 to 407) below.

Attendance at an attendance centre

293. Only two senior attendance centres have been established for the 17 and under 21 age group.[4] The first of these was opened in Manchester in 1958 and the second at Greenwich in 1964. These still operate on what may be termed an experimental basis. The origins and nature of the existing centres were set out fully in paragraphs 87–98 of our report on Non-Custodial and Semi-Custodial Penalties, and are described more briefly in paragraphs 171 to 173 of Appendix B to this report. In our report on Non-Custodial Penalties we discussed the future of senior attendance centres in the light of our recommendation for the introduction of community service, and recommended that there should be no further development of the senior attendance centre system, except for experimental centres for traffic offenders referred to in paragraph 297 below, until it had been possible to evaluate the success of community service.

294. During the House of Lords Committee Stage of what is now the Criminal Justice Act 1972 there was a proposal[5] to extend to the Crown Court the power to commit to attendance centres (which in general is at present available only to magistrates' courts in the relevant areas). This was not pursued, but it was explained that we already had the future of the centres under review, and the Home Secretary asked us specifically to consider this question.

295. We have accordingly reconsidered the question of the future of senior attendance centres in the light of recent experience. It seems to us that the time has come when these centres should be either extended and more systematically developed, or discontinued on the ground that their purposes are served instead by newer forms of treatment, such as community service and arrangements contemplated under the proposed supervision and control order.

296. The first of these courses was cogently urged upon us in evidence, in particular in a memorandum submitted on behalf of the Inner London and South-East London Branches of the Magistrates' Association. In this memorandum it was proposed that the number of senior attendance centres should be increased so as to make one available in every large centre of population; that they should be used increasingly to deal with offenders convicted of vandalism or hooliganism; and that a more effective understanding of attendance centres and a sentencing policy in respect of them should be developed by the courts. It was fairly pointed out in the memorandum that an experiment based on only two senior attendance centres might be thought too small to be meaningful and that even these centres had not been

---

[4] There are 60 junior attendance centres for offenders aged 14 and under 17 in the main centres of population.
[5] House of Lords Official Report, Vol. 333, No. 109, Cols 971–982.

sufficiently used, nor had an adequate evaluation been made of their success with particular types of offender. There was therefore a case for a more widely based and thorough experiment.

297. We have given careful consideration to this argument but have reached the conclusion that an extended experiment based upon the experience of the two existing centres would be less valuable than an attempt to build upon other forms of treatment. The existing centres have, through no fault of their own, developed largely in isolation from the mainstream of social work, having no significant contact with the probation service even where those attending are already on probation, and their staffs have no social work training. Nor have they been given clear guidance about the aims which they should pursue or the methods they should use. It is only as a mildly punitive form of treatment, with few if any constructive aspects, that a case for the attendance centre in its present form can be made. We do not favour purely punitive forms of treatment for young adult offenders and consider that there are more hopeful possibilities in the newer developments to which we have referred.

298. We recognise the thought and effort that have been put into the two existing centres by the officers who have staffed them and we would not wish our criticisms to be taken as being directed at them. *We nevertheless recommend that the existing senior attendance centres should be discontinued. It follows that we would not support the proposal referred to us by the Home Secretary as described in paragraph 294 above.* But while there is not in our view scope for an extension of the present type of senior attendance centre, catering for an unselected group of petty offenders, *we maintain the view expressed in our report on Non-Custodial Penalties (paragraphs 105 to 111) that attendance centres designed for the training of traffic offenders and suitably equipped and staffed for the purpose should be introduced on an experimental basis.* We are concerned only with young offenders between 17 and 21, but there seems to be no reason why such centres should be limited to this age group. We understand that the Government, without rejecting our proposal, has accorded it a low priority among other new non-custodial provisions. We hope that this attitude may be reconsidered.

CHAPTER 11

THE ORGANISATION OF THE CUSTODIAL SYSTEM

299. Our sentencing proposals are designed to bring about a reduction both in the proportion of young adults who are committed to custody and in the amount of time that many of them spend in segregation from the community. But many young adults will continue to be committed to custody and some will need to be detained for a substantial period. Custodial establishments will accordingly retain an important role in the arrangements for dealing with young adult offenders. In this chapter we consider the most suitable means of organising the custodial system for young adults to meet its objectives.

300. It will be apparent from our comments so far in this report how important we consider it to be that custodial establishments should not operate in isolation from the community in which they are situated. We have emphasised the need to treat the period spent in custody as part of a continuum which includes the period subsequently to be spent under supervision after release. It is important for family and friends, and past and future supervisors from the probation and after-care service, to visit the offender. Perhaps even more important is the provision of opportunities for both staff and trainees to relate activities in the establishment to life and opportunities available to the offender after release. It follows that intimate co-operation between the establishments and the supervisory services must be fostered and that custodial staff must have a good understanding of the communities into which offenders will return.

301. We have therefore considered how the organisation of young adult establishments can best contribute to this objective. A question of principle which immediately arises is whether the main aim should be to devise a system which provides, as the existing borstal system has attempted to provide, the widest possible choice of different regimes, coupled with a sophisticated procedure for the appropriate allocation of offenders. Owing to the scarcity of particular skills and to considerations of cost, such a high degree of specialisation can be achieved only among a range of establishments serving wide areas, if not the entire country. The alternative approach is to attach less importance to a wide choice of specialised training programmes and to give higher priority to providing establishments near to the communities from which offenders come and to which they will return. Experience gained within the young adult system and analysis of its results provide a good deal of evidence which is helpful in the resolution of this issue.

302. The assessment of an individual's needs, followed by allocation to the training establishment considered best able to meet them, is a traditional feature of the borstal system for young men, and has become highly developed. There has not been similar allocation of young women sentenced to borstal training only because the numbers of offenders and the range of

choice of establishment have been too small to make it practicable (see paragraphs 322 to 324 below). The same is broadly true of young prisoners of both sexes, where the number of establishments (five centres for young men serving the whole country) leaves little scope for allocation, while in some cases the shortness of the sentence makes lengthy assessment unprofitable. The shortness of sentences of detention, when they were introduced after 1948, was also thought to make elaborate assessment unnecessary. Those sentenced to detention are simply conveyed direct from the court to a detention centre serving the area concerned. It is therefore on the borstal system that an analysis of the advantages and limitations of centralised allocation must be concentrated.

The borstal allocation system

303. At the beginning of the 1930s there were only three borstals—Rochester, Feltham and Portland, all in the south of England. Those sentenced to borstal training were received at Wandsworth Prison, where they were interviewed by the governor and the medical officer, who were assisted by reports prepared on the basis of interviews (and also, in the case of offenders from London, of home visits) by voluntary women social workers. These reports related to social background, work record, home situation and personal characteristics, but the process of allocating people to establishments mainly served to distinguish those who seemed to have some mental instability and to separate those whose criminal record or previous experience of life in institutions for juvenile offenders suggested that they would be a bad influence. "Different types and classes" were sent to different borstals "mainly with the object of keeping the more innocent apart from those with a deeper and longer initiation into evil".[1] Those considered the most committed to crime and those who had previous experience of reformatory schools were sent to Portland; Feltham took the mentally unstable and those for whom borstal was the first custodial sentence; and the rest went to Rochester. The introduction of open borstals in the early thirties created a need to identify those who were least likely to abscond or, if they absconded, were least likely to cause harm and public criticism. By the end of the decade there were two open borstals and five closed borstals and allocation took place at a reception centre at Wormwood Scrubs. Since the Second World War the borstal system has grown to 23 training establishments for young men (one of which was until recently a specialised establishment receiving those recalled or returned to borstal) and two allocation centres, both situated in prisons—Manchester and Wormwood Scrubs.

304. The allocation centres continue to distinguish those who would be best assigned to an establishment such as Feltham or Rochester where psychiatric treatment can be provided. They also continue to separate out those whose records suggest considerable commitment to criminal values or a habitual tendency to revert to crime. Naturally a major consideration is whether an offender can be risked in open conditions. In addition the allocation system operates to limit the age range and range of intelligence dealt with at certain establishments and to take advantage of specialised services, such as full-time education for the more able, or certain kinds of vocational or work

---

[1] *Boys in Trouble*, page 213.

training which are available only at particular borstals. Proximity to a person's home area may play a part in deciding the establishment to which he goes, but the main geographical division is simply between north and south, certain establishments receiving people mainly from Manchester and others mainly from Wormwood Scrubs.

305. Allocation according to such criteria as age and intelligence leads to corresponding variations in the approaches adopted by staff in different establishments, and this in turn has led to the concentration at particular borstals of such facilities as advanced educational courses, high quality vocational training and group counselling which is assumed to be suitable for the more intelligent and those with most insight. For purposes of allocation a great deal of information is collected about each offender. In the fifties the allocation process included an interview with a prison psychologist, who played a major part in deciding the borstal most suited to the offenders needs. Subsequently, as the numbers entering borstal increased, the psychologist's role in the allocation process became one of seeing offenders selectively when referred to him by other allocation centre staff. Growing doubts about the effectiveness of the allocation process and about the participation of psychologists in it led to a programme of research by a team of psychologists at Wormwood Scrubs. We briefly describe the scope of this research and some of the findings from it in Appendix D. The main lessons are that the application of simple rules, without elaborate assessment, could produce allocations similar to those that take place at present in the majority of cases, and that, even if it were possible to devise special regimes which would significantly influence the behaviour of selected groups of offenders, there can be little confidence that existing skills and existing techniques are capable of identifying those groups with any degree of certainty.

306. There is therefore serious ground for doubting whether the present system of allocation, despite all the skills and effort devoted to it, leads to a disposal of young men throughout the borstal system which is more than marginally different from what might be achieved by simpler methods. In any event, it does not succeed in matching the regime to the offender in a way which substantially improves his chance of avoiding reconviction.

307. Moreover the system as at present operated certainly has a number of disadvantages. Its general effect is inevitably to separate many offenders from their home area, and so to hinder the establishments from fostering and maintaining contacts between trainees and their families and future supervising officers. So long as borstal was a selective sentence available only for a small number of offenders at a few widely scattered establishments, the possibility during the course of the sentence of preserving links with the community to which the offender would return was limited. Today there are many more borstals spread throughout the country and, although the spread is uneven, it would be practicable to go a good way towards allocating young men to establishments relatively near to their homes, provided that some loss was accepted in the degree of specialisation offered by different establishments.

308. Already the prison and probation services recognise the need to prepare, while the offender is in custody, for his life on release and supervision in the

community. A young adult who receives a custodial sentence accordingly becomes part of a probation officer's caseload from the time he enters the establishment from which he is expected to be released under supervision. Probation officers are encouraged to visit establishments and become acquainted with those on their caseload during the course of the sentence. But the time required to travel to distant establishments reduces considerably the extent to which this can be done without withdrawal of resources from other important probation work.

309. A further disadvantage of the present arrangements for allocating offenders to borstals is that they usually involve a period of waiting at a local prison immediately after sentence, followed by transfer to a borstal allocation centre for assessment and allocation and transfer yet again to a training establishment. Even when the system is working well, significant periods of time may be spent in unsuitable conditions awaiting transfer. If a young adult is assigned to an establishment where there is already considerable pressure on places he may wait in the allocation centre for some time after the actual process of allocation is complete before being moved to an establishment where staff and trainees will be oriented towards the constructive use of the period of custody and will have the time and facilities to make it possible. A young adult may also previously have spent considerable time in a remand centre or local prison following committal for trial or committal for sentence. Although the position has recently improved considerably, nevertheless at times when there has been a sudden rise in the numbers sentenced to borstal training, delays have built up generally in the progression from local prisons to the allocation centres and from the allocation centres to the training borstals, the offender often being detained during this process in an overcrowded and unconstructive environment.

310. Our impression that undesirable delays are bound to occur where a central allocation point exists to which offenders are referred, and that it is difficult to use the time constructively, was reinforced by our observation of similar systems which we examined on our visits abroad, especially in the United States. In such systems much detailed information is collected, comparatively little of which is necessary to make what is usually a quite limited choice between institutions. It is true that some of this information may subsequently be used, since the assessors may make useful suggestions about the way in which staff might deal with the offender, but such suggestions are necessarily tentative and open to revision in the light of experience. They cannot relieve staff of the responsibility of making their own assessments and judgments. We therefore think it is better for skilled staff to be associated with the establishments where offenders will serve the bulk of their time, so that they can have more direct involvement in dealing with them there than that they should be isolated in a special assessment centre, with relatively little communication with the staff who might benefit by their suggestions and guidance.

A different allocation system

311. These considerations lead us to the conclusion that the allocation procedure has, in the past, been too ambitious. Given the apparent simplicity and predictability of the majority of allocation decisions (cf

103

paragraph 305 above) its ability to achieve the objectives originally set for it is more limited than has been supposed, and it imposes upon the custodial system a degree of centralisation which results in offenders being sent too far from their homes and being subject to undue delays in the process. We have therefore looked for more satisfactory ways in which to perform such of the functions of the present allocation system as appear to be indispensable.

312. One requirement is the ability to separate those whose criminal record or past experience of institutional life will impede the work of staff with less hardened and cynical young men. Such people, however, are recognisable from their record and behaviour, and no complicated system of assessment is required to identify them. Subject to what is said in paragraph 321 below we do not think it would be desirable for young adult establishments to be assigned exclusively to offenders of this kind. People with this type of experience need not have an adverse influence on others if they are in a minority in an establishment where the population is broken up into small manageable groups, and staff have a reasonable chance of establishing among the inmates a culture conducive to co-operation. Experience in certain establishments where some elements of the population have already achieved a degree of maturity shows that it is possible in a well managed unit to control a small number of very difficult trainees with the help of group pressures. Even so, resort to the segregation of such offenders may occasionally be necessary, and we believe that this problem will best be solved by transferring such people to a different wing of the same establishment, rather than by concentrating them in a single establishment. A person may thus be transferred to a different wing if association with people of a different kind seems likely to improve his behaviour or prospects. Concentrating in separate establishments those most committed to crime and those who have the worst problems may seem to have the merit of protecting others from their influence, but it seems likely also to reinforce their own anti-social tendencies, to "label" them as incorrigible institutional troublemakers, and hence to make their return to a normal young adult establishment more difficult. If temporary segregation is necessary this is better done by transfer to a separate wing. It is then still possible for the trainee to participate in a controlled measure of association with trainees of other wings, and at an appropriate time to return to his normal residential wing with the minimum of formality. Since they are the people most likely to contribute considerably to future crime, and therefore those in whom any change in behaviour would have most benefit for society, their isolation in separate establishments is particularly undesirable. It is important that they be treated not as rejects, but as people with whom there is a need to try new methods, possibly requiring a higher staff/inmate ratio than might apply with those who are less committed to crime or less affected by previous institutional life.

313. Another category which will continue to require identification at an early stage is that of offenders who need psychiatric treatment or are able to benefit by specific services which can be provided economically only at certain establishments. This however does not require all those who are sentenced to go to one or two centres for assessment. If the normal procedure were for an offender to go to an establishment serving the area of the court by which he is sentenced, it should be possible for any special needs of this kind to be

identified there and a transfer arranged, if indeed he has not already been identified on remand prior to sentence, as many would be. Certainly the needs of this minority do not provide sufficient reason for maintaining an elaborate centralised system of allocation for all young adults.

314. There will remain the problem of delays and the need to regulate the flow of sentenced young adults to establishments where there are immediate vacancies. It has been one of the incidental functions, though not one of the avowed purposes, of the existing system to provide a place, albeit an unsatisfactory one, where offenders may be immediately lodged until they can be accommodated in their allotted training borstal. In practice, as we noted above, the system has not prevented substantial numbers of sentenced young adults from spending time in local prisons awaiting a place in an allocation centre, although in recent years the period has been comparatively short.

315. We do not consider that a centralised allocation system is needed in order to identify offenders who may be suitable for open accommodation and to separate them from those who will need closed conditions. A period spent on remand in custody could often be used for making a provisional allocation decision in case the offender receives a custodial sentence; and in other cases a decision can be reached soon after the offenders reception into custody on sentence—perhaps initially into a closed induction unit—on the basis of information readily available at the time of or soon after sentence. Many of those who need closed conditions can be recognised very quickly on the basis of their criminal record and no elaborate assessment is needed; some may become suitable for open conditions after they have spent a period in closed conditions and have gained some stability from it. The present system of "once for all" allocation often has the effect of denying the latter group the opportunity of going to open conditions and the more relaxed regime which can be provided in them. We should prefer to see a system in which such offenders were placed initially in closed conditions and were transferred to open conditions at the stage which the staff considered appropriate. Arrangements of this kind already exist at Feltham and its open satellite at Finnamore Wood Camp and we consider that they could be adopted more widely.

316. Under the system which we propose, a young adult ought ideally to be taken direct from court to a nearby training establishment serving that particular area (as happens already with those sentenced to detention in a detention centre) even though subsequent assessment and the offender's own response may result in his having later to be moved elsewhere. In view of what we have learned about the results of using much simplified criteria for allocation, we do not believe that the cases where removal is necessary will be unmanageably numerous. When for any reason immediate committal and transport to a training establishment are not practicable, we consider that the offender should be lodged in whatever Prison Department establishment is most conveniently situated. As we recognise in the discussion in Chapter 15, the poor location of some remand centres means that in our view local prisons may sometimes, in present circumstances, be the most suitable waiting establishment. Detention after sentence pending conveyance to a training establishment should not happen often or involve more than a very brief stay,

provided that there is a reasonable balance between the number of young adults coming into the system and the accommodation available for them. We recognise that the Department will need to provide a margin of spare accommodation in order to meet fluctuations in the numbers whom it has to receive into custody, and hope it will not be deterred from doing so by considerations of cost. Our proposals for a generic sentence for young adults, abolishing the distinction between imprisonment, borstal training and detention in a detention centre, ought to provide the Prison Department with greater flexibility in the use of the available accommodation than it has had in the past.

317. *From our analysis of the problems of allocation we have therefore concluded that the present system, designed to obtain the uncertain benefits of matching offenders to distinctive regimes on a large scale, should be abandoned in favour of a system which would attain the more certain advantage of preserving and developing ties with the home area and the supervising service.*

A new pattern of training establishments

318. Our conclusions regarding allocation are largely based, as we have explained above, upon the results of analysis carried out within or at the request of the Prison Department. It is therefore no surprise to find that the Department has already given a good deal of thought to the possible implications of these findings for the organisation of young adult establishments and the pattern of their distribution throughout the country. We have had the benefit of the Department's thinking on this subject and we revert to it in more detail in Chapter 13 below when considering future building plans.

The "neighbourhood" establishment

319. If, as we propose, young adult offenders who are taken into custody are to be sent to establishments sufficiently near to their home to facilitate continuing contact with their communities, *we should like to see the development of "neighbourhood" establishments having the following characteristics:*

(a) The establishment should serve a limited area. It should be situated in or near to the area from which trainees mainly come: a good test might be whether it can be reached from most parts of the area within one or at the most two hours.

(b) The establishment should take most of the relevant young adult offender population from the area and should therefore be organised so as to provide a fair range of treatment and training facilities, possibly by operating regimes of different types in different wings. Possible exceptions to this would be those who have certain highly specialised requirements which cannot be easily met in every establishment. These might include some particularly dangerous or disruptive offenders, those who are mentally disturbed, or some who could benefit from advanced education. We comment on these exceptions in paragraph 321 below.

(c) The establishment should comprise both open and closed facilities and arrangements for short and medium-term trainees. It should also have associated with it a hostel (as, for example, Hollesley Bay Borstal has Taylor House in Ipswich as a satellite) in which offenders could spend

106

all or part of their period of custody, thus retaining the option of returning them to more restrictive conditions, if their behaviour made this necessary, without resort to formal recall proceedings.

(*d*) Ideally the establishment should be situated on a single site but, where this is not possible, two or more establishments, reasonably near to one another and co-ordinated by a single governor, might be linked to form a neighbourhood establishment containing the necessary variety of facilities.

(*e*) Whether the establishment is on a single site, or whether a range of establishments are grouped under a single governor, the governor should decide the allocation and subsequent transfer of trainees under his control between the establishments or the range of facilities available to him.

(*f*) An establishment fulfilling the above conditions should find it much easier to establish close links with the probation and after-care service. It would probably have to deal with only a small number of local services, each of which in turn would be dealing mainly with the one establishment. The establishment could also develop a more intimate understanding of the local communities from which its trainees came by participating in various ways in local community activities and by making use of the community's provisions for education, including industrial education. In turn, subject to geographical conditions and necessary security requirements, its own facilities could also be made available to the community (for example its sports and educational facilities might be made available to the public at certain times), and outsiders should be encouraged to participate in activities within the establishment.

(*g*) It will be evident that, in order to take the fullest advantage of the neighbourhood concept, the establishment would have to be on an urban or near-urban site and not in the depths of the countryside.

320. We have given this concept of establishment for young adult offenders the title "neighbourhood" because the ideal is that it should serve a limited—and not too large—geographical area, be situated within that area and be able as a consequence to develop links with the local community and draw fully on its resources. We acknowledge that, even when this concept came to full fruition, the area served by a particular establishment would be a good deal wider than is normally connoted by the term "neighbourhood"; but no other term seems to us to convey our intention better.

Specialist establishments

321.

(*a*) *Medical and psychiatric treatment.* There are at present two borstals with full-time psychiatrically qualified staff, and there is also accommodation for young adults at the psychiatric establishment at Grendon. Psychiatrists, like all other specialists in establishments for offenders, operate most effectively in collaboration with other disciplines. Only at Grendon has a regime been developed in which the insights of psychological medicine are fully exploited and staff are integrated into a common and well-organised therapeutic team. In the long term we would

107

hope to see medical and psychiatric resources spread more widely throughout the young adult system; but we recognise that in the short term these resources are limited and that a system of area-based establishments will for some time to come have to be supplemented by some establishments specialising in medical and psychiatric treatment.

(b) *Higher education.* There is a comparatively small number of young adult offenders, including some liable to detention for long periods, for whom advanced education or advanced vocational training will be the best occupation while they are in custody. Certain borstals make special provision for such trainees, and for the time being one or two may have to be maintained for this purpose. The number of offenders who have this requirement is not sufficient to justify the provision of comparable facilities in every neighbourhood establishment. But a fully developed neighbourhood system should be able to meet these needs by drawing on the educational resources of the local community, as well as modern educational technology, and other media such as correspondence courses and courses provided by the Open University.

(c) *Dangerous or disruptive offenders.* We have already made some comment upon this category in discussing allocation (paragraph 312 above). Some special provision may have to be made for such offenders, possibly by providing specially secure accommodation in neighbourhood establishments, together with a particularly high staff/inmate ratio. After considerable discussion with members of the governor grades of the prison service and representatives of the Prison Officers' Association, we have concluded that the re-introduction of a special closed correctional establishment, on the lines of Reading Borstal which was closed in 1969, is not to be recommended.

Establishments for young women

322. The number of young women given custodial sentences has always been comparatively small and the choice of training establishments correspondingly limited. At present, young women sentenced to borstal training (except those who are pregnant) who are assessed as being unsuitable for open conditions are sent to Bullwood Hall (near Southend-on-Sea), and those suitable for open conditions go to East Sutton Park (near Maidstone). There is a training borstal, for those who are pregnant or have babies, in a separate wing of Styal closed prison (Cheshire). Young women prisoners suitable for open conditions go to Askham Grange (near York) or Moor Court (in Staffordshire), while those for whom closed conditions are required are sent either to Holloway or to Styal. Young women prisoners are not placed in separate accommodation from older offenders but are allowed, as experience has shown to be preferable, to take part in the general life of the prison. However, because there is a statutory requirement to separate offenders serving different types of sentence the facilities at Styal for pregnant women and women with babies are divided into two sections, one for women serving sentences of borstal training and the other for prisoners.

323. We do not consider that young women offenders need always be segregated from adults, and we can see no particular merit in the present practice at Styal. The main argument for segregation rests on the danger of

contamination from offenders committed to a criminal way of life, of whom the proportion is much lower among women than among men. We therefore consider that the Prison Department should exercise a wide discretion in permitting the mixing of suitable adult offenders with young adult offenders at establishments for women and girls. This practice seems particularly appropriate for offenders who have been considered suitable for open establishments.

324. Applying this principle, we recommend that as soon as Holloway[2] has sufficient new accommodation it should provide the closed facilities for women and young women in the south of England. We consider that Bullwood Hall is inconveniently placed, far from some of the services which it needs, and that its tightly enclosed and forbidding buildings are unsuitable for its purpose and should cease to be used as a borstal for young women as soon as possible. Open facilities for the south would still be provided at East Sutton Park, where older offenders should also be admitted as they are at present. In the north, Styal should be the closed establishment and Askham Grange should accommodate both adults and young women in open conditions.

325. There is probably scope for experimentation in allowing women in custody the opportunity to associate with men, either within establishments or in the community. We do not recommend the general introduction of "co-education" for young adult offenders, because male and female delinquents are unlikely to provide the best associates for each other. But there may be occasions when young men and women offenders can engage in joint activities in situations which avoid artificiality, such as recreation and group work, and we do not see any argument of principle which need exclude this.

326. Nor do we see any reason why male staff in the governor or discipline grades should not be employed in establishments for women (and vice versa). There have already been some appointments of this kind. We understand that the results have been promising, and that further moves in this direction would be welcomed by governors.

---

[2] Holloway Prison is at present being rebuilt on its present site.

CHAPTER 12

CUSTODIAL REGIMES

327. With the growing use of non-custodial measures which we hope to promote, custodial establishments will increasingly have to control and care for a difficult minority of young people whose conduct has required them to be removed from society for a period. The task of the establishments will be to detain these offenders in whatever conditions of security may be needed for this purpose, and also to make use of this period in whatever way may be to their subsequent benefit. We do not believe that custody as such will confer any particular benefits upon the offenders, but it does nevertheless present opportunities which might not otherwise be available to them and of which they might not otherwise take advantage. These include opportunities for medical treatment, vocational and trade training, and remedial or more advanced education where these are appropriate; and more generally a controlled environment within which an offender can gain some insight into his own situation and his personality, obtain some knowledge of needs and feelings of other people, and receive some guidance which may help him with the problems he will face after release. He will rely to some extent on direct help from members of the staff, but also on the more subtle influence of the establishment as a whole. Staff of all ranks, from governor to basic-grade officer, will need not only to offer direct help when required but also to manage the establishment in such a way that communication takes place freely, that hostility and conflict are avoided or absorbed, and that its total influence is seen to operate in a constructive and helpful way. They will need to keep a proper balance between self-expression and control; to ensure that the offender can maintain his personal identity and his self-respect; and to treat him in an adult and responsible manner while maintaining the degree of care and concern that is appropriate to young men and women whose character is still at a formative stage and whose outlook and circumstances may be subject to rapid change. This task demands a degree of patience, understanding and skill that is perhaps all too little appreciated, particularly in the case of basic grade staff in whose company the trainees spend a large proportion of their time. It requires qualities of management for which there is no similar demand elsewhere.

328. Much consideration has been given in recent years by the Prison Department and by our predecessors on the Advisory Council on the Treatment of Offenders to the many problems involved in adapting the methods of dealing with young adults in custody to the constantly changing environment of modern society. As already explained, thinking on this subject has been concentrated upon the borstal system, whose spirit and principles have spread to young prisoners' centres and also largely to detention centres, which we reviewed in detail in 1968–69.[1] It is therefore the borstal system that we take as our own starting point.

---

[1] See our report, *Detention Centres*.

329. Rule 1 of the Borstal Rules[2] says:

"(1) The purpose of borstal training requires that every inmate, while conforming to the rules necessary for well-ordered community life, shall be able to develop his individuality on right lines with a proper sense of personal responsibility. Accordingly, officers shall, while firmly maintaining order and discipline, seek to do so by influencing the inmates through their own example and leadership and enlisting their willing co-operation. "(2) The objects of borstal training shall be to bring to bear every influence which may establish in the inmates the will to lead a good and useful life on release, and to fit them to do so by the fullest possible development of their character, capabilities and sense of personal responsibility".

330. As a general statement this is unexceptionable and remains broadly valid, and *some similar general statement of objectives should apply to all young adult establishments.* But such generalities require to be re-interpreted in each generation in the light of changed social habits and of the new knowledge and techniques developed by the medical and social sciences. We cannot claim to have discovered entirely new ideas, let alone simple solutions, which have escaped the observation of others, and in the remainder of this chapter we limit ourselves to advancing one or two broad propositions about institutional treatment and to making comments and recommendations on selected aspects of treatment to which our attention has been particularly drawn.

331. The programme of a penal establishment—what is frequently, but in our view inappropriately,[3] referred to as "treatment" or "training"—is on the one hand made up of specific elements such as work, physical training, education, and medical and psychiatric treatment, but also on the other hand embodies broad principles of approach such as providing a degree of independence, encouraging a sense of responsibility, developing constructive personal relationships and providing kinds of support not available outside. We welcome the movement which is already taking place in young adult establishments towards programmes which allow the trainee a greater degree of self-expression, self-determination and personal autonomy. Evidence of this movement is to be seen most conspicuously in such matters as the trainee's personal appearance and the environment which he is allowed to create for himself within the establishment, but also, for example, in the modes of address used by trainees and staff to each other and the kind of behaviour that can be tolerated before it becomes a matter for disciplinary action. By allowing a greater degree of autonomy and adopting a more tolerant approach in these matters the staff try to help the trainee to preserve his dignity and self-respect and at the same time to provide a regime which will so far as possible be free from disturbances, do the least damage to the

---

[2] *The Borstal Rules 1964* (S.I. 1964 No. 387).
[3] The terms "treatment" and "training" are commonly used in discussions of treatment of offenders, especially treatment in custody, and their use is not easily avoided. But their medical, educational and military overtones can easily mislead. We understand by "treatment" no more than the way in which an offender is dealt with from day to day, and have used the term accordingly. We understand by "training" a specific course or programme aimed at improving individual skills, and prefer to use the term only in this sense.

trainee's personality and be helpful to him both during his sentence and also after his release.

332. Traditionally, the philosophy of borstal has been of good men influencing young people through personal relationships. This concept remains valid. Indeed, despite the greater uncertainties today than in the past on the part of borstal staff about their role, probably more importance is attached now than in the past to personal relationships among trainees and between them and staff—especially basic grade staff, the scope of whose relationship with individual trainees has been greatly developed in recent years. Compared with the inter-war period the borstal population now extends across a wider spectrum; the young people in it possess—or at least are seen to possess—more complex problems, perhaps reflecting the greater complexity of modern society; and we suspect that there is a greater awareness than before, in particular among the basic grade staff, of the prime importance of helping those in their charge to develop a capacity for making relationships, as distinct from instilling into them particular skills or attitudes. Modern techniques such as psychiatric treatment, casework and group counselling, as well as work and (even in its stricter sense) education, may all be regarded as means by which helpful influences can be released and people taught to make relationships.

333. Experience shows that surprisingly little of the custodial regime (and this applies even to secure containment) can simply be imposed or ordered without the co-operation of at least the majority of trainees. Where the need to change attitudes and to learn new patterns of response is involved, then clearly the motivation must come from within the individual. The overall objectives of custodial regimes must therefore be to discover, with the help of the offender himself, the direction and extent to which he can realistically be expected to change, taking into consideration his assets and liabilities, and the sort of circumstances to which he will return; and to motivate him to wish to change and therefore to co-operate in planning and carrying into effect processes which may help towards such a change.

334. Much of this has been recognised in the past, and is indeed implicit in the idea of borstal training itself. But there remains a need to move further away from the idea of an offender having things done to him whilst in custody and towards new ways of enabling him to discover how to set realistic objectives for himself.

335. The present state of knowledge is not such as to justify us in attempting any dogmatic statements about how this can best be achieved, but certain general principles have emerged from our discussions. In the first place it is important that, so far as possible, a single culture, shared by staff and inmates, should prevail within the establishment, with a minimum of subcultural influences from anti-social groups. This is likely to require effective communication at all levels and division into manageable living groups. In the second place the regime should be such that the inmates believe it to be genuinely helpful. Crime is frequently a devious means of coping with the individual's own hostility and aggression, and to live in a regime where hostility is not met with hostility may be of very great value.

Thirdly, and closely connected with the two previous points, we believe that it is better to rely on rewards than on punishments. There is now a great deal of hard psychological and clinical evidence that rewards can be an effective means of controlling and changing behaviour, especially that of the more serious types of offender. Indeed, within the limits of available resources and of the unpalatable fact of custody, life in a young adult establishment should aim to be stimulating and even positively enjoyable for both trainees and staff. To some this may seem a large pill to swallow, but it must sooner or later be accepted in any system purporting to have therapeutic and rehabilitative objectives.

336. Finally, success is much more likely if every component of a regime is seen by everyone in the establishment to have a specific purpose, and it is in this respect particularly that we think regimes need to be subject to critical reappraisal. There is an understandable tendency for practices to outlast the objectives that they were designed to serve or to survive after the outside models on which they were based have changed. For instance, rising at 6 am and "lights out" at 9 pm, which has become enshrined in staff work patterns, does not now mirror the habits of the borstal trainee's peers, and one must ask whether it will still help to fit a young man for normal life, if the job to which he goes does not require him to continue in that pattern after his release. If early rising is intended to teach punctuality and regular attendance at work, then it might be better training for normality to give each individual an alarm clock and the responsibility of ensuring that he attends for work punctually. Yet again, drill survives to some extent in borstals and detention centres, at least for new arrivals, but the assumptions on which it has a traditional place in borstal practice may no longer be valid. The role allotted to sport—and perhaps particularly to compulsory sport at weekends— should also be re-examined and its value in particular cases reassessed by comparison with other possible ways of spending the time.

337. The principal elements in the daily routine of a borstal are work, educational classes, and physical training and recreation. Details are given in paragraphs 93 to 106 of Appendix B. We have not looked in any detail at arrangements for physical training and recreation, and have no specific comments or recommendations to make. But other aspects of the training programme raise questions of policy to which we have devoted some attention. (One particular matter which we were asked to consider at an early stage of the review was that of Army Cadet Force training, which formerly took place in two borstals. We made a separate recommendation on this matter to the Home Secretary, the terms of which are recorded in Appendix G.)

338. At present, the borstal time-table has places for activities labelled "work" and "education". For most trainees "work" occupies the greater part of the day-time's activities (there is a 40-hour working week), and "education" is an early evening activity (the Rules specify a normal weekly minimum of six hours). This simple picture needs to be qualified in two ways. First, full-time (or part day-time) education is now provided for an increasing number—mainly those needing remedial education and those doing higher-level courses of education. Secondly, "work" includes vocational training and trade

113

training, in which some 25 to 30% of trainees are engaged at any one time. Nevertheless, "education" and "work" have been seen as particular parts of the programme, rather than as contributing to a common objective which all the activities of the establishment can and should serve. This is an attitude which we have seen to be changing and which we hope will continue to change.

339. Many young adult offenders have a narrow and circumscribed style of life; and it should be the aim of those running establishments to offer them new insights into behaviour and relationships, to make them more aware of opportunities which may be available and to encourage them to equip themselves to exploit them. Many are also "under-achievers", in the sense that their formal educational qualifications and superficial abilities do not match their underlying potential. Some of these would benefit from an increase in the provision made for formal education. Others will benefit more from ways of learning which are not merely those provided in a classroom, but are to be found in living quarters and workshops. Such extra-curricular learning often has a greater effect than what is taught in the classroom. The aim should be to help the individual to mature and to achieve social adequacy. This process involves the whole staff of the establishment whatever the discipline in which they have been trained or the task to which they have been assigned.

340. The role of education in custodial establishments for young adult offenders, and its relationship to vocational and trade training, have received increasing attention in recent years, but it was not until late in the 1960s that effective overall policies began to develop. The system is therefore still in transition and has been handicapped in its progress both by lack of resources and, we were told, by a feeling that our report should be awaited before further steps were taken. From being mainly an evening classroom activity, education in borstals and other custodial establishments is now coming to be accepted as embracing all the experience of learning to be found in the varied activities of the establishment, and, though earlier concepts still persist at some establishments, the education officer is increasingly seen as a fully integrated member of the management team.[4] The scope of education is being widened, through social education and courses in personal relationships, to include general training for life.

341. These are welcome developments so far as they go: but a greater sense of purpose is still needed, and a more determined effort to relate education to the problems of young adult offenders in particular and to contemporary social life in general. In particular discussion of ethical issues within custodial establishments should not be left wholly, or even predominantly, in the hands of chaplains. It cannot be accepted today that genuine and effective religious belief is, for every individual (or for young adult offenders generally), the foundation of personal ethics. Attendance at religious services is no longer obligatory in penal establishments, but it would be regrettable if this had the result that ethical questions, instead of being examined in a secular as well as a religious context, were allowed to drop

---

[4] The "management team" consists of the senior staff of the establishment: the governor, deputy and assistant governors, the chief officer and heads of departments.

out of the picture altogether. We suspect that various forms of "counselling" and "group (or individual) therapy" have been designed to some extent to fill the vacuum left by the absence of belief in a distinctively Christian morality. But concepts of "therapy" or "case-work", derived as their names imply from medical models, are over-occupied with questions of personal relationships and are therefore inward rather than outward-looking. Yet it is well known that offenders of all ages tend to be excessively egocentric. Moreover in the complexities of modern society recognition of impersonal, rather than personal, obligations becomes increasingly important. Vandalism and thefts from corporate bodies or from unknown persons play a very large part in the catalogue of the crimes committed by young people today, many of whom would think it wrong to commit similar offences against known persons.

342. It may be significant that in our visits to establishments for young adult offenders we have listened to numerous discussions of "our problems", but any comparable focus upon the problems created for other people by anti-social behaviour has been conspicuously lacking. We rarely heard any discussion which professed to be primarily concerned with criminality. The legitimate fear among staff that authoritarian moral teaching, whether on a secular or a religious basis, is likely to be counter-productive need not, and should not, result in neglect of discussion of social and ethical issues. Interest in these topics is by no means lacking among offenders, particularly those in the younger age-groups—provided always that discussion starts from the participants' own standards and that any didactic approach is scrupulously avoided. We should therefore hope to see the present rather narrow concept of "social education" greatly expanded along these lines and closely linked with a corresponding extension of community service (to which we refer in paragraph 374 below). The impact of such service on a voluntary basis upon the values both of probationers and of borstal trainees had shown encouraging results even before it became available as a sentence of the courts. We recommend that the development of community service on the one hand, and discussions on social and ethical topics on the other, should be closely related and treated as the practical and theoretical aspects of social education.

343. We recognise that education in establishments for young adult offenders is likely to meet with some resistance on their part. Only a few young adults in custody will have been pursuing further education at the time of their offence and it is understandable that the others will not readily accept "going back to school". Many young adult offenders have failed to respond to experiences in society in general, and in particular they have failed at school. They do not look back upon their schooldays with pleasure and respect, and now wish to be treated as adults. Yet effective learning is essentially a voluntary process, so that the first task, in very many cases at least, is to overcome the psychological resistance to teaching of any kind. Against this background, and despite the enthusiasm devoted to the work by part-time staff, compulsory attendance at evening classes after a day's work— the traditional model of part-time further education for many young people— is not a promising approach.

344. Secondly a relatively short time is available for education or for training

young adults in custody,[5] and our sentencing proposals may at first appear to increase some existing difficulties. The earlier release under supervision of many young adults will make it important that educational courses in custody are not planned in isolation, and it will be necessary to aim at preparing offenders within a relatively short period in custody for further education or training in the community during the period of supervision, rather than equipping them to acquire qualifications while in the establishment.

345. Our proposal to do away with central allocation and to adopt instead a pattern of more locally based establishments, while it should make it easier for offenders to go on with courses after their release, will bring into each establishment offenders with a wider range of educational requirements than has been usual under the present borstal system. We have recognised that some specialised establishments may still be required, for instance for the small minority who are capable of seeking relatively high educational qualifications (eg to GCE Advanced-level standard or the equivalent) and are likely to stay in custody long enough to undertake substantial educational courses. But it will be the task of the new type of establishment to meet the educational needs of all but these exceptional categories. In performing it they may well be able—within the limits set by their geographical location—to make greater use of day release courses in the community: in 1972 out of 5,600 borstal trainees receiving education (including 2,000 in open borstals), only 36 were attending outside classes.

346. Defined in its broadest sense education may mean, for some individuals, spending most of their time at work, for others, spending it entirely in a classroom, while for most it may be a mixing of the two. Not every young adult offender may want or require six hours' formal education per week, and many will need more. We do not think it appropriate for the rules governing treatment to specify a minimum period of hours of education to be uniformly applied. It is important in order to motivate individuals that there should be real choices available to them, and with this in view we consider that the pay received by trainees should not differ according to whether they are engaged in study, vocational training or work.

347. Accordingly we recommend that most educational activity should take place during the day. It follows that more full-time teaching staff will be required, in addition to other staff and voluntary assistance from outside the establishment.

348. It has been put to us in evidence that the Prison Department should establish and employ its own educational service rather than use teachers and education officers employed by the local authority, as it does now. This, it is argued, would reduce the risk of the education officer being regarded in an establishment as an outsider, and would facilitate specialisation and special training. On the other hand, the existing system should better enable education officers to preserve contact and communication with the educational world outside, and to spend some time working in penal establishments without

---

[5] Of those at present in senior detention centres less than one quarter have effective sentences of over eight weeks and very few remain in custody for as long as six months; in borstal the average time spent in custody is about ten months.

appearing to depart from the mainstream of educational work. The adoption of a system of "neighbourhood establishments" and of the principle of continuity between education in custody and education after release reinforces the arguments for maintaining the link with local education authorities. We have therefore concluded that the present system should continue. We would wish to encourage local education authorities to regard a period served in a custodial establishment as an integral part of a teacher's career, and not as a possible handicap to subsequent promotion.

349. While in our view education officers should continue to be drawn from, and to remain part of, the general education service, we also attach importance to their integration into the life of the establishment. The education officer should always be a member of the establishment's management team.[6] Also, education officers need—in addition to the general professional training which is available to them on the same basis as to teachers generally—some specialised in-service training for the particular function which they perform. We understand that the Prison Department already has some measures in hand, and we recommend that consideration should now be given to more comprehensive arrangements which would cater for education officers, teachers, trade instructors and others involved in the varied aspects of education in custody.

350. At an individual level the particular content of education should so far as possible be determined in relation to each offender. The education officer should therefore be versed in assessment methods and in close contact with all those concerned with the individual, and the offender himself should be actively involved in deciding the pattern of education in which he participates. Within the limits of their budget we consider that education officers should be given maximum discretion in the expenditure of money; and the channels through which local education authorities procure their supplies should be made available to them.

351. We would emphasise that no amount of reorganisation of any kind can make up for inadequacy of resources, which has been mentioned by a number of our witnesses as having been a serious obstacle up to the present time. The Prison Department has recently made significant improvements in the educational provision for young adult offenders, including the re-equipment and refurnishing of premises and an increase in the number of full-time education officers and teachers. But the policy is still too modest. We have not thought it helpful to make precise recommendations about the resources which may be needed; such questions would more properly be dealt with in the course of a more detailed investigation which we propose below. While we welcome the advice and assistance which has increasingly been given to the Prison Department by the Department of Education and Science and HM Inspectors, it is nevertheless clear to us that more has still to be done to integrate the provision of education in custodial establishments into the nation's educational system. We are assured that co-operation between the Prison Department and the local authority associations is good, and that this is reflected increasingly in close relations between establishments and individual local education authorities—although in some areas the need for better liaison is clearly

---

[6] See footnote to paragraph 340.

apparent. The integration of educational and other staff within the establishment is improving, though more still needs to be done. This might be made easier if there were designated in each local education authority area an adviser or inspector with specific responsibility for "education of delinquents", both "inside" and in the community. Finally doubts persist about the objectives on which training of educational staffs should be based and about the kind of formal educational curriculum most likely to assist offenders. We recommend that these problems should be formally and intensively investigated by the Home Office and the Department of Education and Science, and the other bodies concerned.

Work and work training

352. Since the end of the Second World War, the Prison Department has devoted significant resources to providing full-time vocational training facilities for selected trainees. There is evidence to suggest that trainees who on release follow the trades for which they have been trained during their sentences are less likely to be reconvicted than either trainees who do not follow vocational training during their sentences, or those who do so but do not pursue upon release the trades for which they have been trained. Regrettably, however, few trainees who undertake vocational training courses do subsequently enter the trade for which they have been trained. The certificates which the Department has issued to trainees at the end of their courses have not been much valued by employers, and over the years the Department's courses have not kept pace with changes in outside industry, and particularly with outside industrial training. There is also a danger of giving trainees an exaggerated idea of their employment prospects, and of training offenders specifically for jobs from which their criminal convictions alone will debar them. Consequently, *we commend the shift of emphasis which is being made, away from the older type of vocational training with its heavy theoretical content, towards more practical training* based on schemes established by Industrial Training Boards and related more directly to employment prospects outside establishments. At the same time we recognise the need to retain really demanding vocational training for those who have an aptitude for it and who are serving long enough terms in custody.

353. In emphasising trade and vocational training we do not under-estimate the value of ordinary institutional work. For some offenders the acquisition of a trade will itself be the best preparation for the future, but for the majority it seems likely that the acquisition of skills which can be generalised, and habits of co-operative effort and commitment, will be of greater importance. In general, *vocational and trade training and ordinary work should all be recognised as being worthwhile in themselves, each an integral part of the institutional programme oriented to future employment.* In addition to teaching simple skills the instructors should aim to encourage understanding and co-operation. Civilian and officer instructors who often spend the greater part of the working day with trainees can exercise a great and permanent personal influence on individual trainees.

354. We commend the efforts of the Prison Department, at every level, to foster good relations with trade unions, which has resulted in significantly easier entry to employment, for example in the construction industry. We understand

that helpful attitudes are encountered at trade union headquarters and we hope that our proposal for neighbourhood establishments will have value in ensuring that equally good communication is effected at local levels with both unions and employers in the areas to which offenders will return.

355. Our remarks above regarding the importance of individual assessment in order to determine the content of an offender's education programme as a whole apply no less strongly to vocational and trade training in particular. The Prison Department recognises that the allocation of borstal trainees to courses has sometimes been haphazard; that some have been allocated to vocational training more in the interests of management in order to fill vacancies than because of their need to undertake it; and that allocation to courses and to types of work has sometimes been made without due reference to the needs, wishes and abilities of the individual. There are dangers inherent in deciding at an early stage to allocate people to particular courses which effectively label them as suitable only for manual work. *We consider that the Department should examine its policies to see how far the choice of training courses provided in young adult establishments takes account of the growth of service trades and the likelihood of employment in, for example, catering, retailing and even office work.* We recognise the need to decide quickly what courses a person might undertake, but we think that the emphasis should be as far as possible on realistic vocational guidance. We do not consider that there is necessarily anything objectionable about a person already qualified for one type of employment working in different employment whilst in custody; and in assessing work history and competence we suggest that it is a mistake to place too much emphasis on the frequency with which a young man has changed jobs in the past, in the light of the habits of the non-offending peers of borstal trainees. It is more important to have regard to the circumstances and motivation for leaving jobs.

356. We would urge that work in young adult establishments should be as constructive as possible, and in particular *we recommend that the Department should review the value of certain kinds of work,* notably metal recovery but also cleaning and other domestic work. We recognise the need to provide basic services, and the value, from the point of view of institutional management, of providing work which can readily be put down and resumed. *But whatever work is performed should be undertaken for a practical and intelligible purpose, using up-to-date methods and equipment and no unnecessary manual labour.*

Medical arrangements
357. The arrangements for the medical care of trainees in young adult establishments do not appear to us to present any conspicuous problem. A few of the larger young adult establishments have full-time medical officers, but the majority of establishments have part-time medical officers. The latter are generally local general practitioners. Few have special psychiatric training but we were assured by the Prison Department that all are able to call upon specialist resources if these are needed.

358. Over the past decade psychiatrists have increasingly been recruited on a part-time basis and appointed as psychotherapists. Within the borstal system three establishments provide psychiatric services and all these have full-time

119

psychiatrically qualified medical officers in charge of medical services. No doubt if psychiatric resources could be found in greater abundance for the young adult system, good use could be made of them: but we have not sought to quantify the unmet demand. Experience at Grendon shows the value of the contribution that psychiatrists can make, not merely by treating those who evidently require their assistance but also by assisting staff and trainees to gain a greater understanding of their own and each others' behaviour in the personal relationships through which staff must try to influence offenders. It should also be borne in mind that deprivation of freedom over long periods imposes strains on the individual with which a psychiatrist may be able to help him to cope. The psychiatrist is not unique in this, and some offenders may find it beneficial to talk things out with another member of staff; but the medical profession has long experience of helping people to adjust to handicaps and limitations imposed by physical injury, psychological strain or emotional or other deprivation.

359. It is not practicable to replicate within a penal establishment the normal outside situation of the surgery on the corner, with its free access to the waiting room and sometimes an appointments system. The establishment assumes total responsibility for the trainee's medical care, and it is inescapable that as a consequence medical arrangements should be to some degree institutionalised. We should like to see them become less isolated from other facets of the establishment. *We believe that at least some medical officers would welcome the opportunity to make a wider contribution to the running of the establishment and we consider that the Prison Department should continue to encourage them to do so.*

360. Finally, we are aware of a continuing debate on the question whether the prison medical service should be integrated into the National Health Service. As a Council we have not considered it in detail. It is a question of organisation which goes beyond the young adult system and indeed bears even more on the treatment of the adult than of the young adult. It will presumably be considered by the Committee on Mentally Abnormal Offenders and accordingly we make no recommendation about it.

Role of the chaplain
361. We were made aware of some uncertainty among chaplains about the role that they should play in young adult establishments (and in the term "chaplain" we include all ministers of religion who serve the establishment). Chaplains can make a distinctive contribution towards the collective effort to change personal attitudes and to help form more effective personal relationships. They also have a traditional function towards those who practise their religion, which is based on the organisation of worship and the administration of the sacraments. This, we suggest, should be carried out with no more departure than is necessary from the normal priest/parishioner relationship. This carries with it the implication that, just as in the outside community, the chaplain may become involved in welfare matters, with the occasional risk of overlapping with other services; but the chaplain, like his outside counterpart, will be alive to this possibility, and to the responsibilities and activities of other specialists. Like their outside counterparts again, chaplains should be free to offer their help to those who are in the parish but not of the congregation: and those

120

approached should have the right to be left alone. Chaplains are not unanimous as to how far they should be involved in the general management of the establishment. We have not sought to frame a general recommendation on this question, which we think best settled in the light of local circumstances and the individual chaplain's own perception of his role.

Rewards and punishments

362. The penalties at present available for misbehaviour in detention centres and borstals are described in paragraphs 65 and 109 respectively of Appendix B. It is clear that certain forms of punishment, eg delaying advancement to a grade, are used for other purposes as well as simply the maintenance of good order or "surface placidity", notably as a disincentive to those who do not make an effort to co-operate in the training programme of the establishment. In one detention centre visited by members, loss of remission also was used for this purpose when other measures failed. It is worth bearing in mind, however, that favourable or unfavourable reactions to behaviour, expressed in the ordinary personal relationships of the establishment, are probably of as much importance as formal sanctions, and that an offender will meet with far more expressions of encouragement or discouragement from his peers in the establishment than from the staff.

363. In a genuinely therapeutic regime, formal punishment is not the means by which control is exercised. At Grendon, for instance, good order is maintained with minimum resort to formal punishment, although the inmates are among the most difficult in the custodial population. Segregation for an unspecified period from the main social unit of an offender whose behaviour is unacceptable in that context is not excluded and certainly the measures employed may bear hard on the individual, but they are not carried to the point where they might have the effect of destroying his co-operation.

364. Grendon, however, is an establishment with a selected intake and an ability to expel the unco-operative. We accept that in most establishments "tariff" punishments, such as specified periods of segregation and loss of remission, cannot be entirely abolished, but *we recommend that wherever possible there should be a change of emphasis in the direction of substituting flexible individual means of control for "tariff" punishments for institutional offences.*

365. Where segregation has to be employed, whether as a "tariff" penalty or otherwise, we think it important that it should not consist simply of solitary confinement. In some establishments staff already adopt a supportive role, visiting the offender frequently; this helps him to prepare for return as soon as possible to the main social group. We commend this approach and would like to see it extended to all young adult establishments.

366. We welcome the Home Secretary's decision to complete the abolition of dietary punishment, and the greater flexibility which is being introduced into the arrangements for punishment generally.

367. The most obvious types of reward are advancement through grades and early release. The grading structure is one of the distinctive features of borstal

training, now carried over into detention centres. We understand that recently many borstal governors felt that the grade system in its old form had become artificial and mechanical in its operation, and more of a hindrance than a help to a constructive regime. It has therefore been replaced in borstals by a modified system,[7] within which governors or Boards of Visitors may still delay a trainee's release by reducing or delaying his grade, but which has little significance in determining a trainee's privileges or the activities in which he is engaged and consists of only two grades. Governors are now free to award privileges, or to select young men for particular activities or responsibilities, by reference only to their likely needs and responses, and the arbitrary limitations of the old grade system no longer apply. We were told how at one borstal the traditional requirement of conformity with the rules of the establishment had been replaced as the criterion for promotion from one grade to another by the recognition by the offender himself of the characteristics which he desired to change and the start of an effort to achieve this goal.

368. We commend these changes towards greater freedom and discretion, and see no objection to the continued use of a grading system so long as it serves a constructive purpose.

Staff uniforms

369. At present officers in the prison officer grades working in borstals wear plain clothes, while those in detention centres and young prisoners' centres wear uniform of the same type as that worn in prisons for adults. In our report on detention centres[8] we recommended that the practice in detention centres should be brought into line with that in borstals, and that officers should wear plain clothes. The Department has taken no action on this recommendation pending our conclusion on this question in this wider review.

370. Uniforms are not necessary for simple identification, since offenders themselves generally wear distinctive clothing. Their function therefore relates to the status of officers within the establishment. Among borstal staff the view has always prevailed that uniforms create an unnecessary barrier between themselves and trainees and discourage the formation of personal relationships; but the view has been put to us that there may be particular circumstances where the wearing of uniform is desirable for the maintenance of discipline—for example, in segregation units or in high security units accommodating serious offenders who at present serve long terms of imprisonment beginning in young prisoners' centres. For our part, we find it hard to envisage circumstances in which there would be advantage in wearing uniforms. For example, the supportive approach which we consider provides the right atmosphere for segregation wings (or establishments if that were found to be necessary) would be hindered rather than helped by the barriers which uniforms would create. *We therefore recommend that officers in all young adult establishments should wear civilian clothes,* and we believe that the great majority of officers would accept this.

Contacts with the community

371. Extramural activities have long been a prominent feature of borstal

---

[7] See paragraph 92 of Appendix B.
[8] *Detention Centres.* Paragraph 93.

training. For the future, we consider that higher priority should be given, throughout the system of establishments for young adult offenders, to contacts with the community. This must be a two-way process: offenders should go out into the community, and "outsiders" should come into young offender establishments, if possible to participate in its activities.

372. Contacts may be permanent or *ad hoc*. The most obvious permanent contact lies in Boards of Visitors, who perform this role with enthusiasm and dedication. In this chapter we have also suggested closer liaison with local education authorities and trade unions; and already members of the public occasionally take part in discussions in establishments, and there are visits from outside sports teams.

373. As regards less formal arrangements, we have not sought to draw up a comprehensive list of possibilities: it is particularly desirable that contacts should be based on real needs and opportunities, as and when they arise.

374. There have been a number of interesting experiments, such as the use of borstal trainees as community service volunteers; the organisation of that name is working with some governors to make this more a regular feature of the borstal regime instead of being confined to a few specially selected trainees. We commend this type of activity on a number of grounds. Community service of all kinds, for example in hospitals and homes for the disabled, in the gardens of old people or decorating their homes, has increasingly been a feature of borstals and more recently of detention centres. These are valuable activities, not only because they help to remove misconceptions about the establishment among the local community, but also because they heighten young adult offenders' awareness of the plight of people less fortunate than themselves. "Outward-bound" activities, both the traditional physical type and, more recently, developments akin to community service are other means, already being employed to some extent by a number of borstals, of helping a person to appreciate his own potentialities and weaknesses and the disabilities of others.

375. One particular barrier to work outside the establishment ought to be removed. At present offenders are only allowed to work for others during normal working hours if the outside bodies or persons pay for their services— which they are often not in a position to do. *We consider that payment should not be sought where the work can properly be regarded as of a charitable kind.*

376. As we have already noted, organising the custodial system in the way we have proposed should facilitate contact with family and friends. At present borstal trainees may under the rules write and receive at least one letter a week; and they may have extra letters as necessary. We welcome the Department's liberal administration of this policy and recent experiments in allowing trainees at certain establishments to send and receive uncensored mail. Similarly, regular visits from families and friends and the opportunity of home leave towards the end of the sentence are of great value. In addition there have recently been experiments in a number of borstals through which offenders have been able to maintain contact by telephone with persons

identified by the probation and after-care service (and who telephone from the probation office) as likely to exert a positive and useful influence on the trainee, notably for example parents and regular girl friends, contact with whom may help to counteract negative peer group influences within the establishment. We particularly welcome experiments of this sort and hope that the Department will extend them.

377. If community links need to be fostered for trainees this is equally true in a different sense with regard to staff. It may be easier to provide staff housing close to an establishment, and to some extent it may be a necessary arrangement as a precaution against emergencies; but it is bound to hinder the integration of staff and their families into local town or village life. We recommend that in planning new establishments consideration be given to dispersing staff quarters to a much greater extent throughout the locality.

CHAPTER 13

MANAGEMENT AND RESOURCES

Central administration

378. The Prison Department is responsible for providing custodial treatment for young adults and for adults, while the probation and after-care service is responsible for providing supervision in the community. The Prison Department is an integral part of the Home Office, and its staff at headquarters, the regional offices and in establishments (including all grades in the prison service) are civil servants. The probation and after-care service is a local service (under the new pattern of local government there will be, broadly speaking, a service for each metropolitan or county area) managed by committees consisting mainly of magistrates. The Criminal Justice Act 1972 has enabled the proportion of the cost of the probation service met from central government funds to be increased from 50% to 80%, the remainder being met from local authority sources. Each local service is under the leadership of a principal probation officer, who is responsible for the day-to-day running of the service in his area. The Probation and After-Care Department of the Home Office has responsibility for policy and development in the probation and after-care field and for the efficiency and well-being of the local services.

379. We recommend no change in these arrangements. In reaching this conclusion we have been aware of other possible approaches to the organisation of the treatment of young adult offenders. In particular, we have considered the pattern in some parts of the United States of America, notably California, where there is a youth authority (and a parallel authority for adult offenders) with a wide-ranging responsibility for the provision of both custodial and non-custodial treatment, and a good deal more autonomy than is enjoyed by the Prison Department as part of a Government department that is responsible to Ministers and to Parliament. Another possibility which we have considered, falling short of the creation of a separate authority, is the separation at all levels of the administration of the young adult custodial system from that for adult offenders.

380. These approaches have their attractions, in particular as a means of securing a concentration of attention on the treatment of young adults. But we believe that this is something that can equally well be secured by other methods. And at the same time, these other approaches would in some respects not be well suited to the general pattern of provision that we favour. In particular, the special advantage of a youth authority would be obtained only if it were responsible for supervision in the community as well as custodial treatment—ie if that part of the probation service which looks after young adults became an agency of the youth authority instead of being an agency of the courts. Our proposed sentencing structure, which distinguishes committal to custody and control from committal to non-custodial supervision and control, and leaves probation as a separate order still available to the courts,

125

would be at least as well served by the present division of responsibility. Moreoever, the separation from the rest of the probation service of a young adult sector would be seriously disruptive at a time when what the service needs is a period of consolidation and continuing growth. We cannot point to any sure advantage which it would be worth pursuing at such a price, and could not be pursued by other means.

381. Similarly, separation of the young adult from the adult custodial system would involve major disruption, especially when a thoroughgoing re-organisation of the Prison Department has only recently been completed. In any event, it would not be sensible or economic to duplicate the large "common services" element in the prison administration. Moreover, while (as we shall go on to show) we are not in all respects satisfied with the present methods of deployment of staff and should like to see more account taken of the desire of staff to specialize in one field or the other, we recognise that the free interchange of staff between adult and young adult establishments has brought advantages to both, and we should not wish to see organisational changes bring about a situation in which there was substantially less interchange. We therefore conclude that the desirable objectives which might be achieved through a separation of the two systems can be more efficiently pursued by means of less fundamental changes, which we now discuss.

Headquarters organisation

382. We have much sympathy with the view put to us by a number of witnesses that the present organisation of the Prison Department does not enable sufficient attention to be given, or at least to be felt to be given, to the special problems of the young adult system. A feeling commonly expressed by governors and other staff of establishments for young adults is regret that there is no longer a Director of Borstal Administration. The holder of this post, who was invariably a former borstal governor, maintained frequent personal contact with governors and was a readily identifiable head of the young adult offender side of the prison service. Of high standing in the Department, he was on the one hand a source of guidance and leadership to governors and on the other hand their spokesman in matters of administration and policy.

383. The post was abolished as part of the recent re-organisation of the Prison Department on functional lines, following a management review. Under the present organisation (which is described in Appendix B) there are Controllers of Planning and Development, of Administration, and of Operations, a Director of Prison Medical Services, and a Chief Inspector of the Prison Service (each of whom is responsible for a section of the headquarters organisation); and a regional organisation. All of them serve both the young adult and adult sectors. Separate concentration on young adults is not found above the divisional level (ie the level of assistant secretary, one below that of controller): and even here work on young adults is combined with work on women offenders and unconvicted persons. Staff in the regional organisation are not allocated specifically to work relating to young adults.

384. This arrangement does not mean either that the young adult system is starved of resources at the expense of the adult system, or that there is a shortage of experience, at any level in the headquarters or regional organisation,

126

of the management of young adult establishments. In regard to resources the young adult system is more generously treated than the adult, whether the criterion adopted is distribution of governor grade staff, staff/inmate ratios, per capita cost of maintenance or capital cost per place of new establishments. As regards expertise at headquarters, the result of the management review has been to create numerous posts, from Controller down, which are currently filled by present or former members of the governor grades, a large number of whom have served in young offender establishments. These staff, we are told, play a fuller part in the management of the system than did the old-style Directors and their subordinate professional staff.

385. Nevertheless it is clear to us and, we believe, to the Prison Department also, that the present arrangements leave those in the field with a sense of a need unmet, and of loss compared with the earlier arrangements. *This is a matter affecting the morale and efficiency of the service, to which we recommend that the Department should give early attention.* The need will be more acute under our proposed new sentencing and treatment structure, and in particular with the development of a new kind of release policy. These changes will call for a concentration of attention on the young adult system at a high level in the Prison Department by a person or persons whose sole responsibility this will be, and will be recognised as being. *It seems to us that such a post might well be established immediately below the Controller of Administration,* where already an existing division is mainly, though not exclusively, concerned with young adult matters.

A standing advisory body

386. *We also recommend the establishment of a standing advisory body whose terms of reference would extend over the young adult offender system as a whole,* and whose membership would be drawn from persons both within and outside the Home Office with responsibilities, training or experience in this field. The case for a body of this kind is in our view the stronger because, while our recommendations call for important developments in relation to young adult offenders, we have decided (for the reasons explained above) against recommending a separate organisation, either within or outside the Home Office, to concentrate exclusively on the young adult system. A body of the kind that we have in mind could act as a forum for the exchange of ideas and information in relation to the whole system of custody, control and supervision of young adult offenders, and would serve the useful function of ensuring regular meetings at which senior officials from the Home Office Prison and Probation and After-Care Departments, and such people as judges and magistrates and representatives of voluntary bodies concerned, could discuss the current problems of the system.

387. It would not necessarily be the function of such a body to report publicly: the Advisory Council for Probation and After-Care has not so far done so, although its proceedings, in which it discusses reports and consultative documents submitted to it, are not normally confidential. Probably an advisory body on the young adult offender system would have most use if its discussions were of the kind in which "outsiders" and "insiders" could exchange views frankly. However that may be, the existence of such a body would help to assure Parliament and others concerned with the penal system that the needs of young adult offenders were receiving the special attention which in our view they require.

Staff movement

388. The other aspect of administration affecting staff which has chiefly caused us concern is that too often in recent years staff at the governor, deputy governor and other senior levels in young offender establishments have been moved too soon; and there have been cases in which the governor and the deputy governor of an establishment have changed in quick succession. *In situ* promotions rarely take place and a person is generally moved to another establishment on promotion. We asked the Prison Department in May 1971 for particulars of the length of stay of governors of young adult establishments. An analysis at that time of the length of stay of up to three previous governors of each training borstal showed that about a quarter had remained in post for over five years and an additional quarter for more than four years: but one third had served for two years but less than four, and one in six had remained for less than two years. The analysis was repeated in July 1973 and showed a broadly similar picture, though in the later analysis a smaller proportion (about one in seven) had remained less than two years in post, and rather more had remained in post for between two and four years. While in general the picture which emerges from these figures is fairly satisfactory, there is no doubt that some moves have taken place more quickly than is desirable.

389. Stability of senior staff is important because it is on them that the maintenance and development of a particular establishment's regime largely depends. To be fully effective, the governor of an establishment needs to assess it; get to know the staff; decide in consultation with headquarters and with his colleagues how and in what direction it should develop; introduce any necessary changes; and administer the establishment for a substantial period in conformity with the agreed policy. If senior staff are moved too soon, while there is much greater stability of staff at lower levels, much of the momentum that a previous governor may have developed will be likely to be lost, and there will be a risk that the establishment will simply drift along. It is particularly important to be able to hold the regime of an establishment steady if there is to be any worthwhile evaluation of different approaches to dealing with young adults in custody.

390. The Prison Department made it clear that they share our concern over the extent of senior staff movement in recent years. They have pointed out that this has occurred in a period of unprecedented expansion in the prison service, creating additional posts at establishments, at headquarters, and in the regional organisation. The growth in headquarters and regional posts has been a consequence of the Prison Department reorganisation with the object of involving the governor grades more closely in the decision-making process, and now that the new organisation has been built up and staffed it may be hoped that the rate of enforced movement of staff will slacken off. The need to man new establishments will of course continue as long as it is necessary for the system to expand. The Prison Department have a nationwide responsibility to see that posts are properly covered, and they follow the principle that posts should be filled by those best qualified for them: a balance therefore has to be struck between the demands of vacant posts and those of maintaining continuity. We understand that the Department are examining ways of reducing the amount of mobility from these causes.

391. But this is not the whole story. It appears to us that some avoidable staff movement is a consequence of the interaction of the grading structure and the promotion system. Each member of the governor grades is in one of five staff grades (Governor Classes I and II and III; Assistant Governor Classes I and II) and has a career expectation of progressing through the grades. Each post in an establishment is assigned to one of these five grades. When vacancies occur in the system (for whatever reason) in any grade above the basic grade, they are bound to generate, in addition to any postings within that grade, a need for promotions from the grade below, which may of course include staff who already hold posts in charge of establishments. The senior or better qualified staff in this lower grade must be reviewed with a view to promotion, and promotion will almost invariably mean a move. These moves on promotion create further vacancies, and the whole process can be repeated one or more grades lower.

392. To canvass the rights and wrongs of this system of grading structure and promotion would take us beyond our obligation to examine the young adult system and indeed beyond the prison service into the wider field of civil service organisation. However, it is our duty to point out the untoward effects of the system on the management of young adult establishments, and to urge that a remedy should be sought by the Home Office in consultation with the staff associations concerned.

393. These untoward effects are of two kinds. The first arises ultimately from the Prison Department's responsibility to man efficiently posts in a nationwide system of establishments. Following the usual pattern in the civil service (which is not unusual among large organisations) each post is graded according to the degree of responsibility that is judged to attach to it. Each vacancy, however arising, is filled by the officer who is considered most suitable for it. He may be already in the grade of the vacant post or be promoted into it in accordance with promotion procedures which have been designed, in consultation with the staff associations, so as to ensure that all officers get a full opportunity of being considered for advancement to the higher graded posts. Staff are promoted not as an abstract recognition of merit but in order to fill vacancies in higher graded posts. Consideration for a higher graded post is automatic and does not require an initiative on the part of the individual—in contrast to the position in some other services.

394. It is not for us to discuss the advantages and the disadvantages of this system save in one respect, which is as follows. It will be seen that if, say, the governor of a young adult establishment is judged to be the most suitable person for promotion to a particular higher graded post (or, if there are several vacant posts, one of the most suitable) he will be promoted and his promotion will normally be to a post at another establishment, thus causing the lack of continuity which we want to see avoided. It seems to us that, within the general framework of the present system of grading and promotion, it ought to be possible by some means (which we have not explored in detail) to treat exceptionally a governor (or other senior member of the staff) who on merits ought to be promoted and moved to a higher graded post, but whose departure at that time would damage the establishment, by promoting him but leaving him for a time in his present post though his promotion has made him over-graded for it. The wholesale adoption of this practice would confuse

the grading and promotion system as a whole; but we believe that it could be done occasionally, where circumstances require it, without having that effect.

395. The second (and related) point is that the relative grading of the governor and deputy governor posts within an establishment can result in a lack of continuity, more particularly if both governor and deputy are moved away within a short space of time. The post of deputy governor is almost invariably graded two grades below the post of governor, so that when a governor is moved the deputy governor is not eligible to be moved up into the post—in contrast to other areas of public service where a deputy is often regarded as the natural person to move up to fill a vacancy at the top. The grading differential between governor and deputy governor posts no doubt reflects a careful assessment of their relative responsibilities. But we consider that in some way or other the system should be made flexible enough to enable a deputy governor to assure continuity by moving up into the vacant governor post where, in the particular circumstances of an establishment, this seems the best course. This is not to say that when a governor leaves it is necessarily, or even normally, the wisest course to promote the deputy. Our point is simply that, when other considerations—in particular the premature departure of the governor—point to the promotion of the deputy governor to fill the vacancy, considerations of grade should not present an insurmountable barrier.

396. We recognise that these shortcomings can be met only by more sophisticated career planning and more looking ahead at the pattern of staff movements. *We should like to see the staff themselves brought more closely into the career planning process.* Our impression is that, as things are, staff can play little part in deciding the course of their own careers. In particular, they have no confidence that they can, without damaging their career prospects, decline a promotion that involves a move if they feel that a move at that time would be particularly detrimental to the operation of the establishment in which they are working. We consider also that governors should be closely associated—as they are not now—in the choice of staff, in particular senior staff, for their establishments.

397. Coupled with the need to give staff a greater say in their career development is a problem which derives from the structure of grades in the prison service. At present the grading of a post (and the pay attaching to it) is related to the management responsibilities that the post is judged to carry; and this in effect means that the larger the population of the establishment the higher the grading and pay of the governor. The relative size of adult and young adult establishments has been such that a member of the governor grades cannot reach the grade of maximum status and pay, Governor Class I, except in an adult prison. Moreover, the Home Office generally requires a man to have had experience at lower levels in prisons as well as young adult establishments if he is to advance to any of the most senior posts. *We consider that it should be possible for a person with a particular aptitude for work with young adults to spend his whole career in that work without thereby losing in status and rewards.* Some young adult establishments at present being planned, and those that we are recommending for the future, with a variety of security conditions at the disposal of the governor, might justify a Governor Class I grading on present criteria of management complexity and size of population. *We consider,*

130

however, that in the grading of governor posts regard should also be had to a wide range of qualities needed in the management of an establishment, including for example the nature of its population and any special problems which they may pose, and not only to the size of the establishment.

Provision of buildings

398. Another area of the administration of the young adult system in which our proposals will have major consequences is the provision of sites and buildings. The general line of the requirement that we foresee, and of changes from the existing pattern of provision, will be apparent from earlier chapters. Particular elements are: the complete withdrawal of young adults (except some of those awaiting trial, sentence or transfer to a training establishment) from adult prisons; the abolition of the centralised borstal allocation system; and the development of establishments which, either on single sites or by means of linking neighbouring establishments, will provide a full range of facilities to meet the needs of all young adult offenders from the area served by the establishment.

399. This adds up to a substantial demand for custodial provision, to be found by a combination of new buildings and re-allocation of existing establishments. The total demand in terms of number of places in, say, five years' time can hardly be forecast. While the future trend of young adult criminality is uncertain, it is certainly our expectation that our proposals, when fully implemented, will reduce the proportionate use of custodial treatment.

400. However, even though we hope that fewer custodial places will be needed in future, it is clear to us that it would not be practicable to rely on a simple re-arrangement of the existing stock of buildings and that a programme of new building will continue to be necessary. For the most part, the existing buildings leave much to be desired. Many of them are overcrowded; their locations are unsuited to present needs and still more to the purpose which we recommend for them; they were not designed with their present use in mind; and their drabness is a hindrance to constructive treatment. Very few young adult establishments, old or new, are purpose-built. Most young adult offenders are housed either in former 19th century convict prisons—which, to whatever extent they are modernised, cannot be transformed into anything suitable for a modern approach—or in camps left behind from other uses. The former policy of reliance on discarded service camps, together with a change in the nature of the population received into young adult establishments, has had the effect that there is now a relative surfeit of open and semi-secure accommodation and a shortage of closed accommodation. A further difficulty is that the pattern of provision is not uniform throughout the country, the north-west for instance being specially deficient. These shortcomings are bad not only for offenders but also for the staff, who have a right not only to decent amenities but also to the physical facilities necessary for effective work with offenders.

401. Early on in our review the Prison Department described to us an ambitious prison building programme, for both adult and young adult establishments, then in its early stages, which if the then forecasts of increased demand (based on a projection of the figures for past years) proved true would at least keep pace with it, and if the influx of offenders proved to be less than forecast

would enable progress to be made in replacing some of the least suitable existing buildings. The Prison Department in developing this programme as it affects young adults have kept closely in touch with our thinking; and we have discussed with the Department in some detail how the establishments now being built, and the existing establishments, could be suited to the needs to which our proposals point.

402. It appears that it should be practicable to divide the country into areas corresponding roughly with the main conurbations and their surrounding districts, and to aim at providing a complete range of establishments in each of them. These would include a remand centre for those who were remanded or committed in custody before conviction or sentence; a short-term establishment intended primarily for offenders whose period in custody is unlikely to exceed, say, four to six months (similar to the existing detention centres); and two or three medium- or long-term establishments providing open and closed accommodation. The assumption would be that a young adult would go to one of the training establishments for his own area unless there were definite reasons to the contrary—for example if he needed specialised medical oversight or formal education of an advanced kind; if he was likely to be a particularly dangerous or disruptive influence; or if the circumstances of his offence or other special reasons made it necessary to separate him from the general run of young adult offenders from his particular area. The medium- and long-term establishments in an area should ideally operate as a single organisation under a common governor and with a number of common services and procedures: this arrangement should certainly be possible where different types of accommodation were available on a single site or were separated by only a short distance (as is intended at Hollesley Bay and Hewell Grange), though more widely separated establishments might have to operate independently.

403. We are encouraged by this indication that, even with existing and already planned accommodation, the Prison Department can (except in the north-west) go at least part of the way towards creating the pattern of establishments that our proposals call for. At the same time, it will be apparent that the full realisation of our proposals would require that the population of a "neighbourhood establishment" should be drawn from the immediately surrounding district, a feature which would be exploited for various training purposes. This means establishments in or very near the large urban areas from which large numbers of offenders come, and presents a problem of finding suitable sites. A few of the existing establishments which are in other ways suitable for development as "neighbourhood establishments" are also appropriately sited. But most are not, and moreover most of the sites for which planning approval has been obtained in the past few years are in rural areas. We know that the Prison Department is fully alive to the need to try to secure urban and near-urban sites, and we understand that many planning authorities recognise at least in principle that such sites are needed for penal establishments. We recognise that these are just the sites that are in demand for many other public purposes and that planning authorities are sensitive to the views of local inhabitants, particularly in regard to open establishments. We do however stress the importance that we attach to the development of near-urban sites for young adult establishments. *The Prison Department should continue to seek such sites;*

132

*and we urge planning authorities and the leaders of local communities to recognise,
and to give proper priority to, the obligation of the community to make provision
for the treatment of young adult offenders in the places where it is most likely
to be effective.*

Probation resources

404. We recognise that implementation of our proposals for an expansion of
non-custodial treatment, and in particular for a new form of non-custodial
supervision order, will demand increased resources. We envisage a greater
proportion of young adult offenders being dealt with under supervision in the
community; and though the periods of supervision may in many cases be shorter
than under existing arrangements, the methods of supervision will be more
varied and in some cases more intensive, with a greater readiness to intervene
in the lives of those under supervision. Clearly these developments will call for
the assignment of more probation officers to carry out work with young adults
and it will be the responsibility of the Probation and After-Care Department
of the Home Office, advised by the Advisory Council for Probation and
After-Care, to quantify these needs and to make specific recommendations
relating to the recruitment and training programmes required to match them.

405. The probation and after-care service has expanded rapidly in recent
years to a present strength of over 4,000 officers, and the existing recruitment
target is a service of 5,350 by the end of 1976. The current forecasts do not,
of course, make specific provision for non-custodial supervision orders. But
they do make provision for a substantial growth of non-custodial treatment
under a number of heads. A further revision of the forecasts will be necessary
to assess, in the light of the various forms of non-custodial treatment which
are becoming available, what addition to the forecasts is necessary in order to
cater for supervision and control orders. In this revision it will be essential to
examine and where necessary reduce probation workloads, which in many cases
we believe are too high for individual offenders to be given the amount of
attention which our proposals would require.

406. The estimated size of the demand on probation resources which our
proposals will make, and the success of the Department in recruiting and
training officers to meet it, must largely determine the rate at which these
proposals in our report can be implemented. While we are anxious to see
implementation at the earliest possible date, equally we are anxious that new
measures are not brought into operation until facilities needed to give proper
effect to them are adequately available. Changes as important as those that we
are recommending must not get off to a limping start. Although our proposals
will cost money, they will cost much less than would be required for equipping
and maintaining at acceptable standards a custodial system for the equivalent
number of offenders.

407. While the investment required by our proposals for non-custodial
treatment is primarily an investment in people, some money for buildings will
also be needed. The main need under this heading is for hostels and other
kinds of residential accommodation within the community, to which we devote
the following chapter. Facilities such as day training centres, which a few
probation departments are already providing experimentally, will also require

an investment, but only on a relatively modest scale as compared with the cost of custodial provision.

Volunteers

408. Voluntary workers are an important addition to the resources available for the treatment of young adult offenders. They are to be valued, not as a means of making good a shortfall of professional staff, but for the qualities and insights that they can bring as ordinary members of the community— and perhaps especially if they are not far removed in age and background from the offenders themselves. There is a long tradition of voluntary involvement with offenders and their problems, which we hope will be developed and consolidated: this is another area in which our proposals should help by reducing the distance between custodial establishments and the home districts of young adult offenders.

409. Within custodial establishments for young adults, voluntary workers can be useful in various parts of the programme, for example in discussions about the problems of everyday life. Community Service Volunteers provide an example of an organisation through which volunteers have spent substantial periods of time playing a part in the general life of penal establishments.

410. But inevitably the voluntary worker can more readily play a part when the offender is in the community and faces the problems of coming to terms with ordinary life. Volunteers have for long been seen as having a particular contribution to make to assisting the resettlement of offenders released from a custodial sentence. This is a stage when an offender may have a jaundiced view of anyone in a position of authority, whether prison officer, police officer or probation officer, and when someone unconnected with the criminal justice system may be in a better position to establish a relationship based on voluntary acceptance and confidence. It is encouraging that the number of volunteers actively engaged in assisting probation officers in after-care work generally rose from 1,200 at the end of 1968 to 2,176 at the end of 1970. Since 1969, probation and after-care committees have been authorised to meet expenditure incurred in the recruitment, preparation and use of volunteers. Recently there has been an increasing trend towards using volunteers in a wide range of probation work.

411. We therefore commend the efforts that have been made by the probation and after-care service to recruit suitable volunteers to assist in work with offenders. We hope that our recommendations regarding treatment in the community will encourage the service to persist in these efforts and to experiment in new ways of deploying voluntary help.

CHAPTER 14

HOSTELS AND OTHER ACCOMMODATION

412. Many times in the preceding chapters we have referred to the great need for hostels and other supportive accommodation for young adult offenders, both those who are released from custody and those who, given the right kind of residential support, do not need to be removed from the community at all. In this chapter we examine this subject in greater detail.

413. We begin with a point of terminology. Discussions of this subject sometimes imply that there is one single model for hostel provision, typified by the small community in the converted Victorian villa under the friendly but watchful eye of the warden. Our own view, which we expound in this chapter, is that there is a need for the widest possible range of residential provision for young adult offenders and for a variety of approaches, differing in the type and degree of support that they provide and in the amount of initiative that they leave to the resident. "Hostel" is no more than a convenient shorthand.

414. The broad case for more hostels—using the term in this wide sense—is now well known and widely accepted—so much so that there is relatively little discussion in specific terms of the particular contribution that hostels can and should make to their treatment. Our approach is to see hostels primarily as an aspect of, and an aid to, treatment in the community. This is in contrast to the view which sees the hostel as a semi-custodial penalty in its own right— a step on the ladder at the top of which is imprisonment. We see in that approach some danger of transferring to hostels assumptions about the advantages of residential treatment which were once made about custodial treatment but are now increasingly doubted or rejected. Our own view is that committal to a hostel, like committal to custody, should be avoided as long as there is any reasonable prospect of dealing with an offender in his own home environment: it is only when this becomes no longer practicable that the advantages of a hostel over a custodial establishment become relevant. And at that point the benefits of hostel treatment should weigh less with those responsible for the decision than the advantages of avoiding total segregation from the community and rupture of community ties.

415. The particular relevance of hostels to the treatment of young adult offenders is that this is an age group many of whose members are in a state of transition from dependence upon a home and its environment to a new state of independence or a new set of relationships. Many young adults find this a difficult transition and need support through it of a kind that the stable environment of a hostel can often supply. The availability or absence of suitable residential provision at this stage of a young adult's development may therefore make or mar him for many years to come. *For this reason we consider that young adult offenders should be given high priority among the many deserving groups with a claim on the resources available for this kind of facility.*

135

The present situation

416. Hostels for offenders have developed in a somewhat piecemeal fashion. Different kinds are provided by different agencies to perform different functions. First there are the approved probation hostels, providing about 400 places for young men and 100 for young women (including some for people extending a little beyond the young adult age range). These hostels, which receive offenders placed on probation whose probation order includes a requirement that they reside at a specified hostel, are described in paragraphs 174 to 195 of Appendix B. They are financed from public funds but up to now have been set up and managed by voluntary bodies: the Criminal Justice Act 1972 contains provision for them to be provided alternatively by the local probation committees.

417. After-care hostels, which may or may not cater exclusively for ex-offenders, have hitherto been provided and managed by voluntary bodies, with representatives from the probation service. Voluntary hostels fulfilling the requirements of the Home Office scheme receive a grant for each place which they undertake to maintain for the reception of offenders. Additionally probation and after-care committees now have a power to make direct provision for after-care hostels. A description of their development is given in paragraphs 196 to 200 of Appendix B.

418. The Prison Department itself maintains a number of pre-release hostels for adult offenders who are approaching the end of a long sentence of imprisonment. There are also three hostels for young adults attached to the borstals at Hollesley Bay (for young men) and at Bullwood Hall and East Sutton Park (for young women). These hostels can receive trainees quite early in the custodial part of the borstal sentence and are seen not simply as allowing the offender to adjust himself to ordinary life after a period in custody but as offering a form of borstal training in its own right. There are plans for two further hostels of this kind. The Prison Department also maintains a post-release hostel for young men who have been discharged from Grendon and there are plans for a similar hostel for adults; but these are regarded as exceptional and the Prison Department does not contemplate any wider provision of after-care hostels.

419. Finally, there has been experimental use of a Salvation Army hostel in London as a bail hostel; and a probation hostel which recently opened in Sheffield under the management of the probation and after-care committee includes provision for people who are required to reside there as a condition of bail.[1] We refer to this topic more fully, in the context of remand, in the next chapter.

The need to expand

420. A good deal of the demand, as expressed in the evidence put to us, for more hostels is for provision of the broad type of the existing approved probation hostels. The objectives of these hostels, and the type of offender for whom they are intended, have varied over the years, but essentially they cater for the offender who is considered suitable for probation on other grounds, but seems unlikely to be able to fulfil the requirements of probation while remaining in his existing accommodation, whether it be his home or elsewhere.

---

[1] The age limits of this hostel are 19 to 25.

421. We agree that there is a need for increased hostel provision for offenders of this type. But *we also consider that the role of hostels should be expanded in terms of the type of offenders which they take, to include some young adult offenders who on existing criteria might not be regarded as at all suitable for a non-custodial sentence, even if suitable accommodation could be arranged.* These are offenders with a number of previous convictions for relatively minor offences and possibly with previous experience of custodial treatment. This is the kind of offender who is being received at the probation hostels for adults that have been provided experimentally since 1970. The experience of these adult hostels with such offenders has been reasonably satisfactory, and this encourages our belief that a wider range of young adult offenders could be taken into probation hostels than has hitherto been considered suitable. For offenders of this kind residence in a hostel has advantages over custody: it disrupts their lives less and gives a better opportunity of developing and maintaining social relationships that will make for a style of life which may reduce the likelihood of future offending.

422. For some offenders with special problems, such as alcoholism or drug addiction, treatment in the community and based on the home may be unlikely to succeed because it is simply not possible to marshal facilities and favourable influences in a sufficiently systematic and intensive way. Such offenders may nevertheless be capable of leading lives which are in other respects normal—perhaps including going out to work—and for them probation hostels may be an appropriate way of making treatment in the community feasible.

423. Personality disorders may mean for some offenders that, however satisfactory their existing homes and other social relationships, something more is needed if they are to be able to lead a life satisfying to themselves or beneficial to the community. A hostel may provide the right degree of support here. As for all hostel residents, the support may consist not only of the influence of the resident staff, but of a group climate and culture conducive to lawful behaviour and to accepting the obligations of ordinary life. A hostel may also have a role to play in freeing an offender from influences, perhaps not connected with the home, which tend to make him unco-operative with his supervisor or to make it difficult to avoid offences.

424. Special mention must also be made of the need for accommodation for homeless young adult recidivists. This can either provide an alternative to custodial treatment or a period of transition after release from custody. Surveys have found a significant proportion of the population of young adult establishments to be homeless in the sense either of having nowhere to go on release (because they had been orphaned or deserted at an early stage or otherwise forcibly separated from their parents), or of having families who refused to have them back, or of not wanting to go home. Many of this last category come originally from broken homes and relationships with such family as they have are extremely bad. Homeless young adult offenders are especially likely to become recidivists and totally dependent on institutional life, and so form a priority class for hostel provision. At present, provision is very limited, an example being Southfield (in North London). *We see a clear need for greater provision of hostels for this group of offenders, both to help them over the transition from custody to community and as an alternative to custodial treatment.*

Hostels for young women

425. On 31 May 1973 only 48 of 85 available places for young women in approved probation hostels were taken up. In one quite small respect a change in the Approved Probation Hostel and Home Rules would be beneficial: at present the Rules preclude the hostels from taking young women who are pregnant, although those found after their arrival at the hostel to be pregnant are normally allowed to stay. *We would support a proposed revision of the Rules to allow for the admission of young women already pregnant.* However, many young women offenders do not settle down easily to normal hostel conditions. Probably the main need of young women is for small hostels with bedsitting rooms, but also with certain communal facilities to ensure that residents do not live in complete social isolation; and for "foster homes". We revert to this point later in this chapter.

Styles of hostel life

426. It does not seem to us that a point has been reached where one approach to the running of hostels for young adult offenders can be confidently recommended at the expense of others. If anything, the need now is for more experimentation and flexibility. The family has generally been taken as a model for probation hostels. This is indeed a model which can provide much in terms of support and security which hostel residents may never have known. But a hostel solely based on the family model may make demands on the staff which even real parents would find it difficult or impossible to meet. Such hostels have, we believe, been successful only because of the exceptional personal contribution of certain individuals. Other models may offer something no less worth copying: for example, the model of the small democratic community in which residents play a full part in decision-making and the running of the hostel. There has been some experience of the democratic approach in the United States: for example, the open homes and apartment complexes of the New York State Division for Youth and the Silverlake Hostel of the Boys Republic exemplify the small democratic community, developed in such a way that peer group pressures can be used to advantage in the treatment of offenders.

427. The basic approach of probation hostels is to encourage the development of a culture in which regular work is a natural expectation. A resident who is not already in employment is expected to look for work immediately after arrival. We believe that this is broadly the right approach provided suitable work is available locally. In the longer term, local unemployment levels must clearly affect decisions about the siting of hostels: we refer again to this question in paragraph 435. As an exception to the general rule, we believe that where residents have the ability and can be inspired with the motivation to engage in full-time education this should be encouraged, and any necessary adjustment made to the Approved Probation Hostel and Home Rules in order to relieve such a resident of the obligation to seek gainful employment in order to contribute to his keep.

428. The retention of adequate spending money by hostel residents is essential if they are to acquire or maintain a sense of responsibility in financial matters and to maintain normal relations with non-offenders outside the hostel. At present residents in most probation hostels who are aged 17 and under 21 are charged £5.50 a week for maintenance and are normally free to dispose of any

balance as they wish, although wardens have a discretion to impose a measure of control over earnings in individual cases. We believe this approach to be correct. The rules applying to residents of Prison Department hostels are more rigid. There is provision for compulsory savings and for a substantial proportion of the amount earned to be paid into public funds; the resident is left with little spare cash. While we recognise that a custodial sentence involves less freedom, less independence and less discretion in all matters including finance,[2] nevertheless if the emphasis is to be on preparing the trainee for life in the community from the start of his sentence, *a more flexible attitude towards earnings within the ambit of a custodial sentence is needed.*

Sanctions for misbehaviour

429. Offenders residing in hostels run by the Prison Department in conjunction with custodial establishments will be serving a custodial sentence and there is a clear sanction available in removal to the parent establishment. In the case of other hostels the ultimate sanction for misbehaviour by a resident is to be taken back to court for a breach of the order or residence requirement. But a clash with staff should not necessarily lead to a further appearance in court, or to a custodial sentence. If hostels are to take in offenders with more severe problems, a single infraction, or even several, need not always be regarded in itself as an indication of failure. Hostel wardens and supervisors of hostel residents should be able to deal with rule-breaking without having to take the offender to court or remove him from the hostel. Wardens of hostels outside the custodial system at present have available a variety of sanctions which they impose, such as restrictions on the use of leisure time and on the availability of spending money. We fully support this approach. In addition, we would expect that the sentencing structure which we have set out in earlier chapters will enable unco-operative hostel residents to be dealt with more easily in the community without the need for recourse to the courts.

The organisation of hostels

430. We see no particular benefit from the "treatment" point of view, and some disadvantage in terms of resource utilisation, in categorising hostels according to the legal situation of the resident, by differentiating between "probation hostels", "after-care hostels" and "bail hostels".[3] But hostels that are within the custodial system will need to be organisationally separate.

431. We are in favour of offenders being placed in hostels where other residents are non-offenders. This already occurs in some voluntary hostels where offenders may be supported by grants from public funds in the same hostels as non-offenders supported by funds from other sources.

432. We consider that hostels should also be "comprehensive" in the sense of catering for people presenting different kinds of problems, provided that the necessary supporting agencies are within reach. The need will nevertheless remain for some specialist hostels providing for those with particular problems

---

[2] Young adults in custodial establishments who work for private employers on outside working parties are paid on the same basis as their counterparts working in the establishment, the rest of their pay going into public funds.

[3] For this reason we particularly approve of the arrangement at the new hostel in Sheffield referred to in paragraph 419 above, where persons remanded on bail may reside as well as offenders who are there as a condition of a probation order.

such as alcoholism, drug addiction and severe instability, for whom intensive specialised treatment is required or particular restrictive measures are appropriate. Experiments in providing different regimes or meeting special needs should continue.

433. We consider that there is a legitimate place for *voluntary* residence in hostels by offenders, where the supervising officer thinks this appropriate. This might take the form of an offender staying on at a hostel voluntarily after a compulsory period of residence, or residing voluntarily after a period in custody, or simply going to a hostel at his own request. Within reasonable limits (which might be time limits) we would welcome this use of public resources in a preventive role, in order to meet a person's needs before an offence, or further offence, is committed, rather than as a result of it. This recommendation has financial implications, since the full cost of a hostel place is beyond the pocket of most offenders; but the principle of public financial support for the housing of potential offenders in the interests of preventing further crime is already established by the placement grants to voluntary hostels accommodating ex-offenders.

434. Because we attach importance to the provision of hostels which will take those who would not normally be acceptable in the community but for whom hostel placement seems to offer the best hope, *we consider that the further hostels needed outside the custodial system should, in the main, be provided and managed by public authorities.* The local probation and after-care committees are clearly the most suitable bodies to take on this responsibility, and now have the necessary powers under section 53 of the Criminal Justice Act 1972. The hostels provided in this way would make up part of a network of which the other component would be hostels provided by voluntary organisations. We prefer this arrangement to the alternative of placing responsibility for all hostel provision under one new authority. It is important that the resources and expertise of voluntary agencies should be retained, provided that there is a sufficient measure of overall co-ordination to secure the aim of a planned system of residential accommodation for young adult offenders in the community.

435. An expansion in public provision will require a thorough assessment of needs and possibilities. *This will involve a survey which we recommend the Home Office should carry out, region by region, of existing supply and demand for hostel places.* The survey should include an attempt to relate the existing situation to predicted changes in demand as a result of the shift in emphasis away from the use of custody which we hope will result from our recommendations.[4] Needs and resources are likely to differ considerably from area to area; for example, unemployed youths in the north-east with a strong regional identity will be different from the young people who make up the rootless floating population of central London. In particular it is important to take account of the existing and long-term employment prospects of an area.

---

[4] A number of the former Regional Group Consultative Committees for After-Care Hostels, which were established following a recommendation in the report of the Working Party on the Place of Voluntary Service in After-Care, undertook surveys of this kind in relation to the demand for after-care hostel places. They did not consider the overall need for accommodation for offenders generally.

Prison Department hostels

436. Hostels within the custodial system are best omitted from the review of needs which we recommend, since their provision is governed by rather different considerations and we have ourselves more specific proposals to make in respect of them. In Chapter 11, in particular, we recommend that hostels should form an integral part of Prison Department "neighbourhood" establishments. Unlike offenders in hostels outside the custodial system, those in hostels within the custodial system are still legally in custody, and unacceptable behaviour in them can therefore be dealt with quickly and informally by a return to the parent establishment ordered by the governor. With this in mind, we think an expansion of Prison Department hostels would have the important advantage of enabling more offenders to be given an earlier chance of proving themselves in a non-custodial situation.

437. In the course of our review we considered arguments that the Prison Department should become more involved in the provision of after-care hostels and that Prison Department staff should be seconded to hostels run by other organisations. We would not wish to rule out occasional experimental postings of this kind, which might have value both for the Prison Department staff and for those among whom they were working. But any greater diversion of effort would, if only in terms of manpower, be at the expense of the custodial system as such, and we do not believe that it would be advantageous to diversify the functions of the prison service to any substantial degree in this way.

The location of hostels

438. We believe that in general and where practicable hostels[5] should serve the locality in which they are sited. It may occasionally be beneficial for a young adult offender to be moved a long way from home, but normally the aim should be to allow him to maintain contact with the environment to which he will return, while keeping him sufficiently detached to allow other influences to come to bear upon him.

439. The success of a hostel depends on links with organisations outside the hostel setting. In the first place, close liaison should be maintained with other arms of the social services. It is desirable, for example, that the local psychiatric hospital should be encouraged to supply a visiting psychiatrist to support the staff and deal with emergencies: such an arrangement will greatly increase the willingness of the staff to accept and persist with difficult residents. For those residents who are unable to compete for work in the community at large, it may also be helpful to establish links with sheltered workshops. More generally, residents should be encouraged to take part in activities outside the hostel which will enable them to establish bonds of friendship and shared interests with non-offenders, from which continuing support can be drawn after the time comes to leave the hostel. Youth clubs, sports clubs and voluntary service organisations are some of the possibilities that we have in mind. All these requirements, together with the availability of outside work, make it necessary that hostels should be sited in urban areas. Many of the factors which in Chapter 13 we have noted as hindering the development of Prison Department

---

[5] As regards Prison Department hostels, questions of location, and of the neighbourhood from which residents should be drawn, are dealt with by our proposals in Chapter 11.

establishments in towns apply equally to hostels, but since hostels are more modest in scale it may prove possible to persuade local authorities to include provision for them in plans for urban redevelopment and renewal: and *we recommend that efforts be made in this direction*. There may also be value in planning individual hostels so that they may be integrated into larger treatment complexes, which might include probation offices and facilities for day training, education and recreation.

Finance

440. The cost of providing and running approved probation hostels managed by voluntary agencies, and hostels and other accommodation provided by probation and after-care committees under the new powers in the Criminal Justice Act 1972, is met from public funds after account has been taken of residents' contributions. We consider this arrangement satisfactory. But the present financial arrangements for voluntary after-care hostels are inadequate in that at present they are limited to a deficit placement grant which goes only part of the way towards meeting costs. *We consider that a higher proportion of the total cost should be met from public funds.*

Staff

441. Hostel staff suffer from low pay and lack of a unified career structure. Voluntary hostels in the after-care field, and approved probation hostels, experience difficulty in recruiting staff, since the conditions of employment compare unfavourably with those available in other areas of social work. A further problem is that hostel staff are isolated from the mainstream of social work and have little opportunity of furthering their career in another field. Changes are therefore needed if a more comprehensive system of residential care within the community is to be created. In view of our recommendations for a system of hostel provision involving more co-operation and co-ordination between the different agencies involved and a system of comprehensive regional planning it is desirable that the needs of staff should be looked at as a whole. Indeed, we see as one of the attractions of a more comprehensive system of residential care, with a unified administration and staff, the fact that it would lessen the danger of a hostel having to close temporarily during an emergency over staff: there would be more chance of calling on reserve staff and so keeping the hostel open.

Other accommodation

442. *The survey which we have recommended above should embrace the provision of specially designated lodgings.* Lodgings are cheaper than hostels and, if developed in each area as part of a coherent and comprehensive range of residential provision in the community, could cater for significant groups of young adult offenders. Lodgings may serve as an alternative to hostel residence for those who are thought, because of a lack of satisfactory home background, to need some sort of stable residential accommodation but who do not require the greater degree of support provided in a hostel. Lodgings may also meet the accommodation need of young adult offenders—perhaps especially young women—who find hostels of the conventional type irksome or who are unco-operative in a large group and therefore unacceptable as hostel residents.

443. Lodgings can also provide a useful service for offenders who, having lived in a hostel, are at the difficult stage of making the transition to an independent existence in the community. A disadvantage which hostels share with custodial establishments (although to a lesser degree) is that residents may become too dependent on communal life and on the staff. For a person for whom this is a risk, a period spent in suitable lodgings, with established links with social workers and the probation and after-care service, will provide a background within which the supervisor may effectively exert his influence. If the lodgings can be near the hostel, valuable relationships with hostel staff and residents remaining in the hostel can be maintained.

444. The accommodation we refer to as "lodgings" might include, for the more stable and mature kind of offender, bedsitting rooms of the traditional type with board provided by a landlady, others with self-catering facilities, and flatlets with someone—who might in some cases be a social worker—available for support.

445. If the use of lodgings is to be developed more effectively, something more is required than merely keeping lists of helpful landladies: and the scope for their recruitment could suitably form part of the regional review of accommodation needs which we have recommended above. It is essential also that the probation service should continue to develop ways of supporting landladies in this difficult role, and that funds should be readily available at need.

446. The London Lodgings Scheme of the National Association for the Care and Resettlement of Offenders, the Hertfordshire Landladies' Project and the Landladies Scheme of the Bristol Association for the Care and Resettlement of Offenders are well established projects from which much can be learnt. In relation to young women the work of the Acorn Trust, which has provided accommodation in a family setting for a number of very difficult girls, is perhaps particularly notable. This kind of friendly background, with un-obtrusive support available, is likely to be especially suitable for girls who do not respond well to hostels. The success of such schemes depends, however, on finding people able and willing to take on the responsibility of accom-modating offenders in this way, and assuring them of support in times of crisis.

CHAPTER 15

REMAND AND ASSESSMENT

447. So far our report has concentrated on sentencing arrangements and on the conditions applying to young adults subject to each sentence. In this final chapter we discuss remand arrangements before trial and sentence, and the preparation and transmission of information about individual young adult offenders to assist in sentencing and in subsequent decisions about their treatment.

REMAND QUESTIONS

448. Remand in custody affects the innocent as well as the guilty. It imports a social stigma and may have adverse practical consequences such as the loss of a job. Like many of our witnesses, therefore, we are concerned that its use should be minimised. There has been a great deal of consideration, both by the Government and by academic writers, of how to make greater use of bail, but general conclusions are not easy to draw.

449. It is probably common ground that a person should be remanded in custody only when the public interest really requires it: for example, where the person would present a danger to the public or to himself if set at large, or if there is reason to suppose that he will not surrender to bail. But these are difficult matters of judgment in the individual case, and it is not easy to frame a provision of law that will have an overall impact without placing tiresome or perhaps even counter-productive restrictions on the discretion of the courts. Section 18 of the Criminal Justice Act 1967 has been criticised on both these counts. The section, which applies only to magistrates' courts, provides that remand should be on bail except in defined circumstances (for example where the defendant has previously failed to surrender to bail, or has no fixed abode, or where the charge involves violence or the use of firearms). We think it better that precise statutory definitions of this kind should be avoided in favour of a general principle, applicable to the Crown Court as well as to magistrates' courts, that *bail should be granted to a person aged 17 and under 21 before he is convicted or sentenced for an offence unless enquiry reveals exceptionally strong reasons for refusing it.*

450. We would add to that general statement comments on three specific issues. First, the courts have held that a person may be remanded in custody under section 14 of the Magistrates' Courts Act 1952 even though the offence is not punishable with imprisonment.[1] *We are strongly of the view that it should not be possible to remand a young adult in custody in such circumstances, and recommend that the law should be amended accordingly.*

---

[1] *Boaks v Reece,* [1957] Q.B.219.

451. Secondly, we do not consider that the likelihood of a custodial sentence is in itself a conclusive argument in favour of remand in custody. Of course, an offender threatened with a custodial sentence may be less inclined to surrender to his bail: if so, this is clearly a factor which the courts will need to take into account. But many courts also think it simply inhumane to release an offender into the community and subsequently to take his liberty away. This is a view with which we have some sympathy, but we should be opposed to an inflexible rule precluding bail in these circumstances. Parliament seems to have taken a similar view: section 20 of the Criminal Justice Act 1967 provides that where a magistrates' court commits an offender convicted summarily to the Crown Court for sentence under section 28 or 29 of the Magistrates' Courts Act 1952—and such a person may often expect to receive a fairly substantial custodial sentence—it may instead of committing in custody commit him on bail. We consider that in these circumstances the courts should continue to apply the general considerations outlined in paragraph 449 above, and that *the prospect of a custodial sentence should be thought of merely as one important factor to weigh in the balance against any other considerations.*

452. Finally, we share the concern of many of our witnesses at the practice, which is said to be adopted by some magistrates' courts, of remanding in custody merely to give people a "taste" of prison life and to achieve the same supposed effect as a very short custodial sentence, before awarding a non-custodial penalty. It is claimed that such remands—usually for three weeks—are ostensibly for the purpose of obtaining a medical report, even though the court has already decided what sentence to impose.

453. Some witnesses with experience of sentencing offenders have expressed the view that this practice can be useful either as a mild punishment, and as a deterrent for the future, or to bring the offender back to court in a more co-operative frame of mind, perhaps readier to consent to a probation order. It is difficult to make a judgment about the effectiveness of this procedure. It is, by its nature, one which does not lend itself to systematic research into its effects,[2] and strong subjective opinions can be found to support both sides of the argument.

454. What we are sure of, however, is that the courts should not seek to achieve their ends in this covert way. Moral issues aside, if a medical report is requested merely as an excuse to commit the person to custody, the time of the doctors and medical staff is wasted and diverted from the care of people who really need their attention. If, therefore, short remands for punitive purposes were thought to be legitimate, this purpose should be recognised openly.

455. We have given a great deal of thought to whether they should be permissible. Our conclusion is that they should not. We are impressed, firstly, by the illogicality of allowing what amounts to a sentence to be passed before the sentencing stage is formally reached, and secondly by the disadvantages of

---

[2] One attempt some years ago is described in "The Choice of Bail or Custody for Offenders Remanded for a Psychiatric Report", *International Journal of Social Psychiatry* Vol. VI numbers 1 and 2, Summer 1960.

short periods in custody, which we have discussed more fully in Chapter 7. We therefore reject the idea of introducing a recognised form of punitive remand. This is not to say that every case in which an offender is given a non-custodial penalty after having been remanded in custody is to be regarded with suspicion; for example, the court might properly take into account, in reaching its sentencing decision, the time that the offender has already spent in custody on remand, and reach the conclusion that his release with a non-custodial measure could be justified. But we strongly urge the courts to avoid using their present powers for the purpose of remanding in custody, as a penalty, someone whom they have already virtually decided they will eventually deal with non-custodially. We repeat our view that unless the offence is so serious as to warrant a custodial sentence of three months or more the use of custody as a penalty should be avoided altogether.

456. During the course of our review a number of administrative measures were introduced to reduce the remand population. First, arrangements were made for police surgeons to examine at court offenders whom the court wished to send to a detention centre, thus obviating the need for a remand in custody for this purpose. Secondly, efforts have been made to reduce the time taken for the preparation of reports on offenders who have been remanded in custody and therefore the period needed for the remand. Thirdly, arrangements are being introduced at, or in association with, a number of prisons and remand centres under which a court may remand an offender on bail with a requirement to attend for psychiatric examination on an out-patient basis.[3] We welcome these developments, and hope that the courts will take full advantage of them.

457. Finally, as a means of reducing remands in custody there has recently been experimental use of a Salvation Army hostel in London as a bail hostel for people who would otherwise have been refused bail because they had no fixed address. In addition a probation hostel recently opened in Sheffield under the management of the probation and after-care committee, to which we referred in paragraph 419 (Chapter 14), includes provision for persons required to reside there as a condition of bail. We commend these developments, and would wish to see the greatest possible flexibility in assessing individual suitability for such schemes. Some of the present restrictions on the type of people admitted to the Salvation Army hostel—for instance on alcoholics and people who have previously served a custodial sentence—could with advantage be relaxed. *We recommend that the provision of hostel places for persons on remand should be expanded within the general framework which we have proposed in Chapter 14.*

458. The majority of young adults remanded in custody are detained in remand centres. The Prison Department's aim for a number of years has been to provide sufficient remand centre accommodation to ensure that all persons under 21 remanded in custody go to a remand centre and not to prison, and their building plans provide for continued expansion of the remand centre system. But in the meantime fairly considerable numbers of unconvicted or unsentenced young people are held in local prisons (at the end of 1972 there were 304 young men).

---

[3] The arrangements apply to the out-patient departments of Holloway, Brixton and Durham Prisons and Risley Remand Centre.

146

459. We endorse the Department's wish to remove young adults from the disagreeable conditions that are all too often to be found in local prisons, and its plans to provide a number of new remand centres for this purpose. At the same time we regard it as important that these new establishments should be accessible (some of the existing centres are not) and that their size should not be such as to require them to serve too large a committal area. What matters most to young people on remand is the ease with which they can be visited—by relatives, friends and lawyers—and the principles on which we have based our proposals in paragraphs 318–320 (Chapter 11) apply to remand establishments no less than to training establishments. In addition, remand establishments have the special feature of relying heavily on part-time specialists whose services are normally available only in the larger centres of population.

460. Some of the Department's existing plans are entirely consistent with this approach, but others may need to be re-examined particularly from the point of view of size. Where existing plans for new remand centres are scaled down, the savings should be used to provide additional remand accommodation, attached where possible to existing establishments, to serve the more remote areas. We recognise however that it may be some years before the number of remand centres is equal to the number of local prisons and until that time a choice will have to be made between committal to a local prison in the defendant's home area and committal to a remand centre which may be as much as 60 or even 100 miles distant. In these circumstances—which may arise for example in parts of Wales and the West Country—we think that the balance of advantage may lie with the local prison.

461. Wherever young people are remanded, every effort should be made to provide a relaxed atmosphere and reasonable facilities for recreation. In a situation in which large numbers of people stay for a short time it is probably too much to hope that anything like a constructive regime can be offered, and we consider that the right of an unconvicted person not to work or take part in the available recreational activities should be preserved. But every effort should be made to provide for activities which people on remand will voluntarily undertake, and we strongly deplore situations of the kind in which young people are simply locked up in cells for a substantial proportion of the day.

462. In the longer term, we hope it will be possible to find a better solution to the problem of accommodating young people on remand than is offered either by local prisons or by the remand centres as they exist at present. The object should be to provide smaller local remand units, perhaps as separate wings of other establishments for young adults, but without detailed study we do not venture to suggest precisely how this might be achieved. *We therefore recommend that the objective should be the provision of remand centres conveniently situated for all the main centres of population; in the meantime, the use of local prisons for the remand of young adults should not be ruled out where the alternative is a very distant remand centre.*

INFORMATION FOR COURTS AND THOSE DEALING WITH OFFENDERS AFTER SENTENCE

463. Our sentencing proposals are designed to achieve a more rational division

of functions between the courts and those who execute their sentences. The crucial decision between custody and non-custody remains that of the court and it is therefore essential that before passing sentence the court should have adequate knowledge of the offender's circumstances. Specifically, it needs to be satisfied that it has sufficient knowledge of his medical and mental condition; his background at home, school and work; his present social environment; and any previous experience of the penal system. Any information about the last is provided in police antecedent reports and reports by the Prison Department; medical information is given in a separate medical report; and information about his social circumstances is contained in a social enquiry report.

464. The Prison Department, for its part, needs information about individuals committed to custody in order to make certain initial decisions about their accommodation and treatment—for example, in order to decide whether an offender is suitable initially for open conditions, or needs to go to a specialised establishment (eg for psychiatric treatment). Within the establishment to which he goes there will be decisions about allocation to a wing or house and to the most suitable form of available instruction or occupation. The abolition of central allocation arrangements should mean that a young adult reaches his training establishment very soon after sentence: this would make it the more necessary that certain information should be available to the custodial system as quickly as possible. Even within the present detention centre system, in which there is direct committal by the courts to a centre serving a single geographical area and no allocation arrangements, we have been told that considerable difficulties arise from the absence of certain information on the offender's reception. These difficulties arise chiefly in relation to information the source of which lies outside the custodial system— the same information, in fact, which is made available to the courts. Securing information already available in a different Prison Department establishment presents few problems.

Social enquiry reports

465. Social enquiry reports are the most comprehensive source of information which the courts have about an offender. They are prepared by probation officers, on the basis of enquiries into (a) the character, personality and social and domestic background of the accused; (b) his record at any educational, training and residential establishments where he has recently been (excluding establishments controlled by the Prison Department) or while receiving after-care; and (c) his employment prospects and, where appropriate, his attitudes and habits as known to his most recent employer.[4] The Criminal Justice Act 1967 (section 57) empowers the Home Secretary to make rules requiring all courts to consider a social enquiry report before passing a custodial sentence, but so far successive Home Secretaries have sought to meet the object of this provision informally by means of recommendations rather than by exercising the rule-making power. The effect of the recommendations, if they are fully implemented, is that only in rare circumstances[5] should a young

[4] Home Office Circulars 28–30/1971.
[5] Theoretically the recommendations do not cover young adult offenders receiving prison sentences of two years or more who withheld consent to pre-trial enquiries, or those receiving prison sentences of six months or less who have previously served a sentence of imprisonment or borstal training.

adult receive a custodial or supervisory sentence without the court considering a report; and in addition, section 15 of the Criminal Justice Act 1972 requires a court to consider a report before making a community service order. Also, in Chapter 8 we have proposed that a court should be statutorily required to consider a social enquiry report before passing a first custody and control order on a young adult. In addition *we recommend that the courts should as a normal practice consider a social enquiry report before making any custody and control order or ordering supervision (whether by means of a supervision and control order or a probation order). Further, we recommend that a report should be considered on conviction of a second or subsequent offence of violence (including common assault), and on conviction of a sexual offence* (ie offences under the Sexual Offences Act 1956 and in addition indecent exposure and soliciting). These last two recommendations should not add substantially to the workload of the probation service, since in many of these cases it is likely that the court would in any case wish to have a report.

466. We have considered whether to recommend that the Home Secretary should now exercise his power to make rules requiring courts to consider a report before passing sentence. We do not feel that at present it is necessary to recommend this. The position needs to be kept under review, and we would certainly hope to see some improvement in the extent of compliance with the recommendations,[6] and the power to make rules should not be given up. But we recognise that in some circumstances courts will feel that the proper course is to deal with the offender immediately without having to adjourn the case for reports, and we therefore think it right that for the present these arrangements should continue to be a matter for the discretion of individual courts except where there already exists, or where we propose, a statutory requirement to consider a report.

467. As regards the contents of social enquiry reports, we see no reason to recommend any change, especially in view of our proposals for correctional assessments (see paragraph 489 below). It has been suggested that the probation officer should summarise the contents of the other reports (eg police, prison, medical etc) to produce a composite document. But the reports of the various disciplines are inevitably written from differing professional viewpoints and we think that where conflicts occur they should be allowed to become apparent to the court and not be built into any composite formula.[7] The probation officer should nevertheless know what is in the other reports, if possible before he draws up his own.

468. The preparation of social enquiry reports forms a substantial part of the work of the probation and after-care service. Rather to our surprise, there does not appear to be any standard arrangement for giving training for this work to new probation officers. This is not a matter on which it would be right for us to make detailed recommendations, but we feel that we should record our view that the inclusion in the initial training of probation officers of training

---

[6] A recent survey by the Home Office Research Department found that reports were considered by magistrates' courts in about 80% of cases in which they made a detention centre order.
[7] The Committee on the Business of the Criminal Courts (the Streatfeild Committee) likewise made no recommendation on a similar suggestion: see paragraph 429 of its report (Cmnd 1289).

in the preparation and presentation of reports is highly desirable. What is important is not the format (where there is already considerable uniformity), but what sort of information is relevant, where to obtain it and how to elicit and interpret it. We suggest that this aspect of probation officers' training should be examined by the Central Council for Education and Training in Social Work.

469. Prison Department establishments, as well as the courts, have a use for social enquiry reports. Staff to whom we have spoken on our visits to establishments have emphasised the need to see them quickly. The social enquiry report forms the basis of the social work record and of the planning of the offender's supervision and resettlement in the community. It is usually the only information which the staff have about his social circumstances, against which to measure his own version of events and from which to ascertain the factors which may have led him into trouble and which could lead to trouble in the future. This further emphasises the importance of a social enquiry report being available before sentence, so that it can be immediately transmitted to staff in the receiving establishment in the event of a custodial sentence. It also shows that where a court declines to order a social enquiry report for fear of wasting the time of the probation service, the loss often has to be made good after sentence is passed. But it seems that even where a pre-sentence social enquiry report is prepared at present there is often delay in it being received by the establishment: it should in our view accompany the offender on the journey from court to custody. The same applies to police antecedent statements where they are available in written form, and medical reports, to which we now turn.

Psychiatric reports

470. In order to determine whether an offender needs treatment for a psychiatric condition the court may remand him, either in custody or on bail, in order to obtain a medical report.[8] Where a person is remanded in custody the report is usually prepared by a prison medical officer. Where he is remanded on bail the report is normally prepared by a consultant psychiatrist at a psychiatric hospital out-patient department or a psychiatric clinic.

471. There are no official statistics of the relative proportions of medical reports which are prepared in custody and on bail. A small survey which we undertook indicated that in some areas few reports are prepared on bail while in others a fairly substantial proportion of reports is prepared on bail, averaging perhaps half overall. There seems to be no shortage of psychiatrists willing to undertake assessments on bail. We understood that courts sometimes complained that psychiatrists outside the prison service take longer to prepare their reports, but in other respects they appeared well satisfied with reports prepared on bail.

---

[8] Magistrates' courts have specific power under section 26 of the Magistrates' Courts Act 1952 to remand for medical examination. The court must be satisfied that the offence has been committed by the accused, but does not at that stage convict him. Where a person is remanded on bail under section 26 it is a condition of the recognizance that he should undergo medical examination by a duly qualified medical practitioner at a specified place and time. Medical reports are also obtained by means of a remand under section 14(3) of the Magistrates' Courts Act 1952. In that case the person is already convicted.

472. *We do not consider that the need for a psychiatric report justifies a remand in custody where bail would otherwise be granted.* Remand in custody would be justified only if it made possible a more intensive observation, but in fact the pressure of numbers prevents this.

473. *Where a psychiatrist recommends psychiatric treatment for an offender we consider that he should be able to accept responsibility* (whether of a direct or supervisory nature) *for that treatment:* an outside psychiatrist should be able to maintain an interest in an offender's treatment in custody, and a prison doctor should similarly be able to be associated with the treatment of a patient who is released on probation. This would have consequences—but not, we think, regrettable consequences—for the organisation of the prison medical service. We consider it undesirable in principle for prison medical officers to spend the whole of their time preparing reports on and treating persons in custody: assessment of those on bail and treatment of those under supervision in the community will provide a balance of more hopeful cases. It is important too that psychiatrists assessing offenders for the courts should be in contact with psychiatric and other services in the community. With this *caveat*, we see no objection to psychiatrists devoting the whole or the major part of their time to dealing with offenders. What we say here should not be interpreted as an encouragement to involve National Health Service psychiatrists to a substantial degree in custodial assessment. Many reports for the courts are prepared by psychiatrists in National Health Service hospitals and clinics, who perhaps have only minimal contact with the prison service, and we see no reason to disturb these arrangements which in many areas work very satisfactorily. The aim should be not so much to bring in people from outside into prison work as to ensure that the permanent full-time staff of the prison medical service have opportunities of involvement outside the prison service.

474. Where psychiatric assessment is undertaken on an out-patient basis at a local prison or remand centre, we think it important that the setting for the examination should be as little as possible like a prison: the usual prison entrance and reception procedures should be avoided. More commonly we would expect examination on bail to take place at a general or psychiatric hospital or at a clinic. Finally it is conceivable, though much less likely, that examination could be undertaken in some form of community treatment facility, such as a hostel or day training centre, if psychiatrists are already engaged in work there. Wherever it is undertaken it is desirable that ample accommodation should be available to enable the patient's family to accompany him so that they can also be interviewed and the psychiatrist can observe his relationship with them.

475. The courts should be able to obtain reports at reasonably short notice. We hope therefore that doctors who do not at present undertake this heavy work will seriously consider whether they cannot make some contribution.

476. As to procedure, we agree with the view that a request for a psychiatric report should have the authority of the clerk of the court, but that arrangements for the examination should be made by the probation officer. Normally a psychiatric report will result from a specific request by the court.

Circumstances may arise, however, in which there is no specific request by the court but the probation officer recognises the need for a medical report during the preparation of the social enquiry report. In these circumstances we consider that it should be possible, with the defendant's consent, to obtain a psychiatric report without reference to the court itself before the resumed hearing, thus obviating the need for a further remand. Court clerks should accordingly have authority to incur expenditure on preparation of reports without specific reference to the judge or to the justices composing a magistrates' court.

477. Although magistrates' courts are required by rules to send the psychiatrist their reasons for requesting a report, courts sometimes give only such reasons as "nature of offence" or "demeanour in court". Naturally this is a handicap to the doctor who does not know quite what the court expects him to investigate. Sometimes, of course, the court may have no more than a general feeling that the offender's behaviour as exhibited in the offence is odd and out of character, but if it has a more precise reason we think it important that this should be stated. Public disclosure may, of course, embarrass the defendant, and equally the arrangement should not be made behind his back. We think that all courts should therefore adopt the practice currently required of magistrates in cases under section 26 of the Magistrates' Courts Act 1952. This is to send a written communication to the psychiatrist, a copy of which should be given to the defendant's legal representative, or to the defendant himself if he is not represented. Where a report is to be prepared at the request of the defence we recommend that they should provide the court with a written statement of their reasons, for transmission to the psychiatrist.

478. It is important that the closest possible links should be maintained between psychiatrists and the probation service, on whom we think the initiative in this must rest. The probation officer should, as soon as possible, inform the psychiatrist of the general contents of the social enquiry report. A psychiatrist may well have the assistance of his own psychiatric social worker, who can visit the patient's home, but the probation service can often provide the psychiatrist with social background information at the outset especially where, as is usually the case, the offender is already well known to the service. This is a well established probation service practice which we endorse.

479. Similarly, as we have said above, we think that the probation officer should be aware of the contents and recommendations of other reports to the court, including psychiatric reports. Some doctors take the view that their reports are a private communication to the court and should not be made available to others. We understand this view but do not agree with it. For one thing the probation officer is himself an officer of the court. But more generally we do not consider that the usual degree of confidentiality between doctor and patient applies to reports prepared for the court on persons found to have committed offences: such reports should in principle be available to any person who has a legitimate interest in their content because of his involvement in giving sentencing advice or in subsequent treatment decisions. It is accordingly desirable that the psychiatrist should stress to the patient at

the outset of the examination that he is preparing a report for the court which may also go to others concerned with his treatment. We noted that a Sub-Committee of the Scottish Health Services Council on Forensic Psychiatry (published in 1969) described and recommended the practice by which the psychiatrist and probation officer tell each other of the general lines of their prospective reports before finalising them. In our view such an arrangement has considerable merit.

480. A copy of the psychiatric report should also go to the defendant or his legal representative, if possible before the resumed hearing, thus obviating the need for a further remand if the defence desire a second opinion.

481. We recommend also that where an offender is made subject to a probation order with a condition of psychiatric treatment the supervising probation officer should be given a copy of the psychiatric report (if he has not already received one under the usual liaison arrangements). The doctor responsible for treatment will normally be the one who prepared the report. (The same should normally be true where a hospital order is made.) Further, where an offender is given a custodial sentence a copy should be sent to the receiving custodial establishment to go on his medical record (which is distinct from the main prison department record).

482. Finally, as regards local arrangements for the preparation of psychiatric reports, *we recommend that a person should be appointed in each area* (this could be each existing probation area) *with responsibility for the efficient operation of the arrangements in the area, and for advising courts and regional hospital boards of developments.* A consultant psychiatrist, for example, might be the most suitable person for such an appointment.

Reports to courts by the Prison Department
483. Prison governors prepare reports on young adults committed to the Crown Court who have previously served a sentence in a Prison Department establishment. In general their reports deal only with behaviour under previous custodial sentences, but a governor or medical officer may occasionally, on his own initiative, report information which he thinks may be valuable to the court—if, for example, some particular abnormality is identified.

484. When a young adult is discharged from a custodial sentence the governor sends the supervising probation officer a report which describes—usually quite briefly—the offender's progress during the sentence and the governor's assessment of his prospects. If the offender is subsequently remanded in custody, the remand centre sends for the previous record. Usually the report to the court from the remand centre is based almost entirely on the discharge report: remand centre staff rightly disclaim any ability to produce a definitive assessment which will guide the court on the most appropriate form of "treatment".

485. This is a cumbersome procedure which achieves comparatively little. *We suggest instead that a report, more thorough than the present discharge report, reviewing progress, problems and prospects, should be prepared by establishment staff at the end of the custodial element of the sentence* (and, incidentally, another

153

at the end of supervision). This report would firstly, and as at present, be to the supervisor. But secondly, it could itself be submitted to the court, without further processing, in the event of a further offence. And finally, looking forward to the system of correctional assessments which we propose later in this chapter, we envisage that such a report would indicate to those who have prepared the assessment how accurate a picture of the trainee the staff found it, and how useful in planning his training. This new arrangement need not preclude the courts from asking the remand centre for a separate report, or the remand centre staff from offering one, if either thought this helpful. Indeed staff of the remand establishment would no doubt undertake some form of assessment as a matter of routine, and *we consider that when a custodial sentence seems a likely outcome the period of remand in custody should be used for the purpose of arriving at a provisional allocation.* This may bring to light special features which should be drawn to the court's attention.

Police reports on the offence

486. There is some difference of view among the staff of Prison Department establishments about their need for information about the offence of which a young adult has been convicted. Some consider that the offence itself is irrelevant and that the important considerations are the offender's actual personal problems, his response to training and his prospects on release. The more common view, which we strongly endorse, is that a police report on the circumstances of the offence is a vital piece of information. It helps the staff to identify those parts of the offender's story which are true and those which are false, thereby helping through discussion to get to the root of his problems; and it is of clear importance in deciding the date of release. A recent Home Office circular[9] invites the police to send information in standard form about certain offenders receiving custodial sentences. The information includes a brief factual account of the case, criminal associates, whether the person is suspected of other offences, and "any habits or peculiarities". These formal arrangements at present apply to prison sentences of more than three months and to borstal sentences. They do not apply to detention centre sentences, but in practice detention centres often receive a brief report. For the future, *we recommend that a police report in the present prescribed form should be prepared in respect of a young adult receiving a custody and control order of six months or more and so far as circumstances allow on shorter sentences too.*

Records of previous custodial or residential experience

487. The present arrangements for obtaining previous custodial records appear to work satisfactorily. At the time when we discussed these matters with custodial staff, however, it was too early to gauge the effect of the transfer of responsibility for the care of juvenile offenders to local authority social service departments. We hope that local authorities will continue to provide the full co-operation which has been given by approved schools and that unnecessary objections of confidentiality will not be raised, since sight of earlier records may often be of great value to staff in assessing, for example, an individual's general development over a period of time, and whether as a result of his institutional experience he is likely to give rise to special problems of management.

---

[9] No. 79/1972.

Exchange of information between the establishment and the after-care supervisor

488. Supervisors produce reports on the progress of offenders who have been released from custody but this information is often given only very limited circulation within establishments. We suggest that governors and the Prison Department might explore what steps could be taken to ensure that staff know how "old boys" are getting on without having to take a special initiative themselves. This applies of course particularly to those who are not house staff, such as civilian instructors.

Correctional assessments

489. We have seen in this chapter that a great deal of information will usually have been collected about an offender before he comes into the care of the probation service or Prison Department. Weaknesses nevertheless remain, partly of substance and partly of procedure. It is at present all too easy, for example, for borstal staff to get a distorted impression of a young man in their care because of misunderstanding or misinformation about his home circumstances or personal history—matters which cannot readily be checked by members of the staff of an establishment. Most of the information available to staff is based on successive interviews, involving tedious repetition of material which the offender may have had to recount many times before and may embroider or distort, perhaps without meaning to do so.

490. *These considerations have led us to our most substantial proposal for improving the range of information available to those working with young adult offenders, both in custodial establishments and in the community: the introduction of a new form of assessment process which we have called a "correctional assessment".* This would be a more systematic and careful attempt than is made at present to record those features of the background and outlook of the offender, knowledge of which seems likely to be of enduring value to those engaged in the treatment process. We see considerable merit in undertaking a really thorough and accurate study of each offender at the stage at which it has become apparent that he is likely to need substantial and continuing help. Resources will, we think, be more productively used in this way than in repeated interviewing and testing each time the offender returns to the system.

491. The resulting dossier will consist to some extent of information of the kind already gathered about the offender's history, social background and educational achievements. The task here will be to cross-check carefully information which is based only on his own version of events, supplementing this where necessary with first-hand enquiry. But the dossier should also contain systematic information, of a kind which is not always available at present, about the offender's personal characteristics—his intellectual status, aptitudes and interests. Finally, all the information so gathered should be carefully synthesised into an overall picture which will provide a useful starting point for treatment.

492. Such a dossier will not be a substitute for the continuing assessment of the offender throughout his career in the penal system. The initial dossier will be continually updated by subsequent assessments by staff—to avoid damaging errors and to give direction to the treatment process. Staff will inevitably continue to be guided in their behaviour chiefly by their own

interaction with the offender. The object in drawing up the correctional assessment should be to provide a sound framework within which the observations and views of those working with the offender (chiefly staff of custodial establishments and probation officers) may be fitted to advantage. The overall picture of the individual offender will therefore become fuller and more meaningful as time goes on; and if the assessments are made on a consistent basis, the information so obtained should be invaluable in subsequent studies of the characteristics of the young adult offender population as a whole.

493. It will already be apparent that we do not envisage the results of this new assessment process being made available to the court before which the offender first appears: the process will be too lengthy to make this practicable. The assessment should therefore be made at an early stage of the offender's first period of custody or supervision. But once it has been prepared we see no reason why a correctional assessment should not be made available to the court in the event of a subsequent offence.

494. The inevitable length of the process, and the fact that it will entail making enquiries outside the immediate ambit of treatment, lead also to the conclusion that it should be performed by a specialist team with adequate time at its disposal; and if the information which is gathered is subsequently to serve as material for comparative research, the team should be the same whether the offender is being supervised in custody or in the community. Small interdisciplinary teams of psychologists and social workers, working closely together but independently of the Prison Department and probation services, seem likely to provide the best combination of talent for this purpose. The psychologists should have experience outside the penal system, and some might continue to do such work at the same time.

495. An important component of this proposal is that those who prepare the assessments should receive "feedback" from those who use them as an indication of their value and accuracy. This process is important if the quality of assessment is to be improved, and advice regarding treatment (and the underlying assumptions) modified, in the light of experience.

496. The resources which such a scheme, properly carried out, would demand over the whole country are bound to seem considerable in relation to the expected benefits, which cannot be measured with certainty before the scheme is put into practice. For this reason *we propose the setting-up of a trial scheme for a period of (say) five years in order to enable the feasibility, value and cost of the scheme to be determined.* If custodial establishments are, as we have proposed, reorganised into area groups, it should be possible to carry out the assessment in relation to all young adult offenders within a defined area, without large numbers of inward and outward transfers to complicate the picture. In this way the experience of staff having the benefit of the scheme could be compared with that of those who do not. We ourselves arranged a small pilot study on a few selected offenders in order to gauge the feasibility of the process we propose. The tests which were employed were not those which we would expect to be used under operational conditions and mainly for this reason the results did not demonstrate indisputably the value of such

assessments. But the pilot study did demonstrate to our own satisfaction that a process of the sort we have in mind could be operated and was worth a fuller trial.

497. It is not possible at this stage to predict the benefits, even of a trial scheme, with greater precision. But the reader should bear in mind that we have had to record, at many points throughout this report, great areas of uncertainty about offenders and their treatment. More useful information, such as we describe here, is the only likely basis for progress in the long term.

KENNETH YOUNGER *(Chairman)*
✠ ROBERT MORTIMER *(Vice-Chairman)*
LEO ABSE[2]
LOUIS BLOM-COOPER[1]
DUDLEY FISKE
GERALD HINES
CORDELIA JAMES OF RUSHOLME[5]
RICHARD LOWRY[4, 6]
R. E. MILLARD
LEON RADZINOWICZ[6]
TIMOTHY RAISON[3]
TERESA ROTHSCHILD
PETER SCOTT
W. R. STIRLING[1]
G. B. TRASLER[1]
GEORGE TWIST[6]
NIGEL WALKER[5]
GEORGE S. WALLER[6]
WOOTTON OF ABINGER[1]

N. R. VARNEY *(Secretary)*
8 November 1973

---

[1] Subject to the Note of Dissent on page 158.
[2] Subject to the Note of Dissent on page 162.
[3] Subject to the Note of Reservation on page 166.
[4] Subject to the Note of Dissent on page 167.
[5] Subject to the Note of Dissent on page 170.
[6] Subject to the Note of Dissent on page 172.

NOTE OF DISSENT

by

*Mr. Louis Blom-Cooper, QC, Mr. W. R. Stirling, Professor G. B. Trasler
and the Baroness Wootton of Abinger*

1. We have signed the report because it appears to us to move in the right direction, but we would have liked it to go much further. In particular we think it is excessively preoccupied with custodial treatment. In our view custody ought never to be inflicted unless this is indisputably necessary for the protection of the public or there are clear advantages that can be secured only by removal from the community. Custody should always be viewed as a method of treatment for buttressing the non-custodial situation, and the decision to use it as part of ongoing supervision within the community should be made at leisure by those who have the day-to-day care of the young offender.

2. We would endorse the view, expressed by the American President's Commission on Law Enforcement and Administration of Justice, that "for the large bulk of offenders, particularly the youthful, institutional commitments can cause more problems than they solve."[1] Treatment in custody has demonstrably failed for many young offenders, as the high figures for recidivism testify, and as the Report itself acknowledges.[2] It is at best a costly way of achieving very little, and all too often has only negative consequences inasmuch as it disturbs the offender's personal and social roots, as well as interfering with his employment. Moreover, it is a common experience that a young person may conform in an exemplary way to a temporary, imposed, environment, without his social relationships as a whole being affected—with the result that the efforts of the prison service (including staff of borstals and detention centres) are largely nullified as soon as the offender is back in his familiar and social environment.

3. Many of the youngsters who come into the penal system have experienced educational failure and social rejection. For them the incentives to conform are weak. In our society we are all bombarded by propaganda which constantly hammers home the philosophy that status and happiness depend upon the possession of money and goods, but the young men for whom we have to frame our proposals have only poor prospects of acquiring much of either through legitimate outlets. They are constantly tempted to grab what they cannot reach by socially acceptable means. Their frustration is manifest in their resort to violence, both as an outlet for aggressive attitudes, and as an attempt to snatch at a social significance otherwise denied to them. It follows that any process of law which makes a young person feel further rejected can only exacerbate the problem it seeks to solve.

---

[1] *The Challenge of Crime in a Free Society*, U.S. Printing Office, 1967, p 165.
[2] See also Appendix D, in particular paragraph 75, where the point is made that research has cast doubt on the effectiveness of custodial treatment.

4. This is not a plea for softness. It is a plea for the insight and attitudes necessary to help a young offender to escape from the snowballing effect of continuing rejection which in turn evokes anti-social behaviour leading to a life of crime. It is also a plea for realism, inasmuch as it recognises that the cures currently attempted more often than not accentuate social rejection and reinforce anti-social life-styles.

5. The report claims that its sentencing proposals are designed to bring about a reduction both in the proportion of young offenders who are committed to custody and in the amount of time that many of them spend in segregation from the community; and it is left to the courts to give effect to this policy. We doubt whether this expectation will be realised, and in any case, as already indicated, we do not think that the courts are well equipped to prescribe, or subsequently to interfere in, the treatment of an offender after the decision has been made that some form of social intervention is called for. We would emphasise the sharp distinction between the sentence of the court, which is a once-and-for-all decision, and treatment which is a continuing process and needs to be adjusted to the offender's progress or changing circumstances.

6. We therefore take a more restricted view of the functions of the court than the report contemplates. We regard these functions as threefold: first, to determine the issue of guilt or innocence; second, in the event of a conviction, to decide whether it is necessary that the offender should be subject to some form of compulsory social intervention; third, in the interests of personal liberty, to fix the maximum duration of any such intervention, whether or not this involves treatment in the community or in custody. The crucial decision to be made by the court is not the choice between custodial and non-custodial treatment. It is the decision whether an offender should be subject to any kind of supervision, custodial or non-custodial, or whether he can properly be dealt with by a fine or discharge.

7. We also think that the courts are mistaken when they assume that sentences can be adjusted to degrees of criminal responsibility, so that the graver the crime, the longer the period during which the offender should be deprived of his liberty. We find this idea inappropriate if applied to the penal system as a whole, and particularly inept for the young offender. When dealing with children and young persons, the juvenile courts act upon the principle that considerations of welfare and of reformation should predominate. Since the main reason for retaining special provisions for the treatment of those between the ages of 17 and 21 is that they are still young enough to be amenable to reformative influences, logic and humanity dictate that the same principle should apply also to this age group.

8. Our endorsement of the report is therefore qualified by the following specific dissents:

(1) Restricted release orders
9. These orders seem to us inconsistent with the principle that the date at which an offender can safely be returned to life in the community can only be properly assessed by those who are in day-to-day contact with him while he is in custody, and that no court at the time of sentencing is in a position

159

to determine this in advance. We hope that we have already made it clear that we regard this principle as fundamental.

(2) Immediate detention under Custody and Control Orders

10. We think that there should be greater flexibility in arranging at what (if any) stage during the currency of a custody and control order an offender should actually be detained. The report's proposals are based on the assumption that when the order is made, the person subject to it should almost always be detained in custody forthwith. Only in exceptional cases do they allow that the operation of the order might be deferred either on account of some imminent event affecting the offender (such as sitting for an examination or undergoing a minor surgical operation) or on the application of the prison authorities. Moreover, the report recognises that in the case of an order of relatively short duration, an offender who has already spent some weeks in custody on remand may be liable for only a few days' or perhaps a week's further detention; and that it will be difficult to arrange any programme that makes sense for so short a period.

11. It seems to us that having gone so far, it would be reasonable to go further, and to admit that there may be cases in which a custody and control order is appropriate as providing the sanction of *potential* detention, but in which a period of supervision in the community may in the first instance be worth a trial. This may indeed establish that detention is not in fact necessary at any time within the currency of the order. On the other hand should this course prove unsatisfactory, the supervisor in the case would be able to substitute a period of detention within the limits prescribed by the order—subject to the offender having the same right of appeal as in cases in which it is proposed that he should be recalled into custody after having been released from an initial period of detention.

12. This comes near to, but is not identical with, provision for a "suspended custody and control order" which a majority of the Council has rejected.[3] The essential difference is that a suspended order could only be activated in prescribed conditions (presumably if the person subject to it committed a further offence) and that this would require further court proceedings. Such a provision is open to the double objection that it is undesirably inflexible and that it also introduces an additional complication into the court's choice of sentence. Our proposal not to insist that a custody and control order must (except in the special circumstances already mentioned) *invariably* mean an immediate period of detention would meet both these objections, while at the same time giving opportunity for any advantages inherent in the concept of a "suspended order" to be realised. It would give greater flexibility to deal with special cases, and it would avoid the absurdity of very short detention in cases where the offender has already been in custody on remand for a considerable proportion of the total period during which he is liable to detention. We submit also that this proposal is more consistent with the underlying philosophy of the report which requires that the decision as to when custodial detention is necessary should in the first instance be a matter to be decided by those who are in day-to-day contact with the offender.

---

[3] In paragraph 239 of the Report; but see the note of dissent by the Lady James of Rusholme and Professor Walker.

(3) Automatic remission

13. We cannot accept the proposal that, subject to good behaviour, a person subject to a custody and control order should be in all cases entitled to remission of one third of his sentence. We find the idea of automatic remission logically incompatible with a wholly indeterminate sentence. If a person is subject to, say, a 12 months' order, and may be released at any time during that period, what is the purpose of allowing automatic release at eight months? If a maximum period of eight months' detention is intended why say 12? True, it may happen that a young offender subject to, say, a three-year custody and control order may find himself confined in the same institution as a prisoner sentenced as an adult, and that the latter will, whereas the former will not, enjoy automatic remission of one third of his sentence subject to good behaviour. But this apparent injustice is, in our view, fully compensated by the fact that the offender subject to a custody and control order may be released at any time, whereas the adult prisoner, whatever his sentence, cannot be considered for parole until he has served one third of his sentence or 12 months, whichever is the longer.

14. The effect of these modifications will be that the imposition of a custody and control order will not necessarily involve the person sentenced being detained in custody at all. The order would carry a *potential* sanction of custodial treatment which may or may not be activated in the light of the offender's progress and circumstances, or of any serious threat to public safety involved in his remaining at liberty. This means that the difference between the custody and control order and the supervision and control order as proposed by the report will be considerably narrowed. We think, therefore, that it would both avoid unnecessary complications for the courts and underline the importance of minimising custodial treatment, if the two orders were combined into a single supervision order, which could be imposed with or without a custodial condition. In the former case the court would merely fix the maximum period for which the offender could be detained in custody. Within that maximum it would be for the supervising authority to determine whether, when and where any actual detention should be enforced (subject to the appeal machinery provided under the proposed custody and control order, as outlined in paragraph 232 of the report). Alternatively if the court attached a nil-custody condition to the order, the offender would be subject to supervision as provided in the supervision and control order proposed by the report; but, apart from the emergency provision for short-term detention in periods of crisis (report paragraph 285), the supervising authority's powers would not include any right to impose detention. An offender under a nil-custody order could only be detained in custody, if after further court proceedings, in which he had been found guilty of a breach of the conditions of the order, a fresh order, with a custodial condition, had been substituted for the original nil-custody order.

NOTE OF DISSENT

by

Mr. Leo Abse, MP

1. I am in sympathy with the opinions expressed in the dissenting note of Mr. Blom-Cooper and others, and, in particular, with their view that custodial sentences ought never to be inflicted unless this is indisputably necessary for the protection of the public or there are clear advantages which can only be secured by removal from the community. This view, however, I believe, compels an examination of the existing powers of the court to give custodial sentences to young offenders: such a scrutiny becomes more urgent in view of the recommendation that the court should now have at its disposal a new non-custodial supervision order which could impose very strict control on an offender while in the community. The granting of this wide ranging new power to the courts should enable us to detract from present powers of imprisonment, and so help to ensure that no young offender is mindlessly detained.

2. In the quest to find a suitable starting point where the powers to administer custodial sentences could, without affront to public opinion or danger to the community, be extinguished, the obvious direction to look is towards certain offences committed by young women offenders. I am of the view that it would be appropriate, coincidentally with the introduction of the new non-custodial supervisory order, to end the present powers of the courts to impose custodial sentences upon young women for offences relating to prostitution, shoplifting, infanticide and child stealing.

3. The present powers of imprisonment of women convicted more than twice of soliciting came into existence as a result of the recommendations of the Wolfenden Committee (Cmnd 247). That Committee expressly stated (paragraph 277) in making its recommendations that it had two purposes in mind. The first was to deter the prostitute. The second was to use the threat of imprisonment as an indirect means of compelling the prostitute to agree to consent to a probation order, since no power existed to make a probation order without the consent of a convicted woman: with imprisonment as the alternative, the Committee believed the woman would rather agree to have the advice and treatment which the probation service would be able to proffer. This second purpose, if the Wolfenden assumption is correct, will now, as far as young prostitutes are concerned, be achieved by the introduction of the proposed non-custodial supervisory order which will be able to be made without the consent of the woman concerned. The first claimed purpose, that of deterrence, in itself surely cannot alone be a justification for continuing to give the courts power to imprison young prostitutes who are found soliciting. In my judgment there is no evidence to establish that the Street Offences Act has had the deterrent effect anticipated by those who wished to have that piece of legislation. The initial effect of the Act may have had the effect of clearing the streets even as it created a class of souteneurs and middlemen, escort agencies, landlords, club owners, taxi drivers, hotel porters and others who have exploited the young

162

prostitutes. But now the convictions for soliciting mount as do the numbers sentenced to prison. In 1970 2,347 women of all ages were convicted of offences relating to prostitution and 264 received immediate prison sentences. In 1971 2,871 women were convicted of such offences and 286 received immediate prison sentences. A significant number of the young women now in prison either by direct sentence or by way of default in payments of fines have been sent there because of their involvement in soliciting offences. Those who are returning to the streets and attracting these sentences are the least "successful", the most inadequate, with a history of mental breakdown, attempted suicide, alcoholism, drug dependency and often burdened with a variety of physical disorders and deformities. To respond to their dilemmas by giving them deterrent custodial sentences cannot in my view be justified by claiming that this is necessary in order to spare the squeamish in the community who find it offensive to see such people walking in public thoroughfares.

4. I believe, too, that the coming into existence of a non-custodial supervisory order will provide the community with an opportunity to draw back from permitting our courts to be used to buttress the irresponsibility of many of the large stores. The question has to be asked, particularly as it is so often the case that shoplifting offences are carried out by a woman who never steals from an individual, whether the community by incarcerating women shoplifters should pay the cost of the deliberate temptations set up by the salesmen to seduce the shopper and maximise the profits. It is known that when pilferage is too low, some stores become not pleased but apprehensive because they fear this means insufficient salesmanship, that goods are not being made tempting enough and sufficiently accessible. I doubt whether the community should collude with the new supermarkets, food halls and the vogueish large stores designed to attract the heavy spending teenagers, which are attracting so many shoplifters. I do not think that stores determined to increase their sales by ostentatiously displaying goods and at the same time determined to have as few shop assistants as possible, are entitled to expect the community to jail those who have become casualties of the stores' recklessness. The insufficiently controlled parade of wares is evidently too overwhelming for many women disposed to depression, or wrestling with the fetishism or masochism, said to be so often the background to an act of shoplifting; and is, too, irresistible to the young au pair girls afflicted with loneliness, relative poverty and social isolation, who form, in some areas, a significant portion of those convicted for shoplifting.

5. In my view, in all these circumstances it would be sufficient to vest in a court dealing with a young woman recidivist shoplifter the power to make a non-custodial supervisory order. The power of the court to make custodial sentences in such cases should be ended.

6. Nor do I consider that the powers of the courts, as at present, to imprison a young woman convicted of infanticide should be continued. Infanticide is an anomalous offence in our criminal calendar: it curiously requires the prosecution, in order to obtain a conviction for that offence, to prove that the wrongdoing consisted of the killing of the child by its mother within 12 months of the birth and that, at the time of the slaying, the mother was also not responsible for her action because her mind was disturbed as a result of lactation or because the mother had not fully recovered from the birth. Although the

163

offence offends against our usual canons of criminal responsibility, it can in theory attract a sentence of life imprisonment. In very recent years the few young women who have been convicted of this offence have not been given custodial sentences but I do not believe it is enough to hope that custodial sentences will simply fall into desuetude. The trial of a young woman charged with this offence is often long drawn out as the offence cannot unfortunately be disposed of in the lower courts, and consequently after the initial proceedings the hapless mother has to await the finalisation of the trial at a higher court. No legal adviser can, during this waiting period, give such a woman a guarantee that she will not be deprived of her liberty. There is in my view no justification in adding such uncertainty to the anguish of a young woman who emerges from the trauma of childbirth to discover she has not a living child to suckle but one she, unknowingly to herself, has strangled or suffocated. If the court possessed the new power of a non-custodial supervisory order it would have sufficient discretion at its disposal: the ending of the availability of a custodial sentence for this offence is in my view overdue.

7. More, I think the widespread disquiet expressed by many sections of the public over the custodial sentences passed on emotionally deprived women, often deluded and schizophrenic, who have been jailed for child snatching has much justification. There is a clear distinction between child stealing by such a young woman and the manipulative stealing of a child by a male, where the child is being used as a pawn in a parental struggle: and the sentencing power of which the court should be seised should reflect the distinction. Indeed, there is a view held by some that the imposition of heavy custodial sentences upon these impulsive women is adding to, not diminishing, the dangers which can fall upon a stolen baby: unstable women who have taken a child may well abandon rather than return the baby if they are aware that returning the child may result in a heavy sentence of imprisonment. The exercise of the supervisory and controlling power possible under the new proposed order should in my view be sufficient to deal with a young woman offender, and a lack of custodial sentencing power in the court may help to make it a little more likely that the stolen baby is returned unharmed.

8. Apart from my view that, with the introduction of the new non-custodial supervisory order, there are offences where custodial sentences become inappropriate for young women, there is a further dissent which I record. I wholly concur in the view that the courts are insufficiently equipped to prescribe the treatment of a young offender and even more ill-equipped to prescribe subsequent treatment after the court has decreed the necessity of some intervention; but I believe that the executive authority which, under the present proposals, will be making the treatment decisions must be insulated from transitory political pressures.

9. The present proposals intend that under a custody and control order and a supervision and control order decisions as to when any offender should serve his sentence in a non-custodial setting within the community, and decisions relating to the degree of control and supervision to be exercised over the offender in the community, will be taken by the Home Secretary. In practice most of these decisions will be taken by local or regional officers with the benefit of advisory bodies; but the responsibility for the release of the offender

out of custody and the degree of control of the offender in the community will fall directly upon the Home Secretary. I believe that such an assumption of responsibility will, from time to time, expose considered penal policies to intolerable pressures.

10. Revulsion against particular highly publicised crimes, ill considered sympathies prompted by manipulating hysterical offenders, escapes by dangerous offenders, a few violent actions by offenders on licence, can all separately or together build up a temporary and irrational public opinion which can overwhelm the most stoical of Home Secretaries. Advising officials are also not cocooned from such gusts of opinion, and I believe grave injustices could result when those called upon to make decisions affecting the personal liberty of individual young offenders are so vulnerable to general political considerations. The most likely consequence of a structure which placed such responsibility on the Home Secretary for so many individual cases is that officials will err heavily on the side of caution, that justifiable releases from custody to community will not take place, and that excessive and unnecessary restrictions will sometimes be imposed on those to be supervised in the community.

11. More, I believe Members of Parliament will be placed in a disagreeable position when it becomes increasingly understood that the individual decisions to detain and control young offenders can be challenged in Parliament. It will be difficult even for the most conscientious of MPs, importuned by parents, to resist requests that the Home Secretary's decisions about their constituent's Johnny should be fought. The floor of the House of Commons is, however, not always a suitable arena for appellate jurisdiction.

12. A transfer of authority in the field of young offenders, from the judiciary to the executive is a necessary but delicate operation. I believe many of the difficulties that result from such a transfer could be minimised if the ultimate responsibility for the decision making affecting individual young offenders rested with a youth authority appointed by the Home Secretary. There are clearly administrative difficulties, which have been canvassed, to such a proposal. I am not, however, finally persuaded that these objections are overwhelming. I am of the view that such an authority should be created, that the Home Secretary should be responsible to Parliament for the general policy pursued by it, but the responsibility for the day-to-day and individual decisions would fall upon the authority alone. Some such distancing of a treatment authority from external pressures is in my opinion necessary if the objectives of the Advisory Council are to be achieved.

NOTE OF RESERVATION TO CHAPTER 8

by

Mr. Timothy Raison, MP

1. Prison and borstals are rare among institutions in that the reasons for sending people to them largely differ from the objectives of the institutions once those people have arrived. We send someone to school or hospital so that he may be educated or treated, and that is what schools and hospitals set out to do. But we send an offender to prison largely to deter him from further offences or to register society's disapproval of his action. But once he is there, we try to treat him. Only keeping the offender out of circulation is clearly common to both sets of objectives.

2. This gulf between the different sets of objectives poses a clear dilemma when we come to consider early release. On the one hand, society—through the courts—wants the offender to be locked up for a while. On the other hand, treatment considerations may suggest that he should be quickly let out. If these latter considerations are valid, the case for allowing early release is obviously strong. On the other hand, if release is allowed too readily, the expressive and deterrent objectives of the court could be undermined—and it is worth pointing out that the deterrent element in a sentence is directed not only at the individual who is being sentenced but at all other potential offenders.

3. This leads me to the view that while the possibility of early release is certainly desirable, the right body to give ultimate approval to such release is a court, rather than the executive. I know that there are practical difficulties about this—not least that the particular members of the court which imposed the sentence will often not be available to review it. I recognise too that there is great pressure on the time of courts. Nevertheless, it is very important to preserve the confidence of both the courts and of the public, and the system which the Council proposes could, in my view, weaken this confidence by giving the impression that the sentence of the court is somewhat nominal. I propose therefore that a court of comparable level to that which imposed the original sentence, ideally the same court though not necessarily with identical membership, should have to determine proposals brought to it by the executive for early release—that is release before the normal period of remission. If this was accepted, I would regard the restriction order as superfluous.

4. If my proposal is not adopted, I would prefer to see the Boards of Visitors acting as the advisory bodies on release. They should certainly sit with the appropriate governor and a probation officer present—or include both as members. But I fear that if we create separate bodies we shall further weaken the existing Boards, whereas giving them this power could help to strengthen them.

NOTE OF DISSENT

by

Mr. Richard Lowry, QC

1. This note of dissent relates to the period of three months which, the Council recommends, should be the minimum period which any court can impose when sentencing a young offender to a custody and control order (Chapter 8, paragraph 188); and to the proposal (Chapter 8, paragraphs 190 and 191) that before making a custody and control order, every court must, as a matter of legal requirement, obtain a social enquiry report.

2. While at first sight these may seem to be matters of detail, they involve, in my opinion, fundamental matters of sentencing philosophy, and of legislative practice.

3. It is stressed in this report that supervision in the community gives the best chance of reforming the young offender. The idea that prolonged training in a regime similar to that found in an English residential Public School is the answer to the young offender problem is out of date. It is now recognised that custody often produces more problems than it solves as far as the person, and the personality, of the offender is concerned. When custody has to be imposed, we should strive to re-introduce the offender into the ordinary mainstream of his life as soon as possible (albeit with supervision and control). More flexible powers of release by the executive are recommended; and it is recognised that some young offenders might stand the best chance of avoiding further offences if they are released after a period of days rather than weeks or months. Agreeing with all these views, as I do, it seems to me to follow that when a court decides that a custody sentence is imperative, the same court should have the power to award a short custody sentence, such as four weeks. Under the custody and control order proposals, this period of custody would be followed by a minimum of six months supervision in the community.

4. Most people think that the human instinct for revenge and retribution should be controlled; it follows that after a custody sentence (which inevitably contains a sharp element of retribution) has been passed, both the offender and the society which imposed the penalty should as quickly as possible put the past (the offence, and the retribution) behind them, and look to the future. But every sentence, even a fine or a probation order, which restricts freedom in any way automatically contains a retributive element. The sharpest dividing line in sentences is that between a sentence involving custody, and one which does not. It follows that the retributive element in a custody sentence is especially present; it exists as a fact of life, and nothing can be done to eliminate it. And so, in my opinion, the courts should have the same power as the executive to make the custody sentence a short one.

5. Fears are expressed that if a sentence of four weeks were possible, severe or illiberal courts will use a sentence of four weeks custody too freely. This is to

assume that a severe court will hesitate to pass a sentence of three months, but succumb too easily to the temptation of passing a sentence of 1 month. This I do not believe to be true. When it is stressed that the constructive part of any sentence is not the time inside, but the time that follows under supervision outside, it seems to me to follow that courts should be encouraged, and empowered, to make the time spent inside as short as possible.

6. At a time when determinate sentences for adults can rise as high as 30 years, it is important to remember that to young people, time, and the scale of time, is very different to that of their elders. It is easier to look back on five years at the age of 50 than it is to look forward five years at the age of 20. Three years, three months, even three weeks, seem in prospect long periods of time to young people. Further, it should not be forgotten by the middle-aged that custody for young people involves confinement with others of the same sex and deprivation of the company of young people of the opposite sex: and this at a time when they have only comparatively recently grown to knowledge and awareness of sexuality.

7. Reference has been made in the report to section 3 of the Criminal Justice Act 1961, which fettered the courts' power to send young persons to prison. The object was to keep young people out of custody, but the result was that some young people were sentenced to longer periods in custody than were really necessary. My fear and expectation is that the three month minimum proposal will have a similar unintended effect.

8. Two examples when courts feel compelled to pass custodial sentences on young offenders are the "football lout" who commits an offence of violence; and the young person who persistently appears in court for offences of dishonesty, and persistently fails to respond to non-custodial supervision. In the absence of facilities for weekend detention, the court should have the power to make the first custodial sentence a really short one. Supervision in the community will follow it.

9. If a court decides on a custodial sentence, it is often better, more effective, and indeed humane to the offender, that the sentence should be imposed as soon as possible; this also means that it will be finished as soon as possible. This factor can, of course, conflict with the desirability of the court having as much information as possible about the offender before passing sentence. In my view courts should be encouraged to obtain, and to consider, social enquiry reports (as they already are, and do); they should not be compelled to obtain them by Act of Parliament. Indeed, while a statute can compel the obtaining of a document, it can not effectively compel anyone to consider its contents, any more than it can compel that person to be charitable, or to be chaste. I also think it is possible to exaggerate the number of courts which jump too quickly to ill-considered decisions. On the other side of the coin, the obtaining of a social enquiry report can mean a delay of weeks, leaving an offender in a limbo of suspense.

10. It is essential that those who sentence should keep abreast of modern thinking and knowledge, including the views of sensible young people; they should not content themselves with reflecting the opinion of the older generation of the public. But courts are not always the bastions of illiberality. In trying to fetter the powers of the harsh court, Parliament can easily prevent the sensible one

from coming quickly to a sensible decision. In my view, such matters as minimum sentences and the consideration of reports are spheres in which Parliament should encourage sentencers, but not seek to fetter discretion entirely by mandatory provisions.

NOTE OF DISSENT

by

The Lady James of Rusholme and Professor Nigel Walker

SUSPENSION OF CUSTODY AND CONTROL ORDERS

The report argues that the principle of the suspended sentence should not be applied to custody and control orders (paragraph 239). We disagree, for the following reasons:

1. The report in effect recommends that the courts should have power to apply to young adults virtually any sentence or measure which can be applied to adult offenders. The only important exception is the suspended custodial sentence. It is true that we recommend that ordinary prison sentences should not be imposable on young adults; but the custody and control order which we recommend instead is—from the formal point of view at least—a very similar substitute. It would be reducible in length by remission and by a form of "junior parole"; and would be followed, like the present prison sentences imposed on many adults and young adults, by compulsory supervision for a period after release. The onus is therefore on those who believe that, unlike short prison sentences, short custody and control orders should never be suspended to produce a convincing argument in support of this view.

2. Two arguments are offered. One is that because young adults change and mature rapidly their needs and characteristics might have changed substantially by the time a suspended sentence fell to be implemented. But does not the Criminal Justice Act 1967 allow a court not to bring the suspended sentence into operation if it is "of opinion that it would be unjust to do so in view of all the circumstances which have arisen since the suspended sentence was passed"?

3. The more impressive argument is that courts should not impose custody and control orders unless they are of the opinion that no method of dealing with the offender other than his immediate—or almost immediate—committal to custody is appropriate. But this is almost exactly what the Criminal Justice Act 1972 stipulates in regard to the imprisonment of an adult offender if he has not previously been sentenced to imprisonment (section 14). Yet in such circumstances a court is allowed to decide that the prison sentence should nevertheless be suspended (section 11(3)).

4. In fact the report's reasoning on this point makes sense only if its underlying but unstated assumption is recognised. This is that there is something different about the sort of custody to which young adults would be subjected: something which makes it inappropriate to use a custody and control order as a threat. Yet elsewhere we have—rightly in our view—disclaimed the optimism of the past about the special virtues of custodial establishments for young adults. Indeed we have said that if there were sufficient resources we should like to see the system which we recommend extended to older age-groups. Would we then recommend the abolition of the suspended sentence for adults?

170

5. This brings us to the heart of the matter. The report has been drafted at a time when the suspended sentence has been under a cloud, partly because the (now repealed) mandatory provisions of the Criminal Justice Act 1967 were unpopular with sentencers, partly because sentencers—without being under any compulsion to do so—had used it where before they would have fined the offender or put him on probation, and partly because its introduction had failed to produce a spectacular reduction in the prison population. Note that there is as yet no evidence to show that it is ineffective; that is, to show that nobody is deterred from a further offence by the knowledge that if reconvicted within the operational period he is almost certain to be imprisoned. The commonsense assumption underlying the idea of the suspended sentence is that *some* people can be deterred in this way, and therefore need not go to prison. If this is assumed to be true of adults of 21 or older, can it be assumed not to be true of young adults of 20 or younger? Or are our colleagues assuming that whereas the threat of a prison sentence would be effective for some young adults, the threat of a custody and control order would not? Surely not, for anyone acquainted with offenders knows that the all-important feature of any kind of sentence[1] is the extent to which it curtails their liberty. The nature of the regime is usually unknown to them, and at best a secondary consideration.

6. It seems to us a cardinal principle of sentencing that unless there is some overriding consideration such as the protection of the public, sentencers ought to try every measure short of custody before resorting to it. One such measure is the suspended custodial sentence.

7. If custody and control orders could be suspended, this would to some extent achieve the objectives which led Mr. Blom-Cooper, Mr. Stirling, Professor Trasler and Lady Wootton to enter their note of dissent; and would do so without taking the decision to impose custody completely out of the hands of courts.

---

[1] We are not of course overlooking the stigma of conviction: but that applies whatever the sentence.

NOTE OF DISSENT

by

The Hon. Mr. Justice Waller, OBE, Mr. Richard Lowry, QC
Sir Leon Radzinowicz and Mr. George Twist, CBE, QPM

1. We are sympathetic with the underlying motive of Chapter 10 that a greater proportion of young offenders should, if possible, be kept out of custody. We are, however, in fundamental disagreement with the proposals for temporary detention contained in paragraphs 283–288.

2. These proposals contemplate a power of detention against the will of the offender for not more than 72 hours where the supervising officer satisfies a magistrate either that a breach of the conditions of the order has been committed, or that he has reasonable grounds for believing that a breach of the order or the commission of an offence is in contemplation. The offender has no opportunity of challenging the supervising officer.

3. Elsewhere in Chapter 10 (paragraphs 279–282) there are specific provisions for dealing with breaches of conditions. Insofar as the above proposal deals with a breach it deprives the offender of the right to a hearing which is given in those provisions. Insofar as the above proposal deals with a contemplated breach or contemplated offence it depends solely on the opinion of the supervisor.

4. Our main reasons for rejecting these proposals are:

   (i) This arrest will be based on the opinion or assertion of the supervisor which the offender has no opportunity of challenging. Arrest which is based on opinion is arbitrary, and the fact that it is limited to 72 hours, is backed by a magistrate's warrant and is made under the authority of an Act of Parliament does not prevent its being arbitrary. We have fought against arbitrary power for centuries. It should not be re-introduced in however limited a manner under the guise of penal reform. Requiring the arrest to be authorised by a magistrate's warrant will be a protection against obvious bad faith, but little else. Once the probation officer forms an opinion which is in good faith the magistrate will normally grant the warrant. He will have no good reason for refusing.

   (ii) The proposal would effect a radical change in the role of the supervisor. At present the probation officer exercises his influence with the consent of the probationer. If the latter does not co-operate the probation officer can take action only if the non-co-operation is a breach of the terms of the order.

   (iii) The proposal would provide opportunity for injustice or, what is more important, a feeling of injustice, eg, where there is a personality clash between supervisor and supervised—the one thinks there is no co-operation, the other thinks there is no understanding. The correctness of the decision would, in practice, be incapable of challenge.

172

5. Speaking generally, much of the Council's thinking on this point is based, as we see it, on assimilating the treatment of the young adult offender to that of the child. In our view this is an extension of childhood which should not be made. The treatment of young adults as a special case does not justify treating them as children. They are adults at 18, free from parental control, and they are entitled to the same protection as other adults.

6. Even if there were strong evidence of the great advantages which would accrue to society, we would hesitate long before supporting such a proposal. But there is, in our opinion, no such evidence. The case for it is simply based on a practice found useful by supervisors, which has grown up in California, of detaining juveniles who are on probation, but releasing them before they have to be charged, ie within 48 hours.

7. Temporary detention in the manner proposed should, in our view, be rejected.

8. Having said that we cannot agree with the temporary detention proposals, it is necessary to consider whether or not there is a case for the supervision and control order without this power.

9. There are three other features which distinguish a supervision and control order from a probation order:

 (i) The absence of formal consent

 (ii) The facility for varying the conditions of the order without reference to the courts

 (iii) The requirement for more intensive supervision and therefore greater resources.

    (a)   When a probation order is to be made the reality of the consent is questionable. When the offender is asked if he agrees to the making of a probation order he knows that the alternative, if he says he does not consent, will possibly be a custodial sentence. Accordingly he says he agrees. But whether the probation order is effective or not will depend on the degree of co-operation which he gives to the supervisor and not on the form of words when sentence was passed. Furthermore, the real sanction will be the power of the supervisor to refer the case back to the court. It seems that the position which would exist under a supervision and control order would be, for all practical purposes, the same. The success of the order would depend on the degree of co-operation attained by the supervisor and the sanction would be the power to refer the case back to the court.

    (b)   The supervisor's ability to vary the conditions is a useful power but we do not see why the present procedure for varying conditions should not be improved to enable variations to be more easily made even where there has been no breach of the existing conditions. Here again success will depend on co-operation.

    (c)   A very important distinguishing feature is the more intensive supervision proposed. This is, in our opinion, the most important part of the proposed order.

173

10. Although, as we have indicated, once temporary detention is removed there is otherwise little to distinguish this order from a probation order, it may well be that there should be a different name for an order which requires more intensive supervision:

(i) So that those courts which regard probation as a soft answer may be encouraged to use a non-custodial remedy,

(ii) So that the public may know that such supervision is required, and

(iii) So that it may be clearly understood that increased resources should be made available.

APPENDIX A

PROCEDURE OF THE REVIEW

1. The terms of the reference made by the Home Secretary to the Council in May 1970 were:

> "to review the arrangements for the treatment of young offenders aged 17 and over, with particular reference to custodial methods of treatment (including after-care arrangements) and the powers of the courts; and to make recommendations."

In contrast to earlier reviews which were undertaken by sub-committees of the Council, the young offender review was carried out by the Council as a whole. However, much of the detailed work was done in small working groups on sentencing and assessment, treatment in isolation from the community, treatment within the community and (at a later stage) treatment of young women offenders. These working groups met in all on 74 occasions. The full Council held 26 meetings for the purpose of the young offender review: these included 2 weekend residential conferences (at Cumberland Lodge, in Windsor Great Park) and 2 two-day meetings.

2. At the outset of the review we issued a general invitation to individuals and organisations to submit written material for the Council's consideration. Those who responded to this invitation are listed at Annex A. The Home Office and other Government Departments contributed preparatory papers and many memoranda on specific matters at our request.

3. Rather than take formal "oral evidence", the Council and the working groups invited numerous persons, as individuals or as representatives of organised bodies, to meet them for informal discussion. Those who assisted the Council in this way are listed in Annex B. This list includes, at the end, a number of officials from the Home Office (Criminal, Probation and After-Care and Prison Departments, including present or former serving members of the "field services") and the Scottish Home and Health Department who regularly attended meetings of the Council and/or the working groups for the purpose of supplying information and otherwise assisting the Council.

4. We were anxious to collect information on how the young adult offender system was viewed by those who are committed to it. We did this in two ways. First, where possible we made arrangements, during our visits to custodial establishments (see below), to meet trainees singly or in groups. Secondly, we asked selected custodial establishments to arrange for groups of trainees to discuss the system under various headings, and the results of these discussions were transmitted to us.

5. We carried out a full programme of visits to young offender penal establishments in this country. Some of these were general purpose visits, others had particular objectives such as the examination of assessment and documentation procedures and participation in a "workshop" (ie a series of discussion sessions in which staff, trainees and others discuss matters such as the problems of resettlement) at Everthorpe Borstal. In the course of the review and the preceding review on detention centres, one or more members of the Council visited each borstal, detention centre and young prisoners' centre in the country, and a number of other prisons and remand centres were also visited. Some establishments were visited more than once. We also visited a number of hostels for persons on probation or released from custody.

6. Information was collected about the practice in dealing with young offenders in a number of other countries in Europe, North America and Australasia. Members of the Council made a number of overseas visits: to Denmark, Finland, Sweden, the Federal German Republic and the Netherlands, and to the United States of America, where time was spent in Washington, New York and California in particular. These overseas visits included long periods of discussion with administrators, field workers and academics, as well as visits to custodial establishments and non-custodial treatment facilities.

7. Members of the Council considered a quantity of material reporting the results of research in this and other countries, and held discussions with members of the Home Office Research Unit and University researchers. The research findings we found of particular relevance are summarised in Appendix D.

ANNEX A

List of organisations and individuals who submitted written material to the Council

Organisations
Apex Charitable Trust
Association of Chief Police Officers of England, Wales and Northern Ireland
Association of Municipal Corporations
Association of Teachers in Penal Establishments
Board of Visitors of Wetherby Borstal
Bow Group
British Association of Social Workers
British Council of Churches
British Psychoanalytical Society
British Psychological Society
British Society of Criminology
Central Council of Probation and After-Care Committees
Church of England Council for Social Aid
Commission for Social Welfare (A Sub-committee of the Roman Catholic Bishops' Conference, representing the Roman Catholic Hierarchy in England and Wales)
Community Development Trust
Conference of Principal Probation Officers
County Councils' Association
Devon, Exeter and Torbay Probation and After-Care Service
Free Church Federal Council
General Council of the Bar of England and Wales
HM Inspectors of Schools
Hampshire Probation and After-Care Committee
Hertfordshire Ecumenical Executive
Howard League for Penal Reform
Institution of Professional Civil Servants (Chaplains' Section)
Institution of Professional Civil Servants (Prison Medical Officers' Section)
Justices' Clerks' Society
Law Society
London Magistrates' Clerks' Association
Magistrates' Association
National Association of Justices' Clerks' Assistants
National Association of Probation Homes and Hostels
National Association of Probation Officers
National Association of Voluntary Hostels
National Association of Youth Clubs
Nottingham Boys' Probation Hostel Management Committee
Police Federation
Prison Officers' Association
Prison Reform Council
Radical Alternatives to Prison
Rainer Foundation
Royal Medico-Psychological Association
St. Christopher's Fellowship
Salvation Army Men's Social Services
Society of City and Borough Clerks of the Peace
Society of Civil Servants, Prison and Borstal Governors' Branch
Society of Civil Servants, Home Office Prison Department (Outstations) Branch
Society of Friends (Penal Affairs Committee)
South West Midlands Housing Association
Tavistock Clinic
Women's Royal Voluntary Service

Individuals

(Here, and in Annex B, those who hold or have previously held a post concerned with the treatment of offenders are so identified. Unless otherwise stated, the post was that held at the time the evidence was submitted.)

Mrs. V. Bennett, JP
Commander E. Bibby
Mr. R. L. Bradley, CBE, MC (formerly a Commissioner of Prisons)
Mr. C. M. D. Burnett, MBE, Governor of Gaynes Hall Borstal
Mr. Justice Caulfield
Inspector I. Claydon, Metropolitan Police (Officer in Charge of Greenwich
    Attendance Centre)
Mr. F. Cork, Deputy Warden, Blantyre House Detention Centre
Mr. R. Duncan Fairn, formerly Assistant Under-Secretary of State, Prison Department
Mrs. S. M. Fulford
Mr. L. Haywood, Prison Officer, Lowdham Grange Borstal
His Honour Judge J. B. Hobson, then Deputy Chairman of North-East London
    Quarter Sessions
Mr. S. Hodson, Prison Officer, Feltham Borstal
Mr. Justice (now Lord Justice) James
Dr. H. V. R. Jones, Visiting Psychotherapist to Cardiff and Swansea Prisons
Mr. Justice (now Lord Justice) Lawton
Mr. D. C. Leach, Deputy Governor, Dover Borstal
Mr. F. Liesching, Deputy Regional Director, Prison Department South West Region
Mr. E. Mallett, Senior Prison Officer, Wetherby Borstal
His Honour Judge Marnan, then Chairman of the North-East London Quarter Sessions
His Honour Judge Peter Mason, QC, then Deputy Chairman of North-East London
    Quarter Sessions
Sir Frank Milton, Chief Metropolitan Magistrate
Mr. A. A. Nicholson, Senior Welfare Officer, Wormwood Scrubs Prison
Mr. K. Parkinson, Senior Officer, Low Newton Remand Centre
Sir James Pitman
Mr. A. F. Rutherford, Deputy Governor of Everthorpe Borstal
Mr. A. Samuels
Mr. O. Smith
Dr. E. Stratta
His Honour Judge Irvon Sunderland, then Chairman of Warwickshire
    Quarter Sessions
Mr. Justice Talbot
Mr. J. P. Taylor
Mr. Justice Thompson
Mr. Justice Veale (since deceased)
Mr. D. G. Waddilove, formerly Director of Borstal Administration, Home Office
    Prison Department
Mrs. E. Warburton, JP
Mr. J. D. Wheeler, Assistant Governor, Wandsworth Prison
Mr. E. V. H. Williams, Deputy Governor of Grendon Prison

In addition the views of a number of Her Majesty's Judges were forwarded to the Council by the Lord Chief Justice.

List of those who, either in a representative capacity or as individuals attended meetings with Council members for discussion*

Home Office

(i) Prison Department Headquarters

Mr. W. R. Cox, CB	Director General of the Prison Service	⎫ Members
Mr. A. Bainton	Controller (Operations)	⎪ of the
Mr. M. S. Gale, MC	Controller (Planning and Development)	⎬ Prisons
Mr. T. G. Weiler	Controller (Administration)	⎪ Board
Dr. I. G. W. Pickering, VRD	Director of the Prison Medical Service	⎭

Mr. D. G. Hewlings, DFC, AFC   Assistant Controller (now Controller (Operations) and a member of the Prisons Board)

Mr. A. S. Baxendale   Chief Education Officer
Mr. W. B. Burkey   Deputy Chief Education Officer
The Rt. Rev. Mgr. A. Cunningham   Senior Roman Catholic Priest
Mr. F. C. Foster   Assistant Director
Mr. W. N. Hyde   Assistant Secretary
The Rev. Canon L. Lloyd Rees   Chaplain General
Mr. K. J. Neale, OBE   Director of Industries and Supply
Mr. A. Pearson   Deputy Chief Education Officer
Mr. T. H. Pool   Senior Vocational Training Officer, Directorate of Works

(ii) Prison Department Establishments and Regional Offices

Mr. W. J. Booth   Principal, Prison Service Staff College
Dr. M. Bull   Now Governor, Holloway Prison
Miss M. A. Carden   Assistant Governor, Risley Remand Centre
Dr. L. Carr   Senior Medical Officer, Ashford Remand Centre
Mr. J. V. J. Donald   Principal Psychologist, Risley Remand Centre
Mr. R. M. Dauncey   Governor, Feltham Borstal
Dr. R. M. L. Dry   Medical Officer, Grendon Prison
Dr. M. J. L. Ellis   Medical Officer, Feltham Borstal
Mr. V. P. Holloway   Principal Psychologist, Wormwood Scrubs Borstal Allocation Centre
Miss J. A. M. Kinsley   Governor, Bullwood Hall Borstal
Mr. L. C. Oxford   Governor, Ashford Remand Centre
Miss O. Parry   Deputy Regional Director, Northern Regional Office
Mr. A. F. Rutherford   Deputy Governor, Everthorpe Borstal
Rev. H. D. Searle   Chaplain, Hollesley Bay Borstal and Detention Centre
Miss J. M. Wilkinson   Welfare Officer, Askham Grange Prison
Mr. E. V. H. Williams   Deputy Governor, Grendon Prison

(iii) Probation and After-Care Department

Mr. E. N. Kent   Assistant Secretary
Miss M. G. Packer   Inspector

(iv) Establishment Department

Mr. J. H. J. Beck   Assistant Secretary

(v) Home Office Research Unit

Dr. C. Banks   Senior Research Officer
Miss N. Goodman   Senior Research Officer

(vi) Statistical Division

Mrs. E. H. Gibson   Chief Statistician

---

* The list does not include the many members of staff of young offender establishments and others whom members met during visits in this country and abroad.

Department of Health and Social Security
Dr. P. Mason
Mr. T. Harris

Staff of local probation and after-care services

Miss J. M. Bickerdike	Probation Officer, Inner London
Mr. J. D. Corby	Assistant Principal Probation Officer, Surrey
Mr. K. L. Howe	Senior Probation Officer, Manchester and Salford
Mr. M. T. Mullany	Senior Probation Officer, Yorkshire West Riding
Miss E. C. Murphy	Senior Probation Officer, Middlesex
Mr. S. Ratcliffe	Deputy Principal Probation Officer, Inner London
Miss G. F. Rawlings	Senior Probation Officer, Inner London
Miss G. M. Stafford	Assistant Principal Probation Officer, Inner London
Mr. D. A. C. Woodward	Assistant Principal Probation Officer, Suffolk

Representative bodies and individuals

Mr. H. Barr — Central Council for Education and Training in Social Work

Mr. G. W. Appleyard
Mr. A. Bannerman† } Conference of Principal Probation Officers
Mr. F. V. Jarvis

Mr. R. Sims
Mrs. J. Williams } Magistrates' Association Working Party of the Inner London and
Mr. M. Wolff } South East London Branch

Mr. R. L. Morrison* } National Association for the Care and
Mr. N. Hinton } Resettlement of Offenders

Mr. W. H. Clarke, JP
Mr. A. Henden Cole } National Association of Probation Homes and Hostels
Miss S. Townson

Mr. T. Bales
Mr. D. S. Bell } National Association of Probation Officers
Mr. C. L. Bruggen

Mr. K. Stoneley, JP — National Association of Voluntary Hostels

Mr. L. J. Barnsdale
Mr. D. Brisco } Prison Officers' Association
Mr. F. G. Castell
Mr. F. W. Money

Mr. A. P. Bishop } Society of Civil Servants, Prison and
Mr. P. Timms } Borstal Governors' Branch
Mr. B. D. Wigginton

Mr. F. Baden-Powell, ARIBA
Mr. L. H. Crew — Principal, Redhill Approved Achool
Mrs. S. Dell
Professor T. C. N. Gibbens, MBE
Dr. A. Graham
Mr. J. K. Halstead
Miss J. H. Hemming
Mr. P. Hodgkinson, ARIBA
Dr. R. Hood
Mr. Hugh Klare
Mr. F. H. McClintock
Dr. R. F. Sparks
Dr. A. Hyatt Williams

---

† Mr. Bannerman also attended a working group meeting in an individual capacity.

* Mr. Morrison, now deceased, attended on a regular basis meetings of the working group dealing with treatment in the community.

Additionally, the following regularly attended meetings of the Council and/or its working groups:

Home Office
    Criminal Department   Mr. M. J. Moriarty

    Prison Department   Mr. D. E. R. Faulkner
                                          Mr. N. C. Honey
                                          Mrs. J. Kelley, OBE
                                          Mr. A. Straker

    Probation and After-Care Department   Mr. M. H. Hogan
                                          Mr. R. W. Speirs
                                          Mr. C. T. Swann

    Scottish Home and Health Department   Mr. D. J. Cowperthwaite

APPENDIX B

THE CURRENT SYSTEM OF TREATMENT OF YOUNG OFFENDERS

NOTE BY THE HOME OFFICE

1. This Appendix describes the existing powers of the courts to deal with young adult offenders aged 17 and under 21,[1] and the treatment facilities. Paragraphs 5–37 set out in simplified form the main statutory provisions governing the powers available to the courts to deal with young offenders aged 17 and under 21, and the consequences of each measure in terms of such matters as release arrangements, supervision, recall and other controls and restrictions. (The reader who wishes to study in more detail the qualifications, restrictions and exceptions relating to the general provisions is advised to look at the relevant statutes.) The use which the courts make of the available powers is examined briefly in the tables in paragraph 39.

2. The Council's terms of reference invite it to concentrate on custodial sentences for young offenders, and accordingly much the greater part of this appendix (paragraphs 40–162) describes in some detail the existing custodial system for young offenders. Paragraphs 40–47 discuss some general and organisational questions; paragraphs 48–140 describe custodial provision for young men; provision for young women is dealt with in paragraphs 141–162.

3. Paragraphs 163–200 deal more briefly with the provision for treatment in the community, including the approved probation hostel system, which is described in rather more detail in paragraphs 174–195.

4. The Appendix concludes with a brief description of the powers to deal with offenders under the age of 17.

THE POWERS AVAILABLE TO THE COURTS TO DEAL WITH YOUNG OFFENDERS

Custodial sentences

5. The custodial sentences available to the courts in dealing with young offenders aged 17 and over are: detention in a detention centre; borstal training; and imprisonment. The relevant statutory provisions are outlined in the following paragraphs. Borstal and detention centre training are available also in respect of offenders under 17, though if the Children and Young Persons Act 1969 were brought fully into effect the minimum age for committal to these establishments would be raised to 17. As regards detention centres there are separate committal arrangements and separate centres for offenders aged 17 and over and those under 17 (with provision for offenders to be transferred between junior and senior centres if their maturity suggests that a transfer would be in their best interests); there is no similar distinction in the borstal system.

(i) *Detention centres*

6. Section 4 of the Criminal Justice Act 1961 enables a court to order an offender aged 14 and under 21 to be detained in a detention centre in any case where it has power, or would have power but for the statutory restrictions on the imprisonment of young offenders (paragraph 17), to impose a sentence of imprisonment. An order cannot be made unless the court has been notified by the Secretary of State that a detention centre is available for the reception from that court of persons of his class or description:

---

[1] From time to time in this Appendix "17–21" is used as a convenient shorthand version of "17 and under 21".

detention centres have been made available to all courts in England and Wales for the reception of young men aged 14 and under 21 but the only detention centre for girls was withdrawn following a recommendation by the Advisory Council in 1968[1]. An order committing to a senior detention centre (for young offenders aged 17 and over) may be for any period of not less than three months nor more than six; and there is a limit of nine months to the period for which an offender may be detained at any one time under consecutive or overlapping orders. There is no power to suspend a detention centre sentence, but there is power under section 40(3) of the Criminal Justice Act 1967 in certain circumstances, where a suspended sentence of imprisonment has been imposed on a young offender and is activated following a subsequent conviction, to direct that the sentence be served in a detention centre.

7. There is no statutory restriction on the number of times that an offender may be sent to a detention centre; but only in special circumstances, and after the court has considered a report by or on behalf of the Secretary of State, may a detention centre order be made in respect of an offender who is serving or has served a prison sentence of six months or more or a sentence of borstal training. An offender aged 17–21 may not be detained in a detention centre in default of payment of a fine unless, at the start of the period in default, he was already serving a sentence of detention in a detention centre.

8. An offender sent to a detention centre can receive up to one third remission of his sentence. Any time spent on remand in custody before sentence does not count towards the sentence (in contrast to sentences of imprisonment). On release he is subject, under section 13 of and Schedule 1 to the Criminal Justice Act 1961, to compulsory supervision for up to one year. Failure to comply with the requirements of supervision can lead to recall to a detention centre for a period corresponding to the amount of remission received, or 14 days, whichever is the longer.

9. *The Sentence of the Court* (a Home Office handbook for the courts which describes the availability, aims and operation of the various sentences available) summarises the object of detention centres as to "provide a means of treating young offenders for whom a long period of residential training away from home is not yet necessary or justified by their offence, but who cannot be taught respect for the law by such non-custodial measures as fines or probation".[2] The handbook reminds the courts that the centres are not suitable for those seriously handicapped physically or mentally.

(ii) *Borstal training*

10. Under section 20 of the Criminal Justice Act 1948, as amended by the 1961 Act, a sentence of borstal training may be passed on a young offender aged 15 and under 21 convicted on indictment of an offence punishable with imprisonment, where the court is of opinion, having regard to the circumstances of the offence, and after taking into account the offender's character and previous conduct, and any report made on him by or on behalf of the Secretary of State, that it is expedient that he should be detained for training for not less than six months.[3] Only the Crown Court can pass a sentence of borstal training. A magistrates' court which considers that an offender whom it has convicted should receive a sentence of borstal training must commit him to the Crown Court for sentence.[4]

---

[1] *Detention of Girls in a Detention Centre.*

[2] Paragraph 99; and the *Supplement on Detention Centres* (HMSO 1971) paragraph 10.

[3] The offence need not necessarily carry a maximum prison sentence of six months or more. The Court of Appeal has stated that the fact that a sentence of borstal training may have the effect of depriving an offender of his liberty for a longer period than the maximum sentence of imprisonment for the offence is a relevant consideration for the court before a borstal sentence is passed, but it does not deprive the court of power and discretion to impose a borstal sentence. (*R v Amos* [1961] 1 All E.R. 191, 45 Cr. App. R 42; *R v Appleyard* [1963] Crim. L.R. 62).

[4] However, a magistrates' court has power to return an offender to borstal—see paragraph 15 below—and a juvenile court may, on the application of a local authority and with the consent of the Secretary of State for Social Services or for Wales, transfer to borstal a person in care who is accommodated in a community home and whose behaviour is detrimental to the other persons accommodated there (section 31 of the Children and Young Persons Act 1969—see paragraph 204(a) below).

11. Magistrates' courts have two powers of committal to the Crown Court for sentence. First, section 28 of the Magistrates' Courts Act 1952 is a specific power to commit to the Crown Court, with a view to a borstal sentence, an offender convicted by a magistrates' court of an offence (whether indictable or summary) punishable on summary conviction with imprisonment. The obligation on the Crown Court to consider character, conduct and any Home Office report before passing a borstal sentence applies to a magistrates' court contemplating committal under this provision. Second, there is a general power under section 29 of the 1952 Act to commit for sentence a person convicted summarily of an indictable offence whom the court, on obtaining information about character and antecedents, considers to need punishment in excess of the powers of a summary court (nb that this is narrower in extent than section 28). In the former case the Crown Court can pass either a borstal sentence or a sentence within the competence of the summary court. In the latter case it can deal with the offender in any way in which it could have done had he just been convicted on indictment. The Court of Criminal Appeal has favoured the use of section 29, when available, in preference to section 28.[1]

12. Section 44 of the Prison Act 1952 empowers the Secretary of State to transfer to borstal a person under 21 who is serving a sentence of imprisonment, if satisfied that he might with advantage be detained in a borstal; it also empowers him, where a borstal trainee is reported by the Board of Visitors to be incorrigible or to be exercising a bad influence on the other trainees, to commute the unexpired term of the sentence to an equivalent period of imprisonment. The power to transfer a young prisoner to borstal has not been used since the passage of the Criminal Justice Act 1961, and the power of commutation is used only rarely.

13. Under section 45 of the Prison Act 1952 (as amended by the Criminal Justice Act 1961) a person sentenced to borstal training may be detained for up to two years from the date of sentence, and, subject to any direction by the Secretary of State, must be detained for at least six months. Between these limits authority for release of an individual offender is given by the Prison Department, on advice from the Board of Visitors of the training borstal, which in turn takes account of recommendations by the governor and staff at the establishment.

14. A person released from borstal training is subject to supervision for a period of up to two years from the date of release, during which time he must comply with the requirements specified in his licence (which may be modified or cancelled). Failure to comply with the requirements of supervision may result in recall to borstal; and an offender so recalled is liable to be detained until the expiration of two years from the date of his sentence or six months from the date of being taken into custody under the recall order, whichever is the later.

15. When a person sentenced to borstal training is convicted, on indictment or summarily, of an offence committed while he is under supervision or unlawfully at large, and the offence is one for which the court has power (or would have but for the statutory restrictions on the imprisonment of young offenders) to pass a sentence of imprisonment, the court (including a magistrates' court) may order his return to borstal (Criminal Justice Act 1961, section 12). An offender returned to borstal under this provision is liable to be detained for the same period as if he had been recalled for a breach of the supervision requirements (paragraph 14 above). This power is to be distinguished from the power to pass a fresh borstal sentence.

16. *The Sentence of the Court* says of borstal training that it is "the only form of medium-term training available for young offenders . . . who need a longer period of remedial treatment than is available in detention centres, and who are not already so recidivist as to be eligible for a sentence of 18 months or more [see paragraph 18 below]. It is designed to achieve recovery from established criminal habits, and, since re-conviction statistics show that this is, for many young offenders, a slow and difficult process which extends over several years, the period of supervision after release . . . is regarded as an important and integral part of borstal training".[2]

---

[1] *R v Dangerfield*, 1959.
[2] Paragraph 108.

(iii) *Imprisonment*

17. Successive statutes have restricted the power of the courts to impose imprisonment on offenders under 21. No court may impose imprisonment on a person under 17, and under section 17 of the Criminal Justice Act 1948 no court may pass a sentence of imprisonment on a person under 21 unless satisfied that no other method of dealing with him is appropriate. A magistrates' court passing such a sentence is required by section 107(3) of the Magistrates' Courts Act 1952 to state the reason for its opinion that no other method is appropriate, and the reason must be specified in the warrant of commitment and entered in the register.

18. Under section 3 of the Criminal Justice Act 1961 a court may impose a sentence of imprisonment on a young offender only for a term of six months or less, or three years or more. This power is subject to the conditions set out in the previous paragraph and the exceptions referred to later in this paragraph. This restriction on the imposition of medium-term prison sentences is subject to the modification that, where a person has previously served[1] a sentence of imprisonment of not less than six months or a sentence of borstal training, the court may impose a prison sentence of 18 months or more; and where an offender is already serving a sentence of imprisonment at the time the court passes sentence no restrictions apply.

19. Section 3 of the 1961 Act also enables the power to impose sentences of six months or less to be removed by Order in Council, subject to the availability of sufficient detention centre accommodation for those offenders for whom such accommodation would consequently be required. No Order in Council has been made.

20. The provisions of section 39 of the Criminal Justice Act 1967 (as amended by section 11 of the Criminal Justice Act 1972), under which sentences of imprisonment of up to two years may be suspended, apply to young offenders as to those over 21 (and the Crown Court can add a suspended sentence supervision order to a suspended sentence of more than six months). The result of the activation of a suspended sentence of six months or less consecutive to an immediate prison sentence of similar length can be that an offender is received into prison with a sentence of an effective length within the range prescribed by section 3 in relation to individual sentences.

21. A young prisoner sentenced to a term of more than one month but less than 18 months is eligible for release on remission after serving two thirds of his sentence, and is subject after release to supervision for up to 12 months as if he had been released from a detention centre (paragraph 8) above. Young prisoners serving sentences of imprisonment of 18 months or more are normally released on licence under section 60 of the Criminal Justice Act 1967, which enables the Secretary of State to direct that (instead of release with remission) a young prisoner should be released on licence until the expiration of the sentence. A young prisoner is also eligible for release on parole after serving not less than one third of his sentence, or 12 months, whichever expires the later. A young prisoner released on licence, whether under the parole scheme or on his ordinary remission date, is liable to recall for failure to comply with any requirement specified in the licence. In the case of those with sentences of 18 months and over, detention on recall may extend to the date on which the sentence expires, but release in lieu of remission after two thirds of the unexpired portion is usual. In the case of those with sentences of 18 months or less, the period of recall may be the unexpired length of the sentence or 14 days, whichever is longer.

(iv) *Detention in a place approved by the Secretary of State*

22. A person found guilty of murder committed while under the age of 18 must, under section 53 of the Children and Young Persons Act 1933, be sentenced to detention during Her Majesty's Pleasure.[2] Offenders subject to the sentence, or to life imprisonment,

---

[1] The courts have held that "served" in this context requires that the offender must have been released on licence. Thus a person unlawfully at large from or still detained under his first borstal sentence remains subject to the restrictions on imprisonment.

[2] The Criminal Law Revision Committee in their interim report in December 1972 on the Penalty for Murder (Cmnd 5184) recommended that persons convicted of murder committed while under the age of 18 should be detained "in such place and for such period and subject to such conditions as to release as the Secretary of State may direct".

may be released on licence subject to conditions on the recommendation of the Parole Board. The date of release depends on the circumstances of the individual case; the Lord Chief Justice and, if available, the trial judge must be consulted before release is authorised.

Non-custodial sentences

23. The non-custodial measures available to the courts to deal with young offenders aged 17 and under 21 are, with one exception, the same as those available in respect of adults, and are set out in the following paragraphs.

(i) *Absolute and conditional discharge*

24. Under section 7 of the Criminal Justice Act 1948 these measures may be used "where a court by or before which a person is convicted of an offence (not being an offence the sentence for which is fixed by law) is of opinion, having regard to the circumstances including the nature of the offence and the character of the offender, that it is inexpedient to inflict punishment and that a probation order is not appropriate". An order for conditional discharge runs for such period of not more than three years as the court specifies. It differs from the probation order (paragraph 27 below) in that it involves no continuing supervision of the offender and only one condition—that the offender does not commit another offence during the period of the order—can be imposed. If he is convicted of another offence committed during the period of conditional discharge he is liable to be dealt with for the original offence.

(ii) *Binding over*

25. Instead of imposing sentence the Crown Court may, except in the case of murder, require the offender to enter into a recognisance to come up for judgment when called upon. The recognisance may also require the offender in the meantime to keep the peace and be of good behaviour; if the offender fails to comply with this require- ment (not necessarily to the extent of committing a further offence) the recognisance may be forfeited, and he may be brought up and dealt with for the original offence. All courts have power in certain circumstances to require either in addition to or in substitution for any other order that the offender should enter into a recognisance to keep the peace and be of good behaviour. In such cases breach of the conditions of the recognisance is punishable only with forfeiture.[1]

(iii) *Fines*

26. The courts can deal with virtually all offences by means of a fine (often there is power to combine a fine and a custodial sentence). In general the Crown Court has power to impose fines without limit, but the powers of magistrates' courts to impose fines are limited by statute, and rarely exceed a maximum of £400. In fixing the level of a fine, the courts take account of the offender's means as well as the gravity of the offence. The courts have various powers of enforcement of fines, the ultimate sanction for wilful non-payment being committal to prison in default.[2]

(iv) *Probation*

27. Section 3 of the Criminal Justice Act 1948 enables a court to make a probation order for not less than one and not more than three years where—

(*a*) having regard to the circumstances, including the nature of the offence and the character of the offender, the court is of opinion that it is expedient to do so instead of sentencing the offender;

(*b*) the court has explained to the offender in ordinary language the effect of the order and that if he fails to comply with its requirements or commits another offence he will be liable to be sentenced for the original offence; and

---

[1] In addition all courts have power, under section 22 of the Criminal Justice Act 1972, to defer sentence for one specified period of not more than six months. This is simply a postponement of the sentencing decision; at the end of the period of deferment the offender has to appear again before the court for sentence to be passed.

[2] Fines are discussed more fully in paragraphs 13 to 21 of *The Sentence of the Court*; and in chapter 2 of *Non-Custodial and Semi-Custodial Penalties*.

(c) the offender has expressed himself as willing to comply with the requirements of the probation order.

In addition to requiring the offender to be under the supervision of a probation officer during the period of the order, the probation order may also require the offender to comply during the whole or any part of the probation period with such requirements as the court, having regard to the circumstances of the case, considers necessary for securing his good conduct or preventing him from committing further offences. Common requirements of a probation order are: to be of good behaviour and lead an industrious life; to notify the probation officer of any change of address; to keep in touch with the officer in accordance with such instructions as he may from time to time give; and, in particular, if the probation officer so requires, to receive visits from the officer at the offender's home. More specifically the Act empowers the court, after considering the offender's home circumstances, to include requirements relating to his residence, and the offender may be required to reside at a specified institution (usually an approved probation hostel[1]) for a specified period of not more than 12 months from the date of the order or any subsequent amending order. Under section 4 of the Act, as amended by the Criminal Justice Act 1972, a probation order may, subject to certain conditions, be accompanied by a requirement to undergo medical treatment, either on an in-patient or out-patient basis. Finally it is also possible, under section 20 of the Criminal Justice Act 1972, to add to a probation order a requirement that the offender should attend a day training centre (provided that the court has been notified that such a centre is available for persons living in the petty sessions area where the offender lives) for a period not exceeding 60 days, at the discretion of the supervising officer.[2]

28. Failure to comply with the requirements of a probation order may be dealt with either by means of a fine not exceeding £50, in which case the order remains in force, or by discharging the order and sentencing the offender for the original offence.[3] Where it appears that a probation order is no longer appropriate it may be discharged or a conditional discharge may be substituted. Subject to certain restrictions, the requirements of a probation order may be varied.

(v) *Community service*

29. Section 15 of the Criminal Justice Act 1972 empowers a court dealing with an offender aged 17 and over convicted of an offence punishable with imprisonment to make a community service order requiring him to perform unpaid work for such number of hours (being not less than 40 and not more than 240) as may be specified in the order. Before a court can make a community service order it must have been notified by the Secretary of State that there are arrangements for community service in the area in which the offender resides or will reside. Initially pilot schemes are in operation in six areas.[4] The court must also be satisfied that the offender is a suitable person to perform community service work and that provision can be made for him in the local community service scheme. In order to satisfy itself on these points, the court is required to consider a report by a probation officer about the offender and his circumstances. An order cannot be made without the consent of the offender. The work must be performed within 12 months of the date of the order. The court does not specify when the work is to be performed, nor the work to be carried out; these are matters for the organising officer.

30. Breach of the requirements of a community service order may be dealt with in the same way as breach of a probation order: that is, the offender may be fined up to £50 or the order may be revoked and the offender sentenced anew for the original offence. The Act also provides for review of community service orders in cases where breach proceedings would be inappropriate, eg where the offender is prevented through illness

---

[1] See paragraphs 174–195 below.

[2] Initially four experimental centres are being provided in Sheffield (opened February 1973), Glamorgan (opened July 1973), Liverpool (opened July 1973) and London (planned for October 1973). The aim of the centres is to meet the needs of the inadequate recidivist, and they are therefore likely to be slanted towards a somewhat older age group than 17–21.

[3] There is also power in the Criminal Justice Act 1972 to empower courts to deal with breaches of probation orders by means of a community service order, but the provision is not being brought into effect during the period of the pilot community service schemes (see paragraphs 29 and 31 below).

[4] Certain petty sessional divisions in Durham, Kent, Inner London, South West Lancashire, Nottinghamshire and Shropshire.

from completing the work within the 12 months of the order. The normal period of 12 months may be extended; or the order may be revoked and the offender dealt with anew for the offence; or the order may simply be revoked without any consequent order.

31. The 1972 Act also provides for a community service order for breach of requirement of a probation order without prejudice to the continuance of that order, or in lieu of imprisonment in default of payment of a fine. But the provisions are not being brought into force during the pilot community service schemes.

(vi) *Driving disqualification*
32. Disqualification from driving applies to young offenders as to adults.

(vii) *Attendance centres*
33. The additional non-custodial measure available in respect of young offenders, which for the 17–21 age group is available in only two areas, is the attendance centre order.[1] Section 19 of the 1948 Act, as amended by section 10 of the 1961 Act, empowers a magistrates' court to order a person under 21 to attend an attendance centre, where one is available to it, in any case where it has power (or would have but for the statutory restrictions on the imprisonment of young offenders—see paragraph 17)—to order imprisonment (including imprisonment in default of payment of a fine), or for failure to comply with a requirement of a probation order. (The Crown Court has the same powers when dealing with a person who has appealed against the decision of a magistrates' court, or has been committed by a magistrates' court for sentence under section 28 of the Magistrates' Courts Act 1952, but not otherwise.) The total number of hours of attendance must be not less than 12 and not more than 24 hours. The sentence is not available in the case of an offender who has previously been sentenced to imprisonment, borstal training or detention in a detention centre, or has been sent to an approved school. For offenders aged 17 and under 21 only two attendance centres are available at Manchester and Greenwich, which serve only courts in the Manchester and Greater London areas.

Mentally disordered offenders[2]
34. Where an offender needs psychiatric treatment, and satisfactory arrangements are available for him to receive it in the community, or in hospital, either voluntarily or compulsorily (under Part IV of the Mental Health Act), the court may in appropriate cases deal with the offender by conditional or absolute discharge. Psychiatric treatment in the community or in hospital may also be provided as a condition of a probation order (see paragraphs 24 and 27 above). An offender whom a court considers to be in need of psychiatric treatment may also be compulsorily admitted to hospital under section 60 of the Mental Health Act 1959 (with or without restriction on discharge under section 65) or admitted to local authority guardianship. A hospital or a guardianship order may be made by the Crown Court for any offence other than an offence for which the penalty is fixed by law, or by a magistrates' court for an offence punishable on summary conviction with imprisonment. Before making an order the court must be satisfied, on the advice of two doctors approved under the Mental Health Act, that the offender is suffering from mental illness, psychopathic disorder, subnormality or severe subnormality, to a nature or degree which warrants his detention for treatment or reception into guardianship as the case may be, and that the hospital or local authority is prepared to receive him.

35. Under a hospital order under section 60 the doctor or the hospital managers may discharge the patient when they consider that he is well enough. A hospital order is effective for one year in the first instance and may be renewed indefinitely at prescribed intervals by administrative action on the advice of a doctor. If the offence is dealt with by the Crown Court and the court thinks it necessary for the protection of the public, the offender may be made subject to a restriction order under section 65 of the Act in addition to the hospital order. The effect of a restriction order is that the offender cannot be discharged or granted leave, or transferred to another hospital, without the consent of

---

[1] Attendance centres are described more fully in *Non-Custodial and Semi-Custodial Penalties*.
[2] An Inter-Departmental Committee under the chairmanship of Lord Butler of Saffron Walden was set up in September 1972 to examine the law in relation to mentally disordered offenders, and the facilities for their treatment.

the Secretary of State, and the authority for detention under the hospital order does not require renewal at intervals on medical advice. A restriction order may be made for a determinate period or without limit of time.

36. A guardianship order returns the offender to the community under some degree of supervision by conferring on the local authority or other medical officer authorised by the authority the powers exercisable by a father on a child under the age of 14. Again a guardianship order is effective for one year in the first instance and may be renewed by administrative action on the advice of a doctor.

37. For offenders made subject to custodial sentences the prison medical service is able to provide psychiatric treatment for some forms of mental disorder, and special centres have been developed within the prison system to provide facilities for such treatment. The prison medical service cannot however usually deal satisfactorily with forms of mental disorder which are so severe, or result in such disturbed behaviour, that treatment in a specialist psychiatric hospital is necessary. The Secretary of State has power under sections 72–74 of the Mental Health Act 1959 to direct the transfer of a prisoner to hospital for treatment if he is satisfied that the prisoner's mental condition is such as to warrant hospital treatment under detention, and persons so transferred are treated as if subject to hospital orders under section 60 of the Act and, usually, restriction orders under section 65.

Social enquiry reports

38. The Secretary of State has recommended courts to consider a social enquiry report as a normal practice before passing certain custodial sentences and before making a probation order;[1] and as noted in paragraph 29 above courts are required by statute to consider a report before making a community service order.

Use made of the available sentences

39. The following tables show the sentences imposed by magistrates' courts and by higher courts[2] in 1971 on young men aged 17 and under 21, indicating the proportion which each sentence represents of the total for each category. Comparative tables for the years 1964–71 are in tables 10–15 of Appendix C.

1971   Magistrates' courts

	Indictable offences		Non-indictable (non-motoring)		Motoring		Total	
	No.	%	No.	%	No.	%	No.	%
Conditional discharge	5,007	9.0	2,380	4.6	596	0.5	7,983	3.6
Probation	6,742	12.1	1,554	3.0	632	0.6	8,928	4.0
Fine	35,588	64.1	44,859	86.4	110,331	96.2	190,778	85.9
Detention Centre	3,987	7.2	1,165	2.2	1,082	0.9	6,234	2.8
Imprisonment (immediate)	702	1.3	246	0.5	183	0.2	1,131	0.5
Suspended sentence	1,753	3.2	550	1.1	367	0.3	2,670	1.2
Otherwise dealt with	1,724	3.1	1,158	2.2	1,467	1.3	4,349	2.0
	55,503		51,912		114,658		222,073*	

* Includes 1,076 (0.5% of the total) returned to borstal.

[1] These recommendations may be traced to recommendations in the reports of the Streatfeild Committee on the Business of the Criminal Courts (Cmnd 1289), and of the Morison Committee on the Probation Service (first report Cmnd 1650); and to the power in Section 57 of the Criminal Justice Act 1967 enabling the Secretary of State to make Rules requiring courts to consider a social enquiry report before passing certain custodial sentences. Current arrangements are discussed more fully in Chapter 15 of the report.

[2] Courts of Assize and Quarter Sessions, which became the Crown Court on 1 January 1972.

	Trial and sentence		Committed for sentence		Total	
	No.	%	No.	%	No.	%
Conditional discharge	513	4.8	103	1.7	616	3.7
Probation	1,803	16.9	797	13.3	2,600	15.6
Fine	1,449	13.6	318	5.3	1,767	10.6
Detention centre	1,523	14.3	647	10.8	2,170	13.0
Borstal	3,072	28.8	2,996	50.2	6,068	36.5
Return to borstal	300	2.8	236	4.0	536	3.2
Imprisonment (immediate)	1,302	12.2	509	8.5	1,811	10.9
Suspended sentence	533	5.0	240	4.0	773	4.6
Otherwise dealt with	180	1.7	128	2.1	308	1.9
	10,675		5,974		16,649	

THE CUSTODIAL SYSTEM FOR YOUNG OFFENDERS

General organisation

40. The custodial establishments for young offenders—detention centres, borstals, prisons and remand centres—are the responsibility of the Secretary of State. The Secretary of State is constitutionally responsible for the management of the prison system generally, of which these establishments form a part, and for decisions taken in his name about the treatment of individuals within that system. The management of establishments of each type is governed by rules made under the Prison Act 1952, and the Secretary of State has a duty to execute the sentences which the courts impose, according to the statutory provisions outlined above. Subject to the limitations imposed by the relevant statutes the Secretary of State has discretion in a number of matters affecting the treatment of individuals. For example, the allocation of an offender to an establishment within the system of institutions of the type to which he was committed is in law a matter for the Secretary of State as is the release of offenders on licence under the parole scheme or from borstal. While the general lines of the Department's policy and a limited number of decisions about individuals are personally approved by Ministers, most of the day-to-day decisions affecting individuals are in practice taken by officials of the Prison Department.

41. The Prison Department was reorganised in 1969 following a review by a management review team which was set up in 1967. The aims of the review were:

(a) to improve the general managerial efficiency of the prison service and, in particular, to establish clearer lines of authority and responsibility;

(b) to speed up the development of a regional administrative structure and to devolve upon it much of the detailed work previously carried out at headquarters;

(c) to set up an organisation able to devote itself to longer term planning and development, free from the heavy pressure of day-to-day work;

(d) to integrate members of the Prison Department who have prison service experience into the executive machinery, instead of their being used primarily as advisers;

(e) to separate the inspectoral functions from executive functions, with the object of raising the level of inspection.

42. Subject to the directions of Ministers and the general supervision of the Permanent Under Secretary of State, the formulation of major policy developments and the general management of the Department is the collective responsibility of the Prisons Board which consists of the Director General of the Prison Service (Chairman); the Controller (Administration); the Controller (Operations); the Controller (Planning and Development); the Chief Inspector of the Prison Service; and the Director of Prison Medical Services.

43. The Director General, who is a Deputy Under Secretary of State, is in overall charge

of the Department. The Controller (Administration) and Controller (Operations) are between them responsible for the day-to-day running of the Department. The Controller (Planning and Development) is responsible for the direction and co-ordination of all medium and long-term planning. The Chief Inspector is responsible for inspecting and reporting on the efficiency of regions and establishments; the Director of Prison Medical Services is responsible for the organisation of these services and for all matters relating to the health of inmates, including physical education.

44. Each of the three Controllers has reporting to him a number of divisions, directorates or specialists with responsibility for particular aspects of the Department's business. In general this responsibility extends over the system as a whole: for example, the divisions responsible for medium and long-term planning, for medium and long-term developments in treatment, work and earnings, for education, for security and for staffing are all concerned with both adult and young offenders and with both men and women. The same is true of the Directorate of Works and of Industries and Supply, and of such specialists as the Chief Psychologist and the Chaplain General. Within the Controllerate of Administration there are however two divisions (P3 and P4) which are responsible for certain aspects of policy and day-to-day administration as they affect certain groups of the population of Prison Department establishments. Of these two divisions, P3 Division is concerned with sentenced adult male prisoners, and P4 Division is concerned with all other inmates including young offenders, women, and all persons who are in custody on remand or awaiting trial or sentence. Matters with which these divisions are concerned include decisions regarding the disposition and treatment of individual offenders; legislation; short-term developments in treatment (including the application of longer-term reviews); and the deployment of the population between establishments. The former posts of Director of Borstal Administration and Director of Prison Administration were abolished as a result of the reorganisation, but experienced governors are included in the staff of P3 and P4 Divisions, as elsewhere in the Prison Department. (Release on parole, after-care and recall of prisoners with sentences of more than 18 months are the responsibility of H2 Division in the Probation and After-Care Department.)

45. The reorganisation of the Prison Department introduced a regional structure between Headquarters and individual establishments. There are now four Regional Directors each of whom is responsible for a list of establishments on a geographical basis. Each Director's list includes establishments of all kinds (both for adults and young offenders) except that most equivalent responsibilities for women's establishments are exercised by the Assistant Director who is a member of P4 Division. The responsibilities of the Regional Director include general oversight of the region in the sense that he is the immediate superior of the governors of all the establishments concerned; the operational activities of those establishments; the general quality of morale and of the regime; and certain matters relating to works, industries, finance and staff training. Regional officers are also responsible for certain decisions regarding the disposition and treatment of adult male offenders; no similar responsibilities have so far been delegated in respect of young offenders or women, but a similar delegation is being considered in relation to male young offenders. The Regional Director's staff includes a Deputy Director (Administration) and either one or two Deputy Directors (Operations); where there are two Deputy Directors (Operations) one has special responsibility for young offenders' establishments.

46. The whole cost of running the custodial system falls on the Exchequer. On the basis of the expenditure shown in Part I of Appendix 4 to the Report on the Work of the Prison Department for 1972[1] (that is, excluding expenditure on maintenance of establishments such as rates, building repairs and rents, and capital expenditure on new buildings, plant, machinery and vehicles) in the financial year 1971–72 the average weekly cost of maintaining a detention centre trainee was £35.28, a borstal trainee £36.89, and a prisoner or remand centre inmate £30.03. The real cost to the community is higher than these figures suggest. As noted they do not include the cost of providing new buildings. (At 1971 prices the estimated amortised annual cost of providing one new place in a young offender establishment was £834.[2]) Nor do they take

---

[1] Cmnd 5375.
[2] Amortisation is a procedure by which capital expenditure is notionally spread over a period of years, rather like the annual payments on a 100% mortgage at the prevailing rate of interest. The figure in the text is amortised over a period of 40 years, at Public Works Loan Board rates.

account of other public expenditure such as social security payments to any dependants (though there would be offsetting savings where the offender had been receiving unemployment pay), nor the forgone potential output by offenders who might otherwise have been in gainful employment. Any comparison with other forms of penal treatment should therefore be made cautiously; but it can be said that the figures quoted above certainly do not exaggerate the cost of custodial treatment.

47. The following paragraphs describe in more detail the facilities available in young offender establishments of each type, the nature of the population they have to deal with, the aims of the regime and the type of training provided. Paragraphs 48–140 deal with arrangements for young men. Provisions for young women are described in paragraphs 141–162.

Provision for young men

48. The custodial system for young male offenders provides separate establishments to deal with offenders under each of the available sentences—senior detention centres (and junior centres for those under 17), borstals and young prisoners' centres. The number of places at present available for young offenders in these establishments is 1,500 in senior detention centres (and 455 in junior centres); 6,002 in borstals (2,196 in open establishments, 3,806 in closed) and 478 in separate young prisoners' centres (in addition to the use of wings in adult prisons for the accommodation of young prisoners). In addition there are remand centres where young people aged 17 and under 21, or in certain circumstances under 17, may be detained in custody on remand or to await trial or sentence, but the number of places is not sufficient to meet demand and some young people have to be accommodated in local prisons.

49. On 30 June 1973 7,627 young men were detained under sentence in Prison Department establishments (other than junior detention centres). These comprised 1,065 in senior detention centres; 5,117 borstal trainees; and 1,445 young prisoners. In addition there were 1,659 young men under 21 including some aged under 17 remanded in custody or awaiting trial or sentence. (The number of borstal trainees includes those who were aged 15 and 16 at the time of sentence. In 1971—the latest year for which information about the population received is at present available—14% of those received under sentence of borstal training were aged under 17 on conviction and a recent estimate indicates that some 10% of the borstal population are under 17—that is there are some 500–550 offenders under 17 in the borstal population, who are included in the borstal and overall population figures given in this paragraph.) In 1972 the daily average population of young prisoners was 1,313; of trainees in senior detention centres 1,351; and of borstal trainees 5,329. The average population of unconvicted and unsentenced persons under 21 years of age was 1,700.

I. DETENTION CENTRES[1]

Types of offenders

50. According to information based on committals during 1971 more than a third of young offenders committed to a senior detention centre are aged 17; and the proportion committed for each year of the age range drops consistently, to 12% aged 20. 11% of those sent to senior detention centres had no known previous convictions and about three quarters had between one and five previous convictions. Less than 5% of those committed to a senior detention centre in 1971 had served a previous sentence in a Prison Department establishment; about 10% had previously been in an approved school, including some who would have to return there. Burglary accounted for about 30% of the convictions of those sent to senior detention centres and, together with theft, for over half of the total committed. The next largest group of offences was taking a motor vehicle without consent, which accounted for almost another 13%. Offences involving violence (including robbery) accounted for 17% of the total.

---

[1] The operation of the detention centre system was reviewed by the Advisory Council on the Penal System in the report *Detention Centres*.

191

Accommodation available

51. There are 13 senior detention centres providing accommodation for 1,500 trainees. These are as follows.

Name	Location	Certified normal accommodation	Date first used for custody of offenders	Date brought into present use	Purpose for which built
Aldington	Rural (7 miles from Ashford, Kent)	115	1947	1961	Former agriculture camp with additional buildings
Blantyre House	Rural (12 miles Maidstone, Kent)	100	1954	1954	Formerly farm house and building (Mr. Fegan's Homes)
Buckley Hall	Urban (Rochdale, Lancs.)	119	1954	1961	Converted country house
Erlestoke	Rural (7 miles Devizes, Wilts.)	92	1962	1962	Country house and former Ministry of Defence camp
Haslar	Urban (Gosport, Hants.)	100	1962	1962	Additions made to former RN Hospital
Hollesley Bay Colony	Rural (17 miles Ipswich, Suffolk)	120	1938	1971	Former LCC agricultural school
Medomsley	Semi-rural (3 miles Consett, Co. Durham)	117	1961	1961	Former local authority building
New Hall	Semi-rural (6 miles Wakefield, Yorks.)	125	1936	1961	Built in 1936 as open prison
North Sea Camp	Rural (5 miles Boston, Lincs.)	152	1935	1963	Built largely by borstal trainees
Send	Rural (7 miles Guildford, Surrey)	116	1962	1962	Former county hospital
Usk	Semi-rural (at Usk, Mon.)	105	1838	1964	Old County Gaol
Werrington	Semi-rural (3 miles Stoke-on-Trent)	115	1957	1957	Former local authority building
Whatton	Rural (11 miles Nottingham)	124	1966	1966	Purpose-built

All courts in the country have power to commit to a detention centre. The Prison Department take the view that the regime of a detention centre cannot be maintained if it is overcrowded; and accordingly courts have been requested to enquire of the centre whether a vacancy exists before they make a detention centre order. On 30 June 1973 there were 1,065 young men in custody in senior detention centres, compared with 1,500 available places. But from time to time it happens that there is no vacancy at a particular centre.

Length of sentences

52. Most offenders committed to a detention centre are sent for a period of three months. This reflects the widely-held view, endorsed by the Advisory Council in the report on detention centres,[1] that three months is the most effective period for this form of training.

Allocation

53. With the short period in custody and the relatively few and similar establishments, no classification or allocation procedure exists or is thought necessary; courts commit direct to the centre made available to them.

The centres and the treatment programme

54. Most detention centres are in relatively new buildings and there is not the same severe problem as to unsuitability of accommodation as exists in both the borstal system and young prisoners' centres. All the detention centres are closed—ie they have perimeter

[1] *Detention Centres*, paragraph 105.

security—except North Sea Camp and Hollesley Bay. These two centres are fairly isolated geographically thereby providing a measure of natural security. Most of the centres are in rural areas, with land outside the perimeter fence, which is generally used for farming and market gardening. Most also have a certain amount of security within the buildings.

55. The conduct of detention centres is governed by the Detention Centre Rules 1952, as amended by the Detention Centre (Amendment) Rules 1968 and 1972. Unlike the Borstal and Prison Rules, the Detention Centre Rules do not lay down the basic principles of treatment at a detention centre. The intention is that the centres should provide for young offenders for whom a long period of custodial treatment has not yet become necessary. In practice however detention centres have received a substantial minority of offenders who have had institutional experience and who are not likely to be responsive to short-term custodial treatment.

56. The Secretary of State appoints a Board of Visitors to each detention centre. The Boards have a general responsibility to satisfy themselves about the state of the buildings, the administration of the establishment and the treatment of inmates. They are required to hold a formal meeting in the detention centre at least once a month, and to arrange for members of the Board to visit the centre frequently and to inspect it. Boards of Visitors provide an important source of independent influence and advice, and the Council's earlier report stressed the need for members of Boards to visit the centres as frequently as possible.[1] Boards of Visitors have disciplinary powers in relation to serious breaches of discipline (see paragraph 65) and hear applications or complaints from the detainees. Each Board of Visitors makes an annual report to the Secretary of State.

57. When statutory provision for detention centres was made in 1948 the emphasis was on the deterrent nature of the establishments, and the relatively punitive nature of the regime. However, experience showed that despite the short length of sentence there was opportunity for a positive treatment approach, and many staff were anxious to develop the centres in that way. The Council's report on detention centres placed emphasis on a constructive regime. Deprivation of the offender's liberty was to be regarded as in itself fulfilling the punitive function of the sentence. Treatment within the centres was to be aimed at bringing about a change in the offender's behaviour through a constructive regime, with increased attention to education.[2] The detention centre system has since continued to develop along these lines.

58. Because of the shorter period of sentence, it is impracticable to emulate the borstal system's provision for trade and vocational training (see paragraphs 102–105). But the senior detention centre system aims at encouraging regular work habits; and there is an 8 hour working day. The detention centre report recognised the problem of providing work that had any real training value during a short period of detention. The aim has been to provide work of a kind which could rapidly be learned such as making sports nets, concrete moulding and metal recovery. In addition, there is the ordinary domestic work of the establishment, and work on the farm or garden or in commercial greenhouse production. Earnings in detention centres are essentially pocket money. They range at present up to 25½p a week and are assessed on a marking system which takes account of the detainee's general response.

59. Trainees at several detention centres undertake outside work for the community, such as assisting at centres for the sub-normal, doing maintenance work at a children's home, keeping local churchyards tidy, and helping old people with their gardening.

60. The Detention Centre Rules provide that, for the 17–21 age group, arrangements should be made for their part-time education either within the normal working week or outside it. In practice, those who are judged to need remedial education receive it during the day; and those who were in full-time education at the time of their sentence are able to continue such studies during the day. There are further education classes for all trainees in the evening. The education officer at each detention centre is recruited in consultation with the local education authority and has a contract of service with them.

[1] *Detention Centres,* paragraph 85.
[2] *ibid,* especially paragraph 63.

The local education authority are responsible—subject to reimbursement by the Home Office—for the education of persons in detention centres. Education arrangements are inspected by local education authorities and HM Inspectors of Schools.

61. A special survey of illiteracy in detention centres undertaken for the Council's earlier inquiry established that about a quarter of those ordered to be detained had a reading age of 10 years or below. In accordance with the recommendation in the Council's report on detention centres[1] provision for remedial education is being expanded to ensure that no one who can benefit from assistance in this way fails to receive it. The Council expressed the general view[1] that the biggest contribution to meeting the needs of the offenders who are sent to detention centres can be made by increased provision for education. Progress has been made in expanding the education programme so far as resources permit.

62. Provision is made at detention centres for an hour's physical education each day and the Council's report made recommendations as to the development of the physical education programme.[2]

63. The staff at detention centres are encouraged to give individual attention to the problems of the trainees. Contact with home is maintained so far as possible through visits and letters and constitutes less of a difficulty than at borstals (see paragraph 112) because of the shorter period in custody, and because in general travelling distances are shorter since each centre serves a local catchment area. Provision was made in the 1972 Rules for trainees to be allowed temporary release, for example to visit a close relative who is seriously ill, to attend a funeral, or for educational purposes.

Religion
64. The Council's report recommended[3] that attendance at a weekly religious service should continue to be regarded as part of the normal detention centre programme, and this remains the position.

Discipline
65. Offences other than those of a serious nature are dealt with by the Warden. The punishments which he may impose are: a caution; removal from specified activities other than work; extra work outside working hours; stoppage of pay; reduction in grade; removal to a detention room (together with appropriate restrictions on activities and stoppage of pay); and loss of remission. (Confinement to a detention room and dietary punishment—both of which were rarely used—were abolished following the recommendation in the detention centre report.[4]) The Board of Visitors, who deal with more serious offences, have similar powers, but their awards may cover longer periods. There is provision for a trainee to be removed from association with other trainees for the maintenance of good order or discipline or in his own interests.

Supervision after release
66. One or more probation officers are appointed to each detention centre as social workers with primary responsibility for arrangements preparatory to release. The social workers take a special interest in the trainee's contacts with his home, and get into touch with the officer who will be supervising him on release and with the appropriate youth employment officer. The practice is so far as possible to appoint women to these posts (the other centre staff generally being men).

67. All offenders leaving a detention centre are under the supervision of a probation officer for a period of up to 12 months and must comply with the requirements of the supervision notice. The normal requirements of the supervision notice are that the trainee should keep in touch with his supervising officer, be of good behaviour and lead an industrious life. The Secretary of State may modify or cancel any of the requirements. Cases are reviewed after half the statutory period of supervision, and sometimes earlier, in order to see whether supervision can be terminated. In accordance with the recommendation in the detention centre report,[5] the emphasis of such reviews has now changed

[1] *Detention Centres*, paragraph 73.   [3] *ibid*, paragraph 81.   [5] *ibid*, paragraph 119.
[2] *ibid*, paragraphs 77–78.   [4] *ibid*, paragraph 86.

towards terminating supervision early, unless there are strong reasons for maintaining it for the full period. In 1972 supervision was terminated early because of satisfactory progress in 1,017 cases. Where the trainee is already subject to a probation order, a supervision order or a care order which is to remain in force, he may be released without licence to continue under the supervision of a probation officer or a local authority social worker as appropriate.

68. The sanction to ensure compliance with the requirements of a supervision notice is liability to recall to a detention centre for the unexpired portion of the original term of detention or for 14 days, whichever is the longer. The procedure is for the supervising officer's report, endorsed by the principal probation officer, to be sent to the Prison Department. In deciding whether recall should be recommended in a particular case consideration is given to the likely effect of further detention, bearing in mind the age of the person concerned, the period for which he may be detained on recall—which in the case of detention centre orders is very limited—the amount of supervision already completed, the extent and effect of previous institutional training, and the overall response and attitude to detention and supervision. Only in exceptional circumstances is a person in regular and honest employment recalled. A trainee can be recalled only once, so that after the limited period of recall has been served there is no sanction during the balance of the period of supervision.

69. The basic criteria for recall to a detention centre are that:
   (a) the trainee is in breach of the terms of his supervision; and in addition either
   (b) his behaviour is placing him at risk and creating a social threat, and his needs and the well-being of society require that he shall be recalled; or
   (c) failure to enforce sanctions for breach of the requirements of supervision is creating difficulty for the supervising officer in his work with other supervised persons.

70. The procedure for recall normally is for a short and final warning of intention to recommend recall to be issued by the principal probation officer. Recall to a detention centre has been used sparingly. The Department consider it to be most effective within three months of the date of release. In 1972, 27 orders of recall to a detention centre were issued. Seven of these orders were cancelled, in six cases because contact with the supervising officer was resumed, and in one case because further charges were preferred.

Staff
71. Each senior detention centre is in the charge of a warden, who is usually a Governor Class III; the function of deputy warden is normally performed by a Chief Officer, Class II.[1] Each centre has a full-time social worker, a full or part-time education officer, a part-time medical officer and a part-time Anglican chaplain, Roman Catholic priest and Methodist minister. Technical staff are employed as required. The discipline staff, but not the warden or deputy warden, wear uniform at most centres. The Council's report on detention centres recommended that all staff should wear plain clothes,[2] but the Department deferred a decision on this issue until it had been further considered in the context of young offender custodial treatment as a whole.

72. The Prison Department do not staff individual institutions on the basis of a fixed staff/inmate ratio, but the ratio can be illustrated by the following example of the staff complement of a fairly representative establishment. Send Detention Centre, with a certified normal accommodation of 116, is authorised[3] to have, in addition to the Warden, 1 Chief Officer Class II as Deputy Warden, 1 Principal Officer, 2 Senior Officers, 19 basic grade discipline officers and 2 temporary officers. Additional officers with specialist functions are a Senior Physical Education Instructor, and a basic grade Physical Education Instructor; 1 Hospital Officer; 2 Officer Instructors; 1 Catering Officer; and 3 Officer

---

[1] These arrangements differ slightly in establishments serving a dual purpose. At Whatton, where there is also a junior centre, an Assistant Governor Class II acts as deputy. At Prescoed, an Assistant Governor Class I acts as warden, under the general control of the Governor of Usk Borstal. And at Hollesley Bay the borstal Governor acts also as warden.

[2] *Detention Centres*, paragraph 93.

[3] Most establishments are in practice below their authorised staff complement.

Trade Assistants. There is also a Civilian Instructional Officer. There is an Administration Officer with the rank of Executive Officer, with supporting clerical and typing staff; a Senior Works Officer with the grade of Engineer Class I; a part-time medical officer; and part-time chaplain, Roman Catholic priest and Methodist minister. There is a social worker, and a full-time Education Officer, with 30 part-time teachers who come in in the evening. Other staff include civilian workmen and night patrols. Altogether the full-time staff amount to about 50.

73. Similar provision exists at the five junior centres for offenders under 17.

Reconviction rates

74. Of the young men released from senior detention centres in 1968—the latest year for which statistics over a suitable period are available—55.9% were known to have been reconvicted within a period of 2 years.

II. BORSTAL TRAINING

Type of offenders

75. According to an analysis of receptions (including those aged under 17) in 1971, the largest single group (46%) of the young men sent to borstal were convicted of burglary, and a further 20% were convicted of theft. About one in six were convicted of offences involving violence (including robbery). Nearly a third had six or more previous convictions, more than two fifths had between three and five previous convictions and only 3% had no previous convictions. More than a third had been in an approved school. Over 40% had been in a detention centre and over 10% had been sentenced to borstal training before.

76. Borstals have in recent years received an increasing proportion of younger and more disturbed offenders—including an increasing proportion who are under the age of 17— many of whom have a long history of institutional experience. This increase has imposed a considerable strain on establishments which cater for this type of offender and at the same time there has been a reduction in the number of offenders who are suitable for open conditions. The result is overcrowding at some establishments while there are vacancies in others, and the Prison Department has a constant problem not only of matching its accommodation to the overall demand but also of matching accommodation in particular types of establishment to the needs of particular types of offender.

Training borstals

77. The borstal system for young men provides a variety of establishments and regimes aimed at meeting the needs of different types of offenders. The following is a list of borstals at present in operation:

Name	Location	Certified normal accommodation	Date first used for custody of offenders	Date brought into present use	Purpose for which built
Closed borstals[1]					
Deerbolt[2]	Semi-rural (½ mile Barnard Castle, Co. Durham)	—	1973	1973	Army camp
Dover	Urban (1 mile Dover, Kent)	282	1953	1957	Nineteenth century fort with new accommodation added
Everthorpe	Rural (15 miles Hull, Yorks.)	338	1958	1958	Built as prison

[1] The secure conditions of closed borstals vary from a fair degree of security in a prison-type building to limited security in, for example, an establishment with little more than a wire-mesh fence round the perimeter. Where perimeter security is most effective it is possible to relax supervision and other security measures to the advantage of the training regime.

[2] Deerbolt, which first received trainees in July 1973, is being converted to borstal use by inmate labour. It currently accommodates about 40 trainees.

Name	Location	Certified normal accommodation	Date first used for custody of offenders	Date brought into present use	Purpose for which built
Closed borstals (contd.)					
Feltham	Urban (Feltham, Middlesex)	306	1910	1910	Industrial school 1856
Grendon Psychiatric Centre	Rural (13 miles Aylesbury, Bucks.)	49	1962	1962	Part of purpose-built prison
Hindley	Urban (4 miles Wigan, Lancs.)	312	1961	1962	Built as prison
Huntercombe	Rural (7 miles Henley-on-Thames)	199	1946	1946	Country house and war-time camp
Manchester Allocation Centre	Urban	346	1869	1966	Part of prison; County gaol, alterations pre-1914
Onley	Rural (5 miles Rugby)	300	1968	1968	Purpose-built
Portland	Semi-rural (8 miles Weymouth, Dorset)	468	1848	1921	Built as convict prison; converted after 1918
Rochester	Semi-rural (2 miles Rochester, Kent)	375	1873	1908	Built as convict prison; extensively reconstructed
Stoke Heath	Rural (5 miles Market Drayton, Salop.)	304	1964	1966	Built as prison
Wellingborough	Semi-urban (at Wellingborough)	224	1964	1964	Purpose-built
Wormwood Scrubs Allocation Centre	Urban (London)	303	1874	1945	Part of prison; completed in 1891, mostly by convict labour
Open borstals					
Finnamore Camp (linked to Feltham)	Rural (3 miles Marlow, Bucks.)	79	1960	1960	Built pre-war as a holiday camp
Gaynes Hall	Rural (9 miles Huntingdon)	180	1946	1946	Country house and war-time camp
Guys Marsh	Rural (2 miles Shaftesbury, Dorset)	265	1962	1962	Former army hospital
Hatfield and Gringley	Rural (9 miles Doncaster) Rural (6 miles Gainsborough)	248	1946	1950	Army camp Land Army hostel
Hewell Grange	Rural (3 miles Bromsgrove, Worcs.)	134	1946	1946	Country house and war-time camp
Hollesley Bay	Rural (17 miles Ipswich, Suffolk)	367	1938	1938	Former LCC Agricultural School, new buildings added since war
Lowdham Grange	Rural (10 miles Nottingham)	290	1931	1931	Purpose-built
Morton Hall	Rural (8 miles Newark, Notts.)	153	1958	1958	Former RAF station
Pollington	Rural (13 miles Pontefract, Yorks.)	140	1950	1950	Former Army camp
Prescoed	Rural (at Usk, Mon.)	100	1939	1939	Purpose-built
Wetherby	Semi-rural (at Wetherby, Yorks.)	240	1958	1958	Former RN Training Establishment

78. There are at present 26 borstals for young men, including two borstals which are satellites to their principal establishments, which provide a total of 6,002 places (2,196 in open borstals; 3,806 in closed). (The occupation of borstals on 30 June 1973 was 1,703 in open establishments and 3,291 in closed—including the allocation centres. The remainder—123—were in local prisons.) Of these 26, 11 are closed training borstals, 12 are open training borstals, two are allocation centres and one is a psychiatric centre.

79. Most training borstals—and all of those which are open borstals—are in rural areas and have a fair amount of land attached. Open borstals are, in general, large country houses which have been adapted, former armed services establishments or permanent hutted camps. Two are purpose-built. In some borstals the sleeping accommodation is in dormitories; in others there are single cells or cubicles.

Allocation

80. Rule 2 of the Borstal Rules deals with the allocation of trainees:

"(1) Methods of training may vary as between one borstal and another, according to the needs of the inmates allocated to them.

(2) Inmates shall be allocated to borstals, as far as practicable, in accordance with their age, character and capabilities and so as to make the best use of training facilities available".

81. Before being sent to a training borstal an offender sentenced to borstal is interviewed and tested at an allocation centre. There are two of these; one for the north at Manchester and one for the south at Wormwood Scrubs. Trainees sentenced by courts in the locality of an allocation centre are sent there direct; the others go first to their nearest local prison and are transferred to an allocation centre as soon as practicable (usually within a week or 10 days). On 30 June 1973, 112 of the borstal trainees in local prisons were awaiting transfer to an allocation centre.

82. The staff of an allocation centre make an assessment of each young offender, in the light of which the allocation decision is taken by an allocation board, chaired by the Assistant Governor Class I in charge of the allocation centre. The board takes account of the offender's background before sentence, his mental and intellectual ability, his age, his degree of criminal sophistication and the likelihood of his seeking or taking an opportunity to abscond. Where alternative training borstals of the type for which a particular trainee is most suited are available, he is allocated to the one nearest to his home. Some borstals concentrate on offenders at the younger end of the borstal age range, including those under 17, but there are no special arrangements for offenders under 17 as such.

83. The two allocation centres are in unsuitable buildings, in wings of adult prisons. Because of pressure of numbers, many trainees—in particular those allocated to closed borstals—cannot be sent to the borstal selected immediately following allocation, but must wait at the allocation centre until there is a vacancy. This delay, added in many cases to a stay of some length in custody on remand and a wait at a local prison after sentence (paragraph 81), constitutes a formidable obstacle to providing a good start to a period of borstal training. The House of Commons Estimates Committee (1966–67) recommended that high priority should be given to the provision of more suitable accommodation for borstal allocation centres, and on the assumption[1] that a central allocation system would be retained the Prison Department has planned two purpose-built allocation centres as part of two new young offender complexes for which planning clearance has been obtained. Both complexes are planned to include a remand centre and a training borstal in addition to the proposed allocation centre.

Staff

84. Each borstal is in the charge of a Governor Class II or Class III according to the size and nature of the establishment. The Governor is assisted by Assistant Governors (one of whom is the Deputy Governor) and by officers in the prison officer grades. Three women assistant governors are serving in male borstals. Most borstals have a

---

[1] But now see the Council's recommendations in Chapter 11.

matron for each of the living units or houses into which a borstal is sub-divided. Originally the role of matrons was primarily domestic but they tend now to perform a wider range of functions in relation to trainees. Specialist staff, including psychologists, are employed at the allocation centres. All training borstals have a full-time or part-time medical officer and chaplain. A Roman Catholic priest and a Methodist minister are also appointed to undertake part-time duties at each borstal. Technical staff, administrative staff and nursing sisters are also employed. Borstal staff do not wear uniforms.

85. It is difficult to describe any borstal as "typical", and the level of staffing is best illustrated by examples. Wetherby is an open borstal with a certified normal accommodation of 240 which was in fact its maximum occupation in 1972. In general it receives young men aged 17–21 of average or below average intelligence; it caters for the more robust, perhaps slightly feckless youth, as well as for the inadequate, and provision is included for remedial education. The authorised[1] staff includes a Governor Class III, an Assistant Governor Class I as Deputy Governor, 4 Assistant Governors Class II, 1 Chief Officer Class I, 4 Principal Officers, 3 Borstal Matrons, 8 Senior Officers, 23 basic grade officers and 8 temporary officers. Other officers with specialist functions are a Senior Physical Education Instructor, 1 Senior Hospital Officer, 1 Senior Catering Officer, 2 Physical Education Instructors, 1 Officer Instructor, 1 Catering Officer and 7 Officer Trade Assistants. There are 5 civilian Instructional Officers, an Engineer Grade I and an Engineer Grade II, an Administration Officer with the rank of Executive Officer who has a supporting staff of clerks and typists, and a part-time medical officer, chaplain and Roman Catholic priest. There is a full-time Education Officer, with 3 full-time teachers, and 35 part-time teachers who provide classes during the evening. The total full-time staff is about 90.

86. Stoke Heath is a closed borstal with a certified normal accommodation of 304; the maximum occupation figure in 1972 was 352. It takes trainees aged 18 to 21 who are not exceptional abscond risks, and who are of good intelligence and maturity. There is heavy emphasis on training in industrial production and the building trades. The authorised[1] staff includes a Governor Class II, an Assistant Governor Class I as Deputy Governor, 6 Assistant Governors Class II, 1 Chief Officer Class I, 6 Principal Officers, 9 Senior Officers and 56 basic grade officers. Additional staff in the prison officer grades with specialist functions are a Principal Officer Physical Education Instructor, 3 Physical Education Instructors, 1 Senior Catering Officer, 1 Catering Officer, 5 Officer Trade Assistants, 1 Senior Officer Instructor and 4 Officer Instructors. There are 15 Civilian Instructional Officers, 1 Foreman of Works, 2 Engineers Class II and an Industrial Manager. The Administration Officer is a Higher Executive Officer, who has appropriate supporting staff. The establishment has a part-time medical officer, a full-time chaplain and a part-time Roman Catholic priest. There is a full-time Education Officer with 3 full-time teacher posts and 23 part-time teachers. The full-time staff numbers some 145. All establishments have other miscellaneous staff such as night patrols, civilian workmen, stokers, etc.

Boards of Visitors

87. The Secretary of State appoints a Board of Visitors to each borstal. The Boards have responsibilities and disciplinary powers (see paragraph 109) similar to those of Boards of Visitors of detention centres (see paragraph 56) and training prisons, and provide a valuable contact between the local community and the establishment. In addition, Boards of Visitors of borstals have duties in connection with the release of trainees under supervision (see paragraph 113).

Training

88. Rule 1 of the Borstal Rules lays down the general principles of borstal training:

"(1) The purpose of borstal training requires that every inmate, while conforming to the rules necessary for well-ordered community life, shall be able to develop his individuality on right lines with a proper sense of personal responsibility. Accordingly, officers shall, while firmly maintaining order and discipline, seek to do so by influencing the inmates through their own example and leadership and enlisting their willing co-operation.

[1] See footnote to paragraph 72.

(2) The objects of borstal training shall be to bring to bear every influence which may establish in the inmates the will to lead a good and useful life on release, and to fit them to do so by the fullest possible development of their character, capabilities and sense of personal responsibility".

89. Borstal training aims at bringing about a development in the trainee's character and capacities and progressively providing increasing scope for personal decision, responsibility and self-control. This means inevitably that there is more opportunity for failures of character to show up than there is in prison with its much more restricted scope for decision making.

90. As the Borstal Rules indicate, borstal training aims at enabling the trainee to develop as an individual. Perhaps the most important aspect is the relationship between staff and trainees. The intention is for staff to be able to get to know each particular trainee for whom they are responsible so that they can exert a personal influence on him. The house system was introduced for that reason, and variations of that system have taken place over the years. Each borstal is divided into houses or units for administrative purposes. The house or unit is generally managed by an assistant governor who is assisted by a principal officer, a matron, two senior officers and an appropriate number of basic grade officers. The assistant governor is responsible for general organisation, mobilising resources and case-work; his training team have responsibilities for interviewing individuals within a particular group and provide reports for the review boards.

91. The aim is to keep to houses organised for no more than about 50 trainees, who can be divided into two groups for training purposes. However, because of the rise in the borstal population and the shortage of staff it has in some cases been necessary to have groups of as many as 60 or even 70 trainees. The organisation of the activities of each house is left as far as possible to individual discretion in order to allow housemasters to develop their own techniques.

92. The Borstal Rules provide for the establishment of a system of grades. Until 1972 there was a system of grades through which a trainee progressed by obtaining credit for conduct and work. Promotion from one grade to another was intended to involve extra responsibility for a trainee as well as more pay and privileges; and one of the most common forms of punishment was reduction in grade or delay in promotion to the next grade. However the view of many Governors was that the system had become artificial and institutionalised in its operation, and was more of a hindrance than a help to constructive training. A modified system of grades has now been introduced: Governors and Boards of Visitors are still able to delay a trainee's release by reducing or delaying his grade, but the grade system as such now has less significance for the training itself and consists solely of a "training" grade and a "discharge" grade. Governors now award privileges or select young men for particular activities or responsibilities by reference to their individual needs and likely response.

93. The daily routine at training borstals generally includes a 40-hour working week; physical training; educational activities; some time for recreation and an opportunity for reading and writing. The staff complement in borstals is such that training and recreational association between trainees can be supported throughout the whole of the day and evening.

94. In most cases a trainee works initially on the domestic work of the borstal itself. According to his capabilities and the facilities available at the borstal he may be selected for

- (a) a vocational training course, or
- (b) construction industry training (or "trade training") leading to building or maintenance work, or
- (c) educational training, or
- (d) production work in a workshop, or
- (e) farm training and work, or
- (f) work in industry outside the borstal or with private farmers, or
- (g) general labouring.

95. The principal types of employment followed at male borstals are: metal work (such as blacksmiths, engineering, wire making); carpentry; laundry work; textile work; concrete moulding; metal recovery; farming and market gardening; in works departments (eg as bricklayers and masons, carpenters and joiners, electricians, fitters, labourers, painters and decorators, plasterers and plumbers); and on domestic work (such as employment as cleaners, jobbers and labourers, cooks and bakers, on gardens and sports fields, as hospital orderlies and as stokers). In addition to work for farmers outside, there is work for a few trainees with private firms, local authorities and other Government departments. On average some 800–900 trainees are engaged in vocational training or trade courses at any one time. Work in borstals, as well as in prisons, is being rationalised to reduce the number of industries and occupations and dispose them round the system in a more rational way. The industries the Prison Department is concentrating on are carpentry, engineering, metal recovery, garment making, weaving and laundering. In borstals the first two are to be given preference.

96. Even at closed borstals trainees may work outside the borstal at local firms, etc. For example, Rochester Borstal has a scheme whereby trainees go out in small numbers to local factories, mainly for engineering work and usually for a minimum of three and a maximum of six months. The steering committee for the scheme comprises representatives of the borstal, the local Chamber of Commerce, management and trade unions and the Department of Employment. At Wetherby Borstal the local Engineering Industry Training Board school is combining with local employers to instruct trainees in the first part of an engineering apprenticeship with the idea that they should continue their training after discharge and eventually take employment with the firm that sponsored their training.

97. No pre-release hostels (such as are associated with adult prisons) have been provided within the borstal system, but 1 hostel has been established for trainees during the main custodial part of the sentence. This is Taylor House, a hostel in Ipswich opened in 1968 which is run from the young men's training borstal at Hollesley Bay. Trainees are selected for the hostel at any time after they have been at the training borstal for a month, and can spend all the rest of the custodial part of their sentence of borstal training there. Misbehaviour or failure to adjust to hostel residence may be dealt with by withdrawal to the parent establishment. The operation of Taylor House is being evaluated, and consideration is being given to the establishment of two additional hostels elsewhere.

98. The earnings of trainees in borstals range from 25½p to 53p a week. Before the modification of the grade system referred to in paragraph 92 above, borstal earnings were related to grades. The intention now is that a trainee's pay should be related to the skill and responsibility of the job he is doing and to his output. Experiments are still in hand to arrive at a standard scheme to put this decision into effect. In the meantime, certain changes have been made in the existing borstal scheme. Two scales—one equivalent to that for the former training grade, and the other equivalent to that for the former senior training grade—have been introduced. Promotion to, or demotion from, the higher pay scale need bear no relationship to the trainee's attainment of the new discharge grade, but reflects all aspects of progress.

99. The provision of education in borstals rests primarily with local education authorities. The Home Office reimburses the authorities in full for their services. Every borstal for young men has a full-time education officer recruited jointly by the Prison Department and the local education authority. He acts as adviser on all educational matters, and the professional teachers at borstals are provided in consultation with the appropriate local education authorities. The educational arrangements in borstals are inspected by HM Inspectors of Schools.

100. The Borstal Rules require that so far as practicable every trainee shall engage in educational activities for at least six hours a week outside normal working hours.[1] They also provide for education within the normal working hours for any inmate who is illiterate or backward. Because borstals differ in the range of trainees for which they are suitable,

---

[1] Arrangements are made for borstal trainees below the statutory school leaving age to receive full-time education.

some establishments have large numbers of trainees in need of remedial education, while at others the need for remedial education is scarcely apparent.

101. The Borstal Rules enable not only those who are illiterate or backward but any other trainee in whose educational interest it is to take part in educational activities during normal working hours. This enables those of sufficient educational attainment to be given the opportunity to study for GCE examinations or even for an external degree. For example at Gaynes Hall Borstal there are courses leading to the Certificate of Office Studies and the Ordinary National Certificate in Business Studies.

102. The education officer's responsibilities include the organisation of vocational training courses. Unlike other education arrangements this instruction is usually provided by civilian instructors who are directly employed by the Prison Department. Nearly 1,500 borstal trainees completed vocational training courses in 1971 or were still under training at the end of the year. Preliminary entrance examinations were arranged by the Department and 743 trainees were entered for external examinations. The pass rate was just over 75%. Vocational training courses in borstals were: baking, brick work, carpentry and joinery, drawing office practice, electrical installation, heating and ventilation, mechanical engineering craft practice, machine operating and setting, motor mechanics work, pattern making, painting and decorating, plumbing, radio and television service, skilled labouring and building operative, and welding (gas and electric arc).

103. Until recently, the vocational training courses tended for the most part to be academically inclined and to lead to examinations of the kind conducted by the City and Guilds of London Institute. In recent years a new form of training, known as construction industry training, has supplemented and in some cases replaced vocational training in building work. These courses are provided by the establishment's works department. They are shorter, place more emphasis on the practical side, and enable the average trainee to be transferred to site work in the borstal before the end of his sentence. The building trade unions have taken a special interest in this practical type of training, and there are agreements with two unions representing building workers (the Amalgamated Union of Building Trade Workers and the Transport and General Workers Union) under which prison and borstal trainees who have reached a reasonable standard in site work as well as in training are considered for union membership immediately before the end of their sentence. The unions have also helped trainees to settle into building jobs when they have been discharged.

104. Borstal trainees are also covered by an agreement made with the Amalgamated Union of Engineering and Foundry Workers. This enables prisoners and borstal trainees who have had a reasonable amount of experience of production work in a prison or borstal engineering workshop to be considered for union membership on their discharge. Membership is in the unskilled or semi-skilled category. It has not been possible to reach a national agreement with the Union about membership in the skilled category for trainees who have completed vocational courses in engineering and welding subjects, but there is a possibility of reaching local agreements.

105. The purpose and scope of vocational training have recently been considered by an inter-departmental working party consisting of representatives of the Prison Department Headquarters, prison and borstal governors, the Department of Education and Science and the Department of Employment. Among its recommendations are that the range of courses available and their relevance to outside needs should be further examined, and that links should be developed with all the industrial training boards responsible for the various forms of vocational training currently available. Relating vocational training to industrial training board recommendations would result in the same type of basic training being available in a number of establishments, so enabling trainees to continue their course of training if they were transferred. Commenting on the division of responsiblities for vocational training and trade training, the working party recommended that there should be only one form of training in the construction trade, reflecting as far as possible the recommendations of the Construction Industry Training Board.

Religion

106. Every borstal has an Anglican chaplain who with the ministers of other denomina-

tions shares in the programme of the establishment. Until 1970 attendance at religious services was required of all borstal trainees unless they put forward strong grounds of conscience. Arrangements in borstal now accord with the practice in adult penal establishments of voluntary attendance. In addition classes in religious instruction are available in young offender establishments as part of the normal education arrangements, and are included in the induction programme, within which they are obligatory for all trainees.

Leisure activities

107. Borstals aim at encouraging trainees to learn how to use their leisure constructively. All borstals have facilities for evening and other leisure time activities. They have their own library and it is usual for the local authority to lend books to an establishment and to change them at frequent intervals. There are facilities for both indoor and outdoor games and matches are arranged against local teams. Many hobbies can be pursued: for example music, drama, painting, home-decorating and boat-building. Trainees from one closed borstal were able to assist in a local archaeological dig. Camps are arranged, and trainees from a number of borstals have taken part in Outward Bound courses. Radio and television are available in borstals. Smoking is allowed, except that in working hours in closed borstals it is permitted only during breaks.

Community service

108. Young men in borstal have traditionally been allowed to go out of the establishment to do what may be described as "good works" in the district—tending old people's gardens or decorating their houses, helping at village functions and so on—and this kind of activity is now being extended to detention centres. It is also coming to demand a greater degree of involvement at a personal level and a greater sense of social purpose: young men may help in youth clubs or community centres, with handicapped or backward children, in hospitals, in socially deprived areas and so on. Sometimes it is arranged by the Governor with the hospital or other agency or institution direct; sometimes it is done under the auspices of an organisation such as Community Service Volunteers, City Challenge or Toc H.

General conduct in borstals

109. The average population of male borstals and the number of offences punished in the years 1968 to 1972 were as follows:

	Average Population	Offences Punished
1968	5,389	8,591
1969	5,368	9,337
1970	5,792	7,913
1971	5,669	8,237
1972	5,192	8,527

The awards which the Governor may make for an offence against discipline are: a caution; removal for any period from any particular activity of the house or borstal; extra work outside working hours; stoppage of earnings; reduction in grade, or postponement of promotion to the next grade; removal from the house; confinement to a room for a period not exceeding three days; and restricted diet.[1] The commonest awards are removal from the activities of the house, reduction in grade or postponement of promotion to a higher grade, and stoppage of earnings. The Governor is authorised to delegate his powers to deal with the more minor offences against discipline to other officers not below the rank of principal officer. More serious cases of offences against discipline are referred to the Board of Visitors. The awards a Board of Visitors may make are similar in kind to those which may be made by the Governor, but may cover longer periods.

---

[1] This punishment is now rarely used and will be formally withdrawn when the Borstal Rules are amended in accordance with the Secretary of State's recent announcement to the Annual Conference of Boards of Visitors.

Absconding

110. Given that the system of training in borstals—even in closed borstals—does not in general involve close custody, some absconding is only to be expected. The average population of open and closed borstals and the number of incidents of absconding in the years 1968 to 1972 were as follows:

	Average Population			Incidents of Absconding		
	Open Borstals	Closed Borstals	Total	Open Borstals	Closed Borstals	Total
1968	1,898	3,491	5,389	891	487	1,378
1969	1,882	3,486	5,368	892	472	1,364
1970	2,024	3,768	5,792	747	224	971
1971	2,015	3,654	5,669	533	262	795
1972	1,797	3,395	5,192	618	214	832

111. Offenders who abscond from borstal are normally dealt with by the Governor or the Board of Visitors and may have their release delayed by an appropriate period. If they have committed criminal offences while at liberty they may be brought before a court with a view to a fresh sentence. Absconders may in addition be returned to the allocation centre for re-allocation to a more secure establishment.

Contact with families and probation officers

112. Increasing emphasis is being placed on maintaining and developing the trainee's relations with his family and his probation officer. All trainees may write and receive one letter a week, with extra letters as necessary; they may receive visits every fortnight; and in certain circumstances they may have access to the telephone. They have the opportunity of a period of up to five days' home leave towards the end of their sentence, and additional journeys can be arranged for visits to probation officers, potential employers or hostels. So far as possible trainees are allocated to borstals which are near enough to their homes for a visit to be made in a single day, but the isolation of many borstals and their geographical distribution are a source of difficulty. Help can be given from public funds if the family is receiving supplementary benefit or its income is at supplementary benefit level, and further help can sometimes be given from a charitable trust.

Release and supervision

113. A person sentenced to borstal training is detained for not less than six months and not more than two years. Traditionally the aim has been to tailor periods of training to the needs of individual trainees, and to arrange release at the time judged to be most favourable to securing the offender's subsequent law-abiding behaviour. Throughout his period of training a trainee's prospects are kept under review. The assessment of his assistant governor and other members of staff are recorded as the trainee progresses and each case is considered by an institution board which is presided over by the Governor. When the Governor and the institution board consider that the trainee could be released under supervision a recommendation is submitted to the Board of Visitors who, if they agree, forward it to the Secretary of State. This is considered and usually endorsed within the Prison Department (P4 Division).

114. In 1960 (at a time when the statutory minimum and maximum periods of detention were nine months and three years respectively) the average length of time spent in custody on a borstal sentence, from sentence to discharge, was 16 months. By 1969 it had fallen to 13 months. The number of young offenders committed to borstal rose sharply in 1969 and 1970. The numbers received under sentence of borstal training in the years 1967 to 1971 were as follows:

1967	5,012	1970	7,171
1968	5,044	1971	6,859
1969	5,839		

The substantial increase in the intake resulted in serious congestion at critical points in the system. Trainees had to wait in the allocation centre after the allocation decision had been taken until a vacancy became available in the particular borstal. In turn large

204

numbers of trainees—at one time as high as 500—had to wait after sentence at a local prison, perhaps for two to three months, until a vacancy became available in the allocation centre. Even after various steps had been taken to improve the flow of trainees and maximise the use of available accommodation, there remained a substantial shortage of places to meet the demand. Faced with the choice of overcrowding training borstals or reducing the average period of training the Department chose the latter. Between the beginning of 1969 and the middle of 1970 the average period of detention from sentence to release on licence dropped by about two months to a little over 11 months. In the period immediately following this reduction in periods served there were some inequalities between establishments but these have now been substantially removed.

115. Most borstals now operate a system of "target dates", under which soon after reception to the training borstal each trainee is given a date on which, subject to subsequent developments during his training, he can hope to be released. Overall the average training period (ie excluding time spent between passing of sentence and arrival at the training borstal) is about 37 weeks for open borstals, and a little longer for closed borstals. The progress of trainees is still assessed individually. Around the average period each trainee has his target date fixed according to individual needs and circumstances, and it may be varied during the period of training. For example release may be delayed as a disciplinary measure, or advanced for good progress or especially favourable circumstances pointing to release.

116. The average period of detention from sentence to discharge is at present about 10 months. However, the range of individual release dates is considerable. The actual distribution of periods of detention served under a borstal sentence naturally changes somewhat from month to month for a variety of reasons. However, the figures for trainees released in July 1973—the most recent month for which statistics are available—provide a reasonable illustration of the present position. In that month 18% of those released had been detained for less than eight months; 56% for eight to ten months; 17% for 10–12 months; and 9% for more than a year.

117. A period of supervision after release is, and always has been, regarded as integral to the borstal sentence. As with other custodial sentences for young offenders, the supervision of trainees after release is a responsibility of the probation and after-care service. The present period of supervision is up to two years from the date of release. The normal requirements of supervision and the provisions for their modification and cancellation are similar to those for detention centre trainees. The probation and after-care service has been encouraged to institute regular reviews with a view to early termination of supervision at the appropriate time and in the expectation that there would need to be positive grounds for its continuance beyond 12 months. Supervision was terminated early in 1,234 cases in 1972.

118. In borstals hitherto the task of maintaining contact with the home, establishing links with the prospective supervisor, and generally making arrangements for resettlement on release has rested not with a specialist social worker (as is the case in prisons and detention centres) but with the assistant governor in charge of the house. Following recent conferences with the probation and after-care service aimed at fostering closer involvement of the service in borstal training, an experimental scheme is being introduced under which probation officers will work in five selected borstals. While there may not be a need in borstals for a welfare officer or social worker on the prison or detention centre model, it seems likely that a probation officer can provide an additional resource which may be valuable in developing and maintaining a constructive and realistic approach to the offender both in the establishment and during his period under supervision in the community.

Recall

119. When a person fails to comply with the conditions of his notice of release under supervision, the supervising officer reports the case through the principal probation officer to the Prison Department which considers whether the person should be recalled under section 45 of the Prison Act 1952. In 1972, 56 orders of recall to borstal training were issued; 30 trainees were apprehended and recalled; ten recall orders were cancelled, in eight cases because contact with the supervising officer was resumed and in two cases because further charges were preferred; 16 recall orders were still outstanding at the end of

the year. A far more common method of being returned to borstal is by order of a court under section 12 of the Criminal Justice Act 1961 following conviction during the period of supervision. In 1972, 1,182 trainees on licence were returned in this way.

120. The procedure for recall to borstal is similar to that for recall to detention centres (paragraphs 68–70). But the sanction is more effective, first because a borstal trainee may be detained on recall until the expiration of two years from the date of sentence or for six months from the date of being taken into custody under the order of recall, whichever is the longer; and secondly because there is a liability to further recall during the balance of the period of supervision.

121. Those who are recalled to borstal by the Secretary of State, as well as those returned to borstal by the courts following a conviction during their period of supervision, have hitherto been sent to a separate recall centre; but the policy now is to return them to their original training borstals, where the staff will be familiar to them from their original period in custody and all concerned can learn from the offender's experience while at liberty.

Reconviction rates

122. Of the young men released from borstal in 1968, 65.1% were known to have been reconvicted within two years. 46.8% were sentenced to imprisonment or borstal training or returned to borstal under section 12 of the 1961 Act.

III. IMPRISONMENT

123. The limited range of circumstances in which a young offender may be sentenced to imprisonment is set out in paragraphs 17–21 above, which deal also with the statutory provisions governing release, licencing and recall.

124. The great majority of young prisoners (about 80%) are aged 19 or 20 when sentenced. About a third of the male young offenders received under sentence of imprisonment without the option of a fine are convicted of burglary and over a quarter of crimes of violence against the person (including robbery). Most have substantial previous records when they enter the young prisoners system: in 1971 over 70% of those whose previous history was known had five or more previous convictions. A few however—in 1971, 4%—have no previous convictions at all: in that year nearly two thirds of the small number with no previous convictions sentenced to imprisonment were convicted of crimes of violence against the person, including violent sexual offences. In addition, 991 young men under 21 were committed to prison in default of payment of a fine, in almost all cases for three months or less.

Classification and allocation

125. Prisoners under 21 years of age at the time of their sentence are classified as young prisoners and so far as practicable serve their sentences separately from adult prisoners. Those serving sentences of 18 months or over go to one of the five young prisoners' centres—allocation being as far as possible on the basis of proximity to home—as follows:

Name	Location	Certified normal accommodation	Date first used for custody of offenders	Date brought into use as YPC	Purpose for which built
Aylesbury	Urban	296	1845	1963	County Gaol, with Inebriates Reformatory added in 1902
*Exeter	Urban	42	1853	1972	County Gaol
*Liverpool	Urban	183	1854	1954	City Gaol, subsequent extensions and rebuilding
*Stafford	Urban	100	1845	1971	County Gaol
Swinfen Hall	Rural (3 miles Lichfield, Staffs.)	182	1963	1971	Purpose-built as borstal

*Wing of prison.

126. Some young prisoners serving sentences of under 18 months are held at Liverpool, Stafford and Exeter; others remain at their local prison (in separate young prisoners wings) or form domestic parties at remand centres.

127. Medium and long-term prisoners may be reclassified as adults once they have reached the age of 18 if the Governor is satisfied that their re-classification is justified on the grounds of the prisoner's character or degree of criminal sophistication, because he would have an undesirable effect on other young prisoners or on grounds of general maturity. They are then transferred to adult training prisons if they have a significant period left to serve. All young prisoners are reclassified at about the age of 21.

128. Under the present arrangements for the allocation of young prisoners those with sentences of less than 18 months imprisonment (most of whom, because of the operation of section 3 of the Criminal Justice Act 1961 described in paragraph 18 above, have quite short sentences) are held at Liverpool, Stafford or Exeter, or at local prisons, where they are segregated as strictly as structural and other conditions permit. Recently, a few local prisons have been able to provide a self-contained unit for young prisoners. But provision for this group of offenders is in general a matter for concern. The shortness of many of the sentences would be an obstacle in the way of moving them to a young prisoners' centre even if places were available; and with the present pressure of numbers, places in these centres must go to those sentenced to longer periods. But to keep them in local prisons—which are almost all overcrowded—is bad for the offenders themselves and presents difficult problems of segregation. The conditions in local prisons are in general such that complete separation cannot be achieved; though young prisoners are accommodated on a separate landing, they cannot be kept from occasional contact with adult prisoners. Neither can satisfactory arrangements be made for their training: for example, they can rarely be employed in a separate workshop.

129. Young prisoners sentenced to life imprisonment are allocated by the Home Office to Liverpool or Aylesbury according to which is nearer to their homes. Young offenders under the age of 18 sentenced to detention under section 53 of the Children and Young Persons Act 1933 on being found guilty of certain grave crimes—only a very small number in any one year—have generally gone to the Borstal Allocation Centre at Wormwood Scrubs or Manchester for classification and allocation. They can be transferred only by order of the Secretary of State. In 1971, 34 young men and one young woman were received with sentences of life imprisonment or detention during Her Majesty's Pleasure.

130. Of the 1,445 male young prisoners in custody on 30 June 1973, 296 were at Aylesbury Young Prisoners' Centre, 173 at Swinfen Hall Young Prisoners' Centre, 245 at the Young Prisoners' Centre at Liverpool, 98 at the Young Prisoners' Centre at Stafford and 42 at Exeter. 45 young prisoners considered likely to benefit from psychiatric treatment there were at Grendon. The remaining 546 young prisoners—over a third—were in local prisons. About 50 young prisoners are serving either life sentences or sentences of detention during Her Majesty's Pleasure. A small number of young prisoners are Category A prisoners who have to be held under special conditions of security.

Training

131. As is indicated above, the real problem with young prisoners lies in the numbers who have to remain in local prisons. For those who are transferred to the centres, there is a regime with a positive character and individual attention of the kind given in borstal. Young prisoners are, however, subject generally to the ordinary Prison Rules as to discipline etc.

132. At Aylesbury and Swinfen Hall trainees progress from one wing to another during training, until they qualify for the "senior" wing, where they have additional privileges and at the same time more responsibility for the organisation of their own activities. A good range of work is available; physical education and vocational training courses are being developed. All offenders under 21 have to undertake some education, arrangements for which are made by the local education authorities.

Parole, supervision and recall

133. The statutory provisions governing the release, supervision and recall of young prisoners are summarised in paragraph 21 above. The conditions of the release licence and the criteria for recall are generally similar to those for other young offenders. As many young prisoners have had considerable experience of institutional training the value of recall for a short period is clearly limited. In 1972 only three recall orders of young prisoners serving sentences of less than 18 months were issued and only two of them effected. However, 52 young prisoners with sentences of 18 months or more who had been released in lieu of remission after two thirds of the sentence were recalled on the advice of the Parole Board. There is no special recall centre for young prisoners. In 1972, 22 young prisoners had their supervision terminated early.

Reconviction rates

134. Of the young male prisoners released in 1968, 70.1% were known to have been reconvicted within 2 years. 54.6% were recommitted to prison or borstal under sentence.

IV. REMAND CENTRES

135. As noted in paragraph 49 above, on 30 June 1973 there were 1,659 young men on remand in custody in remand centres or prisons of whom about half were untried and the other half convicted but unsentenced.

136. The majority of young men in custody on remand are held in special remand centres opened within the last 12 years. The remand centres taking young male offenders are as follows:

Name	Location	Certified normal accommodation	Date first used as remand centre	Purpose for which built
Young men only				
Ashford	Urban (Ashford, Middlesex)	400	1961	Former LCC Residential School
Brockhill	Rural (3 miles Bromsgrove, Worcs.)	176	1965	Purpose-built
Cardiff	Urban	62	1965	Wing of prison
Exeter	Urban	43	1964	Part purpose-built (part old County Court offices)
Latchmere House (overflow for Ashford)	Urban (Kingston-upon-Thames, Surrey)	130	1970	Private residence: war-time interrogation centre
Thorp Arch	Rural (4 miles Wetherby, Yorks.)	101	1965	Purpose-built
Winchester	Urban	78	1965	Purpose-built
Young men, and women of all ages				
Low Newton	Semi-rural (4 miles Durham)	102*	1965	Purpose-built
Pucklechurch	Rural (8 miles Bristol)	93*	1965	Purpose-built
Men and women of all ages				
Risley	Semi-rural (6 miles Warrington, Lancs.)	626*	1965	Purpose-built

*Combined c.n.a. for males and females.

137. Most accommodation in remand centres is in cells. The primary problem in this part of the system also is one of accommodation. More remand accommodation is needed for persons under 21; and there is a programme for building new centres and extensions to existing accommodation. In the meantime, some young adults remanded in custody are accommodated in local prisons. Despite their obvious disadvantages, local prisons have

the advantage that they are near some of the main courts that they serve, and usually have good communications which makes visits by family, lawyers and others much easier.

138. Remand centres have two main purposes. First, they need to detain in suitable and secure conditions those remanded in custody by the courts and to provide the facilities, including those for visiting by solicitors, probation officers and relations, to which an unsentenced person is entitled. Secondly, they provide a service to the courts by the assessment of unsentenced persons by experienced staff including medical staff.

139. Remand centres form part of the overall prison system and their staff are drawn from the general prison service. The Prison Rules apply to remand centres, with any necessary modifications, but untried persons are, so far as possible, separated from all other classes of prisoners. If they wish, they may wear their own clothes. They are not obliged to work, though if they choose to do so they earn money for the work done. Untried persons are allowed to pay for specially furnished rooms and certain domestic services, and to buy newspapers etc; young people make little use of these privileges. They are permitted daily visits and letters. They are also allowed to have their own food sent in; again, young people make little use of this facility, except to receive supplies of chocolates, sweets etc.

140. Given the frequent interruptions in routine through visits from legal advisers etc. and the transient nature of a person's stay in a remand centre, it is impracticable to provide any sort of work, training or education demanding continuity. However, efforts are made to provide educational activity and simple forms of routine work, as well as work in running the establishment.

CUSTODIAL PROVISION FOR YOUNG WOMEN

141. The numbers of young women in custody are small, and it has not been found practicable to provide for them the same geographical spread of establishments as is provided for young men. Nor is it feasible to provide entirely separate accommodation for all young women offenders under 21; there are separate borstals, but elsewhere the trend in recent years has been towards accommodating younger and older women together. Experience of the beneficial influence which offenders of different ages have on each other has led the Department to the view that this is the right approach.

142. The law as regards custodial sentences for young offenders does not distinguish between the sexes, but in practice detention in a detention centre is no longer available for young women (see paragraph 6 above). During their review of the operation of detention centres the Advisory Council, in an interim report, recommended that the detention centre as a method of treatment for young women should be abandoned, short-term custodial treatment in general not being considered suitable for young women, and the detention centre at Moor Court was closed in 1969. Thus the system for young women provides only borstals, prisons and remand centres.

143. It is noteworthy that only some 3% of the total of young offenders in the custodial system are young women. On 30 June 1973 there were 208 young women under 21 serving custodial sentences: 175 in the borstal system (including an estimated 20 girls aged 15 or 16, see paragraph 146) and 33 serving terms of imprisonment. In addition on that date there were 102 young women under 21 on remand in custody at remand centres, about half of them being untried and half convicted but not sentenced. The daily average population of young women in custody in 1972 was 40 young prisoners, 180 borstal trainees, and 90 remanded in custody untried or unsentenced.

144. There are at present seven establishments in which young women under 21 are housed, of which only the closed borstal at Bullwood Hall is exclusively for those of this age.[1] The borstal accommodation is as follows:

---

[1] East Sutton Park also accommodates a number of adult women prisoners.

Bullwood Hall, near Southend—closed borstal -   -   -   -   -   124 places

East Sutton Park,[1] near Maidstone—open borstal   -   -   -   -   45 places

Styal, Cheshire—wing of prison—(for pregnant girls and those with babies)-   -   -   -   -   -   -   -   -   -   -   -   -   32 places

Young women prisoners with sentences of under six months committed by courts in the south are generally held at Holloway, and all others at Styal, both of which are closed prisons. Occasionally a young prisoner suitable for open conditions is transferred to Askham Grange or Moor Court open prisons for women.

145. In addition to Holloway, which takes remand prisoners aged under 21, there are at present three remand centres which take young women—Low Newton, Pucklechurch and Risley. None of these is exclusively for young women, or is able to provide entirely separate accommodation for them.

I. BORSTAL

Type of offenders

146. Two fifths of all the young women received into borstal in 1971 were convicted of theft, nearly one fifth of burglary, and one fifth of offences involving violence (including robbery). Of the 299 received, one tenth had no previous convictions; about a fifth had one previous conviction; one fifth had two previous convictions; and a sixth had three previous convictions. Nearly one in ten had six or more previous convictions. About one in seven of those received in 1971 had previously been in an approved school. Though only six young women were sentenced to borstal training in 1971 for offences relating to prostitution, many had been leading promiscuous lives. About 11% of those received under sentence of borstal training in 1971 were aged under 17 on conviction. It has proved difficult to meet the needs of girls of 15 and 16 within the borstal system where most are aged 17 or over, and the small total numbers make it impracticable to have borstals providing for different age groups.

Reception and allocation

147. The small size of the system does not provide much scope for selection and allocation. Selection for open conditions is done by the staff at Holloway or the remand centres on the basis of the background reports available at the time of sentence and of observation of behaviour while in custody before or immediately after sentence. Bullwood Hall receives all who are unsuitable for open conditions, except those who are pregnant or have small children with them (who go to Styal).

Training

148. The Borstal Rules apply to young women with very few modifications. In particular, the general principles of borstal training set out in Rule 1 (see paragraph 88 above) make no distinction between the sexes, though in practice there are a number of significant variations; for example, young women in all penal establishments wear their own clothes.

149. Emotional disturbance is common among young women who receive custodial sentences, and highly skilled and specialist treatment and care is often needed. They are often in need of psychiatric care and where possible are transferred to a psychiatric hospital; others spend a period in the hospital at Holloway.

150. In putting into effect the general principles of borstal training the staff at the training borstals try to ensure that the period away from home is used constructively. They give a young woman the opportunity to mature into adulthood, to give and receive affection, to make stable relationships, and to learn to recognise what is acceptable social behaviour. Treatment needs to be carefully planned, highly individualised, and to look forward at all times to the period when the young women will leave the establishment.

151. At the main closed borstal, Bullwood Hall, trainees are initially employed on domestic work. The principal employment provided during the main part of the training

---

[1] East Sutton Park also accommodates a number of adult women prisoners.

is in the sewing shop, in a small assembly unit and on the farm, and on domestic work such as in the kitchen or laundry. Remedial education is provided, and there is a wide range of evening classes. Several schemes of community service are in operation. There is within the medical unit a special "community unit" which enables a small group of trainees who are in particular need of supportive community therapy to live and work together and to share psychotherapeutic treatment. Bullwood Hall has a satellite hostel at Hill Hall, near Epping. Like the young men's hostel at Taylor House (see paragraph 97 above) this is a hostel in which selected young women can serve a substantial part of their sentence. The girls go out to employment mainly in Harlow New Town.

152. The only open borstal for young women, East Sutton Park, is a country manor house, the accommodation consisting of bedrooms and small dormitories. Trainees do domestic work and work on maintaining the buildings, in the gardens and on the farm, and there is a good deal of work for the community. There is a pre-release hostel close to but separate from the main house. This is a self-contained flat in which trainees live with little supervision, going to outside employment.

Discipline

153. The available disciplinary awards are the same as those in respect of young men (see paragraph 109 above). The rate of disciplinary offences in closed borstals for young women is relatively high. It is rare for formal punishments to be awarded at East Sutton Park for offences in the establishment; but there is a fair amount of absconding and girls who prove unsuitable for open conditions are transferred to Bullwood Hall.

Supervision after release

154. The provisions and procedures relating to supervision and recall are the same as for young men. In contrast to the borstals for young men the pre-release work is done by seconded probation officers. The distance from home of a large proportion of the young women in borstals—including all those from the north—adds to the difficulty of keeping up family contacts. Where a young woman has a child, there are additional problems if she intends to keep it, and arrangements to be made if she does not.

Recall

155. In 1972 seven orders recalling young women to borstal training were issued; six were apprehended and recalled; one recall order was cancelled because the young woman resumed contact with her supervising officer. In addition 18 were returned to borstal by the courts under section 12 of the Criminal Justice Act 1961 following conviction during the period of supervision. Those recalled or returned to borstal training go to Bullwood Hall.

Reconviction rates

156. Of the young women released from borstal in 1968 38.8% were known to have been reconvicted within a period of two years. 16.3% were sentenced to imprisonment or borstal training or returned to borstal under section 12 of the 1961 Act.

II. YOUNG PRISONERS

157. There were only 33 young women prisoners in custody on 30 June 1973. Of these, 22 were serving sentences of up to and including 18 months, six were serving sentences of over 18 months and up to three years, and five were serving sentences of over three years. About half were at Styal, the remainder being at Holloway or the remand centres.

158. Experience has shown that it is better not to place young women prisoners in their own separate accommodation (as is quite feasible at Styal where there are separate "houses") but to allow them to take part in the general life of the prison. At Styal this includes a domestic training course, a vocational training course in soft furnishing and upholstery, and domestic and garden work.

159. Of the very small number (36) of young women prisoners released in 1968 36.1% were known to have been reconvicted within a period of two years. 13.9% were recommitted to prison or borstal under sentence.

211

III. REMAND CENTRES

160. The number of young women on remand is small and they are divided between four establishments. The fluctuating proportions of young women and adults would make it impracticable to segregate the groups even if experience did not suggest that mixing the age groups is preferable. The small number of establishments means that some young women have to be detained on remand a long distance from the court before which they are to appear, with consequent problems over visits by family, officials, and legal advisers, and with the difficulty both for the prisoner and her escort of long and tiring journeys at the time of a court appearance.

Staff

161. There are Governors Class III in charge of Bullwood Hall and East Sutton Park, with assistant governors at Bullwood Hall. In addition, there is a woman assistant governor in charge of women at Risley remand centre. As in the establishments for young men, there are medical officers and chaplains, technical and professional staff etc. Thus at all establishments for young women there are some male staff, and this is regarded as beneficial to the general atmosphere. The needs of many young women sentenced to custodial treatment are such that the nursing staff is of particular importance in these establishments.

162. The staff/inmate ratio is generous in comparison with that in establishments for young men: this reflects both the special problems of caring for young women and the relatively small size of the establishments with their disproportionate claims on the whole range of staff grades.

Non-custodial treatment

163. This section describes provision for non-custodial treatment of young offenders. It deals briefly with probation resources, then with attendance centres, and at more length with the provision of hostels for young offenders. With regard to community service and day training centres it is not possible at this stage to provide more than an outline.

164. It is not possible from available data to determine with any degree of accuracy the proportion or actual amount of probation service resources devoted to the supervision of young offenders aged 17 to 21 on probation or released from a custodial sentence. On 30 June 1973 there were 4,142 whole-time probation officers in post; and of a total of 130,070 people under the supervision of a probation officer at the end of 1971, whether on probation, on licence following a custodial sentence, or for other reasons, 41,048 (or 32%) were offenders who had been placed on probation while aged 17 to 21 or under supervision following release from detention centre or borstal. It does not follow that precisely 32% of probation service effort and resources are devoted to those in the young offender age group. Probation officers engage in many tasks other than the direct supervision of offenders, notably the preparation of social enquiry reports of which the proportion prepared on young offenders is not known. Moreover a substantial number of probation officers work in prison service establishments as welfare officers, and the work of the service will diversify even further with the new functions under the Criminal Justice Act 1972, such as the administration of hostels, day training centres and community service schemes. In addition, it does not follow that different types of supervision case are equally demanding in terms of time and effort. But the proportion indicated above may certainly be taken as a rough guide to the demands made on probation services resources by young offenders. The approximate average weekly cost of supervising one offender on probation or subject to after-care was estimated for the House of Commons Expenditure Committee[1] at a maximum of £2 per week.

165. *The Sentence of the Court* describes the objects and methods of probation supervision in the following terms:

"The object of probation, as of all methods of treatment, is the ultimate

---

[1] See First Report from the House of Commons Expenditure Committee 1971–72, QQ 1,185–6 page 249. It was estimated then that the cost was between £1 and £2 a week, depending on the stage of the supervision period and hence the time the officer devoted to the case. On the basis explained there and allowing for rising prices the average figure is now probably nearer £2 per week.

re-establishment of the offender in the community. But probation involves the discipline of submission by the offender while at liberty to supervision by a probation officer. It thus seeks both to protect society and to strengthen the probationer's resources so that he becomes a more responsible person. Unlike custodial treatment, which by removing the offender from his family and community tends to suspend his social and economic obligations to them, probation exacts from him a contribution, within the limits of his capacity, to their well-being.

"The probation officer's first task as a social case worker is to win the confidence of the probationer and his family and to develop a relationship which will be a positive influence, regulating the probationer's behaviour and counteracting and modifying the ill effects of past experiences and of irremovable factors in the present. To this end the probation officer keeps in close touch with the probationer, usually both by visiting his home and by requiring the probationer to see him regularly at the probation office.

". . . He encourages the probationer to use the appropriate statutory and voluntary agencies which might contribute to his welfare, and to take advantage of the social, recreational and educational facilities suited to his age, ability and temperament."

The methods of supervision of those released from custody are essentially similar.

166. Among the physical resources associated with probation and after-care work are the approved probation hostels system, and after-care hostels; these are described in paragraphs 174–195 and paragraphs 196–200 respectively below.

167. At this stage little can be said in concrete terms about the new forms of non-custodial treatment being provided under the Criminal Justice Act 1972—day training centres and community service, both of which are being started experimentally in a limited number of areas.

168. The statutory provisions relating to community service are set out in paragraphs 29–31 above. An offender made subject to a community service order is required to report to the officer administering the community service scheme for the area and to inform him of any change of address; he must also perform the number of hours work specified in the order at such times as he is instructed by the officer.

169. It is intended that the work to be carried out by offenders will be of a sort which in the normal way would not be done otherwise than by voluntary effort. In some cases work projects are directly organised by the probation service; in others offenders work on projects run by voluntary organisations and other bodies. Examples of tasks included in the pilot schemes are: work on constructing a community centre; clearing driftwood and debris from tow-paths and foreshores; building adventure playgrounds; preparing a nature conservancy and forest trail recreation areas; and home decorating for elderly and handicapped people. Where possible, offenders work alongside volunteer non-offenders in projects organised by voluntary bodies. If sufficient tasks for offenders cannot be arranged in this way, the probation and after-care service arrange for other work projects. Offenders are supervised at work either by the voluntary agency or other body providing the work or by staff—normally ancillaries—employed by the probation and after-care service.

170. Attendance at a day training centre, which may be included as a requirement of a probation order (see paragraph 27 above) is intended to provide full-time non-residential training for offenders with the aim of equipping them more adequately for the normal demands of modern life. The scheme has been framed with a particular view to the needs of the inadequate recidivist, whose offences often reflect a lack of basic social skills and tend to lead to a succession of short custodial sentences which usually afford little opportunity for the kind of training from which he might benefit. Examples of the kind of training envisaged are remedial education, simple work training, matrimonial counselling and advice on home economics. The centres are to be run by the probation service, drawing on a range of local agencies and resources. Attached to each centre will be a small group of probation officers who will have low case loads consisting of probationers waiting to enter centres, those in attendance, and those who have recently

passed through. While the special needs of young offenders are unlikely to be appropriately met in the centres developed for adult offenders, flexible adaptation of the system to provide specifically for young offenders may be practicable.

Attendance centres

171. The effects of the statutory provisions on attendance centres in so far as they relate to offenders aged 17 to 21 are set out on paragraph 33 above. *The Sentence of the Court* says

> "Attendance centres are designed to deal with young delinquents whose future conduct may be expected to be influenced by the effect of deprivation of leisure time and by what the attendance centre staff teach them about respect for the law and the property of others. In so far as attendance at an attendance centre entails giving up as much as 24 hours of the offender's leisure time, generally on Saturday afternoons, it is calculated to have a deterrent effect both on him and on others. When he attends the centre, the offender comes under the influence of representatives of the law who set before him and require from him a high standard of cleanliness, behaviour and application to the task in hand. The instruction and occupation given at the centres is designed to teach the offender something of the constructive use of leisure and to guide him, on leaving, towards organisations or activities in which he may use what he has learned."

172. Although the 1948 Act envisaged attendance centres providing for offenders aged 14 and up to 21, initially the system provided only for 14 to 17 year olds. Following a recommendation of the Advisory Council on the Treatment of Offenders in their report *Alternatives to Imprisonment* in 1957, two attendance centres were set up experimentally for the 17 to 21 age group, at Manchester in 1958 and at Greenwich in 1964. Hitherto the senior attendance centre system has not been developed beyond those two centres, and the report by the Advisory Council on the Penal System on non-custodial and semi-custodial penalties recommended that there should be no extension until the experimental community service schemes had been evaluated so that it could be ascertained whether there was a continuing need for attendance centres.[1]

173. The two senior centres are open on Saturday afternoons. The Manchester centre is run by prison officers from Manchester prison who have volunteered for the work, and the London centre is run by police officers, who are also volunteers. The period of attendance ordered by the court is normally divided into sessions of two hours each. The scheme of occupation and instruction approved for the senior centres includes a period of physical training or tasks under supervision such as cleaning and upkeep of the premises.[2]

THE APPROVED PROBATION HOSTEL SYSTEM

Purpose and history of approved hostels

174. Probation is essentially a method of treatment in the open and the probationer normally lives at home and remains at work in the community. Probationers may include immature, inadequate and irresponsible people who are socially disorganised and who have lacked appropriate community and family support. They may be assisted to respond to probation by being given initially a stable and supportive environment, in which limits are implicitly set to acceptable conduct, which approved probation hostels are intended to provide. In this environment they can adjust to living with contemporaries and others, including those in authority, acquire basic ideas about acceptable social behaviour, find and keep suitable employment and be introduced to the constructive use of leisure time.

175. Probation hostels began, in the early 1920s, with the concept of providing a substitute home for young persons whose own home had failed to provide the necessary understanding, support and discipline. By 1949 this concept had been developed to the point where hostels were specifically charged with providing training in good social habits and the constructive use of leisure time. The Morison Committee, in its Second Report in 1962[3] which dealt with the approved probation hostel system, defined the role of hostels as

---

[1] *Non-Custodial and Semi-Custodial Penalties* HMSO 1970. Paragraph 103.
[2] A fuller description will be found in paragraphs 87–98 of the Council's earlier report.
[3] Second report of the Departmental Committee on the Probation Service (Cmnd 1800).

catering for young persons who have the potentiality to respond to probation supervision if, for a period, they are removed from their home environment, but whose difficulties are such that they could not maintain themselves successfully in (for example) lodgings, or the comparatively uncontrolled conditions of ordinary hostels for young wage earners. These young persons would have the capacity for work in the community and would not have reached the stage where they needed institutional training in an approved school or borstal, but they could have unusual difficulty in meeting the demands of society because of limitations in their upbringing or home environment or because of undesirable associations. The Committee saw probation hostels as places which provide a sympathetic yet disciplined regime where, with mature adult support and control, a young person could be helped to learn self discipline, acquire more constructive social attitudes and the habit of regular work, personal hygiene and the constructive use of leisure time and, above all, learn to live acceptably with contemporaries and older people.

176. The Departmental Committee on the Treatment of Young Offenders, reporting in 1927,[1] recommended "a greater use of hostels . . . such hostels should be approved and inspected by the central authority and there should be grants from public funds". This recommendation was accepted and the Home Office thereafter contributed towards the maintenance of each probationer sent to an approved hostel, provided the local authority concerned contributed an equal amount. In the pre-war period the assumption appears to have been that hostels could be provided and managed by voluntary organisations without substantial cost to public funds; a modest standard of accommodation and staffing was envisaged. However, by 1948 it had become evident that voluntary funds were not forthcoming to an extent which would maintain reasonable standards of accommodation or provide staff of the calibre necessary and that approved hostels must look to public funds for such part of their income as could not be provided by residents from their earnings. This has been the position since the enactment of the Criminal Justice Act 1948.

The statutory provisions

177. Section 3(4) of the Criminal Justice Act 1948 enables a court to include in a probation order a requirement relating to the residence of the offender. The period for which a probationer may be required to reside in a hostel may not exceed 12 months in all. A residence requirement, like any other requirement of a probation order, cannot be made unless the offender has expressed his willingness to comply with it. Section 46(1) enables the Secretary of State to approve probation hostels "for the reception of persons who may be required to reside therein by a probation order" and who, while in residence, will be employed outside the premises. Section 46(2) enables the Secretary of State to make rules for the regulation, management and inspection of the hostels. The Approved Probation Hostel and Home[2] Rules 1949 have been made under this power. Section 77(3)(b) provides for payment from public funds towards the expenditure of any society or person establishing or carrying on an approved probation hostel. Paragraph 3(1)(d) of the Fifth Schedule to the Act imposes a duty on probation committees to make such payments as may be prescribed in respect of persons required by a probation order to reside in a hostel. Until recently all approved probation hostels were provided by voluntary societies and financed under the statutory arrangements outlined above. However under section 53 of the Criminal Justice Act 1972 probation and after-care committees may now, with the approval of the Secretary of State, themselves provide and carry on probation hostels.

Use of probation hostels

178. In 1971, 12,136 probation orders were made on young men aged 17–21, and 2,731 on girls in this age group. Of these 603 and 188 respectively included a residence requirement under section 3 of the 1948 Act.

Hostels at present available

179. Under Rule 7 of the Hostel and Home Rules the Secretary of State prescribes the age limits and the maximum number of residents for each hostel. There are at present 20 hostels for young men and seven for young women for which the age range on entry is wholly or partially within the 17–21 age range. In addition there are seven hostels taking

---

[1] Cmd 2831. Recommendation (29), page 123.
[2] See footnote to paragraph 179.

only adult men. These are included in the table below in order to provide a complete picture of the available provision.[1] Prior to the enactment of the Children and Young Persons Act 1969 probation hostels also provided for offenders under 17; some have remained available to the juvenile treatment system as community homes, while others have adjusted their age limits and remain within the approved probation hostel system. This has had the result of increasing the accommodation available for probationers over 17, and in particular has made possible the establishment of hostels for adult men. A major expansion of probation hostel places for adults is planned for the next few years. The accommodation at present available is as follows:

Age at entry	Number of hostels	Number of places
Young Men		
17–19	8 ⎫	160 ⎫
17–20	1 ⎬ 16	21 ⎬ 324
17–21	2 ⎪	39 ⎪
18–21	5 ⎭	104 ⎭
Men		
19–25	4 ⎫	59 ⎫
21–30	4 ⎬ 11	68 ⎬ 174
25–35	3 ⎭	47 ⎭
Young Women		
17–19	3 ⎫	45 ⎫
18–21	2 ⎬ 7	38 ⎬ 118
18–25	1 ⎪	18 ⎪
19–25	1 ⎭	17 ⎭

These figures relate to the total amount of accommodation provided, but the number of places available at any given time may vary for a number of reasons. For example, a hostel may have to close temporarily because of major structural alterations or staffing difficulties.

Location of hostels

180. The present location of hostels has been determined to some extent by the initiative of the voluntary organisations which have provided them. Most are in the large conurbations or cities such as London, Birmingham, Liverpool, Manchester, Leeds, Newcastle and Nottingham, but following a recommendation of the Morison Committee some of the new hostels have been located in smaller towns, such as Ipswich, Oxford, Maidstone, Redditch and Windsor. An important consideration is the availability of an adequate supply of employment of a kind suited to the capabilities of the average hostel resident and a reasonable supply of alternative employers, but the area should also offer satisfactory further educational and recreational facilities.

Premises

181. Most of the existing hostels are large Victorian or Edwardian houses built as family residences which have been considerably adapted and extended to serve their present purpose. A few are purpose-built on the sites of such residences. In some cases, notably in London, areas are being completely redeveloped and new purpose-built hostels are being provided as part of the redevelopment scheme. The older hostels were based mainly on large dormitories for the residents with recreational and dining facilities and minimal quarters for the staff which offered little in the way of privacy. A substantial programme of modernisation has been carried out in the last few years, in addition to the provision of new premises, and most hostels now provide about 20 places for residents (rather fewer in hostels for young women); accommodation for between a third and a half of the residents is in single bedrooms, the remainder being in rooms for three or four. In addition to

[1] There are also three approved probation homes providing 76 places for young adult offenders. This Appendix does not deal in detail with probation homes. The administrative arrangements are generally the same as for approved probation hostels. However the primary object of placement in a probation home is to instil the habit of regular work. For this reason, while probation homes resemble hostels in other respects, residents in homes are employed on the premises for the greater part of their stay and move only in their last few months into employment in the outside community.

the usual kitchen, laundry and dining facilities the hostels now provide a sitting room (with TV), a games room (which can be used for dancing), a hobbies room and sometimes a quiet room. The staff are provided with an administrative office and individual quarters consisting of a three bedroom flat with sitting room, kitchen and bathroom for the warden; a similar flat with two bedrooms for the deputy warden; and a bed sitting room or separate bedroom and sitting room with simple self-catering facilities for the assistant warden. Flexibility of provision to take account of the employment of non-resident supervisory staff is a feature of recent development.

Management

182. Hitherto all approved probation hostels have been under the management of voluntary committees (referred to in the Rules as Managing Committees) who may be either self-appointed or appointed by some parent organisation or public body. The Secretary of State has no control over the appointment of Managing Committees and cannot nominate members. As noted in paragraph 177 above probation committees now have statutory authority to provide and manage probation hostels.

Finance

183. Residents in approved probation hostels are required to contribute towards the cost of their maintenance according to their earnings; the maximum amount of this contribution is prescribed by the Secretary of State and is reviewed annually. For 1973–74 it is fixed at £5.50 a week for those under 21. Up to 31 March 1973 the balance of the cost of providing and running probation hostels and probation homes was shared equally between the Exchequer and local authorities on behalf of probation committees. On 1 April 1973 the Exchequer share was increased to 80%. Since the cost of providing and maintaining hostels and homes varies from one to another a "flat rate" system is in operation so that the local payment is the same irrespective of the hostel or home used. The net running cost of each hostel, after allowing for residents' maintenance contributions and flat rate payments from probation committees, is met by Home Office grant. The "flat rate" paid by probation committees is reviewed annually with the object of maintaining the agreed ratio between local authorities and Exchequer payments. The combined "flat rate" for 1973–74 is £18.20. The responsibility for paying individual flat rate contributions rests with the probation committee for the area in which the court making the original probation order is situated. The Home Office exercises a substantial measure of control over the expenditure of hostels by the examination and approval of preliminary and revised estimates; by requiring committees to obtain prior approval to any expenditure not included in the estimates or in excess of the amounts approved in the estimates; and by issuing annually a list of "pro-rata" allowances for various items such as food, clothing and household requisites. The average net weekly cost to public funds per head for residents in hostels for youths (after taking contributions from earnings into account) was estimated to be £25.19 in 1972–73. In hostels for girls the net cost was estimated to be £28.80. The building of some new hostels and most major structural alterations to existing hostels has been financed by way of loans negotiated by the managing committees and the servicing and repayment of these loans is reflected in the figures of net costs above. Capital costs of this kind are not included in the calculations of net costs of prison service establishments, and therefore the net cost figures of places in probation hostels and prison service establishments are not directly comparable.

Staff

184. Under the provisions of the Hostel and Home Rules the managing committee of each hostel is responsible for the appointment and supervision of staff, but an appointment as warden requires the consent of the Secretary of State. The warden is responsible to the committee for the efficient conduct of the hostel and, subject to their directions, determines the duties of the other members of the staff. A typical hostel will have a staff of warden and matron (who will usually be husband and wife) a deputy warden and an assistant warden. Hostels for young women have a staff of warden, deputy warden and one or two assistant wardens. In the past supervisory staff have usually been resident but a proportion of non-resident staff is now employed. In addition to the supervisory staff a hostel will usually have a non-resident cook, part-time domestic staff and a part-time clerk/typist. The pay and conditions of service of supervisory staff are prescribed by the Standing Joint Advisory Committee for Staffs of Children's Homes (which also has within its purview matrons, house-masters and certain other staff in community homes

217

and—while they still exist—approved schools). Probation officers seconded to act as wardens retain their existing salary scales and conditions of service.

Admission to hostels

185. If a hostel has a vacancy it may not, except with the consent of the Secretary of State, refuse to accept a person who is required to reside there by a probation order, is within the category of persons for whom the hostel is approved and is not debarred from admission on specified grounds.[1] The courts have, however, been advised to consult a hostel, through a probation officer, about the suitability of a particular individual before making an order for him to reside there, and this is the general practice. Where there are more applications than there are vacant places a measure of selection is exercised by most wardens, usually in consultation with the liaison probation officer. Hostels for young offenders are not at present assigned to particular catchment areas and since one of the objects of placement in a hostel may be to make a break with unsuitable associates or with an unsatisfactory home it is not uncommon to seek a hostel some distance from the offender's home. (For their part hostels may be reluctant to admit an offender who lives in the vicinity since they feel that the opportunity of frequent visits home not only keeps fresh the problems which led to his removal but has an unsettling effect on other residents who are unable to enjoy this facility. Nevertheless the practice of the probation and after-care service is in general to seek placements within a reasonable distance of the community to which the probationer is expected to return.)

The hostel regime

186. The Rules provide that residents shall as soon as possible and in any case within two weeks of admission be assisted in finding suitable employment outside the hostel. It is generally expected that residents will not needlessly change their employment and will in any case not do so without the consent of the warden. Since residents are in general not available for local employment for more than 12 months it is not easy to find progressive and satisfying work for them, and they are generally dependent on work of an unskilled, or at best semi-skilled, nature.

187. Residents are encouraged to participate in worthwhile leisure pursuits and are generally free to pursue leisure activities of their own choice in consultation with the hostel staff.

188. Residents usually have control of their earnings, simply paying over to the hostel their weekly maintenance charge. They are encouraged to consult the staff about the spending of their earnings, and to save. In some hostels for young women provision is made for residents nearing the end of their stay to live in a bed/sitting room or shared flat, purchasing and cooking their own food, being responsible for laundry and cleaning and paying only a rental charge for accommodation.

189. Discipline is maintained by the personal influence of the warden and staff. Residents in hostels are not in legal detention and cannot be compelled to remain there or to return if they abscond. A probationer who absconds can, however, be brought back to court under section 6 of the Criminal Justice Act 1948 for breach of the requirement of the probation order. The court may then impose a fine or deal with the probationer for the offence in respect of which the probation order was originally made in any manner open to it if it had just convicted him of that offence.

Training

190. The formal requirement in the Rules that each approved hostel should provide a

---

[1] Rule 8 of the Approved Probation Hostel and Home Rules provides that a person shall not be received in a hostel:
  (a) if he is on remand;
  (b) if he is subject to an order under the Children and Young Persons Act 1933 (section 67) relating to temporary detention in a place of safety;
  (c) if he is mentally defective;
  (d) if he is suffering from epilepsy to such a degree that he cannot be accommodated without detriment to himself or other residents;
  (e) in the case of a woman or girl if she is pregnant.
New Rules which simplify and reduce the excluded categories are in a stage of final preparation.

218

scheme of training approved by the Secretary of State is no longer invoked. When the 1949 Rules were made the hostel system generally catered for a younger age group than it now does—in 1949 only one hostel accepted youths as old as 19 on admission. By the time more hostels were available for young men of up to 21 on admission there had already been a movement away from providing classes of various kinds on the premises and towards encouraging residents to take part in activities in the community, eg to join youth clubs. The practice in the hostels now that they provide for an older age-group is to allow considerable freedom of choice of evening activity, within or outside the hostel. The Statutory Rules are being revised to reflect the general change of emphasis which has developed.

191. Wardens of hostels make it their business to find out how residents propose to use their leisure time and will guide and encourage them in worthwhile pursuits. Although they can exercise little control over what a resident does when he is away from the hostel in the evenings a resident who persistently abused the freedom allowed him would have it curtailed. The opportunities of "training" in any formal sense are minimal, and are largely confined to seeing that residents get off to work in good time, ensuring reasonable social behaviour within the hostel, encouraging worthwhile leisure pursuits and keeping some kind of control over relationships with other residents. However the possibilities of the informal influence of a mature and integrated personality upon the doubts and uncertainties of the offender are considerable, and may well be the principal benefit conferred by residence in a hostel.

Length of stay

192. The period for which a probationer may be required to reside in a hostel may not extend beyond 12 months from the date of the order or amending order. It is the general practice for the courts to stipulate a maximum period of 12 months' residence. A former obligation on the supervising court to review the need for continued residence beyond 6 months was repealed by the Criminal Justice Act 1967, but supervising probation officers keep the period of residence under review, and a court will usually be prepared to cancel the requirement when satisfied that the resident's progress warrants this course. Excluding those who abscond or are removed as the result of further offences, the average length of stay in hostels is between 10 and 11 months.

193. The Rules enable the Secretary of State to authorise residence in a hostel for a period exceeding 12 months. This power has been sparingly used in the past to allow continued residence on a voluntary basis, usually for a few days or weeks in exceptional circumstances or when extra time is needed to complete resettlement arrangements. In view of the demand for places it has not been thought right to encourage the idea of a person making a probation hostel his permanent home. Moreover there is little evidence that residents themselves wish to stay longer and the few cases where extended stay has been allowed on grounds that the extra time would materially affect the success or failure of the hostel placement have not lent any support to the suggestion that an extension of stay measured in terms of two or three months is likely to affect the outcome. Nevertheless such requests are viewed sympathetically where circumstances permit. A difficulty in the wider use of the power is that the full cost of maintenance is much greater than a resident can afford; some probation and after-care committees are willing to continue maintenance payments beyond 12 months but they have no general authority to do so and must obtain specific approval in each case.

The probation officer's function

194. One or more of the probation officers in the area where the hostel is situated has responsibility for supervising the residents; this automatically follows from the inclusion of the requirement of residence in a probation order. The local officer (known as the liaison officer) keeps in close touch with the residents under his supervision, and the rules entitle him to see them privately at any reasonable time. This may be either at the hostel or at the probation office. Apart from formal interviews, which are not likely to take place more often than once every three or four weeks, a liaison officer usually makes a point of attending the hostel on at least one evening a week to mix informally with residents and staff. A probation officer in the resident's home area meanwhile keeps in touch with his parents or guardian and supplies a report on the home conditions for the supervising court if it is considering terminating the requirement of residence. The supervising

probation officer and the home probation officer will, together with the warden, be concerned at an early stage in planning for the resident's future when the time comes for him to leave the hostel. The supervising probation officer must, of necessity, work closely with the staff of the hostel and is expected to give them support and advice. Regular case discussion groups in which the probation officer and hostel staff participate, often with the assistance of a consultant psychiatrist, are a regular feature of most hostels.

Inspection

195. Probation hostels are subject to inspection by the Home Office; this is undertaken by the Probation and After-Care Inspectorate, whose particular concern with the use made of the hostels as part of the probation system and with the duties of the liaison probation officer has been extended to embrace all other aspects of hostel life and management.

AFTER-CARE HOSTELS

196. After-care hostels are also provided and managed by voluntary bodies. Probation and after-care committees have hitherto had no specific power to provide them, but section 53 of the Criminal Justice Act 1972 now enables them to provide, in addition to the specific types of establishment mentioned there, "other establishments for use in the rehabilitation of offenders". Local authorities have general powers under sections 21(1) and 26, of the National Assistance Act 1948 to provide residential care for persons who by reason of age, infirmity or any other circumstances are in need of care and attention which is not otherwise available to them and section 26 enables them to act through voluntary bodies. These powers have not been used to provide accommodation specifically for offenders, but offenders are frequently accommodated in eg reception centres provided under this Act. Local authorities also have power under section 65 of the Health Services and Public Health Act 1968 to help voluntary bodies providing hostels for alcoholics and drug addicts, and grants are being made in a few cases to hostels provided by voluntary bodies for alcoholic and drug offenders.

197. The Secretary of State has power under section 77(3)(e) of the Criminal Justice Act 1948 (as amended by section 96(1) of the Criminal Justice Act 1967) to make grants to voluntary bodies engaged in supervising or assisting persons convicted of offences with a view to their rehabilitation. Grants are made under this authority to voluntary bodies providing after-care hostels. The principles underlying this reliance on voluntary bodies were recognised by the Working Party on the Place of Voluntary Service in After-Care in its report on Residential Provision for Homeless Discharged Offenders published in 1966. One is the need to educate public opinion to the special problems and difficulties of discharged offenders by the involvement of the community in practical measures for their rehabilitation. Another is the preference of many discharged offenders for facilities which are not manifestly provided by the official authorities. It was assumed by the Working Party that residents would contribute from their earnings about one fifth of the running costs of after-care hostels and it was felt that it would be appropriate to divide the balance of the running costs equally between the voluntary bodies and the Exchequer. The grant system now in force was designed to meet this principle. The normal rate of grant is a maximum of £175 a year for each place specifically reserved for offenders. The actual amount paid depends on the difference between on one side the running costs and on the other the contributions from residents. Subject to the overriding maximum of £175 a place the grant is limited to what is necessary to close this gap—in other words it may in some cases be less than £175 a year a place. A higher rate of grant, not exceeding £275 a year for each place, is available for hostels providing facilities for alcoholics, drug addicts or other special categories of resident needing a higher level of support than is provided in the ordinary after-care hostel. (Responsibility for grant aid to hostels catering specifically for alcoholics was transferred to the Department of Health and Social Security on 1 April 1973, but the system and the rate of grant remain the same.)

198. At the outset of the grants scheme it was assumed that the individual voluntary bodies providing hostels might find difficulty in raising funds to meet capital costs and that this might act as a brake on the rate at which the additional places necessary would be forthcoming. The Government therefore sponsored the formation of the Bridgehead Housing Association in the expectation that a national body of evident standing would be

in a better position to negotiate loans from local authorities and building societies than would local voluntary bodies. The Association, which was incorporated in August 1967, was intended to purchase properties, adapt them for hostel use and then lease them to local voluntary organisations. As the Association would not be able to raise loans to meet the full cost of purchase and adaptation of properties it was decided to make available limited capital grants to bridge the gap. A grant of £30,000 is being made for 1973–74. Grant totalling £115,246 has been paid in respect of the provision of 24 projects providing 316 places. Six projects came into service in 1972–73. A grant, currently £7,000 a year, is also made towards the administrative expenses of the housing association.

199. The Home Office does not maintain such close financial supervision of after-care hostels as it does of probation hostels, which are wholly supported from public funds, but it is a condition of grant that a representative of the probation and after-care service must be a member of the managing committee. A liaison probation officer is appointed to maintain contact with residents, the warden and other probation officers. The hostel and its records must be open to Home Office inspection.

200. It is difficult to classify after-care hostels, or to obtain an accurate account of the number of places available to any particular category of offender, because many of the general purpose hostels are prepared to accommodate one or two residents who are younger or older than the normal age range and some will occasionally assist those with special problems. Subject to this qualification, there are 38 hostels receiving grant in respect of 336 places for young offenders, and these hostels offer facilities for those between 17 and 25 years of age. In addition, there are 11 hostels which provide 54 places for young women and five hostels providing 20 places for young mothers and their babies. Residents are normally selected by the warden in consultation with a liaison probation officer who provides professional guidance and support to both residents and staff. Some residents come direct from penal establishments; others are referred by probation officers or voluntary social workers. There is no uniformity of method in the process of resettlement but all hostels try to provide support for the offender in an understanding and caring family atmosphere. At one extreme, a hostel for highly disturbed young men released from borstal has offered a sophisticated regime and intensive treatment by psychiatrists, social workers and laymen wholly committed to the concept of surrogate parental care which, in theory at least, lasts indefinitely. At the other extreme is a hostel run by a motherly housekeeper with a flair for containing the unruly outbursts of youth.

PROVISION FOR JUVENILE OFFENDERS AND JUVENILES IN NEED OF CARE OR CONTROL

201. It is conclusively presumed that no child[1] under the age of 10 years can be guilty of any offence (Children and Young Persons Act 1933, Section 50, as amended by the Children and Young Persons Act 1963, Section 16(1)). A juvenile[1] aged 10 or over who is alleged to have committed an offence may be the subject of criminal proceedings or of care proceedings under the provisions of the Children and Young Persons Act 1969. The Act contains power to raise the minimum age for criminal proceedings to 14. The present Government has announced its intention to raise the minimum age to 12 in due course, but not higher.[2] When this takes effect only care proceedings will be available for children aged 10 and 11.

202. For many years the philosophy underlying the treatment of children in trouble has increasingly been to blur the distinction between those who come to notice because they have committed an offence and those who are in trouble for some other reason; this philosophy is inherent in the 1969 Act, which is the result of a review of the arrangements for the treatment of children in trouble initiated by the previous Administration.[3] The aims

[1] "Juvenile" is used to mean a person under the age of 17, "child" a person under the age of 14, and "young person" a person who has attained the age of 14 and is under the age of 17. For convenience in this Appendix, the term "child" is also used in respect of a person in care, irrespective of his age.
[2] eg in an address by Mr. Mark Carlisle, then Parliamentary Under-Secretary of State, Home Office, to the Annual Conference of the Association of Children's Officers on 1 October 1970.
[3] The philosophy underlying the 1969 Act and the main proposals on which it was based were discussed in the White Paper *Children in Trouble*, published in 1968 (Cmnd 3601).

of protecting society from the consequences of juvenile delinquency and of protecting the young and helping them to grow up into mature and law-abiding persons are seen as complementary rather than as distinct and contradictory. Criminal behaviour in children and young persons is seen less as a problem in itself, to be treated in isolation, than as one of several factors in a child's personality, history and background, the existence of any of which might point to a lack of care or control requiring social intervention.

203. Section 1 of the Children and Young Persons Act 1969 is a comprehensive provision relating to care proceedings in juvenile courts in respect of persons under the age of 17. For an order to be made the juvenile court must be satisfied that any of a number of conditions is met, one of which, in the case of a child or young person over the age of 10, is that an offence has been committed; the court must also be of opinion that the child or young person is in need of care or control which he is unlikely to receive unless an order under the section is made. Care proceedings, where an offence is alleged, may be initiated by a local authority or the police if they reasonably believe that there are grounds for making an order under section 1.

204. The following orders are available to the court in both care and criminal proceedings:

(a) *A care order*

A care order commits the child or young person to the care of the local authority in whose area he appears to the court to live (or, if he has no fixed residence, the local authority in whose area the offence was committed). The order places the local authority in loco parentis, with a prior right to the custody of the child and an additional power to restrict his liberty if necessary; a person who has attained the age of 18 will still be subject to this latter power while the care order remains in force. The local authority may board the child out with foster parents; maintain him in a community home (see paragraph 206 below) or a home provided under section 64 of the 1969 Act;[1] or make such other arrangements as seem appropriate to them. The authority has power (similar to the previous power in relation to children subject to "fit person orders") to allow a child in its care to be under the charge and control of a parent, guardian, relative or friend, eg to provide a trial period, at home or elsewhere, while the child remains legally in local authority care. A care order, unless it is changed or extended, ceases to have effect when the child attains the age of 18 years or, if he has already attained the age of 16 when the order is made, when he attains the age of 19. The local authority has a duty to review the case of every child in care not less than every six months and, if the child has been committed to care by a care order, to consider whether to make an application for the discharge of the order. A juvenile court has power to discharge a care order on an application by the local authority, the child, or the parent or guardian on the child's behalf. A juvenile court also has power, on the application of the local authority, to extend to the 19th birthday a care order which would otherwise expire at 18. This may be done only if the child is accommodated in a community home or a home provided under section 64 of the Act and it appears to the court that, by reason of his mental condition or behaviour, it is in his interest or the public interest for him to remain there after he attains the age of 18. As noted in the footnote to paragraph 10 above, with the consent of the Secretary of State for Social Services or for Wales a local authority may bring before a juvenile court a person who has attained the age of 15 who is subject to a care order and who is accommodated in a community home. The court may order removal to borstal if satisfied that the person's behaviour is such that it would be detrimental to the persons accommodated in any community home for him to be accommodated there (section 31 of the 1969 Act).

(b) *A supervision order*

A supervision order places a juvenile under the supervision of a local authority or

---

[1] Section 64 empowers the Secretary of State for Social Services to provide homes "for the accommodation of children who are in the care of local authorities and are in need of particular facilities and services which are . . . unlikely to be readily available in community homes" (for example those who need long-term psychiatric treatment or who because of their behaviour present special problems of management). Three such homes are planned to serve the whole country, and one is already in existence.

a probation officer. It lasts for three years or for such shorter period as may be specified by the court and, except where the order is made in criminal proceedings, may not expire later than the supervised person's 18th birthday. The court may designate as supervisor either a local authority or, for a child aged 12 or over and provided that certain requirements are met, a probation officer. The supervisor has a duty to advise, assist and befriend the supervised person. A supervision order may include:

   (i) a requirement to reside with an individual, eg a relative;

   (ii) a requirement to submit to treatment for a mental condition, similar to the requirement which may be included in probation orders;

   (iii) in due course, a requirement to comply with any directions given by the supervisor to live at a specified place, or to present himself to a specified person at a time and place specified and/or to partake in specified activities. These requirements relate to what is commonly called "intermediate treatment"—see paragraph 207 below.

(c) An order requiring the child's parent or guardian to enter into a recognisance to take proper care of him or exercise proper control of him.

(d) A Hospital Order
(e) A Guardianship Order } For the effects of which see paragraphs 34–36 above.

(f) Payment of compensation to the aggrieved person. In care proceedings an offence must be proved and the maximum amount which can be ordered is £100.

205. The following additional orders are available to the courts in criminal proceedings. (Certain powers, (f) and (g) below, may be exercised only by the Crown Court.)

(a) Binding over (see paragraph 25 above).

(b) Absolute or conditional discharge (see paragraph 24 above).

(c) Fines (see paragraph 26 above). Under section 6(3) of the Children and Young Persons Act 1969 a young person tried summarily may not be fined more than £50; and under sections 6(3) and 34(5) of the Act a child may not be fined more than £10.

(d) Attendance centre order, if the offender is a boy and a centre is available to the court. There are 60 junior attendance centres (for boys aged 10 and under 17) situated mainly in the larger centres of population.

(e) Detention centre order, if the offender is a boy aged 14 or over and a centre is available to the court. (At present all courts have a centre available to them.)

(f) Borstal training if the offender is 15 or over and is either convicted by the Crown Court or committed there for sentence.

(g) In the case of grave crimes, ie those carrying a maximum prison sentence of 14 years or more for an adult, detention under section 53 of the Children and Young Persons Act 1933 in a place approved by the Secretary of State; this can be ordered only by the Crown Court.

206. The Children and Young Persons Act 1969 abolished the power to commit to an approved school, to place an offender under the age of 17 on probation and to make a fit person order. The Act provides for approved schools and remand homes to become part of a comprehensive system of community homes available for all children in care. England and Wales have been divided into 12 areas for the purpose of planning the community homes system, and the local authorities in each area have formed a Children's Regional Planning Committee to plan the system in conjunction with the voluntary bodies concerned. Approved schools and remand homes continued in being for an interim period. Following approval by the Secretaries of State for Social Services and for Wales the community homes system came substantially into effect on 1 April 1973. On that date all remand homes and the great majority of approved schools became community homes in accordance with the regional plan. The remaining approved schools are expected to be incorporated in the system by October 1973.

207. The Children's Regional Planning Committees are also responsible for drawing up schemes of "intermediate treatment" for juveniles under supervision, which must be either in a category approved by the Secretary of State or individually approved by him.

Intermediate treatment is the term used (though not in the Act itself) to describe new forms of treatment for children under supervision to be made available to juvenile courts and supervisors under Part 1 of the Children and Young Persons Act 1969. The provisions are intermediate between the previous two alternatives of removing a child from his home or relying on supportive social work with the child and his family in the community. The child may either spend up to 90 days (single period) in a residential treatment centre or attend a non-residential centre within reach of his home for up to 30 days in any one year. Schemes are on a regional basis and will consist of a wide variety of recreational, educational and other socially valuable activities which, while allowing the child to remain in his own home, will bring him into contact with a new environment, interests and experience in company with other children in his community. The Children's Regional Planning Committees were asked to survey voluntary and statutory agencies in their areas which might be able to contribute to intermediate treatment schemes. The Committees have assessed the resources available and are submitting schemes to the Secretaries of State for Social Services and for Wales, who decide when they should be made available to the courts. *Intermediate Treatment, a guide for the Regional Planning of new forms of treatment for children in trouble*, illustrates in Appendix C the types of activity which might be included in schemes of intermediate treatment.[1] Intermediate treatment is now available to a number of courts, and it is hoped that further schemes now being considered by the Secretaries of State may be approved by the end of 1973.

208. The Children and Young Persons Act 1969[2] provides power eventually to withdraw the power to send offenders to attendance centres and detention centres, and the power to commit (and transfer) to a borstal may be withdrawn by stages, raising the lower age limit for a borstal sentence first to 16 then to 17. The present Government have indicated their intention not to withdraw these powers until it is possible to gauge the adequacy of the new provisions being established under the Children and Young Persons Act, and until they have been able to consider the consequences of the Council's recommendations relating to the treatment of offenders aged 17 and over for the future of borstal and detention centres.

Home Office

September 1973

---

[1] The Guide was published by H M Stationery Office in 1972. Examples of activities mentioned there include sailing, canoeing, climbing, handicrafts, canal reclamation and various other forms of community service activity, and attendance at evening classes.

[2] Section 7(1) and (3).

APPENDIX C

STATISTICS

1. This Appendix is intended to illustrate and amplify what is said in the report (in particular in Chapter 5) about the incidence and nature of crime for which young adults are convicted, and how the courts use the sentencing options open to them in dealing with young adult offenders. A more detailed and comprehensive statistical survey of crime and the ways in which offenders are dealt with by the courts can be obtained from two annual Home Office publications, the Criminal Statistics and the report on the Work of the Prison Department—Statistical Tables. The following paragraphs draw attention to a number of the factors which need to be borne in mind in interpreting the tables which form the main part of the Appendix and give a brief account of some important points which the tables illustrate.

2. The information available from the regularly collected statistics about the extent of criminal activity in a particular age group, and its relation to that of other age groups, is in terms of persons proceeded against, or cautioned by the police for, criminal offences. In this context a caution is defined as a written or oral caution given by, or on the instructions of, a senior police officer as an alternative to taking criminal proceedings. If different age groups are being compared there is some advantage in aggregating—as has been done in tables 1 to 4—the figures of persons found guilty of indictable offences and of persons cautioned for indictable offences. This is because of the high proportion of juveniles who, especially since the coming into effect of the Children and Young Persons Act 1969, are dealt with by way of caution and not by court proceedings. For example, in 1971, 44,059 boys and 5,102 girls aged 14 and under 17 were found guilty of indictable offences, and a further 20,756 boys and 5,771 girls were cautioned for indictable offences. The proportion of persons cautioned to persons found guilty is much less for older age groups. While it is possible to question whether all those cautioned would otherwise have been found guilty of an offence, nevertheless figures comparing the younger age groups with the older which ignored cautions would present a very incomplete picture. Separate figures of persons found guilty and persons cautioned are given in the annual volumes of Criminal Statistics; those for 1971 are given in table 5.

3. But whether or not cautions are included, the figures of persons in a particular age group dealt with for criminal offences cannot be taken as a reliable guide to the proportion of total crime—or even of recorded crime—for which that age group is responsible. More than half the indictable offences recorded by the police are not cleared up,[1] and so cannot be attributed to a particular person or a person of particular age; nor is there any exact correspondence between offences cleared up and persons prosecuted. It cannot be assumed that any comparison made on the basis of the figures in the tables of the behaviour of offenders of different ages would remain valid if the full picture were available: it is possible that the proportion of cases in which steps are taken to bring an offence home to a particular person, and indeed the detection rate itself, may bear an uneven relationship to the age of the offender.

4. A further necessary qualification is that, while the tables accurately reflect the number of occasions on which proceedings against a person were completed resulting in at least one finding of guilt, they do not show the number of *different* offenders dealt with during the year or the number of offences involved. If a finding of guilt is recorded against a person on two or more separate occasions in the same calendar year, this is recorded in the statistical tables on each occasion. The effect of this feature of the tables is therefore to exaggerate the number of different individuals who are dealt with in a particular year.

---

[1] Offences known to the police which are said to be cleared up include those for which a person is arrested or summoned, or for which he is cautioned, those attributed to children under the age of criminal responsibility, those taken into consideration by a court when the offender is found guilty on another charge, and certain of those of which a person is known or suspected to be guilty, but for which he cannot for some reasons be prosecuted (eg because he died).

But if, on the other hand, two or more findings of guilt are recorded against a person at the same court appearance, only one offence, known as the principal offence, is selected for tabulation and the others are ignored. The offence selected as the principal offence is the one for which the heaviest punishment is awarded or, if that does not distinguish between the offences, the one for which the maximum penalty available to the court is the heaviest. (An exception to this rule is that where findings of guilt are recorded against a person in respect of both indictable and non-indictable offences at the same court appearance, one finding of guilt is recorded in the indictable offence section and one in the non-indictable offence section of the tables.) The impact on the statistics of the recording practice described above can to some extent be gauged by comparing the number of principal findings of guilt recorded in the statistics with the number of additional findings of guilt ignored for purposes of these statistics: in 1971 for example, there were in all courts 277,308 principal findings of guilt in respect of indictable offences committed by males and 160,561 additional findings of guilt.

The Theft Act 1968

5. The tables contain figures extending over varying periods of years up to and including 1971. It is, however, important to note that, because of changes in the law concerning theft and related offences made in the Theft Act 1968 (which came into force on 1 January 1969) no direct comparison can be made between the criminal statistics for 1969 onwards and those for previous years. The range of indictable offences was increased by the addition of certain offences which were formerly non-indictable, the most significant being the offence of taking a motor-vehicle without the consent of the owner. Further complication was caused by the re-definition of some offences so that their classification in criminal statistics changed. In those tables where the Theft Act is a complicating factor this is indicated by the insertion of a line between the 1968 and 1969 figures in order to avoid false comparisons being made, since the effects of the Theft Act may make a significant contribution to the difference between the figures for those years. Another effect of the Act is that it is not possible to provide a precise figure for the percentage change between the base year of each table and 1971. In those tables in which such a comparison is of relevance, an *estimated* percentage change has been calculated by the Home Office Statistical Department, for the purposes of this Appendix only (the figures are not comparable with any which appear in annual volumes of the Criminal Statistics).

Age of criminal responsibility

6. A further change in the law to be borne in mind when comparing figures for different age groups is the Children and Young Persons Act 1963 which raised the age of criminal responsibility from 8 to 10 with effect from 1 February 1964.

What the tables show

7. Tables 1 and 2 show, for the two sexes separately, persons found guilty or cautioned for indictable offences, in different age-groups. They give some indication of the scale of the problem presented by young adult offenders. Of all the age groups shown (which, it will be noted, are not bands of equal width), young adults now have the largest absolute number of findings of guilt and cautions recorded against them.

8. Tables 3 and 4 relate these figures to the number of persons "at-risk", that is, they show the proportion of people of that age within the population as a whole who are dealt with for indictable offences. These tables therefore give—subject to the important qualification made in paragraph 3 above—an indication of relative criminality in the different age groups, and illustrate strikingly that criminal involvement is a characteristic of youth which diminishes steadily with increasing age. A cause for concern in table 3 is the rate at which it suggests that criminal involvement has recently increased: this is true for all ages but particularly for young people aged 14 to 20. The criminal justice and penal system through which young adult offenders are dealt with has therefore assumed an increased importance in terms both of dealing adequately with the young adult offender problem as it exists, and of attempting to divert the sharply rising number of offenders in this age group from criminal behaviour as they get older.

9. Tables 6 and 7 reveal a few important differences among the age groups in terms of the types of offences for which persons are found guilty. Theft (or larceny before 1969) is the most frequent offence in all age groups for males and (even more so) females, except

226

that for males under 14 burglary is as common as theft. For both males and females burglary becomes proportionately less common in older age groups (and similarly, before 1969, for breaking and entering). Offences involving fraud are proportionately more frequent in older age groups than among males under 21; among females fraud was as frequent in the 17–20 age group as in older age groups. Crimes of violence become proportionately more frequent with age for males up to the 17–20 age group, where the figures are similar to those for older age groups; among females, they are proportionately most frequent in the 14–16 age group.

The choice of sentences

10. Tables 10–15 show first that the fine is the most commonly used method of dealing with offenders. Sanctions involving "social intervention"—custody and supervision—are used only in a minority of cases, albeit a substantial minority where the offence is indictable. Tables 12 and 13 show that the fine has been increasing in relative importance as a sanction used by magistrates' courts dealing with offenders found guilty of indictable offences. The probation order—during the period covered by these tables the one option open to the courts involving supervision in the community—has consistently been declining in relative importance as a method of dealing with young adult offenders: tables 12–15 show that this decline has occurred in relation to both young men and young women, and in both magistrates' and higher courts. Table 10 shows a slight decline in the absolute number of probation orders passed on male offenders between 1969 and 1971. The introduction of the suspended sentence in 1968 was accompanied by a significant reduction in unsuspended sentences of imprisonment imposed by magistrates' courts (see table 12) on young adult males, but in general the use of the suspended sentence power has not been accompanied by a corresponding fall in the use of custodial sentences. Indeed, in the case of young men, it can be seen from table 10 that the number of borstal sentences and detention centre sentences passed rose over the period at a faster rate than other sentencing options open to the courts.

227

TABLE 1

**Males found guilty of, or cautioned for, indictable offences:
distribution by age group**

1960–1971   Percentages

Year	Total number	Age group					
		Under 14	14–16	17–20	21–24	25–29	30 and over
1960	163,719	24.0	17.6	16.2	11.2	9.1	21.8
1961	178,923	23.3	18.3	16.4	11.5	9.0	21.5
1962	196,852	20.6	18.0	17.1	11.9	9.8	22.6
1963	206,480	19.2	18.9	17.6	11.7	10.0	22.5
1964	198,385	17.0	19.6	19.1	12.1	10.1	22.2
1965	209,173	15.6	18.5	20.5	12.5	10.7	22.2
1966	224,659	14.6	17.5	21.3	13.2	10.9	22.4
1967	233,194	14.4	16.8	21.3	13.2	10.7	23.5
1968	249,831	14.2	17.1	21.6	13.7	10.8	22.6
1969	302,078	13.5	18.1	22.9	14.1	10.2	21.2
1970	323,737	13.4	18.4	22.5	14.0	10.2	21.6
1971	335,034	13.9	19.3	22.3	13.3	9.8	21.3
Estimated percentage change in absolute number 1960 to 1971	91.2	16.6	103.1	145.8	125.6	111.5	97.1

Note: Some 20,000 of the increase in total number between 1968 and 1969 resulted from the
Theft Act 1968 which, amongst other changes, made the offence of taking a motor vehicle
without consent indictable. The increase was largely in the age groups 14–16, 17–20 and
21–24 and accounts for much of the change in percentage distribution between the two
years. See paragraph 5 of the introduction to this Appendix.

228

TABLE 2

Females found guilty of, or cautioned for, indictable offences: distribution by age group

1960–1971   Percentages

Year	Total number	Age group					
		Under 14	14–16	17–20	21–24	25–29	30 and over
1960	23,635	17.2	14.7	12.6	7.8	7.6	40.0
1961	27,856	17.1	15.3	12.4	7.9	7.2	40.0
1962	32,231	15.2	15.0	11.6	7.9	7.6	42.7
1963	32,710	14.6	15.6	11.9	8.1	8.2	41.7
1964	34,222	13.4	17.1	12.5	7.8	7.8	41.3
1965	37,234	13.2	17.8	12.6	7.4	7.9	41.0
1966	38,204	12.7	18.3	13.5	8.4	8.0	39.1
1967	40,021	12.4	15.4	14.1	8.9	8.7	40.6
1968	42,422	12.4	15.7	13.9	9.5	9.0	39.6
1969	49,669	12.6	15.7	14.0	10.3	9.2	38.2
1970	54,847	13.3	16.2	14.3	10.3	9.4	36.5
1971	61,236	14.0	17.8	14.1	10.0	8.9	35.2
Estimated percentage change in absolute number 1960 to 1971	156.8	110.7	207.2	182.5	224.7	198.4	127.9

Note: Some 450 of the increase in total number between 1968 and 1969 resulted from the Theft Act 1968 which, amongst other changes, made the offence of taking a motor vehicle without consent indictable. The increase was largely in the age groups 14–16, 17–20 and 21–24, but was small in comparison to the total increase between the two years. See paragraph 5 of the introduction to this Appendix.

TABLE 3

Males found guilty of, or cautioned for, indictable offences:
rates per 100,000 population by age group

1960–1971   Rates per 100,000 population

Year	All ages*	Age group					
		Under 14*	14–16	17–20	21–24	25–29	30 and over
1960	850	1,786	2,842	2,323	1,588	1,039	290
1961	919	1,957	2,924	2,379	1,779	1,113	311
1962	1,000	1,960	3,004	2,580	2,002	1,302	356
1963	1,044	1,957	3,253	2,693	2,060	1,381	371
1964	1,029	2,412	3,446	2,603	1,982	1,317	350
1965	1,083	2,448	3,635	2,829	2,084	1,471	368
1966	1,163	2,462	3,826	3,110	2,245	1,620	398
1967	1,196	2,487	3,890	3,199	2,251	1,649	432
1968	1,280	2,572	4,246	3,692	2,346	1,746	446
1969	1,541	2,862	5,441	4,953	2,789	1,976	505
1970	1,644	2,962	5,906	5,344	2,914	2,053	550
1971	1,708	3,044	6,155	5,502	2,908	1,983	572
Estimated percentage change 1960 to 1971	87.7	68.2	94.5	106.8	69.7	83.5	94.2

*The lower age limit is the age of criminal responsibility (ie 8 before 1 February 1964 and 10 thereafter).
Note: See note on table 1.

TABLE 4

**Females found guilty of, or cautioned for, indictable offences:
rates per 100,000 population by age group**

1960–1971   Rates per 100,000 population

Year	All ages*	Age group					
		Under 14*	14–16	17–20	21–24	25–29	30 and over
1960	113	193	358	260	159	128	67
1961	132	235	397	284	189	144	78
1962	152	249	428	292	218	174	96
1963	154	246	445	294	226	185	96
1964	165	345	547	302	222	184	99
1965	179	387	655	320	221	199	106
1966	183	382	713	345	246	207	104
1967	191	386	639	372	265	236	113
1968	201	400	691	409	279	254	117
1969	235	464	812	508	339	298	132
1970	258	527	921	585	369	326	139
1971	289	590	1,088	657	401	338	151
Estimated percentage change 1960 to 1971	153.6	205.1	198.3	146.2	149.3	162.3	125.4

*The lower age limit is the age of criminal responsibility (ie 8 before 1 February 1964 and 10 thereafter).
Note: See note on table 2.

TABLE 5

**Persons found guilty of, or cautioned for, indictable offences in 1971:
proportion to population in each age group**

Age	Estimated number of persons of each age or age group in England and Wales	Number of persons found guilty of indictable offences	Number of persons cautioned for indictable offences	Number of persons found guilty per 100,000 of the age or age group	Number of persons cautioned per 100,000 of population of the age or age group	Number of persons found guilty or cautioned per 100,000 of population of the age or age group
MALES						
10	397,000	1,311	5,129	330	1,292	1,622
11	384,000	2,745	6,537	715	1,702	2,417
12	377,000	5,407	7,822	1,434	2,075	3,509
13	370,000	8,519	9,037	2,302	2,442	4,745
14	360,000	12,980	9,609	3,606	2,669	6,275
15	354,000	15,168	7,027	4,285	1,985	6,270
16	339,000	15,911	4,120	4,694	1,215	5,909
17	344,000	20,733	1,450	6,027	422	6,449
18	345,000	19,682	1,003	5,705	291	5,996
19	333,000	16,606	676	4,987	203	5,190
20	339,000	14,174	555	4,181	164	4,345
21 and under 25	1,535,000	43,400	1,239	2,827	81	2,908
25 and under 30	1,651,000	31,988	757	1,937	46	1,983
30 and under 40	2,875,000	36,787	874	1,280	30	1,310
40 and under 50	3,004,000	19,059	527	634	18	652
50 and under 60	2,844,000	9,038	401	318	14	332
60 and over	3,767,000	3,800	963	101	26	126
TOTAL	19,618,000	277,308	57,726	1,414	294	1,708
FEMALES						
10	375,000	70	736	19	196	215
11	365,000	194	1,364	53	374	427
12	356,000	495	2,061	139	579	718
13	351,000	953	2,707	272	771	1,043
14	339,000	1,535	2,853	453	842	1,294
15	336,000	1,806	1,896	538	564	1,102
16	322,000	1,761	1,022	547	317	864
17	326,000	2,357	214	723	66	789
18	330,000	2,192	127	664	38	703
19	326,000	1,857	101	570	31	601
20	333,000	1,703	90	511	27	538
21 and under 25	1,520,000	5,722	372	376	24	401
25 and under 30	1,616,000	5,137	333	318	21	338
30 and under 40	2,794,000	7,276	499	260	18	278
40 and under 50	3,034,000	5,270	427	174	14	188
50 and under 60	3,020,000	4,178	516	138	17	155
60 and over	5,451,000	2,022	1,390	37	25	63
TOTAL	21,194,000	44,528	16,708	210	79	289

Note: The figures shown above are as published in the Criminal Statistics for 1971 (Introductory Note pp liv–lv), except that slight revisions have been made in the light of further information subsequently made available to the Home Office.

232

TABLE 6

Males found guilty of indictable offences: distribution by offence group within age groups

1960, 1968, 1969 and 1971 — Percentages

Age group and year	Total number	Violence against the person	Sexual offences	Breaking and entering	Larceny	Receiving	Frauds and false pretences	Robbery	Burglary	Theft and unauthorised taking	Handling	Fraud	Other offences
Under 14													
1960	27,622	1.2	1.0	31.4	58.4	3.8	0.3	0.5	—	—	—	—	3.5
1968	22,031	1.0	0.7	37.0	53.2	5.6	0.3	0.6	—	—	—	—	1.6
1969	22,173	↓1.2	0.8	—	—	—	—	0.7	44.3	45.9	5.1	0.4	1.5
1971	17,982	1.8	0.6	—	—	—	—	1.2	45.9	41.5	5.7	0.6	2.7
14–16													
1960	24,749	4.9	3.8	30.7	52.6	4.5	0.4	0.6	—	—	—	—	2.6
1968	35,136	4.3	2.7	33.1	52.2	5.4	0.5	0.8	—	—	—	—	1.4
1969	42,778	4.2	1.7	—	—	—	—	0.9	35.1	51.0	5.4	0.6	1.2
1971	44,059	6.7	1.4	—	—	—	—	1.4	35.0	47.3	5.5	0.7	2.0
17–20													
1960	25,068	10.8	4.1	22.9	53.2	3.3	1.1	1.1	—	—	—	—	3.5
1968	51,106	9.6	2.1	25.6	52.4	5.0	1.8	1.4	—	—	—	—	2.2
1969	65,903	8.5	1.6	—	—	—	—	1.3	25.7	53.8	5.2	2.0	2.0
1971	71,195	9.3	1.6	—	—	—	—	1.3	24.1	52.4	5.4	2.5	3.4
21–24													
1960	17,648	11.4	3.8	20.6	52.6	4.1	2.6	1.3	—	—	—	—	3.7
1968	33,317	10.2	2.2	21.7	51.2	6.4	4.0	1.3	—	—	—	—	3.0
1969	41,467	9.4	2.1	—	—	—	—	1.1	22.8	50.5	6.4	4.6	3.1
1971	43,400	10.8	2.0	—	—	—	—	1.2	20.8	48.5	6.9	5.0	4.7
25–29													
1960	14,496	8.8	4.1	16.7	56.1	5.0	4.1	0.9	—	—	—	—	4.1
1968	26,337	9.8	3.0	18.5	51.4	7.7	5.2	0.9	—	—	—	—	3.5
1969	30,293	9.6	2.6	—	—	—	—	0.9	19.8	49.1	8.0	5.9	4.1
1971	31,988	11.1	2.7	—	—	—	—	1.0	17.7	47.4	8.2	6.0	5.9
30 and over													
1960	34,282	6.6	7.0	8.7	59.7	6.0	6.5	0.3	—	—	—	—	5.1
1968	54,680	8.5	5.1	10.7	56.6	8.6	6.7	0.5	—	—	—	—	3.3
1969	61,861	8.5	4.6	—	—	—	—	0.4	12.8	53.0	9.0	7.3	4.4
1971	68,684	9.6	4.5	—	—	—	—	0.4	11.7	51.3	9.6	7.0	5.9

*The offence groups were changed in 1969 because of the Theft Act. See paragraph 5 and the note on table 1.

TABLE 7

Females found guilty of indictable offences: distribution by offence group within age groups

1960, 1968, 1969 and 1971   Percentages

Age group and year	Total number	Offence group*											
		Violence against the person	Sexual offences	Breaking and entering	Larceny	Receiving	Frauds and false pretences	Robbery	Burglary	Theft and unauthorised taking	Handling	Fraud	Other offences
Under 14													
1960	2,319	0.7	0.1	14.1	79.6	2.5	1.0	—	—	—	—	—	1.9
1968	2,504	1.1	—	11.2	80.8	4.7	1.0	0.4	—	—	—	—	0.9
1969	2,537	1.3	—	—	—	—	—	0.9	16.6	74.3	5.3	0.8	0.7
1971	1,712	1.7	0.2	—	—	—	—	0.2	17.4	73.5	4.3	0.9	1.8
14–16													
1960	2,670	1.0	—	6.7	85.4	3.6	1.3	0.1	—	—	—	—	1.8
1968	4,700	2.5	—	6.3	81.8	6.4	1.1	0.3	—	—	—	—	1.6
1969	4,957	3.1	—	—	—	—	—	0.9	9.3	77.7	6.4	1.1	1.5
1971	5,102	5.6	—	—	—	—	—	0.6	9.5	72.8	7.0	1.9	2.5
17–20													
1960	2,703	1.8	0.1	4.9	80.4	3.3	3.2	0.6	—	—	—	—	5.8
1968	5,484	2.2	0.1	5.5	78.0	5.5	4.5	0.5	—	—	—	—	3.7
1969	6,436	2.3	0.1	—	—	—	—	0.5	6.5	74.7	6.1	5.6	4.1
1971	8,109	3.4	—	—	—	—	—	0.4	6.2	72.2	7.2	5.7	4.8
21–24													
1960	1,681	3.6	0.4	3.6	76.7	2.9	5.0	0.3	—	—	—	—	7.5
1968	3,795	4.4	0.2	2.9	76.2	4.9	6.3	0.2	—	—	—	—	4.9
1969	4,788	3.5	0.1	—	—	—	—	0.3	4.4	74.4	5.2	6.2	5.9
1971	5,722	3.7	0.1	—	—	—	—	0.2	3.5	73.5	5.8	7.5	5.8
25–29													
1960	1,628	4.4	0.3	1.4	75.2	3.4	6.7	0.1	—	—	—	—	8.6
1968	3,549	4.9	0.1	1.7	78.7	4.1	4.8	0.3	—	—	—	—	5.3
1969	4,288	4.1	0.1	—	—	—	—	0.3	2.1	74.6	4.5	5.9	8.4
1971	5,137	4.3	0.1	—	—	—	—	0.1	2.5	75.2	5.2	6.1	6.5
30 and over													
1960	8,616	2.8	0.3	0.8	83.9	3.1	4.5	—	—	—	—	—	4.6
1968	14,688	2.9	0.7	0.7	87.1	3.3	3.2	—	—	—	—	—	2.7
1969	16,589	2.6	0.1	—	—	—	—	0.1	1.2	84.9	3.7	3.6	3.9
1971	18,746	2.6	0.1	—	—	—	—	0.1	1.2	83.6	4.4	3.8	4.2

*The offence groups were changed in 1969 because of the Theft Act. See paragraph 5 and the note on table 2.

TABLE 8

**Males aged 17–20 found guilty of non-indictable offences:
distribution by offence group**

1960, 1968, 1969 and 1971   Numbers

Offence group	Year			
	1960	1968	1969	1971
Assault	1,944	2,495	2,549	2,605
Offences against Highways Acts	8,847	4,644	4,935	5,479
Taking vehicle without consent	4,827	9,985	—	—
Drunkenness offences	6,680	9,711	10,398	11,261
Malicious damage	2,887	4,668	5,207	5,884
Disorderly behaviour	4,636	3,965	3,576	3,184
Offences against revenue laws	2,098	3,381	3,680	3,634
Motoring offences	71,738	123,076	118,763	115,710
Other offences	10,003	15,133	15,557	20,476
TOTAL	113,660	177,058	164,656	168,233

Note: Because of the Theft Act 1968 figures for 1969 and 1971 are not precisely comparable with
those for earlier years.

TABLE 9

**Females aged 17–20 found guilty of non-indictable offences:
distribution by offence group**

1960, 1968, 1969 and 1971   Numbers

Offence group	Year			
	1960	1968	1969	1971
Assault	85	126	105	160
Offences against Highways Acts	459	278	348	367
Taking vehicle without consent	44	215	—	—
Drunkenness offences	249	307	315	551
Malicious damage	49	128	143	183
Disorderly behaviour	207	137	138	133
Offences against revenue laws	29	68	72	95
Motoring offences	1,448	4,701	4,375	4,377
Other offences	1,494	2,181	2,360	2,977
TOTAL	4,064	8,141	7,856	8,843

Note: Because of the Theft Act 1968 figures for 1969 and 1971 are not precisely comparable with
those for earlier years.

TABLE 10

Males aged 17-20 sentenced at all courts: distribution by sentence

1964-1971

Numbers

Year	Total	Sentence or order								
		Conditional discharge	Probation	Fine	Detention centre	Borstal	Returned to borstal	Imprisonment (immediate)	Suspended sentence	Other
1964	195,209	4,875	8,102	165,088	4,926	3,177	*	2,289	—	6,752*
1965	217,552	5,078	9,022	183,823	5,990	3,685	913	2,534	—	6,487
1966	230,028	5,121	8,908	193,502	6,297	4,542	983	3,156	—	7,519
1967	237,131	6,045	9,565	198,848	6,344	4,649	1,175	2,834	—	7,671
1968	232,820	7,382	10,265	189,793	6,529	4,484	1,212	2,090	3,092	7,972
1969	235,963	8,145	11,678	186,822	7,478	5,425	1,324	2,462	3,358	9,271
1970	241,413	7,978	11,273	189,222	8,383	6,283	1,385	2,804	3,542	10,543
1971	245,402	8,599	11,528	192,545	8,404	6,068	1,605	2,942	3,443	10,268
Estimated percentage change 1964 to 1971	18.2	79.6	35.3	14.6	61.7	91.1	64.1	24.4	—	36.0

*In 1964 figures for "returned to borstal" were included with "other".

Note: See note on table 1. The net effect of the Theft Act on the figures in this table was small.

TABLE 11

Females aged 17–20 sentenced at all courts: distribution by sentence

1964–1971

Numbers

Year	Total	Conditional discharge	Probation	Fine	Detention centre	Borstal	Returned to borstal	Imprisonment (immediate)	Suspended sentence	Other
						Sentence or order				
1964	9,631	816	1,724	6,486	59	98	*	80		370*
1965	10,647	914	1,944	7,202	45	98	22	87		335
1966	11,835	1,043	2,078	7,946	79	146	14	92		437
1967	13,377	1,196	2,156	9,270	67	126	20	95		447
1968	13,795	1,420	2,251	9,198	90	122	26	53	207	428
1969	14,510	1,677	2,421	9,436		186	9	72	196	513
1970	15,908	1,792	2,548	10,396		216	18	88	277	573
1971	17,237	2,087	2,682	11,206		228	19	94	284	637
Estimated percentage change 1964 to 1971	74.1	146.3	54.3	59.5		132.7		17.5		54.4

*In 1964 figures for "returned to borstal" were included with "other".

Note: See note on table 2. The net effect of the Theft Act on the figures in this table was small.

237

TABLE 12

Males aged 17–20 sentenced at magistrates' courts for indictable and non-indictable offences: distribution by sentence

1964–1971

Numbers and percentages

Offence class and year	Total number	Sentence or order																
		Conditional discharge		Probation		Fine		Detention centre		Imprisonment (immediate)		Suspended sentence		Returned to borstal		Other	
		No.	%	No.	%	No.	%	No.	%	No.	%	No.	%	No.	%	No.	%
Indictable offences																	
1964	28,178	2,838	10.1	4,708	16.7	16,545	58.7	2,233	7.9	836	3.0	—	—	*	*	1,018	3.6*
1965	31,919	2,960	9.3	5,290	16.6	19,048	59.7	2,668	8.4	881	2.8	—	—	438	1.4	634	2.0
1966	35,188	3,067	8.7	5,285	15.0	22,041	62.6	2,741	7.7	1,046	3.0	—	—	428	1.2	610	1.7
1967	36,603	3,567	9.7	5,666	15.5	22,560	61.6	2,741	7.5	890	2.4	—	—	520	1.4	659	1.8
1968	39,994	4,270	10.7	5,754	14.4	23,774	59.4	3,022	7.6	526	1.3	1,485	3.7	514	1.3	649	1.6
1969	52,441	4,938	9.4	7,118	13.6	32,574	62.1	3,813	7.3	663	1.3	1,806	3.4	637	1.2	892	1.7
1970	54,358	4,732	8.7	6,710	12.3	34,803	64.0	4,088	7.5	692	1.3	1,861	3.4	648	1.2	824	1.5
1971	55,503	5,007	9.0	6,742	12.1	35,588	64.1	3,987	7.2	702	1.3	1,753	3.2	734	1.3	990	1.8
Non-indictable offences (including motoring offences)																	
1964	155,462	1,765	1.1	1,575	1.0	147,942	95.2	1,652	1.1	790	0.5	—	—	*	*	1,738	1.1*
1965	172,040	1,833	1.1	1,732	1.0	163,937	95.3	1,957	1.1	868	0.5	—	—	243	0.1	1,470	0.9
1966	178,438	1,815	1.0	1,558	0.9	170,400	95.5	1,823	1.0	1,093	0.6	—	—	299	0.2	1,450	0.8
1967	183,677	2,169	1.2	1,694	0.9	175,124	95.3	1,915	1.0	900	0.5	—	—	340	0.2	1,535	0.8
1968	175,071	2,661	1.5	2,182	1.2	164,989	94.2	1,906	1.1	426	0.2	982	0.6	323	0.2	1,602	0.9
1969	163,010	2,734	1.7	2,001	1.2	152,963	93.8	1,890	1.2	405	0.2	839	0.5	298	0.2	1,880	1.2
1970	163,746	2,720	1.7	2,042	1.2	152,965	93.4	2,106	1.3	403	0.2	949	0.6	290	0.2	2,271	1.4
1971	166,570	2,976	1.8	2,186	1.3	155,190	93.2	2,247	1.3	429	0.3	917	0.6	335	0.2	2,290	1.4
Total																	
1964	183,640	4,603	2.5	6,283	3.4	164,487	89.6	3,885	2.1	1,626	0.9	—	—	*	*	2,756	1.5*
1965	203,959	4,793	2.3	7,022	3.4	182,985	89.7	4,625	2.3	1,749	0.9	—	—	681	0.3	2,104	1.0
1966	213,626	4,882	2.3	6,843	3.2	192,441	90.1	4,534	2.1	2,139	1.0	—	—	727	0.3	2,060	1.0
1967	220,280	5,736	2.6	7,360	3.3	197,684	89.7	4,656	2.1	1,790	0.8	—	—	860	0.4	2,194	1.0
1968	215,065	6,931	3.2	7,936	3.7	188,763	87.8	4,928	2.3	952	0.4	2,467	1.1	837	0.4	2,251	1.0
1969	215,451	7,672	3.6	9,119	4.2	185,537	86.1	5,703	2.6	1,068	0.5	2,645	1.2	935	0.4	2,772	1.3
1970	218,104	7,452	3.4	8,752	4.0	187,768	86.1	6,194	2.8	1,095	0.5	2,810	1.3	938	0.4	3,095	1.4
1971	222,073	7,983	3.6	8,928	4.0	190,778	85.9	6,234	2.8	1,131	0.5	2,670	1.2	1,069	0.5	3,280	1.5

*In 1964 figures for "returned to borstal" were included with "other".

Note: See note on table 1. The main effect of the Theft Act on this table was to cause a transfer of some 9,000 persons from the non-indictable class to the indictable class.

238

TABLE 13

Females aged 17–20 sentenced at magistrates' courts for indictable and non-indictable offences: distribution by sentence

1964–1971

Numbers and percentages

Offence class and year	Total number	Conditional discharge		Probation		Fine		Detention centre		Imprisonment (immediate)		Suspended sentence		Returned to borstal		Other	
		No.	%	No.	%	No.	%	No.	%	No.	%	No.	%	No.	%	No.	%
Indictable offences																	
1964	3,644	609	16.9	1,341	37.3	1,463	40.6	31	0.9	37	1.0	—	—	*	*	119*	3.3*
1965	3,962	665	16.8	1,450	36.6	1,686	42.6	30	0.8	42	1.1	—	—	17	0.4	72	1.8
1966	4,324	730	16.9	1,561	36.1	1,865	43.1	46	1.1	38	0.9	—	—	7	0.2	77	1.8
1967	4,801	852	17.7	1,622	33.8	2,156	44.9	26	0.5	27	0.6	—	—	13	0.3	105	2.2
1968	5,031	987	19.6	1,633	32.5	2,130	42.3	51	1.0	14	0.3	105	2.1	16	0.3	95	1.9
1969	5,866	1,199	20.4	1,771	30.2	2,646	45.1	—	—	21	0.4	106	1.8	8	0.1	115	2.0
1970	6,611	1,260	19.1	1,827	27.6	3,244	49.1	—	—	25	0.4	139	2.1	8	0.1	108	1.6
1971	7,371	1,505	20.4	1,887	25.6	3,662	49.7	—	—	22	0.3	137	1.9	11	0.1	147	1.0
Non-indictable offences (including motoring offences)																	
1964	5,584	188	3.4	210	3.8	5,019	89.9	13	0.2	33	0.6	—	—	*	*	121*	2.2*
1965	6,171	237	3.8	283	4.6	5,502	89.2	4	0.1	36	0.6	—	—	4	0.1	105	1.7
1966	6,820	294	4.3	274	4.0	6,068	89.0	10	0.1	34	0.5	—	—	3	0.1	137	2.0
1967	7,896	321	4.1	288	3.6	7,089	89.8	11	0.1	47	0.6	—	—	4	0.1	136	1.7
1968	8,092	407	5.0	374	4.6	7,055	87.2	11	0.1	30	0.4	79	1.0	4	0.1	132	1.6
1969	7,821	436	5.6	370	4.7	6,770	86.6	—	—	29	0.4	64	0.8	3	—	152	1.9
1970	8,277	487	5.9	379	4.6	7,119	86.0	—	—	41	0.5	93	1.1	3	0.1	155	1.9
1971	8,781	527	6.0	432	4.9	7,490	85.3	—	—	49	0.6	112	1.3	4	0.1	167	1.9
Total																	
1964	9,184	797	8.7	1,551	16.9	6,482	70.6	44	0.5	70	0.8	—	—	*	*	240*	2.6*
1965	10,133	902	8.9	1,733	17.1	7,188	70.9	34	0.3	78	0.8	—	—	21	0.2	177	1.7
1966	11,144	1,024	9.2	1,835	16.5	7,933	71.2	56	0.5	72	0.6	—	—	10	0.1	214	1.9
1967	12,697	1,173	9.2	1,910	15.0	9,245	72.8	37	0.3	74	0.6	—	—	17	0.1	241	1.9
1968	13,123	1,394	10.6	2,007	15.3	9,185	70.0	62	0.5	44	0.3	184	1.4	20	0.2	227	1.7
1969	13,687	1,635	11.9	2,141	15.6	9,416	68.8	—	—	50	0.4	170	1.2	8	0.1	267	2.0
1970	14,888	1,747	11.7	2,206	14.8	10,363	69.6	—	—	66	0.4	232	1.6	11	0.1	263	1.8
1971	16,152	2,032	12.6	2,319	14.4	11,152	69.0	—	—	71	0.4	249	1.5	15	0.1	314	1.9

*In 1964 figures for "returned to borstal" were included with "other".

Note: See note on table 2. The main effect of the Theft Act on this table was to cause a transfer of some 180 persons from the non-indictable class to the indictable class.

239

TABLE 14

Males aged 17–20 sentenced at higher courts: distribution by sentence

Mode of trial and year	Total number	Conditional discharge		Probation		Fine		Detention centre		Borstal		Returned to borstal		Imprisonment (immediate)		Suspended sentence		Other	
		No.	%	No.	%	No.	%	No.	%	No.	%	No.	%	No.	%	No.	%	No.	%
Trial on indictment																			
1964	5,077	238	4.7	1,312	25.8	546	10.8	648	12.8	1,516	29.9	176	3.5	509	10.0	—	—	132	2.6
1965	5,797	244	4.2	1,328	22.9	724	12.5	900	15.5	1,710	29.5	170	2.9	543	9.4	—	—	178	3.1
1966	6,453	197	3.1	1,336	20.7	876	13.6	1,036	16.1	1,935	30.0	177	2.7	745	11.5	—	—	151	2.3
1967	6,797	266	3.9	1,434	21.1	958	14.1	981	14.4	2,087	30.7	181	2.7	722	10.6	—	—	168	2.5
1968	7,592	377	5.0	1,707	22.5	855	11.3	1,046	13.8	2,109	27.8	219	2.9	731	9.6	404	5.3	144	1.9
1969	8,846	403	4.6	1,804	20.4	1,059	12.0	1,200	13.6	2,663	30.1	227	2.6	913	10.3	427	4.8	150	1.7
1970	10,009	429	4.3	1,693	16.9	1,217	12.2	1,496	14.9	3,026	30.2	250	2.5	1,243	12.4	482	4.8	173	1.7
1971	10,675	513	4.8	1,803	16.9	1,449	13.6	1,523	14.3	3,072	28.8	300	2.8	1,302	12.2	533	5.0	180	1.7
Summary trial																			
1964	2,930	34	1.2	507	17.3	55	1.9	393	13.4	1,661	56.7	65	2.2	154	5.3	—	—	61	2.1
1965	3,661	41	1.1	672	18.4	114	3.1	475	13.0	1,975	53.9	62	1.7	242	6.6	—	—	80	2.2
1966	4,742	42	0.9	729	15.4	185	3.9	727	15.3	2,607	55.0	79	1.7	272	5.7	—	—	101	2.1
1967	4,836	43	0.9	771	15.9	206	4.3	707	14.6	2,562	53.0	134	2.8	322	6.7	—	—	91	1.9
1968	4,656	74	1.6	622	13.4	176	3.8	555	11.9	2,375	51.0	156	3.4	407	8.7	221	4.7	70	1.5
1969	5,395	70	1.3	755	14.0	226	4.2	575	10.7	2,762	51.2	162	3.0	481	8.9	286	5.3	78	1.4
1970	6,151	97	1.6	828	13.5	237	3.9	693	11.3	3,257	53.0	197	3.2	466	7.6	250	4.1	126	2.0
1971	5,974	103	1.7	797	13.3	318	5.3	647	10.8	2,996	50.2	236	4.0	509	8.5	240	4.0	128	2.1
Total																			
1964	8,007	272	3.4	1,819	22.7	601	7.5	1,041	13.0	3,177	39.7	241	3.0	663	8.3	—	—	193	2.4
1965	9,458	285	3.0	2,000	21.1	838	8.9	1,375	14.5	3,685	39.0	232	2.5	785	8.3	—	—	258	2.7
1966	11,195	239	2.1	2,065	18.4	1,061	9.5	1,763	15.7	4,542	40.6	256	2.3	1,017	9.1	—	—	252	2.3
1967	11,633	309	2.7	2,205	19.0	1,164	10.0	1,688	14.5	4,649	40.0	315	2.7	1,044	9.0	—	—	259	2.2
1968	12,248	451	3.7	2,329	19.0	1,031	8.4	1,601	13.1	4,484	36.6	375	3.1	1,138	9.3	625	5.1	214	1.7
1969	14,241	473	3.3	2,559	18.0	1,285	9.0	1,775	12.5	5,425	38.1	389	2.7	1,394	9.8	713	5.0	228	1.6
1970	16,160	526	3.3	2,521	15.6	1,454	9.0	2,189	13.5	6,283	38.9	447	2.8	1,709	10.6	732	4.5	299	1.9
1971	16,649	616	3.7	2,600	15.6	1,767	10.6	2,170	13.0	6,068	36.4	536	3.2	1,811	10.9	773	4.6	308	1.8

TABLE 15

Females aged 17–20 sentenced at higher courts: distribution by sentence

1964–1971 · Numbers and percentages

Mode of trial and year	Total number	Conditional discharge		Probation		Fine		Detention centre		Borstal		Returned to borstal		Imprisonment (immediate)		Suspended sentence		Other	
		No.	%	No.	%	No.	%	No.	%	No.	%	No.	%	No.	%	No.	%	No.	%
Trial on indictment																			
1964	207	17	8.2	132	63.8	2	1.0	2	1.0	36	17.4	—	—	9	4.3	—	—	9	4.3
1965	226	11	4.9	156	69.0	12	5.3	8	3.5	24	10.6	1	0.4	5	2.2	—	—	9	4.0
1966	277	16	5.8	164	59.2	10	3.6	15	5.4	44	15.9	2	0.7	14	5.1	—	—	12	4.3
1967	275	19	6.9	172	62.5	20	7.3	10	3.6	33	12.0	3	1.1	9	3.3	—	—	9	3.3
1968	316	24	7.6	189	59.8	13	4.1	15	4.7	44	13.9	2	0.6	5	1.6	17	5.4	7	2.2
1969	380	34	8.9	204	53.7	19	5.0	—	—	75	19.7	1	0.3	11	2.9	19	5.0	17	4.5
1970	442	38	8.6	252	57.0	24	5.4	—	—	81	18.3	6	1.4	5	1.1	29	6.6	7	1.6
1971	497	50	10.1	266	53.5	46	9.3	—	—	78	15.7	1	0.2	18	3.6	24	4.8	14	2.8
Summary trial																			
1964	122	2	1.6	41	33.6	—	—	13	10.7	62	50.8	1	0.8	1	0.8	—	—	2	1.6
1965	144	1	0.7	55	38.2	2	1.4	3	2.1	74	51.4	—	—	4	2.8	—	—	5	3.5
1966	208	3	1.4	79	38.0	3	1.4	8	3.8	102	49.0	2	1.0	6	2.9	—	—	5	2.4
1967	211	4	1.9	74	35.1	5	2.4	20	9.5	93	44.1	—	—	12	5.7	—	—	3	1.4
1968	170	2	1.2	55	32.4	—	—	13	7.6	78	45.9	4	2.4	4	2.4	6	3.5	8	4.7
1969	218	8	3.7	76	34.9	1	0.5	—	—	111	50.9	—	—	11	5.0	7	3.2	4	1.8
1970	285	7	2.5	90	31.6	9	3.2	—	—	135	47.4	1	0.4	17	6.0	16	5.6	10	3.5
1971	286	5	1.7	97	33.9	8	2.8	—	—	150	52.4	3	1.0	5	1.7	11	3.8	7	2.4
Total																			
1964	329	19	5.8	173	52.6	2	0.6	15	4.6	98	29.8	1	0.3	10	3.0	—	—	11	3.3
1965	370	12	3.2	211	57.0	14	3.8	11	3.0	98	26.5	1	0.3	9	2.4	—	—	14	3.8
1966	485	19	3.9	243	50.1	13	2.7	23	4.7	146	30.1	4	0.8	20	4.1	—	—	17	3.5
1967	486	23	4.7	246	50.6	25	5.1	30	6.2	126	25.9	3	0.6	21	4.3	—	—	12	2.5
1968	486	26	5.3	244	50.2	13	2.7	28	5.8	122	25.1	6	1.2	9	1.9	23	4.7	15	3.1
1969	598	42	7.0	280	46.8	20	3.3	—	—	186	31.1	1	0.2	22	3.7	26	4.3	21	3.5
1970	727	45	6.2	342	47.0	33	4.5	—	—	216	29.7	7	-1.0	22	3.0	45	6.2	17	2.3
1971	783	55	7.0	363	46.4	54	6.9	—	—	228	29.1	4	0.5	23	2.9	35	4.5	21	2.7

APPENDIX D

RESEARCH

Introduction

1. This Appendix briefly surveys some of the research which we found to be of particular interest and of relevance to our review, including studies carried out at our own request. It is not a full survey of the research results available, and the description of those projects to which it refers amounts to no more than a sketch. For a fuller survey and for more detail the reader should consult some of the useful general literature in this field[1] and the reports of the projects themselves.

2. We have concentrated on research into the effectiveness of treatment after sentence rather than research into the causes of crime: are some forms of treatment generally more effective than others, and is it possible to identify particular "types" of offender for whom particular forms of treatment are especially effective? It is not possible to discover the absolute effectiveness of any form of treatment, since this would require knowledge of what would have happened if there had been no intervention at all in the offender's life. Studies are therefore more of the *relative* effectiveness of different forms of treatment. These depend on a measurement of the proportion of offenders who are afterwards reconvicted, or of changes in attitudes or personality. Since offenders differ in their likelihood of committing further offences, care must be taken that like is compared with like, either by comparing categories whose risk is known to be similar or by controlling (either in the sampling or the analysis) for those variables known to be associated with reconviction.

3. The form of this Appendix is as follows. Section I (paragraphs 4 to 10) refers to three small-scale studies, of direct relevance to questions which arose in our review, which were carried out for us by the Home Office. Section II (paragraphs 11 to 34) surveys some existing work relating to the borstal system and the characteristics of the young offender population in this country. Section III is concerned with research in the United States of America, and describes a number of projects relatively fully because summaries of the American material are not so easily available to British readers. Paragraphs 35 to 55 outline some attempts in the United States to develop means of "matching" offenders to particular types of treatment in an effective way. Paragraphs 56 to 70 describe some attempts there to compare the effects of custodial treatment with those of treatment in the community. Finally, Section IV summarises some conclusions that may be drawn from the research previously described.

I. STUDIES CARRIED OUT FOR THE COUNCIL

4. A study was made of the "standard" reconviction rates (over a period of three years following the year of release) for young prisoners and those released from borstals and detention centres. In recent years these have been recorded by reference to the age of the offender when released, and to his previous criminal history. On the basis of these statistics the Home Office Research Unit carried out for us an analysis, by individual establishment, of offenders released in 1966 and 1967. The analysis took account of the differences between one establishment and another in the proportion of offenders in each category with differing degrees of previous criminal involvement. The method was to identify the distribution of different categories of offender within each establishment, and also throughout the whole borstal system and the whole detention centre system. An estimate was then made of what numbers of "good risks" and "bad risks" each establishment would have had if the proportions within the establishment had been the same as the average for all borstals or all detention centres. The success rates which the establishment actually achieved with each category were then applied to these "notional" numbers of offenders, thus putting every establishment so far as possible on an equal

---

[1] See, for example, D. J. West: *The Young Offender* (Pelican, 1967); R. Hood and R. Sparks: *Key Issues in Criminology* (World University Library, 1970).

footing as regards the criminality of its intake. This enabled some comparison to be made of the relative "success" of different establishments that was not simply a reflection of differences in the make-up of their offender population.

5. There appeared, before adjustments of this kind were made, to be large differences between the success rates of different borstals and different detention centres. Of offenders released from the different borstals in 1966, the actual proportions who were not reconvicted within three years varied from one establishment to another between 53% and 22%; and for 1967 between 50% and 15%. After adjustment in the manner described above the range within which the success rates varied narrowed, but remain significantly large: the "notional" ranges of success rate were between 48% and 25% for 1966 and between 50% and 20% for 1967. For offenders released from detention centres both in 1966 and 1967, the unadjusted rates ranged between 47% and 34%, while the adjusted rates ranged between 45% and 35% for 1966 and between 46% and 34% for 1967.

6. In the case of detention centres the difference between 1966 and 1967 in success rates which remained, after adjustment to take account of the characteristics of the population of each centre, was not statistically significant; and when detention centres were ranked according to "success rates" the rankings changed sufficiently between the two years to suggest that there was no consistent pattern. When the "success rates" for borstals were adjusted to take account of the differences in the characteristics of the population some changes took place in the ranking also; but, in contrast to detention centres, the differences which remained between individual borstals were statistically significant. There was also considerable consistency in the rank order of borstals for the two years. This may indicate that allocation between institutions divides people according to their inherent probability of reconviction to a greater degree than can be adjusted for simply by reference to previous criminal history. On the other hand, it may be that certain borstals are more effective than others, either in general or for particular subgroups selected for the borstals concerned or highly represented among the class of persons deliberately selected for those borstals.

7. It would be a considerable research task to discover how far these differences are the results of selection factors ignored (intentionally or unintentionally) in the analysis, and how far they may be attributed to the regime. Our conclusion was that the results need not significantly affect our preference for abandoning the present system of borstal allocation. The analysis does show, however, that under the present system there are certain establishments which have a consistently better record than others. Most noticeable is the superiority of the open borstals, and particularly of Gaynes Hall, an open borstal providing educational programmes and high level vocational training; in the context of a relaxed social structure, for borstal trainees of above average ability. Gaynes Hall was the most "successful" establishment (after the results had been adjusted to allow for character of intake, in the way described above) in both 1966 and 1967 (and also in 1965, for which year the Research Unit made a partial analysis).

8. The second study, referred to in paragraph 132 of the report, was an attempt to see whether the existence of detention centre training and borstal training had led to a greater use of custodial sentences for young adult offenders than for those over 21. The Home Office Statistical Department compared sentences imposed on males aged 19 and 20 in 1968 and 1969 with those imposed on males aged 21 and 22 in the same years for malicious wounding and burglary (in its various forms). For the purposes of comparison, a distinction was made between those with no previous convictions, those with one previous conviction and those with two or more previous convictions, and between sentences by higher and lower courts. While the courts did not appear to differentiate between young adults and those over 21 in the extent to which they used custodial sentences for wounding, they did make greater use of custody for young adults convicted of burglary.

9. The figures varied between higher and lower courts, from one type of offence to another, and according to the previous criminal history of the offenders. In a number of the sub-categories, the chances of a non-custodial sentence[1] were higher for the 21–22s than for the 19–20s. For example, of first offenders convicted of burglary in a building other than a dwelling in 1969, in the higher courts 71.4% of those aged 19–20 received a

---

[1] A suspended sentence was treated as a non-custodial measure.

non-custodial sentence and 85.7% of those aged 21–22; in magistrates' courts the percentages were 94.2 for the younger age group and 98.0 for the older age group. Of offenders with two or more previous convictions convicted of the same offence in the same year, in higher courts 25.0% of the younger age group and 32.5% of the older, were dealt with non-custodially; in magistrates' courts the corresponding percentage figures were 56.3 and 64.5. It can be argued, however, that this difference is accounted for (or partly accounted for) by the obligation which existed in both years under section 39 of the Criminal Justice Act 1967 to suspend short sentences of imprisonment under certain circumstances. There was no similar obligation to suspend detention centre sentences or sentences of imprisonment for violent offences.

10. The third study was prompted by the fact that there is no statutory provision confining sentences of borstal training[1] or detention centre training, in contrast to prison sentence,[2] to cases where the court concludes that no other way of dealing with the offender is appropriate. We asked all borstals and senior detention centres to provide information about those received between 1 February and 31 July 1972 who had not previously been found guilty of an indictable offence since reaching the age of 14. (The total number of files received, 334, was rather less than Prison Department statistics would have led us to expect, but we have no reason to think that the sample was unrepresentative.) In all but a small minority of cases the sentence was entirely explicable in terms of other sentencing criteria than a need for reformative training. The nature and circumstances of the offence, the number of offences taken into consideration, findings of guilt before the age of 14 or the response to measures ordered as a result of such earlier offences, were sufficient to explain the majority of decisions, on the assumption that the courts wished to express public disapproval of a serious offence, deter other people from similar conduct or afford the public a period of immunity from offensive behaviour.

II. RESEARCH IN ENGLAND AND WALES

Prediction methods[3]

11. An early attempt in this country to develop systematic methods of predicting "success" or "failure" for particular offenders was in a study by H. Mannheim and L. T. Wilkins, published in 1955.[4] They showed that it was possible, on the basis of information already collected about the background and characteristics of each borstal trainee, to draw up "prediction" or "experience" tables which afforded a better guide to the likelihood of future reconviction than the forecasts of staff based on their experience and observation of the trainees. (It is important to note that the fact that certain characteristics and circumstances may indicate or be associated with a certain likelihood of future conviction does not necessarily imply any causal relationship.)

12. Categorising their samples of borstal trainees according to their probability of success, Mannheim and Wilkins found that the system of allocating trainees among establishments was effective in ensuring that open borstals contained more of the better risks than closed borstals; but that even within each prediction category (ie when high-risk, low-risk and medium-risk groups were examined separately) those trainees who were allocated to open borstals proved to have a consistently higher success rate than those allocated to closed borstals. Again, a possible explanation is that the allocation process, in some unrecognised and indefinable way, discriminated between good and bad risks to a greater extent than the Mannheim-Wilkins formula.[5] This would mean that the apparent superiority of open borstals was due not to any characteristics of the establishments themselves but to some differences between particular offenders which had continued to escape the notice of the observers. But even if it is assumed that their formula was adequate

---

[1] Except in relation to those aged under 17.

[2] Criminal Justice Act 1948, section 17: see paragraph 140 of the report.

[3] For a wider review of prediction methods as a research technique, and of a large number of prediction studies (in relation both to custodial and non-custodial treatment), see F. H. Simon's *Prediction Methods in Criminology* (HMSO 1971).

[4] *Prediction Methods in relation to Borstal Training* (HMSO 1955). A somewhat fuller summary of this study is given, for example, in the book referred to in footnote 3 above.

[5] This hypothesis was subsequently explored by R. Cockett in "Borstal Training: A Follow-Up Study" (*British Journal of Criminology*, Volume 7, No. 2, April 1967).

to take account of the different prospects of individual offenders, and thus that open borstals did in fact show a superior performance, there is still room for debate about how this superiority should be explained. Wilkins himself was inclined to attribute the superiority of open borstals to the impact upon the general institutional atmosphere of its containing a high proportion of those less likely to commit further offences.

13. A further finding of interest concerned the effect of different lengths of detention. Taken in isolation the time that a young man spent in borstal was prognostic of success or failure (ie a longer stay was associated with a poorer chance of success); but when account was taken of likely success or failure according to other criteria, length of time in borstal ceased to be of significance, neither adding to nor subtracting from his overall chance of success. (It must be noted, however, that one result of the later study by Bottoms and McClintock, described in paragraphs 27 to 29 below, cast considerable doubt on this finding. Apart from their study of Dover Borstal, they analysed the subsequent careers[1] of a random 20% of young men discharged from all borstals in 1962 and 1966, observing that when allowance was made for age, previous convictions, institutional experience, type of offence and nature of previous employment, their probability of reconviction was *greater* the longer the time they had spent in borstal, whether of the open[2] or closed type.)

14. Finally, the study by Mannheim and Wilkins confirmed that the longer a young man was able to keep out of trouble after discharge from borstal, the less likely it was that any eventual failure would be a serious one.

Characteristics of young adult offenders

15. One of the most comprehensive recent studies of the characteristics of young men in English penal establishments—prisons, borstals and detention centres—has been conducted from University College, London from 1961 onwards, under the direction of Dr. Charlotte Banks,[3] and is still unpublished although some preliminary results have been made available to the Council in a number of papers. The research was designed principally to distinguish particular classes of offender with special needs. Dr. Banks developed four scales based on factor analysis: a scale of introversion—extroversion; an "adverse family score", made up largely of items describing parental discord, rejection and homelessness; an "adverse personality score", made up of items such as deprivation, hostility and instability; and a "criminal score" derived from psychologists' ratings of degree of criminal involvement. As is normally the case with such characteristics, scores on these measures showed a rather small degree of dispersion. It proved impossible to place most of these offenders in distinct categories, since only those with extreme scores on these measures could be said to constitute easily recognisable types. It was possible, however, to identify certain combinations of characteristics which distinguished offenders who were particularly at risk: for example, homeless and deprived young men with a good deal of earlier experience in penal institutions[4].

16. As regards matching offenders to treatment, the main conclusions of the research are so far largely negative: in general success and failure, however assessed, tend to follow expectations based on the offender's own characteristics and experience. There is, however, some evidence to suggest that those classified as abnormal and introverted tend to do better on release from borstal than after imprisonment or detention in a detention centre.

17. In the University College research the highest association with reconviction was provided by time previously spent in penal institutions. It found that different sentence-lengths did not appear to affect failure rates and confirmed the finding of Gibbens and Prince[5] that reconviction rates over a long period following release may show a different picture from those relating to the periods of two, three or five years that are usually chosen.

---

[1] As ascertained from the Home Office's borstal index.

[2] The effect was less marked but still significant for those who had been in open borstals.

[3] Who joined the Home Office Research Unit in 1966.

[4] A similar finding was made by Roger Hood, in his study entitled *Homeless Borstal Boys* (1966): his conclusion was that the primary need in such cases was to help trainees to adjust to life in the open community.

[5] See footnote to paragraph 138 of the report.

Allocation methods

18. Another research project which has substantially influenced our review is the Borstal Typology Study carried out by the staff of the Psychology Department at Wormwood Scrubs Prison[1]. This consisted of a number of related investigations of current allocation practice and of the effect of various aspects of different borstal regimes. The studies extended over a number of years up to 1971. Of particular significance for our review are a study of allocation practice and a study of "pooled allocation"; we have drawn to a large extent on the results of these studies in considering the future pattern of establishments for young adult offenders.

19. In the course of the Borstal Typology Study relationships were analysed between 71 items of information relating to a sample of 1,100 young men received for borstal training. Most of these factors were objectively defined attributes of background and history, but they also included the results of psychological tests. The analysis showed no large correlation between data relating to criminality (for example, the nature of the most recent offence and previous criminal history) and other, "non-criminal", data (relating for example to family structure, social relations and answers to personality questionnaires).

20. The study of allocation practice grew out of an increasing awareness by the psychologists at the allocation centre that the nature of the allocation decision was obscure. They therefore attempted to discover whether any specific "rules" underlying the process, as then carried out, could be discerned. The method adopted was to "mimic" the process, in the sense of drawing up tables of comparatively simple rules, the application of which would give the same final result as the full allocation process itself. The psychologists used information in existing records about previous offences and sentences and information in medical records or gained from a medical examination about mental condition, any previous suicide attempts and previous medical treatment. On this basis it proved possible in 85% of cases to predict the decision of the allocation board as to whether the trainee should go to an open or a closed establishment—which in itself had been regarded as one of the most important functions of the allocation centre. A further study showed that once an offender had been found suitable, in general, for open conditions, it was possible, in a similar proportion of cases, to predict the allocation board's decision between three open borstals.

21. These findings suggested that a few simple facts determined most of the decisions, and in the great majority of cases the application of simple rules, without elaborate assessment, could produce allocations similar to those made by the board. It does not necessarily follow that a more effective allocation process could not be devised. This was not a question with which the researchers concerned themselves directly, though it is fair to say that they themselves discovered no more effective basis for matching offenders to particular types of treatment than that which was already in operation at the allocation centre.

22. The study of "pooled allocation", carried out between 1964 and 1967, was made possible by the existence of three open borstals, of roughly equal size, exemplifying three different treatment approaches: Pollington, using group counselling methods; Hewell Grange, applying "casework" principles, and Morton Hall which could be said to be operating a "traditional" borstal regime. Normal borstal rules applied in all three establishments, but steps were taken to reduce the turnover in staff in order to minimise changes in the regimes. All three establishments were accustomed to receiving trainees who were relatively young and intelligent and had few previous convictions.

23. Instead of allocating trainees to a particular one of these three establishments the allocation staff allocated to a common "pool" all those considered suitable for any one of the three. From this pool trainees were then assigned by random selection to a particular establishment. But first they were interviewed and assessed by a prison psychologist. On the basis of the interview and of documentary information the psychologist made a general assessment of each trainee's prospect of success. Three other predictions were also made, to take into account each of the establishments to which he might be allocated. A 4-point scale was used, ranging from probable success to probable failure. In addition

---

[1] This research has not as yet been published, but copies are obtainable on application to the Chief Psychologist, Home Office Prison Department, 89 Eccleston Square, SW1.

to these prognoses the psychologists assessed, on a similar 4-point scale, the degree of disturbance of each trainee.

24. It is of interest that there was a difference between the success rates of the three establishments, although, since this was essentially research into allocation, and did not attempt to test the reliability of the descriptions which had been attached to the three establishments, it is difficult to generalise from this finding. Judging by the proportion of inmates who were reconvicted within two years of release, the establishment using "case-work" was the most successful with a reconviction rate of 51% compared with about 63% for both the other establishments.[1] In addition to this general result, the psychologists determined the final failure-rate for those from each establishment in each of the categories of disturbance according to which each trainee had initially been classified. As regards the two middle categories (which accounted for a high proportion of the total) each regime showed a consistent relationship between disturbance and failure. But for those who had been assessed as being most disturbed, the traditional regime did better than either of the other two; while for the least disturbed, the traditional regime did worst.

25. Of greater significance is the fact that the case-work regime did not do especially well with those cases assessed in the allocation centre as amenable to or requiring case-work. When the psychologists' original prediction of probable success or failure, made before allocation to a specific establishment, was compared with the actual results, there proved to be a consistent relationship between predicted success and actual success: thus the psychologists had been able to estimate fairly well the probability of an offender's being reconvicted, given only information about him and not about the regime to which he would go. But those predictions made by the psychologists which took into account the establishment to which each trainee eventually went proved less reliable. Not only did the additional information not increase the ability to predict outcome: it actually reduced it.

26. These results appeared to us to throw considerable doubt on the contribution of the allocation process in operation at that time to maximising the success of the borstal system.

Comparison of borstal regimes

27. A deliberate attempt to develop a borstal regime with a view to evaluation by systematic comparison with treatment prior to its development, and with treatment in other institutions, was the subject of a study by F. H. McClintock and others from the Institute of Criminology at Cambridge. The study centred on a regime developed at Dover Borstal and a sample of those who entered it between January 1965 and March 1966.[2] The modifications which were made to the regime did not involve a new and radical treatment approach, but took the form of an adaptation of the existing regime with greater emphasis on an individualised approach. Individual training plans were drawn up, and more discussion took place between staff and trainees about problems relevant to criminality. These changes were buttressed by changes in organisation and in the approach to breaches of discipline. The training plan for each individual specified what should be attempted during the period of institutional treatment. The possibilities included, firstly, individual discussion or group discussion to assist the offender in gaining insight into his problems and to influence his attitudes; and secondly, rather more intensive efforts in the fields of education, the provision of occupational skills, matching offenders to suitable supervisors within the institution, and improving relationships with relatives or friends outside who might give support on release. Formal arrangements were made for noting progress in the implementation of the training plan; they included discussions of it at intervals with the offender. The average duration of training was less in the "modified" stage.

28. For various reasons, the modification in the regime did not extend as far as the originators of the research proposal had hoped. The project cannot, therefore, be said to have compared totally different regimes, nor to have tested out the form of treatment

---

[1] These figures relate to trainees discharged from the three establishments; they therefore take no account of trainees transferred to other borstals. Apparently, however, the difference between success rates was "substantially sustained" in a straight comparison of all allocations.
[2] A. E. Bottoms and F. H. McClintock: *Criminals Coming of Age* (Heinemann, 1973).

which the researchers had hoped to see developed: the latter would have involved greater resources and greater continuity between institutional treatment and after-care supervision. The senior staff of the borstal and the researchers did, however, claim that under the modified regime there had been developed certain features of the system for facilitating individual training and new ways in which this was carried out such as to distinguish it from the traditional regime.

29. The experimental sample who went through the modified regime were compared, on the basis of 18 months' follow-up, with borstal trainees who had undergone their training at Dover during the traditional regime. No statistically significant differences in re-conviction rates were found. This result was unaffected when allowance was made for different degrees of risk by using a predictive instrument developed in the research, and the general conclusion was that the two regimes were similar in their outcome with respect to reconviction. Nor was any difference found when various aspects of social adjustment apart from delinquency were considered. No clear evidence was found of an interaction between particular types of offender and type of regime. A tendency was found for those with low scores on measures of "social problems" and "penal problems" (ie those whose social problems were fewer and/or less acute; and those with less history of previous criminal involvement and/or penal treatment) to do better in the modified regime than the traditional regime and for those with high scores on these measures to do better after the traditional regime; but the differences were not statistically significant. Mr. McClintock has observed that if such a trend had continued on more prolonged differentiation of the two regimes, one of the possible implications would be that the modified regime, with its individual training programmes, could improve upon the results of traditional borstal training methods for those whose social problems and penal history were not the most extreme, while for those with more serious problems it might produce even worse results.

Probation research

30. The Home Office Research Unit has been carrying on research on probation for over a decade. A number of reports have been published, two of them being of direct relevance to the young adult age group. These are both descriptive studies and, while it cannot be said that recommendations in the Council's report derive directly from them, they deserve a mention as being a source of interesting research information about this group of offenders and their problems. Mention should also be made of a probation pre-diction study, the object of which was to provide a "risk classification" of young adult men placed on probation which could be used elsewhere in the programme by probation research. This study is described in *Prediction Methods in Criminology*.[1]

31. *Probationers in their Social Environment*[2] is a detailed description of a sample of 507 young men in the 17–20 age range in eight probation areas who were placed on probation in the latter part of 1964. The object of the study was to identify those parts of the environment which are most likely to present difficulties for male probationers in this age group and those which are most likely to be related to reconviction. The findings of the study, which are summarised in a final chapter, include the following:

    (a) In the sample of probationers, 37.3% were reconvicted within 12 months of the beginning of the probation order.

    (b) Nearly three quarters of the probationers in the sample were living with parent(s) or parent substitute(s). 8% lived in hostels, lodgings etc and homelessness was a problem for less than 5%: both these groups had above average reconviction rates, greater than one in two.

    (c) The material standards of the probationers in the sample were generally high: over a third were completely free from material stress and the majority of probationers and their families were "well in the main stream of Britain's economic affluence in the 60s". Where probationers suffered material stress, it was material factors connected with inadequate family functioning (eg dirty and untidy homes) rather than those beyond the family's control (eg overcrowding) which were linked with a high probability of failure.

    (d) Parental over-indulgence was common, and was linked with reconviction.

[1] Home Office Research Studies, No. 7, by F. H. Simon (HMSO 1971).
[2] Home Office Research Studies, No. 2, by M. Davies (HMSO 1969).

(e) Being unemployed and having a poor work record were both linked with failure on probation. 40% of those in the sample had unsteady work records, and about the same number were unemployed at the time they were placed on probation. Of those in work at that time, nearly half had held their present job for less than three months. A high proportion had in the past been sacked from jobs, or had left for no good reason, and this fact was linked with failure on probation.

(f) More probationers were said to mix mainly with non-delinquents (40%) than mixed mainly with delinquents (33%); the latter group had a failure rate of one in two, and were more likely to be out of work and to have quarrelling parents.

(g) Almost all leisure activities were essentially passive. Less than a quarter were actively involved in organised youth clubs, and nearly a third claimed that there was no specific place in the community where they spent a lot of their time.

32. The second report[1] describes studies of approved probation hostels for young men. The studies were based on various samples of young men, aged between 15 and 21, who had passed through probation hostels between 1954 and 1963 and on surveys of hostel staff and hostel regimes.

33. The studies suggested that rootless offenders were more likely to be reconvicted while still at the hostel than those with home ties, and that those from unsatisfactory homes settled down relatively well in the hostel though a high proportion of them were likely to be reconvicted on their return home. The regime found most likely to be successful, at least with the younger offenders who comprised the bulk of the population study, was one that combined firm consistent discipline with warm relationships between staff and offenders. It appeared that the warden played the vital part in producing this atmosphere. However, the differences in reconviction rate between the more successful and less successful hostels applied in general to the period of residence in the hostel and not to the period after residents had left. The studies drew attention to various problems of probation hostels, notably the difficulty of obtaining and keeping suitable staff, the need for closer professional support for them, the severe difficulties posed by hostel residents and the difficulty of bringing about changes in home background such as would prevent a relapse into further delinquency after the offender's return.

34. The field work for the research ended in August 1966, and since then there have been a number of important developments relating to hostels. Additionally, many of the offenders studied in this research were below the age range of offender to which the Council's report refers.

III. RESEARCH IN THE USA

35. We turn now to a brief description of some projects in the United States of America, in particular in California, which are of interest as being quite sophisticated attempts to measure the effect of differential institutional regimes, and to compare institutional and non-institutional treatment. The first of these approaches, in the United States as in this country, has not so far been able to establish conclusively that some forms of regime are more effective (in terms of avoidance of future reconviction) than others; the results of the latter approach, though these again are not so far fully conclusive, form part of the basis for the belief that treatment in the community is not less effective than institutional treatment.

36. A development in California which has aroused widespread interest is the use of the *Inter-Personal Maturity Level* (integration level or I-level) classification, which postulates seven levels on a scale of increasing maturity of a person's relationships with others. In the application of the theory to delinquency only three I-levels—2, 3 and 4—have been used to any extent, and within each of these three I-levels a number of sub-types have been established, to take account of differences in the nature of the reaction which the individual makes to his perception of the world. People are assigned to an I-level and sub-type either according to the original method of subjective judgment by staff after interview or by a method (known as the sequential method) devised by Dr. Carl Jesness,

---

[1] *Hostels for Probationers,* Home Office Research Studies No. 6 (HMSO 1971).

which involves the offender in completing a psychological questionnaire known now as the Jesness Inventory; this is supplemented if necessary by an interview.

37. Criticisms have been levelled against the I-level classification on both theoretical and practical grounds. The theory provides no adequate definition of "potential for change" or maturation during an individual's normal psychological development, so that it is difficult to distinguish normal maturation from maturation or change as the result of treatment intervention. On a practical level, the most serious criticism has been of the subjective nature, mainly using interview material, of the method of assigning individuals to the various I-level types. Attempts, by research workers outside the Californian school, to find objective methods of applying the classification, have not so far been successful. It therefore seems unlikely that the classification could be widely used as a routine method of classifying offenders for particular treatment programmes.[1]

38. The I-level classification has, however, been used in a number of interesting ways. In some projects different treatment strategies have been offered to offenders according to their I-level classification, while in others the same treatment has been offered to offenders in different categories, the classification then being used to search for differences in response. Californian research projects using the I-level classification have received a great deal of public notice, and from time to time claims have been made that they have demonstrated particular forms of treatment to be more successful than others.

Camp Elliott

39. The first reported study that appeared to show differential response to treatment according to I-level type was a study of naval personnel in detention for disciplinary reasons at Camp Elliott in California.[2] Three types of training regime were compared, the criterion being the proportion of persons going through each regime who were restored to military duty. Groups of 20 of high, low and mixed maturity levels were randomly allocated to three types of regime, each of which had essentially the same daily routine but differed in the manner in which the supervisors approached their task and in particular in the approach to group discussion sessions. The researchers rated the supervisors according to the degree of effectiveness they expected; they expected "internally oriented" attitudes to be more effective than those stressing outward observance of recognised standards of behaviour. For the living group which the researchers had predicted would be most effective, the success rate for high maturity subjects was significantly higher than for those of low maturity level. There was a similar, but less marked, difference for the second group; while in the regime predicted least effective there was no difference in the success rates of the two types of offender. Overall the high maturity subjects did significantly better than the low maturity subjects, but neither the high maturity subjects nor those of low maturity did significantly better in one regime than in another. In fact, those of low maturity level had an above-average success rate in the living group predicted least effective and a below-average success rate in that predicted most effective. These results, however, were not statistically significant, and cannot be said to have proved that one form of treatment was better than another for any particular type. They offered partial confirmation, however, of the hypothesis that some people of relatively low maturity may do worse in a regime oriented to introspection and self-analysis than in a regime run on more authoritarian lines which places greater emphasis on satisfactory outward behaviour.

Preston Typology Study

40. In a typology study at the Preston Industrial School in California, directed by Dr. Jesness from 1965 until 1968, residents were assigned to living accommodation in six groups, according to their I-level type, so that on the whole people of the same type were accommodated together. The staff of the six units approached their task with differently formulated aims, designed to meet the particular needs of the different groups.

---

[1] For a detailed critique of the I-level classification (and of the Community Treatment Project, which is described below) see "A critical appraisal of the California differential treatment typology of adolescent offenders", by Beker and Heyman (*Criminology,* Vol. 10, No. 1, May 1972, pages 3-59).

[2] C. E. Sullivan, J. D. Grant and M. Q. Grant, "A Group Dynamics Approach to the Treatment of Non-Conformists in the Navy", *Annals of the American Academy of Political and Social Science* 1959, 322, 126-135.

41. The most immediate effect of introducing the "I-level" system was a decrease in institutional management problems. Comparison with a control group not allocated by I-level type showed a decrease for both in the number of reports of serious misbehaviour during the project, but the decrease was greater for the experimental units. There was, however, an increase in reports of serious incidents for the house where those at the lowest I-level (I-2) were housed. Only minor differences were found between the failure rates on parole of the various sub-types and between the failure rate for the experimental and control groups. Psychological measures appeared to show some changes in behaviour for the better among those in the experimental sample.

Youth Center Research Project: OH Close and Karl Holton Schools

42. In the Preston Typology Study, "treatment" still rested on the capacity of staff to influence offenders through the strength of their personal relationships with them: it involved no particular theory as to how behaviour should be changed. In order to formulate more explicit guidelines for treatment, experiments were made in the course of the project with two distinct treatment strategies: one which made use (inter alia) of the group treatment technique of transactional analysis, and the other employing the technique of behaviour-modification. These techniques were later introduced as an integral part of research in a recent project of major importance, the Youth Center Research Project at the Northern California Youth Center, Stockton.[1]

43. Two of the component institutions of the Northern Youth Center at Stockton, OH Close and Karl Holton Schools, were used for the development of the two experimental regimes. From September 1968 a pool was formed of offenders aged 15 to 17, and from the pool they were randomly assigned to one or the other institution.

44. The regime at Karl Holton was based on behaviour-modification theory. The most important aspect of a behaviour-modification programme is its emphasis on the behaviour itself, rather than on hypothetical psychological states: what happens immediately after an item of behaviour is seen as being of prime importance. Since the emphasis is on overt behaviour, the establishment of good relationships between staff and inmates, which is so much stressed in most approaches to the treatment of offenders, is regarded as having no positive importance in itself, and is even liable to interfere (for example, by sympathetic response to a plea for attention expressed through anti-social behaviour) with attempts to ignore or (if unavoidable) penalise unacceptable behaviour.

45. The method of implementing this treatment strategy at Karl Holton School was through a token economy. Specified good behaviour resulted in the award of points (known as behaviour change units) which entitled a resident to "currency" for use in buying various privileges within the institution and, when earned in sufficient number, to a recommendation for release. Three different kinds of behaviour were taken into account: "convenience behaviours", ie behaviour relating (favourably or adversely) to the orderly and efficient running of the institution (though not necessarily related to avoiding future delinquency); achievements in the institution's educational programme; and behaviour contributing to the correction of "critical behaviour deficiencies"—patterns of behaviour that could be expected on the basis of theory and past empirical research to be associated with failure on parole. Specified achievements in these three areas were the subject of "contracts" made with members of staff, performance of which would be rewarded by a definite number of behaviour change units.

46. The range of penalties applicable to undesirable behaviour was limited. Serious misbehaviour was brought to the attention of the Youth Authority board when release was under consideration. Less serious misbehaviour could result in an addition to the number of behaviour change units required for recommendation for release or in deprivation of certain privileges until a specified series of contracts relating to the behaviour had been completed. They could also be dealt with by fines in the token currency or by brief periods of isolation in a separate room.

47. This system, despite extensive staff training, proved very difficult to implement.

---

[1] Conducted from April 1968 to March 1972 and fully reported in C. F. Jesness, W. J. De Risi, P. McCormick and R. F. Wedge, *The Youth Center Research Project*, California Youth Authority 1972.

Fewer than half the contracts examined by the staff who were monitoring the experiment were rated as relevant and as referring to overt behaviour—the essential feature of a behaviour—modification approach.[1] In practice it proved necessary to make some use of penalties (instead of relying, as behaviour-modification theory prescribes, upon rewards alone). This was particularly the case in dealing with "convenience behaviours", since objectionable behaviour in this category was conspicuous, while desirable behaviour was necessarily less obtrusive.

48. The experimental regime at OH Close School was based on fundamentally different theories. Transactional analysis deals with much broader patterns or units of behaviour than those with which the practitioner of behaviour-modification would ordinarily be concerned. The theory assumes that, in order to change behaviour, attention must be paid to the inner person, and that people react to events more in terms of their interpretation of events than in terms of the objective reality of the external world. Transactional analysis is to be distinguished from the normal form of psychoanalysis: it is not primarily concerned with unconscious mechanisms, but assumes that people are capable of recognising the influence of the past on their present behaviour. Speech and behaviour can be regarded as exhibiting three approaches to oneself and to others, those of the parent, the child and the adult. When in the adult "ego state" the person is able to choose effectively the most appropriate response to the occasion. But childhood experiences and relationships with parents may establish routines and patterns in a person's relationships with others which he adopts automatically because they are familiar and habitual but which may be damaging to him or others. Other people may be so manipulated that they inadvertently find themselves playing a part in such a "game", so that for example a well-disposed and friendly member of staff may be continually provoked until he begins to fit more closely the guise of an aggressive and vindictive authority figure against whom the delinquent is used to playing a corresponding role, as a result of a relationship with his parents. Transactional analysis is concerned with identifying such "games" and helping to free the patient from the restrictions they impose on his capacity to live as an adult.

49. The principal vehicle for transactional analysis at OH Close School was the small group counselling meeting, where chains of transactions were analysed as they occurred. But all staff were encouraged also to use the theories of transactional analysis in all their contacts with residents and with each other. A system of contracts was again used, setting precise goals to be achieved either in education or in small group meetings or in ordinary behaviour within the institution. The contracts relating to social behaviour were concerned with the correction of unsatisfactory relationships with members of staff or other residents.

50. Once again there were difficulties of implementation. Despite the high degree of staff training Dr. Jesness and his colleagues did not consider that the institution was fully successful in producing a treatment regime consistently based on transactional analysis.[2]

51. The reports on the Youth Center Research Project available included, during the Council's review, information regarding parole violation for only some of those who received the experimental treatment over follow-up periods of only 15 months or less. Future reports must therefore be awaited before an attempt can be made to draw reliable inferences from the reconviction rates for the two regimes. But some comparisons were made both of the performance on parole of offenders released from the two experimental regimes and on parole for at least 12 months, and between them and offenders released from the schools before the introduction of the experimental programme. A similar percentage from each institution, 31% from OH Close School and 32% from Karl Holton, had been

---

[1] Some members of the Council who visited this institution noticed this: contracts sometimes referred to the name of the behaviour or the deficiency to be corrected, for example "obtrusiveness", rather than to specific behaviour to be performed or avoided with a view to remedying the deficiency.
[2] Some Council members who visited OH Close School observed a group meeting in which the leaders made use of psycho-therapeutic tactics which seemed objectionable and possibly harmful. But it was not clear whether these methods were acceptable practice in transactional analysis, or merely unfortunate improvisations on the part of the leaders concerned.

removed from parole, compared with failure rates of 44% and 42% for the control samples released from the two schools before the experiment began. Comparison with those released from two other Youth Authority schools after adjustments for different proportions of persons of each age in the population showed rather larger differences in favour of the two experimental regimes. These comparisons, however, included no adjustment for previous criminal record and penal history which might have accounted for at least some of the differences. No firm inferences can be drawn from an analysis of outcome by reference to I-level sub-types until parole data are available for the whole sample, but Dr. Jesness and his colleagues believe that some differences may then be found. Results so far suggest that low maturity "social passives" and "cultural conformists" tend to be more successful after the behaviour-modification regime, while "manipulators" have less failure after transactional analysis. It is perhaps particularly interesting that low maturity, social passive subjects should seem to do better in a regime concentrating on conformity in external behaviour. Of interest too are some of the conclusions drawn by the researchers which are not necessarily related to subsequent success on parole. The results of administering the Jesness Inventory, a self-report questionnaire, and a "behaviour check-list" before and after treatment showed changes in the residents of both institutions in a variety of ways that most people would consider desirable with respect to their attitudes to themselves and others. A psychological measure of the social climate of the institution, as seen through the eyes of staff and inmates, showed that the new methods of treatment changed perceptions considerably and that they produced two very different social climates. This result partially reflected some dissatisfaction with the behaviour-modification regime, which offered no rewards except for behaviour precisely defined by staff.

52. The effect of the experiment on disciplinary incidents is interesting. In both institutions there was an initial increase in the number of incidents of misconduct reported followed by a decline to something like the level before the experiment started. In both institutions, however, this higher level of misconduct was accompanied by a much smaller use than before of detention as a punishment. The detention rate dropped by more than 60% and staff agreed that detention was being used differently, for briefer periods and to promote positive changes in behaviour.

Kennedy Youth Center

53. An alternative strategy for providing differential treatment is to be found at the Kennedy Youth Center, an open Federal institution in West Virginia, where different treatment approaches are in operation in each of the living units within one open institution. The institution employs a classification of offenders developed by Professor Quay: inadequate-immature, neurotic-conflicted, unsocialised aggressive, psychopathic and socialised, and sub-cultural delinquent. This classification may be thought to be related to the I-level categories, but no correlation between the two typologies has in fact been found. Whereas the I-level classification was developed originally by a synthesis of different theories regarding the development of human behaviour, the behaviour categories of Professor Quay's classification are intended to be empirical in origin rather than theoretical.

54. Offenders are assigned to different housing units on the basis of the behaviour categories listed above. The differentiation in treatment consists not so much in the mode in which the regime is conducted as in the "preferred style" of the staff and the objectives they set for themselves—objectives related to what seem to be the most damaging characteristics of the offender. Different theoretical frameworks—behaviour-modification, transactional analysis and "reality therapy"—are, however, drawn upon. It was initially intended that the behaviourist approach should be the basis of treatment throughout the institution. In practice, however, only one of the regimes is now based clearly on specifying and rewarding precise changes of behaviour. (When, in a separate research project, offenders of all behaviour categories were randomly assigned to this housing unit, the results tended to show that those in the "unsocialised aggressive or psychopathic" category benefited most.) The token economy system survives to some extent throughout the whole institution, in the form of points earned by educational performance, which have monetary value, and of "cottage points", for what at Karl Holton School would be called "convenience behaviour", which carry an entitlement to privileges. Some use is also made of the system of contracts but these are not fundamental to the programme.

253

55. A long-term study is in progress comparing a cohort of offenders who went through the Kennedy Youth Center with trainees going through other institutions, and the samples will be big enough to enable analysis by the behaviour categories of the Quay classification. An assessment of the relevance of the classification for treatment purposes and of the treatment approaches adopted must await the outcome of this study.

California Community Treatment Project

56. The best known recent California research project is probably the California Community Treatment Project. The project compares offenders undergoing the ordinary treatment provided in the Californian Youth Authority (a period of custodial treatment of a similar length to borstal training followed by a period on parole) with offenders released on parole immediately after assessment and supervised by parole agents aware of the "I-level" type of the clients and taking this into account in their manner of supervision. It has three phases, the last of which is still in progress, and these are best described separately. Phase 1 of the project from 1961 to 1964 involved people committed to the Youth Authority for the first time by the juvenile courts of the towns of Sacramento and Stockton. After elimination of certain categories these formed a pool from which random allocation was made to (i) an experimental group who were released to the I-level "differential treatment" low-caseload supervision in the community and (ii) a control group who went through the ordinary Youth Authority programme. It can be said that, broadly speaking, the effect of the initial process of selection was that those who participated in the project were comparable to those young adult offenders sentenced to custody in this country who might be considered suitable for an open establishment. In terms of the offences for which they were committed to the Youth Authority the population involved does not seem to have been very different from those receiving custodial treatment here, but they were a little younger than the age group with which we are primarily concerned (mean age of 16.6 years for the experimental group and 15.3 years for the control group).

57. A number of measures were used to compare the effects of the two types of treatment, including parole revocation, to which most attention has been given. Among those on parole for at least 15 months there was a parole failure rate of 31% for the experimental group and 50% for the control group. The rate for the experimental group was also significantly better than the failure rate for a state-wide cohort released from the Youth Authority in 1966. Similar differences were found in comparing the experimental and control group who had been on parole for at least 24 months (39% and 61% respectively) and those who had been on parole for 36 months (46% and 63%).

58. Some differences were found for particular sub-types. On the basis of all three periods of follow-up the failure rate for the "neurotic acting-out" sub-type was significantly lower in the experimental sample than in the control sample. This applied also to the "neurotic anxious" sub-type after 24 months follow-up. The "conformist immature" sub-type in the experimental sample had a significantly lower failure rate after 15 months' follow-up and after 36 months' follow-up, while the "conformist cultural" and "manipulator" had a lower failure rate after 24 months' follow-up.[1]

59. Judged by the criterion of revocation of parole, therefore, those receiving differential treatment performed significantly better than the controls. But this may not be a wholly reliable indicator of performance on release, since there seem to have been inconsistencies in the standards applied in deciding whether to recommend a revocation of parole. There are alternative sanctions used by supervisors in the event of a breach: an offender may be detained temporarily[2] and then either released or brought to the attention of the Youth Authority Board—who may order restoration to parole. A method of assessing success or failure which takes account of all these possibilities is to compare favourable discharge from parole, resulting simply from reaching the maximum age or from earlier termination of supervision because it is judged no longer necessary, and unfavourable discharge, resulting from further serious offences or major breaches of parole.

60. Thus, although according to the criterion of revocation of parole those receiving

---

[1] At a confidence level of less than 0.1.
[2] See paragraph 284 (in Chapter 10) of the report.

differential treatment performed significantly better than the control group, investigation showed that in fact they committed offences at approximately the same rate as those in the control sample; the explanation was that for breaches of parole of a comparable nature a lower proportion in the experimental sample than in the control sample had their parole revoked. The breaches leading to parole failure were significantly less serious for the control sample than for the experimentals. This need not be regarded as telling against the success of the project: the ability to tolerate misbehaviour and to try to cope with it while retaining the offender in the community is one measure of success.

61. During Phase II of the Community Treatment Project, from 1964 to 1969, the experiment already described was extended and a further experiment was begun in San Francisco. The latter involved random assignment of offenders to two experimental samples in the community and to a control sample going through the ordinary Youth Authority programme. One of the experimental samples was dealt with by the differential treatment strategy devised on the basis of I-level theory and applied in the Sacramento/ Stockton experiment. The other sample was treated by staff following the theory and philosophy of a group counselling method known as guided group interaction. This approach seeks to exploit the fact that young people are subject to many more pressures from their peers than from treatment staff, even in custody.

62. This experiment, unlike the Sacramento/Stockton experiment, included some juveniles committed for a second time and some who had been released from the ordinary Youth Authority programme and had had their parole revoked. When investigated by the Council results had been reported for the period to December 1969 at which time relatively few of the experimental samples and very few of the control sample had been on parole for as much as two years. The percentage of each sample who had failed on parole was lower for differential treatment than for guided group interaction or ordinary parole. There was little difference between the sample who received guided group interaction and the control sample with respect to the percentage failing on parole; among those on parole for at least 15½ months the control sample had, in fact, slightly fewer parole failures. The full implications of this research will not be clear until a larger proportion of the experimental and control samples have been on parole for a greater length of time.

63. In both phases of the Community Treatment Project comparisons were made with respect to changes in character and personality measured by the Jesness Inventory and the California Psychological Inventory. In general, changes regarded as desirable were greater among those undergoing differential treatment than others.

64. Phase III of the Community Treatment Project, now in progress, is designed to develop further the I-level typology, the treatment strategies based upon it and the matching of parole agents to offenders. In particular it is intended to test the suitability of these methods for dealing with people committed by the criminal courts rather than the juvenile courts and to develop forms of treatment for certain types of offenders who performed badly both in I-level differential treatment and in the ordinary Youth Authority programme during Phases I and II of the Community Treatment Project. One hypothesis being tested is that for certain types of offender differential treatment will be more effective if it begins with a period of full-time residence. The project provides for a short period of residential treatment followed by parole, with continuous responsibility taken by the parole agent from the beginning of the period of sentence. Random allocation provides four groups for comparison. Those committed to the Youth Authority for the first time by the juvenile or adult criminal courts of Sacramento county are eligible for the pool from which the allocation is made, with exceptions similar to those applying in the earlier phases of the Community Treatment Project and the exclusion of some additional categories, for example those involved in earlier stages of the project and those with a history of previous institutional treatment. Those judged as suitable for immediate release into the community are selected at random for immediate release or for an initial period of detention, and the same is true of those judged unsuitable for immediate release into the community. Only some of the parole case-loads are being matched to the preferred style of the parole agent, as was the case in earlier phases of the Community Treatment Project, and this should enable the value of the matching process to be assessed.

65. The results of the Community Treatment Project so far available have been interpreted as a vindication of the view that offenders may be treated not only more cheaply but more effectively in the community than in custody. While, because of the difficulties of evaluation which have been noted above, it is questionable whether this has been demonstrated, it can fairly be claimed that the project has demonstrated that, at least for the type of offender dealt with in it, treatment can be provided in the community which is no less effective. Some of the results suggest that certain more mature offenders may do significantly better when dealt with in this way than when dealt with by more traditional penal methods of custodial treatment.

The Provo Experiment

66. A more definite suggestion that treatment in the community can be superior to custody is given by the results of the Provo Experiment,[1] designed to provide an alternative to custody for persistent juvenile offenders. The experiment was in relation to offenders aged between 14 and 18 coming before the juvenile court in Provo, Utah, between 1959 and 1964 who had one or more previous convictions or were appearing before the court for several serious offences.

67. The intention was that those who would normally have been put on probation, and those who would normally have been sent to an industrial school, should be treated as separate populations; and that from each of them an experimental group (undergoing experimental treatment) and a control group (undergoing the same treatment that they would normally have received) should be created by random selection. (This plan eventually foundered because the number of offenders whom the judge indicated that he would normally have sent to the custodial training school was not sufficient to enable the creation of experimental and control groups by random methods. It was therefore decided, in 1962, to include in the experimental programme all those on whom the judge was inclined to pass a custodial sentence and to establish a group for comparison from other offenders with similar characteristics to those in the experimental sample who were committed to the state industrial training school from other courts.) The experimental treatment programme did not use any testing, analysis of case history, or clinical diagnosis, but relied on the interchange of experiences and information in group meetings as the source of information about those in the experimental samples and their delinquency. There were two phases to the treatment. The first was an intensive programme of work, schooling and group meetings. During the winter those who were still at school continued to attend, while those who were not at school were employed in a programme of paid work for the city. On Saturdays all boys worked. Late in the afternoon of each day, after school or work, the boys attended a group meeting at the centre and then returned to their homes. During the summer every boy attended an all-day programme of work and group discussions. The second phase was intended to provide assistance after release from the intensive programme. It consisted of maintaining a group to which he could relate and from which he could obtain support, and using community resources to find him employment.

68. The first analysis of results indicated that, by criteria related to behaviour during a 4-year follow-up, the experimental programme did not seem to be greatly superior to ordinary probation. But those in the experimental group who would otherwise have gone to the industrial training school were less delinquent during the follow-up period than their control group. Moreover, a more complex comparison between the experimental and control groups in the experiment appears to show greater differences in favour of the experimental programme. This analysis was designed to exclude differences in success resulting from differences in social class and age. The study also appears to show that penal treatment did have an appreciable effect upon behaviour, helpful for those in the experimental programme and the probation control group (though to a lesser degree for those in the experimental programme who would otherwise have been committed to custody) but damaging in the case of custodial treatment in the sense that it increased the tendency to delinquency.

---

[1] L. T. Empey and M. L. Erickson *The Provo Experiment:* evaluating Community Control of Delinquency (Lexington, Massachusetts, Lexington Books, D. C. Heath and Co., 1972).

69. The experiment illustrates the ethical difficulties involved in random allocation;[1] and the eventual abandonment of random allocation between the experimental programme and the industrial training school inevitably casts some doubt on the results.

Silverlake

70. Random allocation was maintained throughout a later project in which Empey was engaged: the Silverlake Experiment.[2] This project also used group counselling and guided group interaction. Boys were randomly assigned between Boys' Republic, a traditional training school for delinquents, and Silverlake, a house in a Los Angeles suburb, acquired by the school to be a hostel from which the residents would go out to the local school. By the criterion of any arrest in the 12 months following release there was no significant difference between the experimental sample who passed through Silverlake and the control sample who went to the main Boys' Republic institution.

IV. CONCLUSIONS

71. There have been few systematic attempts to compare different forms of penal treatment. Most of them have shown little difference in outcome when like offenders are compared with like by the use of random sampling, prediction categories or matching, and there appear so far to be no instances of a full interaction effect being demonstrated—that is, where a particular category has an above-average level of success in one regime and a below-average level of success in another.

72. Some of the research surveyed above—particularly the study at Dover Borstal and the Youth Center Research Project—has illustrated the difficulties of maintaining consistently an innovatory regime. What has also been shown, however, is that, even if it is impossible to prove that a new regime is better than the old, there may be beneficial effects which are in a sense incidental to this main purpose. The most obvious of these relates to the manner in which discipline is maintained. Some of the studies have shown an increased tolerance of offences committed in the community, a decrease in incidents of misbehaviour within institutions, and greater flexibility in handling misbehaviour.

73. It has also emerged that, even if the programme of which they were a part led to no obviously superior outcome, new treatment approaches—such as the use of the Jesness Inventory—may give staff a greater sense of understanding and of purpose; the use of different elements of particular approaches, as and when they seem useful, may be of value in management terms.

74. The relative lack of success so far ought not to discourage future attempts to elucidate the treatment process by means of research. Given the powerful effect of environmental influences on the behaviour of offenders, it is necessary to try to reach a clearer understanding of what the treatment process is, and how it achieves whatever effect it may have, as well as to seek to measure the effect of different forms of treatment on different categories of offenders. Pointers towards further research that emerge from this survey include: the tendency of those with serious social problems and a long penal history to do worse in the modified regime at Dover; the apparent relative success of "casework" at Hewell Grange; and the differences in American studies between the reactions of the more and less mature to certain forms of treatment. Our recommendation (in Chapter 15) of a field trial of a system of assessment would make possible research by means of "matching". Random allocation to different forms of treatment raises greater problems, but its use within reasonable limits should not be discouraged: for example, the random selection of offenders for a less unwelcome measure or regime than they would otherwise have experienced is obviously open to less objection of an ethical nature than random selection for a *more* unwelcome regime.

---

[1] For a discussion of the difficulties of random allocation (including certain practical difficulties affecting the administration of institutions) see *The Controlled Trial in Institutional Research* by R. V. G. Clarke and D. B. Cornish (HMSO 1972).

[2] L. T. Empey and S. Lubeck: *The Silverlake Experiment* (Chicago, Aldine Publishing Co., 1971).

75. Finally—and most significantly—such research as there has been has cast great doubt on the effectiveness of custodial treatment as opposed to treatment in the community. Custodial treatment seems to achieve no more—except the immediate prevention of offences—and the cost, at least in the long term, is very much higher. Where custody is imposed, a long sentence seems to be no more effective as regards future behaviour than a short sentence. These findings point to the more sparing imposition of custodial sentences, except so far as these are considered necessary on other sentencing criteria, and to a major effort to develop more effective ways of controlling the behaviour of offenders in the community.

SUPPLEMENTARY PROVISIONS OF THE CUSTODY
AND CONTROL ORDER SCHEME

1. This Appendix, which relates to the proposals in Chapter 8 about the custody and control order, sets out our recommendations for dealing with young adults who receive custody and control orders which extend beyond their 21st birthday, and for providing some measure of flexibility in the application of the general age limits which we have proposed for the young adult system (see paragraphs 240–241).

Transfer to prison and reclassification as adults of offenders subject to custody and control orders

2. A considerable number of young adults will still be detained under custody and control orders for some time after reaching the age of 21, because they are subject either to an order of substantial length or to one that began just before their 21st birthday. These will include some offenders with long custody and control orders who may not be considered suitable for release until their middle or late twenties, or in a few cases possibly even later. Some will be physically and mentally more mature than the bulk of young adult offenders. On a variety of criteria staff might conclude that certain young adults should be accommodated with adult prisoners and receive similar treatment. While we should not wish to discourage controlled mixing of young adults and older offenders on an experimental basis if the Prison Department considered it had merits, we do not think that it would be right as a general rule to retain in young adult establishments men in their middle or late twenties who seem, and themselves feel, out of place, or are a source of difficulty to staff. We also recognise that it would seem unjust for those sentenced as young adults and released well into their twenties to be subject to compulsory supervision and liability to recall in the final third of their sentence when their contemporaries, released from sentences of imprisonment passed after the age of 21, have no such liability, and are completely free after two thirds of their sentence (assuming good behaviour). This is a considerable source of current grievance. The following paragraphs contain proposals for the status and liabilities of offenders sentenced as young adults who attain the age of 21 during the currency of their custody and control orders to be assimilated progressively to those of adult prisoners.

3. *We recommend that it should be possible to transfer a young adult to an adult prison at any time after the age of 19, if it is considered that his needs can thereby be better met, provided that transfer before the age of 21 should take place only if his sentence is of such a length and his personal circumstances and character seem of such a nature that he is likely to be still in custody for a considerable period after reaching that age.* It is to be stressed that we see this measure being used only in circumstances where it is clear that it would be in the best interests of the offender for him to be dealt with in company with older people on grounds of maturity. It should not be used as a disciplinary measure; but we can envisage circumstances where the adverse effect of an offender's conduct on discipline and control, along with other factors, might lead to the quite proper conclusion that relocation in an adult prison should not be postponed until after 21. This power corresponds to the existing power to reclassify young prisoners as adult prisoners and the Secretary of State's power to commute a sentence of borstal training to one of imprisonment.

4. *We recommend that, after the age of 22, an offender subject to a custody and control order should not be subject to greater restrictions after release than would apply if he had been sentenced when over 21 to imprisonment.* This means that, if an offender who receives a custody and control order is in custody on reaching the age of 22, his liability to supervision on release, to licence conditions and to recall should cease when two thirds of the order has expired. If an offender over the age of 22 and subject to a custody and control order is released before two thirds of the sentence has expired he should be subject to supervision, licence requirements and recall only until two thirds of the sentence (plus any additional days ordered as disciplinary awards) have expired, on the analogy of

parole of prisoners over 21. If he is on licence under a custody and control order on reaching the age of 22 and the date of his entitlement to release has already passed, supervision, licence conditions and liability to recall should automatically lapse.

5. The Secretary of State's discretion to release at any time during the course of a custody and control order, subject to the procedures described in paragraphs 198 to 205 of the report and any restricted release order, should apply to all offenders sentenced to custody and control, whether they are accommodated in a young adult establishment or in a prison, until the age of 23.[1] *At that age the status and liabilities of a person sentenced to custody and control should become the same as those of a person sentenced to imprisonment for the same length of time.* If he is still in custody at the age of 23 and has not already been transferred to an adult prison this should now be done. His expectations of release, whether by parole or through the operation of remission for good behaviour, would become the same as if he had been sentenced to imprisonment. Any postponement of his entitlement to release ordered through disciplinary proceedings in a young adult establishment would be converted into a loss of remission, for purposes of calculating the earliest date of release. (This is an incidental but substantial advantage of the arrangements proposed in paragraphs 204–205 which separate loss of time for disciplinary reasons from the operation of the discretion to release on criteria related to future conduct.)

6. If the power we propose in Chapter 4 (paragraph 91) to raise the general upper age limit for young adults is exercised, the age points of the transitional arrangements proposed in the foregoing paragraphs should be increased accordingly.

Exceptions to the age limits

7. Finally we have considered whether it should be possible, exceptionally, to sentence persons above the maximum age of the young adult age range as if they were within it and persons over 17 as if they were under 17. One of the most common themes in witnesses' discussions of age limits is the need for "flexibility" and for recognition that chronological age is often of very little use in determining the nature of the individual and the best way of altering his behaviour. Emotional maturity is often a more relevant factor in deciding how to treat an offender, and it seems likely that some immature offenders above the normal age limit would derive particular benefit from treatment arrangements and support on release of the type to be provided for young adults, whereas they might pass through an adult establishment almost unnoticed and with their problems exacerbated. There is therefore a good case for the courts to have discretion to deal with an adult offender near to the young adult age limit either as a young adult or as an adult according to his needs.[2]

8. It would be wrong, however, to use such a power for reasons other than the special characteristics of the offender, for example to use it in order to give identical sentences to joint offenders. Under our proposals the staff of young adult establishments will have in any event to deal with a great many offenders who will be difficult to reach and influence. It would be particularly unhelpful to add to their responsibilities offenders over the age of 21 whom they considered too mature, or too committed to a criminal way of life, to be suitable to be dealt with as young adults. The decision to sentence an adult as a young adult should be made only very exceptionally on the basis of the offender's personal characteristics and the Prison Department's assessment of his suitability for a young adult establishment. *We therefore propose that a magistrates' court or the Crown Court should have power to make a custody and control order on an offender over the age of 21 on the recommendation or with the agreement of the Prison Department.* Such a provision might be especially suited to offenders over 21 who had already been subject to a custody and control order. We would expect this power not normally to be used for any offenders over the age of about 24.

---

[1] In the case of those in prison the powers of the licence advisory committee should be exercised by the parole local review committee for the prison.

[2] An arrangement of this sort is similar to that applying to the special sentences of young persons' imprisonment in a number of European countries where there is a normal upper age limit and above that a two year band in which the court may use the sentence exceptionally if it specifies that the sentence is obviously more appropriate than adult imprisonment—although those sentences are in any event "selective" sentences even within the young adult offender age range, as was the borstal sentence in earlier days, and not a generic custodial sentence for all young offenders.

9. To deal with cases where the courts exercise this power, some modification is needed of the proposals in paragraphs 2–6 above for the progressive assimilation of the conditions of the custody and control order to those of adult imprisonment, since otherwise the automatic application of those changes on the age points proposed would defeat the objects of this proposal. We suggest that the right course is to provide for a person sentenced to custody and control at any age over 21 to graduate to adult status by the same stages and after about the same length of time as would apply if he had been sentenced to custody and control immediately before his 21st birthday. That is to say, after one year he should cease to be liable to compulsory supervision, licence conditions, or recall after two thirds of the order (plus any period of deferment ordered in disciplinary proceedings); after two years he would be transferred to a prison and treated for purposes of release as if he had been sentenced to imprisonment. This would not prevent the offender's transfer before that date to an adult establishment if his progress suggested that he was after all better dealt with among adults, nor his reclassification in less than two years if that seemed appropriate.

10. We do not see any need for a corresponding power to sentence young adults over 17 as juveniles, that is to make a care order or a supervision order under the Children and Young Persons Act 1969 or to remit the case to the juvenile court for sentence. Offenders suitable for such an arrangement are less easy to identify than adults above the upper limit who ought to be treated as young adults, in that towards the lower age limit there is a much greater spread of ability and maturity levels.

11. However, it is clearly important that if an offender has recently been in the care of a local authority his response to treatment under that order should be carefully considered by the court before deciding how to deal with the case. There are a number of provisions enabling local authorities to assist young people who have formerly been in their care, and an appropriate course might be for the court to defer sentence or make a probation order or conditional discharge, on the understanding that the offender concerned would seek and receive the local authority's assistance. Alternatively the court might make a probation order with a condition of residence if the plan were for him to return to lodgings or a foster home where he had been before, or if the local authority were prepared to accommodate him in a community home (available up to the age of 21 under section 50 of the Children and Young Persons Act 1969).[1]

12. In order to determine whether such measures would be realistic in the circumstances *we recommend that where an offender has been in the care of a local authority within 12 months preceding his court appearance (which should be evident from the social enquiry report) the court should be obliged to consult the local authority concerned before making any order.* We do not consider that it would be sufficient to rely on routine information collected for purposes of a social enquiry report on any offender who has been in care, since what is in mind is whether the local authority will use powers of a special nature in exceptional circumstances. Formal consultation by a court prior to sentencing in a limited category of cases is likely to have a different impact from informal enquiries by a probation officer to see whether financial or other support would be available in the event of the court dealing with the case by a conditional discharge or a probation order, or deferring sentence.

---

[1] A local authority also has power, under section 58 of the Children and Young Persons Act 1963, to advise and befriend and, in exceptional circumstances, give financial assistance to a person under 21 if so requested by him and if he was in care on or after his 17th birthday. Under section 20 of the Children Act 1948 it has power to contribute to the accommodation and maintenance of a young person who was in care after ceasing to be of compulsory school age.

APPENDIX F

APPEALS AGAINST SHORT CUSTODY AND CONTROL ORDERS

1. During our visits to detention centres, both during this review and during our earlier enquiry into the detention centre system, we have been told that cases occur in which offenders subject to detention centre sentences—ie usually for three months, but sometimes up to six months—are deterred from appealing by the fact that delay in dealing with the appeal, and the courts' general reluctance to grant bail pending appeal, often have the result that the offender has already largely or completely served his sentence by the time the appeal has been determined.[1] For example an offender with a detention centre sentence (or in future a custody and control order) of three months would have a maximum period of detention of two months. With the delays which can at present occur in dealing with appeals the offender may well judge it more worth his while to see out his custodial sentence and after-care, rather than risk serving the greater part of it and then receiving in substitution (or in effect in addition, though naturally one would expect the appeal court to take proper account of that part of the sentence which the offender had already served) perhaps a fine or a probation order resulting in a longer period of supervision.

2. There is thus an obvious possibility of serious injustice, and it is one which we have been concerned to overcome by seeking to encourage arrangements for the speedy determination of appeals against short custody and control orders. The problem is one independent of our proposal for a custody and control order, and should in our view be put right whether or not our general sentencing proposals are accepted.

3. *Accordingly we propose that arrangements should be developed which would ensure that as far as possible appeals against short custody and control orders are dealt with speedily, as an ideal within 48 hours of sentence, and at worst within two weeks.* We must stress that to do this requires the co-operation of all concerned, not only those responsible for court administration in collecting, copying and transmitting documents and accepting notice of appeal within this time, but also defence solicitors in providing notice of appeal and in expediting preparation of their case. Our proposal applies both to appeals against sentence alone, and to appeals against conviction and sentence. Clearly a convicted person is unlikely to be deterred by the shortness of his sentence from pressing his innocence if he believes there has been a miscarriage of justice. But appeals against conviction and sentence often go together, and it is not easy to maintain a distinction of principle between appeals against sentence on the one hand and appeals against conviction on the other.

4. In practical terms there are two forms of appeal to be considered: appeals from magistrates' courts which go to the Crown Court for hearing; and those from the Crown Court which go to the Court of Appeal (Criminal Division). An appeal from a magistrates' court will in the ordinary way go to the Crown Court. Under the Courts Act 1971, and Rules made under it, the court hearing such an appeal must include two lay magistrates. The court of first instance will have considered the facts of the case, the antecedents given by the police and a social enquiry report. There may also have been other documentary evidence, such as a school report, and witnesses may have been called on behalf of the defendant and prosecution. Where the appeal is against sentence only,[2] witnesses need not be recalled, and it should not be difficult to get the necessary documents duplicated for the use of the Crown Court. But there may be difficulties about establishing a properly constituted court without our ideal time scale. We would hope that in general it should be possible to achieve a hearing within 48 hours or so, but informal enquiries which we have

---

[1] The same may well be true of appeals by adults against short prison sentences, but this is not a matter within our terms of reference. In any event we believe we can make a case for giving young adults preferential treatment in this respect—though naturally speedy consideration of all appeals is the ideal—in that if a young adult has a short sentence it is likely to be his first custodial sentence and because, since a 3-month sentence cannot be reduced, it is more likely than an adult's to be quashed on appeal.

[2] Appeals to the Crown Court against conviction are by way of rehearing.

made suggest that this ideal may be too difficult to achieve over the country as a whole. Taking everything into account however we see no reason at all why it should not be possible to hear appeals everywhere in the country within a maximum of 14 days, given as we have said the co-operation of all concerned, including defence solicitors. In the case of appeals to the Court of Appeal there may be slightly more difficulty, but with few exceptions there is a court in session and therefore available within 14 days. Even in exceptional times such as the Long Vacation there will probably be a court sitting within 14 days.

5. Nevertheless cases may still occur for various reasons in which it will be clear that in the circumstances it will not be possible to determine the appeal within the time scale we have in mind. There is a difference between appeals from magistrates to the Crown Court and appeals from the Crown Court to the Court of Appeal. In the former case bail can be granted by the magistrates. In appeals from the Crown Court, however, bail can be granted only by the Court of Appeal and this is rarely done.[1] We would wish to see some relaxation of the principles laid down by the Court of Appeal relating to the granting of bail pending appeal, the general effect of which is at present that bail is granted only where it appears prima facie that the appeal is likely to be successful or where there is a risk that the sentence will have been served by the time the appeal is heard.[2] Instead we propose that in such circumstances *the court considering the application for bail should apply the general criterion relating to the granting of bail pending trial or sentence which we propose in paragraph 449 of the report.*[3] *We propose also that power should lie with the court of trial to grant bail pending appeal, where notice of appeal is entered early enough to enable them to do so.*[4] It is true that the result of this may be that some offenders whose appeals in the event fail will be incarcerated, released and then rearrested. While this is perhaps one humanitarian reason why the courts have been reluctant to grant bail pending appeal against a custodial sentence, most of us see no objection to this practice;[5] and the risk of later incarceration, and hence delay in his final release from restrictions, is one factor which the offender would have to take into account in deciding whether to apply for bail pending appeal. Granting bail is however no substitute for speedy determination of appeals, which remains the main object of the proposals in this Appendix.

[1] In 1972 bail was granted in four cases in which appeals were lodged against detention centre sentences.

[2] The Court of Criminal Appeal laid it down that bail should not be granted after conviction except in very special circumstances (see for example *R v Gordon*, 7 Cr App R 182). This principle has frequently been repeated by the Court of Appeal (see for example *R v Lang and Rowe* [1969] Crim. L R 97). See also the report of the Interdepartmental Committee on the Court of Criminal Appeal (Chairman: the Rt. Hon. Lord Donovan) (Cmnd 2755) paragraphs 207–215.

[3] That as a matter of general principle bail should be granted, by a court of whatever level, to a person aged 17–21 accused or convicted of an offence unless enquiry reveals compelling reasons for refusing bail.

[4] Of section 20 of the Criminal Justice Act 1967, which permits magistrates' courts to commit to the Crown Court on bail for sentence where the offender has been convicted summarily.

[5] The Court of Appeal has in fact held that there is no general principle that once an appellant has after conviction been released on bail there is never any question of sending him back to prison (*R v Cullis, R v Nash* [1969] 113 S.J. 51 C.A.).

APPENDIX G

ARMY CADET FORCE TRAINING

1. At the time when the Council began its review of the treatment of young offenders, in 1970, two borstals in England had Army Cadet Force Units. One unit was started during the Second World War; and the other soon after it. The training provided by these units, participation in which was on a voluntary basis, included some training in the use of firearms.

2. After the matter had been raised in Parliament[1] the Home Secretary asked the Council to give specific attention to it as part of the young offender review. The Council decided that it could deal with this question in advance of its main report. Its conclusion, that this form of training should be discontinued, was conveyed to the then Home Secretary in the following terms.

4 May 1971

Sir,

As requested we have considered the question of Army Cadet Force Units maintained in establishments for young offenders. We have received the views of the Prison Department and of the Governors of the two borstals in England and Wales where units are maintained, Lowdham Grange and Rochester.

We have also received evidence from the Army Cadet Force Association which, like the two borstal Governors directly involved, favours the maintenance of these units; and on the other hand have been informed that the Police Federation has expressed to you its anxiety about this form of training.

The Governors of Lowdham Grange and Rochester borstals stress the voluntary nature of the cadet corps activity and consider it valuable, partly because it offers the volunteers an opportunity to join with other cadets outside the borstal in various activities and to compete with them, often with success. The Governors make the point that weapon training plays only a small part in cadet training, emphasising the care which is taken to ensure the security of the weapons and the limited amount of ammunition available for practice. They consider that the military type of discipline, organised marching and military excercises are of value in the training of offenders. We do not doubt the ability of the present Governors and their staffs to make a success of this activity, in whose merits they obviously believe.

Having paid full regard to these views we nevertheless feel that, at a time when the type of discipline based upon army methods, including formal parades, marching, etc., is no longer rated as highly as it once was in the routine of young offender institutions, it is somewhat inappropriate to perpetuate military cadet training, including weapon training, for young men whose subsequent recruitment into the armed forces, while not wholly ruled out, is not seriously envisaged. The situation has entirely changed in this respect since the end of National Service. Indeed, the military life for which cadet training is primarily designed is now remote from any conditions which young offenders are likely to encounter after release.

On the question of weapon training, which was the principal reason for this matter being raised in the House of Lords, we do not wish to exaggerate the dangers involved. We feel, however, that at best this is an irrelevant form of training for young offenders who are not going to enter the armed forces; while at worst it invites a familiarity with firearms which could well be misapplied.

---

[1] House of Lords Official Report, Volume 312, cols. 924–928, 17 November 1970.

We would therefore suggest that borstal institutions should withdraw from cadet training and that the Prison Department should discuss with the Governors alternative ways of retaining some of the advantages claimed for the present units which would not involve training in the use and care of firearms. The Fire Fighting and First Aid Unit which we understand has been formed at Hollesley Bay Borstal may provide an example of what we have in mind.

I am, Sir,

Your obedient Servant,

K. G. YOUNGER,

Chairman,
Advisory Council on the Penal System

The Rt. Hon. REGINALD MAUDLING, MP
Her Majesty's Principal Secretary of State
for the Home Department

3. The Home Secretary accepted this recommendation and announced on 17 May 1971,[1] in reply to Questions in the House of Commons, his decision that the units should be disbanded.

---

[1] House of Commons Official Report, Volume 817, Written Answers, cols. 232–233.

Printed in England for Her Majesty's Stationery Office by McCorquodale Printers Ltd.
HM 6579   Dd 504334   K40   4/74